Global Tourism and COVID-19

T0300408

This comprehensive book focuses on how the COVID-19 pandemic is transforming travel and tourism, globally. Despite the devastation caused by COVID-19, authors argue that within the ongoing crisis, there is also an opportunity to positively transform the tourism sector in ways that contribute to a more hopeful future for tourism practitioners, tourists and host communities.

As the world emerges from the shadow of COVID-19 there will not be a return to the 'normal'. Rather, the volume shares a vision of global transformation that is driven at least in part by the changing ways people in the post-COVID-19 era may travel and encounter each other and their environments. Individual chapters explore topics such as regenerative economies, transformational travel, critical perspectives on pandemics and tourism, sustainable development and resilience post-COVID-19, re-discovering and re-localising tourism, global (im)mobilities, transforming tourism management, as well as new value systems for travel and tourism including the chance to strengthen social equity and social justice as tourism returns after COVID-19. In this edited volume, a series of senior and emerging scholars engage with debates on how to best contribute to more substantial, meaningful and positive planetary shifts within the tourism industry.

The chapters in this book were originally published as a special issue of the journal *Tourism Geographies*.

Alan A. Lew is Professor Emeritus at Northern Arizona University and is the founding Editor-in-Chief of the journal *Tourism Geographies*. His background encompasses human geography, urban planning, and tourism studies. His recent interests and writings have focused on place making, resilience, and consciousness studies as they relate to travel and tourism.

Joseph M. Cheer is Professor, Center for Tourism Research, Wakayama University, Japan; and Visiting Professor, AUT, New Zealand and UCSI Malaysia. He is Co Editor-in-Chief of *Tourism Geographies*. Recent books include *Masculinities in the Field: Tourism and Transdisciplinary Research* (2021) and *Travel and Tourism in the Age of Overtourism* (2021). He is an Australian Research Council Linkage Project (ARC LP) grant recipient with colleagues at University of Melbourne.

Patrick Brouder holds the British Columbia Regional Innovation Chair in Tourism and Sustainable Rural Development at Vancouver Island University, Canada. He works closely with stakeholders across western Canada on Indigenous tourism, creative economies, and long-term regional evolution. He is an editor of *Tourism Geographies* and co-managing editor of *Tourism Geographic*.

Mary Mostafanezhad is Associate Professor, Department of Geography and Environment, University of Hawai'i at Mānoa. She is the co-editor-in-chief of *Tourism Geographies* and the co-founder of the Critical Tourism Studies Asia-Pacific Network. Her scholarship is broadly focused on tourism, development, and socio-environmental change.

Global Tourism and COVID-19

Implications for Theory and Practice

Edited by
**Alan A. Lew, Joseph M. Cheer,
Patrick Brouder and Mary Mostafanezhad**

Routledge
Taylor & Francis Group

LONDON AND NEW YORK

First published 2022
by Routledge
2 Park Square, Milton Park, Abingdon, Oxon, OX14 4RN

and by Routledge
605 Third Avenue, New York, NY 10158

Routledge is an imprint of the Taylor & Francis Group, an informa business

© 2022 Taylor & Francis

British Library Cataloguing-in-Publication Data
A catalogue record for this book is available from the British Library

ISBN13: 978-1-032-12136-9 (hbk)
ISBN13: 978-1-032-12138-3 (pbk)
ISBN13: 978-1-003-22325-2 (ebk)

DOI: 10.4324/9781003223252

Typeset in Myriad Pro
by codeMantra

Publisher's Note
The publisher accepts responsibility for any inconsistencies that may have arisen during the conversion of this book from journal articles to book chapters, namely the inclusion of journal terminology.

Disclaimer
Every effort has been made to contact copyright holders for their permission to reprint material in this book. The publishers would be grateful to hear from any copyright holder who is not here acknowledged and will undertake to rectify any errors or omissions in future editions of this book.

Contents

Citation Information

The chapters in this book were originally published in the journal *Tourism Geographies*, volume 22, issue 3 (2020). When citing this material, please use the original page numbering for each article, as follows:

Introduction
Visions of travel and tourism after the global COVID-19 transformation of 2020
Alan A. Lew, Joseph M. Cheer, Michael Haywood, Patrick Brouder and Noel B. Salazar
Tourism Geographies, volume 22, issue 3 (2020) pp. 455–466

Chapter 1
Transforming the (tourism) world for good and (re)generating the potential 'new normal'
Irena Ateljevic
Tourism Geographies, volume 22, issue 3 (2020) pp. 467–475

Chapter 2
"We can't return to normal": committing to tourism equity in the post-pandemic age
Stefanie Benjamin, Alana Dillette and Derek H. Alderman
Tourism Geographies, volume 22, issue 3 (2020) pp. 476–483

Chapter 3
Reset redux: possible evolutionary pathways towards the transformation of tourism in a COVID-19 world
Patrick Brouder
Tourism Geographies, volume 22, issue 3 (2020) pp. 484–490

Chapter 4
COVID-19, indigenous peoples and tourism: a view from New Zealand
Anna Carr
Tourism Geographies, volume 22, issue 3 (2020) pp. 491–502

Chapter 5
Regenerative tourism needs diverse economic practices
Jenny Cave and Dianne Dredge
Tourism Geographies, volume 22, issue 3 (2020) pp. 503–513

Chapter 24
The transformational festival as a subversive toolbox for a transformed tourism: lessons from Burning Man for a COVID-19 world
Ian Rowen
Tourism Geographies, volume 22, issue 3 (2020) pp. 695–702

Chapter 25
A mindful shift: an opportunity for mindfulness-driven tourism in a post-pandemic world
Uglješa Stankov, Viachaslau Filimonau and Miroslav D. Vujičić
Tourism Geographies, volume 22, issue 3 (2020) pp. 703–712

Chapter 26
The novel spaces and power-geometries in tourism and hospitality after 2020 will belong to the 'local'
Lucia Tomassini and Elena Cavagnaro
Tourism Geographies, volume 22, issue 3 (2020) pp. 713–719

Chapter 27
COVID-19 leads to a new context for the "right to tourism": a reset of tourists' perspectives on space appropriation is needed
Sabrina Tremblay-Huet
Tourism Geographies, volume 22, issue 3 (2020) pp. 720–723

Chapter 28
From high-touch to high-tech: COVID-19 drives robotics adoption
Zhanjing Zeng, Po-Ju Chen and Alan A. Lew
Tourism Geographies, volume 22, issue 3 (2020) pp. 724–734

Conclusion
Reflections and discussions: tourism matters in the new normal post COVID-19
Patrick Brouder, Simon Teoh, Noel B. Salazar, Mary Mostafanezhad, Jessica Mei Pung, Dominic Lapointe, Freya Higgins Desbiolles, Michael Haywood, C. Michael Hall & Helene Balslev Clausen
Tourism Geographies, volume 22, issue 3 (2020) pp. 735–746

For any permission-related enquiries please visit:
http://www.tandfonline.com/page/help/permissions

Notes on Contributors

Derek H. Alderman Department of Geography, University of Tennessee, Knoxville, USA.

Irena Ateljevic Institute for Tourism, Zagreb, Croatia.

Stefanie Benjamin Department of Retail, Hospitality & Tourism Management, University of Tennessee, Knoxville, SA.

Patrick Brouder College of Management and Economics, University of Guelph, Quebec, Canada.

Anna Carr Department of Tourism, University of Otago, Dunedin, New Zealand.

Elena Cavagnaro Academy of International Hospitality Research, NHL Stenden University of Applied Sciences, Leeuwarden, The Netherlands.

Jenny Cave Department of Business, School of Management, Swansea University, Wales, United Kingdom.

Natasha Chassagne University of Tasmania, Hobart, Australia.

Joseph M. Cheer Center for Tourism Research, Wakayama University, Japan.

Po-Ju Chen The W. A. Franke College of Business, Northern Arizona University, Flagstaff, Arizona.

Helene Balslev Clausen Aalborg University, Aalborg, Denmark.

J. A. Cooper Department of Geography, The University of Tennessee, Knoxville, USA.

Émilie Crossley Otago Polytechnic, Dunedin, New Zealand.

Alana Dillette L. Robert Payne School of Hospitality and Tourism Management, San Diego State University, USA.

Dianne Dredge The Tourism CoLab, Australia.

Johan Edelheim International Media and Communication, Hokkaido Daigaku, Sapporo, Japan.

Phoebe Everingham University of Newcastle, Callaghan, Australia.

Viachaslau Filimonau Talbot Campus, Faculty of Management, Bournemouth University, Poole, United Kingdom of Great Britain and Northern Ireland.

Adriana Galvani Free University Mediterranea, Nola-Naples, Italy.

Stefan Gössling Department of Service Management and Service Studies, Lunds Universitet, Helsingborg, Sweden; School of Business and Economics, Linnaeus University, Kalmar, Sweden.

Szilvia Gyimóthy Copenhagen Business School, Department of Marketing, Frederiksberg, Denmark.

C. Michael Hall University of Canterbury, Christchurch, New Zealand. Department of Service Management and Service Studies, Lunds Universitet, Helsingborg, Sweden; School of Business and Economics, Linnaeus University, Kalmar, Sweden.

K. Michael Haywood College of Management and Economics, University of Guelph, Canada.

Freya Higgins-Desbiolles Business School, University of South Australia, Adelaide, Australia.

Dimitri Ioannides Mid-Sweden University, Ostersund, Sweden.

Dominic Lapointe Université du Québec à Montréal, Montreal, Quebec, Canada.

Alan A. Lew Geography, Planning and Recreation, Northern Arizona University, Flagstaff, USA.

Mary Mostafanezhad Geography and Environment, University of Hawai'i at Manoa, Honolulu, Hawaii, USA.

Sanjay K. Nepal Professor of Geography and Environmental Management, University of Waterloo, Canada.

Piotr Niewiadomski Geography & Environment, School of Geosciences, University of Aberdeen, UK.

Anja Pabel School of Business and Law, Central Queensland University, Cairns, Australia.

Maria Sotelo Perez University Rey Juan Carlos, Madrid, Spain.

Tomas Pernecky School of Hospitality and Tourism, Auckland University of Technology, New Zealand.

Bruce Prideaux School of Business and Law, Central Queensland University, Cairns, Australia.

Jessica Mei Pung University of Hawaii at Manoa, Honolulu, USA.

Luc Renaud Université du Québec à Montréal, Montreal, Quebec, Canada.

Francesc Romagosa School of Tourism and Hotel Management & Department of Geography, Autonomous University of Barcelona, Cerdanyola (Barcelona), Spain.

Ian Rowen Sociology, Geography and Urban Planning, Nanyang Technological University, Singapore.

Noel B. Salazar Vancouver Island University, British Columbia, Nanaimo, Canada; KU Leuven, Leuven, Belgium.

Daniel Scott Geography & Environmental Management, University of Waterloo, Canada. School of Hospitality and Tourism Management, University of Surrey, Guildford, UK.

Uglješa Stankov Faculty of Sciences, Department of Geography, Tourism and Hotel Management, University of Novi Sad, Serbia.

Simon Teoh Murdoch University, Australia.

Michelle Thompson School of Business and Law, Central Queensland University, Cairns, Australia.

Lucia Tomassini Academy of International Hospitality Research, NHL Stenden University of Applied Sciences, Leeuwarden, The Netherlands.

Sabrina Tremblay-Huet Faculty of Law, University of Sherbrooke, Sherbrooke, Canada.

Miroslav D. Vujičić Faculty of Sciences, Department of Geography, Tourism and Hotel Management, University of Novi Sad, Serbia.

Zhanjing Zeng School of Geography and Ocean Science, Nanjing University, China.

Visions of travel and tourism after the global COVID-19 transformation of 2020

Alan A. Lew ⓘ, Joseph M. Cheer ⓘ, K. Michael Haywood, Patrick Brouder and Noel B. Salazar ⓘ

> The future belongs to those who believe in the beauty of their dreams.
>
> — Eleanor Roosevelt

This special issue is a reflection by tourism scholars on the initial impacts of the COVID-19 pandemic on the world, with travel and tourism being among the most significant areas to bear those impacts. However, instead of an analysis of the impacts of COVID-19 on tourism places and sectors, as is the emphasis for many other journal special issues this year, the papers in this issue focus on visions of how the pandemic events of 2020 are contributing to a possibly substantial, meaningful and positive transformation of the planet in general, and tourism specifically. This is not a return to a 'normal' that existed before – but is instead a vision of how the world is changing, evolving, and transforming into something different from what it was before the 2020 global pandemic experience. Comments from the guest editors for this special issue are individually identified in this introduction editorial.

Resilience issues

Alan Lew

Resilience theory postulates that change is fundamental and the only constant that we can depend on (Butler, 2017; Cheer & Lew, 2017; Hall et al., 2017). Because all things change with time, systems (from a single entity to the entire planet) must adapt to their changing context or perish in some way. The resilience adaptive cycle suggests four general phases of a change event:

Phase 1: (Re-)Organization (innovation and creativity),
Phase 2: Growth (exploiting opportunities that arise from phase 1),
Phase 3: Consolidation (establishing fixed institutions and rules for phase 2),
Phase 4: Collapse (failure of fixed institutions in phase 3 to adapt to context changes),
  which results in a return to the Re-organization (phase 1) or, alternatively, the com-
  plete dissolution of the system.

Systems do not need to move through all four of these phases. The collapse phase
could, theoretically, be avoided if the system maintained a culture of constant innovation to match its changing context (i.e. staying in phases 1, 2 and 3 only). Similarly, a
system can be 'stuck' in a collapse sequence if it is unable to effectively exploit its
opportunities and resources (i.e. staying mostly in phases 1 and 4). In addition, the
intensity of each phase can vary considerably. For example, a collapse (phase 4) can
be minor and easily overcome, or it can be a pandemic; and it can be a common
occurrence or a rare, once-in-a-lifetime event.

The COVID-19 pandemic event has caused a significant, although not total, collapse
of the human-earth system. At the time of writing (May 2020), the collapse is still
taking place, and the re-organization of the system is just barely beginning. We are
probably, therefore, starting to enter a Re-organization phase of innovation and
creativity, which is necessary for our human system to transform itself to adapt to the
new context of the planet we inhabit.

Phase 1 innovation, for example, is seen in the many ways that people are seeking
to connect with one another in the context of social/physical distancing policies
implemented to control the COVID-19 pandemic. From this perspective, the deeper
lesson of physical distancing has to do with expanding the integration of the planet
in new directions. Humans are social animals and if they cannot connect physically
they will find other ways. These other forms of connecting are creating new pathways
to knowledge, understanding and empathy across the globe.

This is the goal of this special issue: to contribute, hopefully innovatively, to the Re-
organization of the planet. As travel and tourism may be the single most impacted
sector of the global economy under the COVID-19 pandemic, it makes sense for
tourism scholars to be central to this innovative and creative re-organization process.
The commentaries in this special issue are based on many years of focus and scholarship on travel and tourism around the globe. These writings are not based on
deep dives and analyses of the COVID-19 pandemic, as data for such an understanding is not yet available.

What is most important at this early innovative stage of Re-organization is to be
open to all ideas and to be willing to make mistakes. Innovation requires that
we hold our judgements and acknowledge the potential value of every proposition.
That means, for example, acknowledging some potential value in neoliberal economics,
as well as sustainability. Unfortunately, the potential futures that we envision can only
be based in some way on the pasts that we know. The new organizational structure(s)
that will ultimately emerge post COVID-19 cannot really be known at this time, but will
be formulated through the Re-organizational phase 1 of the resilience adaptive cycle,
and tested and proven through the Growth phase 2.

'Growth' (phase 2) does not need to be GDP growth but could instead be, for example, growth in well-being. Many people have come to realize, in recent years, that things need to change, not just for tourism, but for the planet overall. The planet is simply delivering on that desire. Change is not easy, nor does it guarantee more fecund outcomes. But this time is the best chance yet to move the planet in a new direction. People are endlessly creative, and they will need to use their creativity to build a more meaningful, more benign, and less disruptive 'new normal' for our evolving global society. This is what the contributors to this special issue seek to nudge us all towards, in expressing their voices at this still very early time in the COVID-19 pandemic's change cycle.

Noel Salazar

The widespread crisis surrounding the outbreak of the COVID-19 pandemic is laying bare the fragility and unsustainable nature of the current global economic system, in which travel and tourism play a crucial role. We should not forget that it was in great part due to international tourism and business travel that this coronavirus spread so rapidly across the planet. Not surprisingly, tourism is also one of the economic sectors most hit by the lockdowns and travel restrictions that countries have imposed to keep their citizens 'in' and travelers from abroad 'out'. While many still hope to return to 'business as usual' as soon as everything is over, others are seriously doubting that this will be possible.

The more significant question is what kind of world we envision for ourselves and future generations. A crisis gives us a unique opportunity to seriously reflect on this. While it is essential to dream about hopeful future scenarios, we should not forget that our social world is heavily marked by inequalities of various kinds. These inequalities existed before the crisis, have been exacerbated during the crisis, and will certainly not disappear after the crisis. It is within this general context that we need to re-envision the travel and tourism of the future, and the future of travel and tourism.

Michael Haywood

Nobody expects the status quo to remain. While certain policy changes are bound to occur, rather than being pre-determined, they will occur in response to: (1) the needs, demands, and changing habits and behaviors of the traveling public; (2) changing business models and practices; and (3) better preparedness for prevailing exigencies, such as a continuation of evolving zoonotic viruses and possibly other global and regional disruptions.

Actual innovation and revival will take place in the tourism trenches of everyday enterprises. But so many questions remain: Where are the blind spots in communities-as-destinations? How can they be identified and corrected? What needs to be done to dissipate the 'fear of disruption', which can be more damaging than the disruption itself? What needs to be done to protect employees, customers, suppliers and communities, and what is required to effectively communicate with these stakeholders, through the post COVID-19 cycles, particularly about the changes that will, or needs to, occur? What is urgent and needed as cities, communities, and destinations adapt to, for example, car-free zones, revisions to placemaking and gatherings, and the design and planning of markets, events, and festivals?

The COVID-19 pandemic certainly has caused utter devastation. But crises often bring people and communities together. With time, and as the desire for connectivity and sociability is re-manifested, hope will return. Innovation and entrepreneurialism will reveal what is indeed possible and aspirational. The pause in economic activity has been eye-opening in that it has provided a glimpse of what the world could look like when the excesses of touristic activities are reined in. Social innovation needs to take place creatively at the community level to find the best balance between the benefits and excesses of tourism development.

This is what most of the articles in this special issue seek to address. But we must be cautious in what we wish for. In reference to climate change, a green economy, clean energy, and sustainability, for example, I encourage everyone to search for and examine all the facts and varying perspectives, and not just those to which you may seem ideologically attached.

Future forecasting

Alan Lew

Prognosticating the future is risky, especially in these still early days of not knowing how the pandemic will progress, and just as mysterious, how the Re-organization resilience phase will pan out. With that caveat, Figure 1 models the COVID-19 transition from the current pandemic Collapse through the four phases of the resilience adaptive cycle. At a minimum, this exercise offers a starting point for discussion of where we are now and where we might go next.

In the short term, possibly for the coming two to five (or more) years, efforts will be made to 'Return to the Past' by governments, the travel industry, and many tourists who are anxious to stretch their wings again after being locked down. This seems to be occurring to some degree in China, which is several months ahead of the rest of the world in terms of the COVID-19 pandemic experience. As the virus situation begins

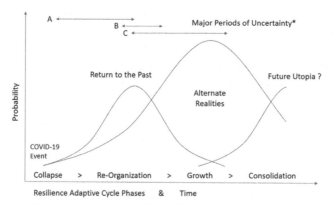

Figure 1. Resilience adaptive cycle phases and possible post COVID-19 pandemic scenarios.
*Note: A = Current Uncertainty (2 to 5+ years); B = Abandoning the Past; C = Alternative Experimentations.

to become better understood and stabilized there may be a big jump in proximity tourism to easily accessible destinations.

For a time, it might seem like nothing has changed at all. With time, however, the dominant values of the past will be less supported and ultimately abandoned as new values arising from the COVID-19 experience become more prominent (Kruglanski, 2020). This will give rise to an explosion of innovative and creative experimentation with 'Alternate Realities' (Figure 1), incuding new business models and government policy alternative, as the Re-organization phase transitions into a Growth phase. Some of these alternate experiments in organizing human societies already emerged in isolated ways prior to the pandemic. These may become more prominent, along with newer innovative alternatives that have yet to be imagined.

The world will change, as it always does. Some of the major values that might drive innovative alternative social systems in an emergent post COVID-19 world include:

– Peace (within and between countries and peoples);
– Love, Health and Happiness (as basic human rights);
– Equity, Fairness and Cooperation (in government and business policies and relations, and in ensuring protection of the most vulnerable populations and places); and
– Green Economies (such as full-cost life-cycle pricing and local sourcing), and perhaps a Gift Economy (where people pay what they can afford).

How these values will be achieved is unknown at this time, as they need to emerge from experimentation and consensus decision making. This may be the most important work to undertake during this COVID-19 transition period – how to facilitate change that has agreed upon values, while encouraging experimentation without an agreed upon method.

Eventually, a mostly global consensus will form over which approach or mix of approaches works best for a future utopia on Earth. What this alternative utopia looks like is impossible to know now, as it will emerge through the experiments with alternate realities as the resilience adaptive cycle moves from the Growth to the Consolidation phases (Figure 1). The best we can do at this time is to focus on the alternative values that we personally feel should form the basis of a future 'new normal' by defining and living them in our daily lives and careers.

Things could get worse before they get better. There are a lot of people and cultures on our planet and diversity is likely to expand, especially in the Re-organization and early Growth phases of creative innovation. But if we can hold our vision for what is possible, we can achieve it, at least in some measure and form. The old social-economic system will not be upended entirely, but its silencing during the pandemic has been an opportunity for alternative voices to be heard.

Michael Haywood

In refining Figure 1, I propose that the resilience 'Re-organization phase' will progress through the following stages, leading into the new 'Growth phase' for tourism businesses and communities.

1. Everyone trying to establish their local truth and the reality as it is being experienced by others;
2. Continuing efforts to build integrative awareness and engagement in collective sense-making;
3. Remaining in a state of pause as enterprises try to remain solvent, and divert capacity and resources in attempts to address the myriad of issues brought about by the crisis;
4. Identifying temporary measures to buy time, address the churn, manage the disruption taking place, and develop collective resilience;
5. Examining the new realities to clarify, if not revise, the purpose of tourism and communities-as-destinations (their core reason for being);
6. Undertaking a deep-dive assessment to clarify the current situation and discern critical shifts;
7. Engaging in aspirational thinking of what could or should be;
8. Deciding to stop certain activities, particularly those that in a post COVID-19 world are deemed obsolete or no longer fit-for-purpose;
9. Managing the transition period by accelerating re-structuring and re-strategizing, and the revision of policies;
10. Engaging in innovative programming, that will cut through years of institutional and systemic inertia, presenting the imperative and possibility for change;
11. Pushing through an agenda for change and transformation;
12. Creating new measures or metrics that identify how well tourism and all associated activities are performing for visitors and communities-at-large … creating value and 'wellth' for all.

Taking stock, hope and change

Alan Lew

Mother Earth is forcing people to stay home and to become introspective – to ask themselves what is important in their lives? What is truth to them? What are they fearing, denying, or resisting? What do they want to do about these questions? This is the great *reset* of 2020, for the world, and especially for travel and tourism.

Joseph Cheer

The many discussion threads within this special issue suggest a myriad of questions and possible pathways forward for the post COVID-19 milieu. It is reminiscent of philosopher Bertrand Russell's enquiry into human potential where he asks:

> Is there a way of life that is good and another that is bad, or is it indifferent how we live? If there is a good way of life, what is it, and how can we learn to live it? Is there something we may call wisdom, or is what seems to be such mere empty madness? (Foules, 1959, p. 8)

In a sense, we are broadly countenancing what is 'desirable tourism' and what is not. These are clearly value judgements and assessments based around consistent thinking that we have reached social and ecological tipping points that must be turned around. Will we have the capacity and willingness to make the changes necessary? Is this wisdom or is it madness, as Russell expounds? Are we overthinking all of this and underestimating the extent to which systems can self-correct and adapt accordingly, or are we barking at passing cars as it were, where no amount of intellectual parrying can enforce the changes we so desire?

Running a rapid thematic analysis of the collection of papers for this special issue reveals a coalescence around two key themes:

- *Taking Stock* – How did we get here?
- *Future Proofing* – What are we going to do now?

'Taking Stock' is really an evaluation of the status quo amidst the still unfolding crisis. What have we learned so far from what was previously in place and how has the COVID-19 pandemic propelled us into necessary rethinking? This is a deep reflection and unpacking of just how we came to be in the position we find ourselves in.

Conversely, 'Future Proofing' is more forward thinking and considers the conditions and approaches that are required to make the so-called paradigm shift from what was, to a more hopeful, regenerative, and sustainable future, among other outcomes. Perhaps future proofing is an apt description for the hope of remaking tourism.

Patrick Brouder

There is another two-theme categorization to consider in the papers in this special issue: *Hope* and *Change!*

There is a group of papers which are hopeful that this is the moment of change. (Even the more skeptical papers seem to share that common hope of a better world, although they claim it is unlikely to materialize any time soon!) That sense of hope for a 'better world' and that something good can come out of tourism's return from near zero is central to our rationale for publishing this special issue.

The other set of papers is focused on how change may occur in a COVID-19 world (the more hopeful papers address change to a greater or lesser extent, as well). The change papers align with the resilience projection sketched out in Figure 1. Change is desirable, but how it comes about is a messy, place-specific process that will be seen through a myriad of contemporaneous realities in a global patchwork. How these realities resolve themselves (assuming they do) will decide which alternate future will manifest. As tourism scholars, we are all well aware of the complexities that lie ahead, and even as some of us focus on hope and others on change, it seems clear that we can all agree that, at the end of the day, we all *hope for change!*

Overview of contributions

The authors contributing to this special issue were mostly either members of the *Tourism Geographies* Editorial Board, or members of an informal group of tourism scholars with research interests in 'Transformational Tourism'. Most of the papers are 'commentaries' which underwent editorial review and revisions prior to formal submission and acceptance by the journal.

Joseph Cheer

The essence of papers in this collection centers on the yearning to glean lessons and move purposefully forward from the pandemic in a manner that allows tourism to optimize its potential as a benefit to humankind. In a sense, almost all the papers, as should be expected from critical scholars, take the view that the status quo before COVID-19 was unsustainable.

Renaud's long association with cruise tourism is rather revealing in that he infers that everything that is not right about tourism is easily encapsulated in cruising. An enduring problem is that a portion of the travelling public loves cruising and many destination managers and policy makers see advantages in associations with the sector. This passion is found in many other sectors of the tourism and leisure economy, such as professional sports, which **Cooper and Alderman** point out have been similarly halted by the COVID-19 pandemic. Can we be so sure that the human penchant as a creature of habit will not return to former consumptive ways after a vaccine is developed (if not before)? Hopefully, the COVID-19 era will not be looked back upon fondly as 'the time we thought we had woken up from our slumber but promptly went back to sleep again'.

Nepal's paper is rather wistful, and understandably so looking at adventure tourism's past with fondness and lamenting what it has become declaring, 'Annapurna is no longer a classic trekking destination'. Is this an inevitability and is this what happens necessarily when tourism is introduced? Nepal is confident that COVID-19 gives adventure tourism a chance to reset. The question that begs is whether adventure tourism is even interested in resetting, akin to the cruise tourists that Renaud discussed. What unfolds as Nepal suggests, might not only be up to the communities and policy makers, but more so the provinces of the tourism global supply chain that might roll on regardless, at least for the short term.

While we might already know what needs doing, does the broad tourism stakeholder group have the capacity and willingness to follow through? **Brouder** opines that transformation might remain a pipe dream unless 'sufficient institutional innovation' emerges – but these are the same institutions that were instrumental in getting us to where we are in the first place. Brouder's summation that 'the likelihood of a transformation of tourism is low and there is evidence of past moves towards sustainable tourism being ultimately undone by the dominant development path coming back' is daunting and depressing all at once. **Niewiadomski's** linking of globalization and the rise in international tourism suggests that deglobalization can have an adverse impact on any future recovery. However, COVID-19 is 'giving the global tourism industry a unique chance for a re-boot' and that there are 'unlimited path-shaping opportunities'. The extent to which COVID-19 will shape path-creation is undoubted, but the question regarding what this pathway might be remains open.

Tomassini and Cavagnaro's conflation of power and 'the local' poses very timely considerations – can tourism rebalance the disproportionate power relations between the travelling classes and those who host them? Rethinking neoliberalism is very much allied to the reshaping of tourism in the post COVID-19 milieu, but how confident can we be that the markets will undergo behavior change? Will it always be 'about the economy, stupid', as Bill Clinton is said to have uttered, and will that dictate terms of engagement above that of social movements against it? **Higgins-Desbiolles** follows on from this, proposing that socializing tourism where the public good is prominent might form a realignment potential. One way forward is seen in **Everingham and Chassagne's** plea for values reshaping, for which the Buen Vivir tradition from South America might offer some salient instructions on how tourism limits might be better acknowledged.

Remaking tourism features prominently throughout the articulations in this collection and based around a unified appeal for positive transformation. **Ateljevic** calls for new ways of thinking, doing and being underlined by regenerative economics where land use and global food systems are transformed and more in sync with natural world systems and away from hyper driven production systems. **Edelheim** also appeals for a revaluation structured around tourism higher education where 'we equip our students, through the education we provide them, with tools not only to transform themselves but also to transform the realities they will inhabit'. Hope underlines much of what **Pernecky** holds true to advocating that as critical scholars, 'We ought to have *hope-as-utopia* and draw on the imaginative capacities of tourism scholars, students and professionals to envisage and articulate social realities vis-à-vis tourism that are more just, equitable and considerate'.

Romagosa considers finding a middle way that rebalances the weighting between economic, social and ecological priorities in a redefined sustainability paradigm. The annual Burning Man festival in the US, according to **Rowen,** presents a potentially ideal platform from which to rearticulate the urgency for finding the sustainability sweet spot that Romagosa suggests. Rowen's rendering of the Burning Man festival is very relevant to the transformation of tourism because as he says: 'the exemplary and creative response of some of its participants to this and past waves of disaster and crisis can offer lessons for the formation and maintenance of community and connection that may support more sustainable social and environmental economies'. Rowen is ebullient that *Burners'* 'pro-social behavior could be of use for a reimagined and reconfigured tourism'. Fair to say that they are the converted and the question that begs is whether the philosophies and subversive actions of Burners extends beyond what might be iconoclastic interests at best.

Ioannides and Gyimóthy articulate the sentiments of almost all contributors by highlighting travel and tourism's so-called fork in the road. Are we able to 'grasp the opportunity and to rectify an otherwise defective global system' as they suggest, while noting that tourism remains subject to larger, overarching agendas beyond tourism circles? Are the solutions we need going to lie in technology and the wider smart tourism movement as many think? **Zeng, Chen and Lew** offer what they consider to be likely response, suggesting that in a high-touch industry like tourism, solutions to make us more secure in the event of future pandemics lie in low-touch or no-touch technologies, which would also create a new potential for high-touch opportunities for tourism workers.

In elucidating the impacts of the COVID-19 pandemic on Indigenous peoples, **Carr** argues that it 'accentuates the cumulative impacts from mass tourism, overtourism, colonialism and racism on Indigenous peoples as it has disrupted livelihoods'. Indeed, this accords with the argumentation that in times of crisis, the most vulnerable tend to pay the biggest price. Indigenous peoples and their encounter with colonization are manifold but as historical entreaties have proved, the spread of hitherto unprecedented illnesses is embedded in colonial narratives. Carr is piercing in her assertions that 'The virus, like colonialism, extends a legacy beyond this generation to future generations'.

That the COVID-19 pandemic has created an inflection point is certain. **Cave and Dredge** suggest that the diverse economies framework may offer any insights for a post COVID-19 tourism system. They describe this framework 'as systems of coordinated exchange through which value is produced, consumed and accumulated – organized into types of economic practice'. In essence, it flags how economic considerations and the refiguring these might be the key to the post pandemic tourism landscape. **Haywood** similarly places tourism's post COVID-19 recovering within the framework of an existing and yet diverse economic system, but sees innovative hope in the tourism sector's 'desire and ability to work collaboratively, as a collective unit'.

While a great deal of attention in foreshadowing the 'post-pandemic new normal' is spent on reforming the industry and policy making, much less attention is given to the role that tourists themselves should play in all of this. Where this has been apparent, behavior change is considered vital, and for **Stankov, Filimonau and Vujičić**, the key might lie in cultivating mindfulness in travellers. As they argue, 'a post-pandemic tourism industry could benefit from more conscious consumers, that are more aware of their unconscious behaviors, purchasing patterns, and increased ability to resist the promise of false happiness'. Similarly, in calling for the cultivation of a new global consciousness, **Galvani, Lew and Sotelo Perez**, adjudge that this is needed because 'True sustainability will only occur when it is valued as a part of the take-for-granted daily life of individuals and cultures across the globe'.

Mostafanezhad articulates the conundra that COVID-19 presents us, the inhabitants on planet Earth, stating 'we must denaturalize the political-economic drivers of disasters and their human and non-human consequences in ways that not only reveal the open wounds of structural inequality, but also offer more than a band-aid to heal them'. This appeal resonates through all the contributions in this collection, and in the whole scheme of things, the rights to travel seem trivial when so many lives have been lost and public health concerns remain central. Mostafanezhad is realistic in opining, 'While there are reasons to be hopeful, who will benefit from this restructuring is still an unsettled question'.

The remaining contributions in this collection traverse the continuum of despair and hopelessness at one extreme, and ebullience and optimism at the other. **Hall, Scott and Gössling's** wide sweep of the status quo suggests that complexity and messiness, rather than straight-up circumstances, makes prognosticating and future forecasting tricky. Notwithstanding, humans, non-humans and the planet might be in for the fight of their collective lives in the post pandemic transformation. While COVID-19 is seen as a harbinger of what's to come, **Prideaux, Thompson and Pabel** argue that climate change presents a far greater threat to humanity, and that the pandemic may provide some insights into how the planet and tourism might shift toward a carbon neutral economic production system.

Crossley's rendering of ecological grief deftly illustrates the way a sense of considerable loss has become an overriding emotion. That nature is appearing to benefit from a lighter human touch is a silver lining amidst overwhelming cumulonimbus. This aligns with **Lapointe's** interweaving of alterity and what this means for tourism. If indeed Lapointe's sense of alterity is so, when 'the transformation of the tourism sector within the striated zones, and simultaneous deterritorializing movements in the smooth corridors of 6 ft-tourism products' takes place, will this be stomached so acceptingly by a tentative travelling public?

Tremblay-Huet meditates on the issue of power and privilege in regards to space appropriation suggesting that reinstating local agencies might signal a shift to a transformed status quo for host communities. Indeed, human flourishing as a touchstone is raised by **Cheer** who argues that any new normal must have this as a fundamental tenet.

In the end, while contributors have made stirring appeals for how we might see things changing, ultimately, transformation requires solutions and actions that are not only tolerable and viable, but have the capacity to puncture the policy maker and practitioner bubbles, and also entice the traveling public to embrace the pandemic's lessons to shift their past values to better align with those of planet. Whether or not the stampede for greater resilience building in tourism destinations can be achieved or not remains a quest that has taken on greater urgency than ever before (Lew & Cheer, 2017; Saarinen & Gill, 2018). That said, are we humans even capable of recognizing our self-harming failings and transform accordingly? On this, Bertrand Russell offers us yet another point for reflection:

> And what are we to say of man? Is he a speck of dust crawling helplessly on a small and unimportant planet, as the astronomers see it? Or is he, as the chemists might hold, a heap of chemicals put together in some cunning way? Or finally, is man what he appears to Hamlet, noble in reason, infinite in faculty? Is man, perhaps all of these at once? (Foules, 1959, p. 8)

Acknowledgement

The editors of this special issue wish to thank the following lecturers and scholars for their assistance in translating the abstracts from English to Chinese in an expeditious manner.
Xuewang Dong – Zhejiang Gongshang University, Hangzhou
Cui Feng – Nanjing Agricultural University, Nanjing
Tian Fengjun – Jiangxi University of Finance and Economics, Nanchang
Guosheng Han – Shandong University at Weihai
Yexinghan Hu – Hebei Finance University, Baoding
Zhongjuan Ji – Sun Yat-Sen University, Guangzhou
Qinglian (Melo) Li – Huangshan Vocational & Technical College, Huangshan
Wenjing (Essie) Li – Sun Yat-Sen University, Guangzhou
Shu Tang – Jingling Institute of Technology, Nanjing
Jia (Jane) Wang – Nanchang University, Nanchang
Li (Shine) Wang – Anhui Normal University, Wuhu
Wenrui Wang – Lanzhou University, Lanzhou

Ying (Ellen) Xue – Hangzhou Normal University, Hangzhou
Dongbin Yan – Hebei Finance University, Baoding
Ke Yin – Chongqing Normal University, Chongqing
Ziping (Alice) Yu – Nanjing Xiaozhuang University, Nanjing
Zhanjing Zeng – Nanjing University, Nanjing
Yan (Isabelle) Zhang – Zhejiang Gongshang University, Hangzhou
Xun (Diane) Zhang – Zhejiang University of Finance and Economics, Hangzhou
Xingming Zhong – Qingdao University, Qingdao

ORCID

Alan A. Lew ⓘ http://orcid.org/0000-0001-8177-5972
Joseph M. Cheer ⓘ http://orcid.org/0000-0001-5927-2615
Noel B. Salazar ⓘ http://orcid.org/0000-0002-8346-2977

References

Butler, R. W. (Ed.). (2017). *Tourism and resilience*. CABI.
Cheer, J. M., & Lew, A. A. (Eds.). (2017). *Tourism, resilience and sustainability: Adapting to social, political and economic change*. Routledge.
Foules, P. (Ed.). (1959). *Bertrand Russell: Wisdom of the West*. Crescent Books.
Hall, C. M., Prayag, G., & Amore A. (2017). *Tourism and resilience: Individual, organisational and destination perspectives*. Channel View Publications.
Kruglanski, A. (2020). 3 ways the coronavirus pandemic is changing who we are. The Conversation (March 20), https://theconversation.com/3-ways-the-coronavirus-pandemic-is-changing-who-we-are-133876
Lew, A. A., & Cheer, J. M. (Eds.). (2017). *Tourism resilience and adaptation to environmental change: Definitions and frameworks*. Routledge.
Saarinen, J., and Gill, A. M. (Eds.). (2018). *Resilient destinations and tourism: Governance strategies in the transition towards sustainability in tourism*. Routledge.

Transforming the (tourism) world for good and (re)generating the potential 'new normal'

Irena Ateljevic

ABSTRACT

With or without the global COVID-19 pandemic to promote and envision a meaningful and positive transformation of the planet in general, and tourism specifically, a wake-up call is long overdue. The 300-years old industrial and modern paradigm of ruthless and selfish exploitation of natural resources has separated us from nature and ultimately ourselves to such an extent that the crises of our economic, political, environmental, social and healthcare systems do not come at any surprise. Yet, in juxtaposition to (post)modern pessimistic views, the positive transmodern paradigm shift with its holistic perspectives and practices can be observed. Led by 'the silent revolution' of cultural creatives, new worlds are emerging, although still kept at the margins. 'Transformative travel and tourism' as an ever-growing trend, appears to be an important medium through which these cultural creatives reinvent themselves and the world they live in. Inner transformation is reflected in the outer world. New ways of being, knowing and doing in the world are emerging as conscious citizens, consumers, producers, travellers, entrepreneurs, and community leaders are calling and acting upon the necessary transformation towards the *regenerative* paradigm and *regenerative economic systems*. Based on the natural cycles of renewal and regeneration, this circular approach is underpinned by regenerative land practices. The vision of connecting regenerative agriculture and transformative tourism is offered to reset the global tourism system for good.

摘要

无论是否出现新型冠状病毒肺炎全球大流行, 警钟早就应该敲响以促进和展望整个地球, 尤其是旅游业发生重大和积极的转变。历时300年野蛮而又自私地开采自然资源的工业和现代范式, 将我们与自然分开, 以至于当我们的经济、政治、环境、社会和保健系统的危机到来时, 我们一点不惊讶。然而, 与 (后) 现代悲观主义观点同时存在的是我们也可以观察到跨现代范式及其整体视角和实践的积极转变。在文化创意"无声革命"的引领下, 仍处于边缘的新世界正在崛起。"改造式旅游和旅游业"作为一种不断发展的趋势, 似乎是这些文化创意者重塑自己以及他们生处世界的重要媒介。外在世界反映了内在的转变。伴随着有上述意识的公民、消费者、生产者、旅行者、企业家和社区领导人呼吁并采取行动实现向可再生范式和再生经济体系的必要转变, 新的存在、认识和行动方式正在出现。基于可恢复和再生的自然循环, 这种循环方法以再生土地实践为基础, 提出将再生农业和改造式旅游相结合的愿景, 以期永久性地重置全球旅游体系。

Introduction

We will not go back to normal. Normal never was. Our pre-corona existence was not normal other than we normalised greed, inequity, exhaustion, depletion, extraction, disconnection, confusion, rage, hoarding, hate and lack. We should not long to return, my friends. We are being given the opportunity to stitch a new garment. One that fits all of humanity and nature (Renee Taylor, 2020).

This special TG issue has been designed to promote '**a substantial, meaningful, and positive transformation of the planet in general, and tourism specifically.**' A call to not return to a "normal" that existed before COVID-19 but rather to provide a vision of how the world can or is evolving into something different. I have been 'obsessed' with these kinds of issues most of my life and academic career. From my personal traumatic experience of the civil war in Croatia to my PhD in critical economic geography in New Zealand, to co-founding the global Critical Tourism Studies movement and promotion of an Academy of hope, I've called upon new ways of being, knowing and doing not only in tourism studies and practice but also in the world (e.g. Ateljevic, 2009, 2011). Thus, I feel I cannot say anything new here, but will aim to instead mainstream previously marginalised ideas allowed by the unprecedented global standstill. To potentially move what was considered either radical, over positive or naïve into the centre of (y)our attention and (y)our consideration. During this great pause, we could potentially embrace the holistic paradigms and practices that have been waiting on the margins. In our humbled state, we could bring them into the centre and build a new system around them (Eisenstein, 2020). In some parts of the world, we already are. I thank Alan Lew on this initiative to wave the flag of what **radically** different and potentially positive outcomes can come out of this huge predicament. We need to see a vision of what's desirable and possible so that we are able to commit to a paradigm shift.

I imagine all sectors surrounding or embedded in tourism practice will be in a desperate need for a new and meaningful sense of direction. In such desperate need and ambitious aspiration, I recall Charles Eisenstein (n.d.) when he states: 'We don't need smarter solutions. We need different questions'. Indeed, we need to look at the values underlying, pre-existing and exacerbating the crisis that may drive us to ask questions like, what do we really want? What does a beautiful life look like? What do we want to leave behind and what do we want to take forward? If we are able to stop almost everything to save sick humans, why don't we do the same for a sick planet? That's the invitation that crises in general can offer - that is to deeply reflect on our dominant worldview and our value system. Anderson and Ackerman-Anderson (2010), in their extensive experience with change management at the organisational and systemic levels, distinguish processes of *change* and *transformation* whereby the *change* happens within the existing world view, while *transformation* in fact 'is the emergence of a new order out of existing chaos … <which> begins with ever-increasing disruption to the system, moves to the point of death of the old way of being, and then, as with the phoenix, proceeds toward an inspired rebirth' (p. 61).

Transformative travel and tourism

In 2009, I wrote a chapter for Tribe's book on *Philosophical Issues of Tourism*, entitled: *Transmodernity: Remaking Our (Tourism) World?*, in which I summarised my academic journey from being a pessimistic, critical theorist to a more positive and hopeful academic. In juxtaposition to the structural relations of injustice created by the worldview of 'the survival of the fittest', I reviewed the emerging promising discourses of the transmodern philosophical, economic, political and socio-cultural shift. The shift that moves us from the story of separation from ourselves, nature and each other - to a narrative of *inter-being*, the one that sees the mutual interdependence of all living forms (Eisenstein, 2013). Ghisi (2008) described transmodernity as a planetary vision in which humans are beginning to realize that we are all (including plants and animals) connected into one system, which makes us symbiotic, vulnerable and responsible for the Earth as an indivisible living community. The current pandemic crisis could not be a greater case in point.

Magda (1989), the Spanish philosopher who first coined the term, uses Hegelian logic whereby modernity, postmodernity and transmodernity form a dialectic triad that completes a process of thesis, antithesis and synthesis. As expressed in her own words: 'the third tends to preserve the defining impetus of the first yet is devoid of its underlying base: by integrating its negation the third moment reaches a type of specular closure' (p. 13). In other words, transmodernism is critical of modernism and postmodernism while at the same time drawing elements from each. In a way it is a return to some form of absolute 'logic' that goes beyond Western ideology and aims to connect the human race to a new shared story, which can be called a *global relational consciousness* (Rifkin, 2005; for the full review of transmodernity paradigm see Ateljevic, 2013).

The paradigm shift is being carried by the growing population of so-called transmodern 'cultural creatives' who are acquiring new ways of looking at and being in the world — ways that are consistent with a sustainable global future and in doing so forming and shaping new cultures of conscious living (Ray & Anderson, 2001). They provide and demand products and services based on their values of social and environmental justice, and travel appears to be a powerful medium through which these conscious citizens seek to re-invent themselves and the world they live in. They travel in order to volunteer and make a difference; they value what is slow, small and local (especially food); they are connected and communicative; and they seek meaningful experiences, which help them develop personally and collectively (Ateljevic et al., 2016).

Observing and researching new travel trends, I argued they are indicators manifesting the emerging global shift in human consciousness rather than just 'special interest' market segments. Elsewhere, I have further reformulated this transmodern perspective into the concept of *hopeful tourism scholarship* (Pritchard et al., 2011). This values-led, humanist perspective that strives for the transformation of our way of seeing, being, doing and relating in tourism worlds, called for the creation of a less unequal, more sustainable planet through action-oriented and participant-driven learnings and acts.

Since then, a growing number of studies have begun to emerge to reaffirm 'transformative travel and tourism' as a potential means of making the world a better place. Claimed to create conditions conducive to personal and social transformation necessary for a radical change in worldview, transformative tourism has become a new buzzword in tourism studies (Reisinger, 2013; 2015; Lean et al., 2014; Lean, 2016; UNWTO and Institute for Tourism, 2016; Kirillova et al., 2017a; 2017b; Soulard et al., 2019). In a similar vein, Pollock (2015) uses the term 'conscious travel' which assists this transformation towards a life-affirming, place-based *regenerative* economy in which all stakeholders and all living forms can thrive and flourish.

Parallelly, the tourism sector has reflected this trend. For example, the Transformative Travel Council (TTC) was formed in 2016, which comprised of 'guides and conveners of a global movement which maximizes the power of travel to positively transform how we live our lives, how we live with others, and how we live on our planet' (TTC, n.d.). A trendy Vogue magazine article (Trimble, 2017) claimed that 'transformational travel is the next evolution. It has similar elements of experiential travel, but taken a step further—it's travel motivated and defined by a shift in perspective, self-reflection and development, and a deeper communion with nature and culture'. In 2018 Skift (the agency that invented the term *overtourism*) published a report 'Transformative travel: Shifting toward meaning, purpose and self-fulfilment', claiming that 'travelers today are increasingly drawn to travel as a form of self-actualization and personal transformation and growth. They want more than a simple visit to a new destination or spend their days merely relaxing on a beach. Instead, the travel they're seeking is an experience of the world that goes deep — one that changes them in ways they may not even be aware of' (p.3). To this end, Sheldon (2020) examines how the ultimate human journey is an inner one towards the state that gives us a sense of peace and unity and connectedness with all living beings, and how tourism destinations and providers might design tourism experiences to assist tourists on the path to this ultimate inner destination.

During the same years, I conducted a longitudinal (2015–2019) research project titled: '*Trans-tourism: an integrated approach for the study of the transformative role of tourism in the 21st century*'*. Designed to run for the period of 4 years through a multi-method approach, the project further investigated these claims of tourism being a transformative catalyst towards a more caring and sustainable human existence on our beautiful planet. This proposition was analysed from three aspects, by capturing: a) the transformative power of past and present travel experiences of the cultural creatives, b) the motivations and practises of pioneering change-makers who create transformational travel products, and c) tourism stakeholders' receptiveness to integrate a transformational view of tourism into the organisational design of their businesses and products. The project was underpinned by my immersion into a whole variety of transformative travel programmes and experiences and the subsequent maintenance of connections with the participants (mostly through closed social media groups). Moreover, I have also become a social entrepreneur who established her own transformative tourism enterprise (see my Instagram handle: @terrameeracroatia). While it goes beyond the scope of this short paper to elaborate on all findings (for more, see e.g. Ateljevic & Tomljenovic, 2017; Tomljenovic & Ateljevic, 2017), some generative conclusions will be highlighted here.

All co-creative informants expressed a desire to live more fully and authentically with a meaningful life purpose and in the greater harmony with nature and humanity. Most of them at some point in their lives, felt 'stuck' in a system in which they no longer believe; by running the 'rat race' of climbing a career ladder and working exclusively for money. Their internal shift happened either when they experienced a huge personal life change or through 'unusual' travel experiences that touched upon this suppressed sentiment and helped them to reflect and make the necessary changes in their lives. Once they reached 'the point of no return' as Ross (2010) explains from his therapeutic view, the inevitable question posed itself: 'how do I live now when I do not believe in such a system anymore?' As a consequence of this urge, many leave their established careers behind and become social entrepreneurs, community leaders, activists, volunteers and often establish their own transformative tourism enterprises (that either combined their hands-on skills, hobbies or moving to a rural setting). These entre-preneurial initiatives then serve as venues to manifest their commitment to change their life-style and live more close to their own truth, while at the same time providing a fairly sustainable livelihood (albeit living more simply then in their previous overtly urban and con-sumerist lifestyle). The key motivation that was solidly expressed by all informants can be sur-mised as: 'I need to live what I believe in', however challenging that may be as the dominant system continues pushing the old paradigm of separation, consumerism, competition, and sta-tus achievement. As expressed by one of the informants in one of closed Facebook groups:

> We are curious how the fire, that has ignited something precious and something potent in many people since The Journey at Embercombe, can be rekindled. A fire will go out if not kept an eye on and given space, air and fuel - and a spark!

> We intend to create a space for reconnection with ourselves, each other and given airtime to be heard, whatever the inner voices may be thinking, it's a place that intends to move past any limiting fears by listening and learning from each other. Moving above and beyond our expectations and allowing transformation to be brought about, however small and simple, big and complex.

From transformative to regenerative: Invitation for 'the new normal'

> If you've never heard about the amazing potential of regenerative agriculture and land use practices to naturally sequester a critical mass of CO_2 in the soil and forests, you're not alone. One of the best-kept secrets in the world today is that the solution to global warming and the climate crisis (as well as poverty and deteriorating public health) lies right under our feet, and at the end of our knives and forks (Ronnie Cummins, Regeneration International Steering Committee Member).

The cutting-edge research of medical Dr Zach Bush's ** team (n.d.; Bush, 2018; 2019) has shown that human health is dependent on the connections between cells and on the cooperation and communication with microorganisms such as bacteria, fungi, and viruses. This community of vital microorganisms or the *microbiome* living inside of us largely determines the state of our health and is directly strengthened by our inter-action with the earth, and more specifically the soil in which we grow our food. Yet, we have disconnected ourselves from nature and our food supply, and that outsourc-ing has resulted in toxic farming practices and chemicals contaminating our food and killing the microbiome on which we are dependent for our bodies' healthy functioning. Consequentially, the impact on human health has been disastrous. In the USA, where chemical, industrial farming now dominates over 80% of agricultural land, Dr Bush (2018; 2019) cites parallel medical studies that provide disturbing health statistics. In 1965, 4% of the total US population had a chronic disease, while as of 2015, 46% of American children have a chronic disease diagnosis. The horrific statistics continue where 1 in 4 Americans live with diabetes; 1 in 3 are obese; 1 in 2 live with major depression; 1 in 2 men and 1 in 3 women suffer from cancer; and lastly 1 in 3 men and 1 in 4 women are infertile. Dr Bush (n.d., 2019) points out how this array of conditions is on near identical trajectories of increase since 1996, corresponding to the release of the toxic herbicide glyphosate (the active ingredient in 'Roundup'). This water soluble weed killer has not only been pushed for farming in the US and all over the world, but has also been adopted by vast amount of American households in order to rid lawns and gardens of weeds, consequentially poisoning groundwater.

Similarly, Dr Aviva Romm, MD (2017) in her book on the adrenal thyroid revolution connects autoimmune diseases with the unregulated release of numerous toxins and chemicals into our environment. Not only through chemical farming but also around all aspects of industrial production that is creating a vicious cycle of disastrous impacts on our health, our ecosystems and all other living beings. This is a mirror of our current linear economic paradigm of ruthless and selfish exploitation of natural resources that has caused separation between and within ourselves, thus resulting in the crises of our economic, political, environmental, social and healthcare systems.

It is of no surprise that the regenerative paradigm and the regenerative economy have emerged as welcome alternatives with 'holistic worldview, which recognizes that the proper functioning of complex wholes (like an economy) cannot be understood without understanding the ongoing, dynamic relationships among parts that give rise to greater "wholes"'(Fullerton, 2015, 13). More precisely, David Korten (2013), former professor at the Harvard Business School and prominent critic of corporate globalization, gives us an eloquent and simple definition: 'The only valid purpose of an economy is to serve life. To align the human economy with this purpose, we must learn to live as nature lives, organise as nature organizes, and learn as nature learns guided by a reality-based, life-centred, intellectually-sound economics'.

One of the first economic sectors that has been using this approach is regenerative agriculture and soil science (Shiva et al., 2015). This 'no spray, no toil' agriculture not only 'does no harm' to the land but actually improves it, using technologies that regenerate and revitalize the soil and the environment. In doing so, it leads to healthy soil, capable of producing high-quality, nutrient-dense food while simultaneously regenerating land, and ultimately leading to productive farms and healthy communities and economies (Regeneration International, n.d). Following this circular approach of soil economy, based on natural cycles of renewal and regeneration Shiva et al. (2015) use the analogy of the relationship between soil and society as a relationship based on reciprocity, on the 'Law of Return'. The ecological law of return maintains the cycles of nutrients and water, which becomes the basis of real sustainability. In social terms, the law of return ensures mutuality, respect, human solidarity, equality, democracy and peace.

Fortunately, this story does not stop at theory as thousands of new, local, community-based initiatives, as well as cooperatives, social enterprises and neighbourhood associations are mushrooming around the world. A good example is the European Network of Community-led Initiatives on Climate Change and Sustainability (Ecolise) whose members include international networks of community-based initiatives such as the Transition Town Network (representing over 1200 transition initiatives world-wide), the Global Ecovillage Network (15,000 ecovillages), the Permaculture movement (3 million practitioners globally), ICLEI - Local Governments for Sustainability (a global network of more than 1,750 local and regional governments (in 100+ countries) committed to sustainable urban development; national and regional networks; and other specialist bodies engaged in European-level research, training and communications to support community-led action on climate change and sustainability (Ecolise n.d.).

Departing from the grounds of such inspiration and to finally answer the question of what could be a positive and meaningful way forward for the future of tourism? I propose the correlation to regenerative agriculture practices for two key reasons. Firstly, it gives us a framework of regeneration rather than just sustaining the existing worldview. Secondly, food is one of the key ingredients underpinning tourism consumption. Can you imagine if all flights, hotels, restaurants, resorts ... would use local organic produce coming from regenerative farms? If the total contribution of travel and tourism to global GDP in 2018 was US$8.9 trillion (World Travel & Tourism Council, 2019) and 1.5 billion people travelled internationally in 2019 (UNWTO, 2020) - the positive global impact of the industry on the regeneration of the world would be huge. Satish Kumar, a founding editor of Resurgence Magazine and a key leader behind Schumacher college (Devon, the UK) beautifully reinforces my point here. In his recent interview (2020, April 16) on what will need to change in the post-COVID-19 world, he points explicitly to the notion of mass tourism and industrial agriculture as two key examples of unsustainable human activity disconnected from nature (he gave his interview one day after I wrote the final draft of this paper). Kumar then calls upon the need to return to the original meaning of travel as a journey of purpose, meaning, adventure and exploration, and growing small-scale food as the nurturing bedrock for human health rather than a commercial commodity.

What a beautiful new sense of purpose for each of us, as we stand at this crossroads to choose between the path toward greater isolation and separation or *the more beautiful world our hearts know it is possible* (Eiseinstein, 2013). As Eiseinsten (2020) brilliantly expressed in his article on what he described our collective coronation: 'We can normalize heightened levels of separation and control, believe that they are necessary to keep us safe, and accept a world in which we are afraid to be near each other. Or we can take advantage of this pause, this break in normal, to turn onto a path of reunion, of holism, of the restoring of lost connections, of the repair of community and the rejoining of the web of life'.

Notes

*The Croatian Science Foundation had awarded funding to a research team of the Institute for Tourism in Zagreb.

** Dr Zach Bush, MD is a triple board certified physician specialised in internal medicine, endocrinology and hospice care and an internationally renowned educator on the microbiome as it relates to health, disease and our food production systems.

Disclosure statement

No potential conflict of interest was reported by the author(s).

References

Anderson, D., & Ackerman-Anderson, L. (2010). *Beyond change management: How to achieve breakthrough results through conscious change leadership* (2nd ed.). Wiley.

Ateljevic, I. (2009). Transmodernity – remaking our (tourism) world? In J. Tribe (Ed.), *Philosophical issues of tourism* (pp. 278–300). Elsevier Social Science Series.

Ateljevic, I. (2011). Transmodern critical tourism studies: A call for hope and transformation. *Revista Turismo em Análise, 22*(3), 497–515.

Ateljevic, I. (2013). Transmodernity: Integrating perspectives on societal evolution. *Futures, 47*(2013), 38–48.

Ateljevic, I., Sheldon, P., & Tomljenovic, R. (2016). The new paradigm of the 21st century: Silent revolution of cultural creatives and transformative travel of and for the future. In *Global report on the transformative power of tourism: A paradigm shift towards more responsible tourism traveller* (pp. 12–20). UNWTO & Institute for Tourism.

Ateljevic, I., & Tomljenovic, R. (2017). The crisis world and a journey into the transformative potenal of tourism: an ethnographic approach. In M. Knezevic, B. Brumen, & M. Goranek (Eds.), *Refugees travel on a tourist road* (pp. 31–64). Pearson Education.

Bush, Z. (2018, July 8). Nourish Vermont: Our role in today's disease epidemics. (Video). YouTube. https://www.youtube.com/watch?v=O1aD5NpTLXY

Bush, Z. (2019, January 8). *Food independence & planetary evolution: Zach Bush/Rich Roll Podcast.* https://www.youtube.com/watch?v=O1aD5NpTLXY

Bush, Z. (n.d.). *Glyphosate + toxins.* https://zachbushmd.com/gmo/glyphosate-toxins/.

Ecolise. (n.d.). *About Ecolise.* https://www.ecolise.eu/about-ecolise/

Eisenstein, C. (2013). *The more beautiful world our hearts know it is possible.* North Atlantic Books.

Eisenstein, C. (2020, March). *The coronation.* https://charleseisenstein.org/essays/the-coronation/?_page=5

Eisenstein, C. (n.d.). *Short course: Unlearning for change agents.* https://charleseisenstein.org/courses/unlearning-for-change-agents/

Fullerton, J. (2015). *Regenerative capitalism: How universal principles and patterns will shape our new economy.* Capital Institute.

Ghisi, L. M. (2008). *The knowledge society: A breakthrough towards genuine sustainability.* Arunachala Press.

Kirillova, K., Lehto, X., & Cai, L. (2017a). Existential authenticity and anxiety as outcomes: The tourist in the experience economy. *International Journal of Tourism Research, 19*(1), 13–26.

Kirillova, K., X., Lehto, X., & Cai, L. (2017b). What triggers transformative tourism experiences? *Tourism Recreation Research, 42*(4), 498–511. https://www.tandfonline.com/doi/abs/10.1080/02508281.2017.1342349?journalCode=rtrr20

Korten, D. (2013, January 18). What would nature do? Not Wall Street: Models for a healthy down-to-earth economy are all around us. *Yes Magazine.* http://www.yesmagazine.org/issues/what-would-nature-do/inside-the-down-to-earth-economy

Kumar, S. (2020, April 16). *Resilience, patience, equanimity & solidarity.* https://www.facebook.com/42acres/videos/599239047468148/

Lean, G. (2016). *Transformative travel in a mobile world.* CABI.

Lean, G., Staiff, R., & Waterton, E. (Eds.). (2014). *Travel and transformation.* Current Development in the Geographies of Leisure Series. Ashgate Publishing.

Magda, R. M. R. (1989). *La sonrisa de saturno: Hacia una teoria transmoderna.* Anthropos.

Pollock, A. (2015). *Social entrepreneurship in tourism: The conscious travel approach.* Tourism Innovation Partnership for Social Partnership (TIPSE), UK.

Pritchard, A., Morgan, N., & Ateljevic, I. (2011). Hopeful tourism: A new transformative perspective. *Annals of Tourism Research, 38*(3), 941–963.

Ray, H. P. and Anderson, S. R. (2001). *The cultural creatives: How 50 million people are changing the world.* Harmony Books.

Regeneration International. (n.d.). *Why regenerational agriculture?* https://regenerationinternational.org/why-regenerative-agriculture/

Reisinger, Y. (2013). *Transformational tourism: Tourist perspectives.* CABI.

Reisinger, Y. (2015). *Transformational tourism: Host perspectives.* CABI.

Renee Taylor, S. (2020, April 2). *We will not go back to normal.* @sonyareneetaylor; https://www.sonyareneetaylor.com

Rifkin, J. (2005). *The European dream: How Europe's vision of the future is quietly eclipsing the American dream.* Penguin Group.

Romm, A. (2017). *The adrenal thyroid revolution.* HarperCollins.

Ross, S. (2010). Transformative travel: an enjoyable way to foster radical change. *ReVision, 32*(1), 54–64.

Sheldon, P. (2020). Designing tourism for inner transformation. *Annals of Tourism Research, 18*(3), 473–484. Forthcoming.

Shiva, V., Lockhart, C., & Schroff, R. (2015). *Terra Viva: Our soil, our commons, our future: A new vision for planetary citizenship.* Navdanya International.

Skift. (2018). *Transformative travel: Shifting toward meaning, purpose and self-fulfilment.* http://skiftx.com/wp-content/uploads/2018/04/The-Rise-of-Transformative-Travel.pdf

Soulard, J., McGehee, N. G., & Stern, M. (2019). Transformative tourism organizations and glocalization. *Annals of Tourism Research, 76*(2019), 91–104.

Tomljenovic, R., & Ateljevic, I. (2017). Transformative tourism, social entrepreneurs and regenerative economy. In A. M. Tonkovic (Ed.), *Serial proceedings of the 6th international scientific symposium economy of Eastern Croatia - vision and growth* (pp.577–587). Faculty of Economics. https://www.dropbox.com/s/gpkdqlirbhv9hqx/Zbornik%202017.pdf?dl=0

Transformative Travel Council. (n.d.). *Transformational travel.* https://www.transformational.travel/about-tt-page.

Trimble, M. (2017, January 3). Why 'transformative travel' will be the travel trend of 2017? *Vogue.* https://www.vogue.com/article/transformative-travel-trend-2017.

UNWTO & Institute for Tourism. (2016). *Global report on the transformative power of tourism: A paradigm shift towards more responsible tourism traveller.* UNWTO. http://cf.cdn.unwto.org/sites/all/files/pdf/global_report_transformative_power_tourism_v5.compressed_2.pdf

UNWTO. (2020, January, 20). *International tourism growth continues to outpace the global economy.* https://www.unwto.org/international-tourism-growth-continues-to-outpace-the-economy

World Travel and Tourism Council. (2019). *Economic impact report.* https://wttc.org/Research/Economic-Impact

"We can't return to normal": committing to tourism equity in the post-pandemic age

Stefanie Benjamin, Alana Dillette and Derek H. Alderman (iD)

ABSTRACT

Tourism transformation must bring an actionable focus on equity. A new normal openly recognizes the crises and tensions inhabiting tourism well before the COVID-19 pandemic along with the holistic and integrated nature of a pro-equity agenda. A resilient post-pandemic tourism must be more equitable and just, in terms of how it operates, its effects on people and place, and how we as scholars teach, study and publicly engage the travel industry— particularly in preparing its current and future leaders. A commitment to equity is about making specific changes in practices and decisions at multiple levels, along with growing a wider ethical framework. This pivot of a mindset requires us, as tourists, corporations, and educators to step away from a selfish perspective and critically change our perception and understanding of tourism to a truly equitable focus. Consequently, these actions force us to question the consumerism and capitalistic lens that has contributed to mass growth across the touristic landscape and instead, choose a system that fosters sustainable and equitable growth - which in turn, 'slows down' our ways of *consuming* the world around us - transforming our values and experiences of what tourism is and should be.

摘Z要

旅游业转变必须切实地注重公平。作为一种新的公开的常态, 人们已经意识到在新冠状病毒来临之前, 提倡公平旅游的迫切性就和危机、紧张一起共存于旅游业中。就后疫情时期旅游业怎样运作, 及其对人们和地方的影响, 还有我们学界的教学研究, 公众参与旅游的方式, 尤其是为当前和未来的主流准备而言, 后疫情时期旅游业的韧性发展, 必须更公平公正。对旅游公平的承诺与在不同层面上的旅游实践和决策中做出具体的改变相关, 同时还z要培育更广层面上的道德构架以实现旅游公平。这种思路构建的关键z要求我们作为旅游者、企业和教育工作者们, z要摒弃自私的视角, 批判性地改变我们对旅游的看法和理解, 使之成为真正公平的焦点。因而促使我们去质疑促进了整个旅游业的大规模增长的消费主义和资本视角, 反过来选择一种促进可持续和公平增长的体系。这会"减慢"我们消费周围世界的方式, 改变我们与旅游本质有关的价值观和体验。

Now is the time for academics, practitioners, travelers, and humans to take a pause, reflect, unite, then reset the tourism industry. As we write this piece, the world is in the middle of the global pandemic that is COVID-19 (World Health Organization, 2020). The virus has had a highly damaging effect on tourism, forcing travel-related businesses around the world to lay off employees and close temporarily if not for good. Job loss in tourism is predicted to be as much as 50 million jobs worldwide (World Travel and Tourism Council, 2020). However, the industry has been a major agent in its own undoing, helping spread COVID-19 through the unwitting travel and over-tourism patterns of people, the blatantly poor decisions made by some authorities refusing to close destinations, and the refusal of some travelers, such as infamous spring breakers, to ignore social distancing and 'stay at home' guidelines.

Once this pandemic reaches its peak, our hope is that we will see it decline, or eventually level off enough to allow us to return to some *normalcy*. Yet, what do we want to accept as 'normal'? And do we want to settle for and return to the industry's old 'normal'? Perhaps the situation is best captured by a graffiti message spray painted on a wall in Hong Kong, first inscribed amid pro-democracy protests but even more appropriate in the current crisis: "We can't return to normal, because the normal that we had was precisely the problem." Over its history, tourism has normalized a series of systemic inequalities that contributed in part to the dilemma in which the industry and its communities now find themselves (Higgins-Desbiolles, 2010).

There is an opportunity—if not an outright necessity—not just to regain travel and tourism dollars and market position once the pandemic recedes, but to reform and repair the industry in meaningful ways. As the co-directors of a progressive initiative called Tourism RESET, we are scholars interested in advancing a new, transformative *normal* in post-pandemic tourism. We use 'post-pandemic' cautiously since it is likely that the epidemiological and social footprint of COVID-19 will not soon go away, if at all. For us, transformation must bring an actionable focus on equity. As we detail in this commentary, a new normal openly recognizes the crises and tensions inhabiting tourism well before the pandemic along with the holistic and integrated nature of a pro-equity agenda. A resilient post-pandemic tourism must be more equitable and just, in terms of how it operates, its effects on people and place, and how we as scholars teach, study and publicly engage the travel industry—particularly in preparing its current and future leaders. A commitment to equity is about making specific changes in practices and decisions at multiple levels, which we discuss below, along with growing a wider ethical framework to make real the possibility of tourism being "a servant to building society, citizenry and well-being" (Tourism Alert and Action Forum, 2020)

COVID-19 exposes an already sick industry

Important to developing the new normal is to recognize the destructive if not violent dimensions of travel and tourism as a means of capitalist accumulation (Devine & Ojeda, 2017). On the surface it appears COVID-19 is creating a crisis for tourism, but we assert that the pandemic is also exposing crises and tensions that have historically existed in the industry. Ongoing mass job loss magnifies the vulnerabilities and injustices long facing tourism workers in the form of low wages, lack of benefits and 'right on time' labor practices (Baum et al., 2016).

COVID-19 has intensified criticism of previously unchecked exploitative management practices, forcing a company like Darden Restaurants (the parent company of Olive Garden) to offer a sick leave policy for employees amidst the virus outbreak (Lucas, 2020). The strict market-driven ideology of many tourism businesses and their over-reliance on capital makes this pandemic-induced economic downturn especially painful (Borden, 2020). For example, the negative impact of the virus on short-term vacation rentals exposes stark inequities underlying housing markets in some tourist destinations (DuBois, 2020). Booming metropolitan cities like San Francisco and Toronto, where these vacation rentals previously thrived, are now ghost towns leaving homes empty and mortgages unpaid amid a still pervading housing crisis (Schaal, 2020).

As the pandemic hollows out highly visited destinations, it exposes the degree to which we have allowed an over-dependence on tourist dollars and large numbers of tourists to go unchecked for far too long. A mass tourism paradigm continues to dominate as numerous entrepreneurs, planners, students, and faculty perceive that it is *beneficial* and *worthwhile* to the economic prosperity of a destination and its culture (Weaver, 2007). Over-tourism now appears deadly in light of COVID-19 in addition to the mandates to avoid crowded conditions. However, has this type of development ever really made sense in terms of sustainability and social responsibility? Pre COVID-19, widespread promotion of over-visited excursions via social media were normalized – perpetuating glorified but unfulfillable ideas of what a vacation *should* look like. Consequently, these actions encouraged travel to already environmentally fragile destinations (Miller, 2017) and persuaded participation in inauthentic and culturally offensive practices (Hauanai-Kay, 2000) – acting like some type of badge of honor magnified through platforms like Instagram or Facebook.

However, in the face of the pandemic, tourists are not able to travel and instead, are forced to stay home and quarantine. Their absence from sites like Venice bring into focus what can be regained in suspending over-tourism; the vacant city's iconic canals are being granted an environmental reprieve and allowed to be cleared of pollution and waste (Clifford, 2020). With numerous restrictions in place like 'social distancing', more people are escaping to 'return to nature', taking time to 'slow down', and with continued international travel restrictions, engaging more with domestic travel. However, with National Parks strained with overpopulation before COVID-19 (Lake & Rulli, 2019), what will this look like in the post-pandemic era? Gabe Saglie, Senior Editor for *Travelzoo,* posits that there will be a resurgence of regional travel venturing to lesser known or populated destinations and attractions (Travelzoo, 2020). Perhaps even, a return to a time where travelers *enjoyed the journey not the destination* - and participated in what is known as 'slow tourism'.

What could a 'new normal' look like? A tourism RESET code

Especially at this pivotal moment, the measure of our science as scholars of tourism will be judged not by how detached we are from everyday realities and injustices but by our level of engagement with a world in need of leadership. We argue for a call to arms that challenges our purpose as scholars and educators to drive the conversation, to critique, and to take action in planning a post-pandemic tourism. This planning is a multi-dimensional enterprise and requires intervention in the principles and code of ethics of the industry, tourist, and educator.

Industry

Now is the time to redesign our tourism landscape and industry to be more sustainable and equitable. We've all heard it before - sustainability - ecotourism - over tourism - but who was really listening? Sure, steps were taken with select hospitality and tourism businesses and destinations to limit plastics, increase recycling, and provide counter-narratives and experiences - but was it enough? With this global pandemic, there is an opportunity for a true RESET of the tourism industry. Such a RESET should be more than lip service or greenwashing of brochures; rather, it should be about planning a tourism future not fueled solely by demand but guided by an *ethics of care*, *social and environmental justice*, and *racial reconciliation*. The latter issue is especially salient given how hard COVID-19, the disease itself and its economic aftermath, has hit communities of color in the United States (Breslow, 2020).

The post-pandemic tourism industry will need to confront its historical role in perpetuating *structural inequalities* and implement policies and practices in daily operations to ensure a safe, clean and just environment for all employees. This may include reasonable sick leave and health benefits, fair and consistent scheduling and equitable wages. Destinations will grapple with how to quickly 'bounce back' while also dedicating significant resources to developing a more resilient, equitable and sustainable tourism industry. They may consider encouraging social and spatial equity in tourism development by moving towards a marketing plan to encourage 'slow' and 'local' tourism that focuses on supporting locally and minority owned and operated tourism businesses. Policy makers need to work tirelessly to consider how best to protect the rights and livelihoods of tourism workers rather than exploiting them in the post-pandemic financial recovery. They will need to consider the benefits of policies like industry-wide collective bargaining agreements and increasing the minimum wage to an actual 'living wage' in order to protect tourism workers in the next time of crisis (Glasmeier, 2020). A true industry RESET will require commitment from a variety of players and deep critical analysis of the flaws in our current policies and practices.

Tourist

Now is the time to be critical of the social values communicated and realized through our own actions, both in traveling for personal reasons and for business. Once travel resumes, will you jump on the first opportunity to jet across the globe or pause and consider how your next trip may truly support the local economy you are visiting? As travelers, we all have the responsibility of considering how we spend each of our tourism dollars, especially in a post-pandemic world where finances may be more fragile. Consider this - is the destination you have chosen to visit traditionally over-touristed? If so, is there an alternative destination that you may consider? Not only in consideration of your own health and well-being, but also for those local communities and hosts that may be even more precarious in a post-pandemic world. Is the vacation rental you'd like to patronize located in a neighborhood that suffers from high levels of housing insecurity or inequity? Perhaps you could choose a locally owned or minority operated boutique hotel as an alternative.

If you were planning to go on a cruise, you might now reconsider—not just because of COVID-19 fears but because of the industry's long injurious record. The three major cruise lines that make up 70% or more of the market (Carnival, Royal Caribbean, and Norwegian Cruise Lines) have a history of not paying federal income taxes, poor workforce conditions, and environmental pollution (O'Kane, 2020). Perhaps you can find another way to visit one of those destinations and make sure to support the local community - from your transportation, to where you stay, what you eat, your touristic activities, and the gifts you purchase. Maybe international travel is completely out of the picture for the foreseeable future to help ease the amount of environmental impacts of air travel (Irfan, 2019). Are you willing to sacrifice the international vacation for closer, perhaps lesser known destinations to experience and learn about the beauty and culture closer in your own backyard? Right now, we may all be dreaming of the day when things return to 'normal', when we can finally take that vacation that we had to cancel. While we have the time, consider how your next travel dollar can contribute to a more equitable and sustainable RESET of the tourism industry.

Educator

Now is the time for scholars, educators and students to be critical of what caused this pandemic, the contributing role of travel, and how our own teaching and scholarship are complicit in perpetuating the social and environmental inequities in tourism. Let's challenge ourselves, as educators, to provide critical pedagogy to transform rather than merely maintain the current tourism industry. What should we do institutionally and intellectually in the academy to keep this actionable critique flowing, even as we advocate for tourism development? As educators, it is our responsibility to facilitate difficult conversations that encourage an 'unlearning' of the old *normal* of tourism and a re-learning of what might be possible and more equitable.

The 'critical turn', dubbed by several scholars, explores the increasing tide of research conducted through critical epistemologies that question power relations in tourism, reflecting the rising prevalence of industry critiques (Ateljevic et al., 2007; Bianchi, 2009). This 'critical turn' and its associated scholars "seek to stimulate their audience to transform society and thereby to liberate themselves and others" (Bramwell & Lane, 2014, p. 2). Consequently, in order to seek this stimulation and transformation, tourism researchers and educators must recognize tourism as more than an industry, focusing instead on tourism and travel as a social force capable of positive and just impacts (Higgins-Desbiolles, 2006). Therefore, we suggest departments, schools and colleges critically examine their current course curriculum and revise their learning approaches to include case studies, strategies, debates, and community service projects that actively disrupt the hegemonic landscapes of tourism - a curriculum that challenges the status quo and forces us all to get comfortable with being uncomfortable.

A commitment to equity

At the 2019 Travel and Tourism Research Association Conference in Australia, Dr. Pauline Sheldon argued in her keynote address, "it is clear we need to shift our thinking about tourism … we need a new relationship with capitalism … put the wellbeing of the planet, people, and places-not just profits and growth-on the agenda" (personal communication, 2019). By conceiving of tourism as a social force (rather just a market opportunity) and empowered by studies of humanities and their critical epistemologies, one can see how tourism has the power to change people and societies and, to quote Sheldon, the power to shift from a "me to we" economy (personal communication, 2019). This pivot of a mindset requires us, as tourists, corporations and educators to step away from a selfish perspective, critically change our perception and understanding of tourism to a truly equitable focus. Consequently, these actions force us to question the consumerism and capitalistic lens that has contributed to mass growth across the touristic landscape and instead, choose a system that fosters sustainable and equitable growth - which in turn, 'slows down' our ways of *consuming* the world around us - transforming our values and experiences of what tourism is and should be.

Disclosure statement

No potential conflict of interest was reported by the author(s).

ORCID

Derek H. Alderman (iD) http://orcid.org/0000-0002-5192-8103

References

Ateljevic, I., Pritchard, A., & Morgan, N. (2007). *The critical turn in tourism studies*. Routledge.

Baum, T., Kralj, A., Robinson, R., & Solnet, D. J. (2016). Tourism workforce research: A review, taxonomy and agenda. *Annals of Tourism Research, 60*, 1–22.

Bianchi, R. V. (2009). The 'critical turn'in tourism studies: A radical critique. *Tourism Geographies, 11*(4), 484–504.

Borden, T. (2020, April 13). *The coronavirus outbreak has triggered unprecedented mass layoffs and furloughs*. Business Insider. https://www.businessinsider.com/coronavirus-layoffs-furloughs-hospitality-service-travel-unemployment-2020

Bramwell, B., & Lane, B. (2014). The "critical turn" and its implications for sustainable tourism research. *Journal of Sustainable Tourism, 22*(1), 1–8.

Breslow, J. (2020, April 10). *Why misinformation and distrust are making COVID-19 more dangerous for Black America*. NPR. https://www.npr.org/sections/coronavirus-live-updates/2020/04/10/832039813/why-misinformation-and-distrust-is-making-covid-19-more-dangerous-for-black-amer

Clifford, C. (2020, March 18). *The water in Venice, Italy's canals is running clear amid the COVID-19 lockdown*. CNBC. https://www.cnbc.com/2020/03/18/photos-water-in-venice-italys-canals-clear-amid-covid-19-lockdown.html

Council, World Travel and Tourism. (2020, March 18). *Coronavirus puts up to 50 million Travel and Tourism Jobs at Risk*. Skift. https://skift.com/2020/03/13/coronavirus-puts-50-million-tourism-jobs-at-risk-says-wttc-report/

Devine, J., & Ojeda, D. (2017). Violence and dispossession in tourism development: A critical geographical approach. *Journal of Sustainable Tourism, 25*(5), 605–617.

DuBois, D. (2020, March 11). *The impact of the Coronavirus on global short term rental markets*. AirDNA. https://www.airdna.co/blog/coronavirus-impact-on-global-short-term-rental-markets

Glasmeier, A. (2020). *Living wage calculator*. https://livingwage.mit.edu/pages/about

Hauanai-Kay, T. (2000, March). Tourism and the prostitution of Haiwain culure. *Cultural Survival Quarterly Magazine*. https://www.culturalsurvival.org/publications/cultural-survival-quarterly/tourism-and-prostitution-hawaiian-culture

Higgins-Desbiolles, F. (2006). More than an "industry": The forgotten power of tourism as a social force. *Tourism Management, 27*(6), 1192–1208.

Higgins-Desbiolles, F. (2010). The elusiveness of sustainability in tourism: The culture-ideology of consumerism and its implications. *Tourism and Hospitality Research, 10*(2), 116–129.

Irfan, U. (2019, Novemeber 30). *Air travel is a huge contributor to climate change*. Vox. https://www.vox.com/the-highlight/2019/7/25/8881364/greta-thunberg-climate-change-flying-airline

Lake, Z. & Rulli, M. (2019). *National parks officials grappling with high volume as Instagram tourism booms*. ABC News. https://abcnews.go.com/Lifestyle/instagram-tourism-booms-horseshoe-bend-national-parks-officials/story?id=64638198.

Lucas, A. (2020, March 19). *Olive Garden's parent begins offering paid sick leave to all employees amid coronavirus outbreak*. CNBC. https://www.cnbc.com/2020/03/19/darden-restaurants-dri-q3-2020-earnings-beat-estimates.html

Miller, C. (2017). *How instagram is changing travel*. National Geographic. https://www.national-geographic.com/travel/travel-interests/arts-and-culture/how-instagram-is-changing-travel/

O'Kane, S. (2020, March 12). *Carnival's Princess Cruises to shut down for two months due to coronavirus*. The Verge. https://www.theverge.com/2020/3/12/21176538/carnival-princess-cruise-coronavirus-covid-19-cancel-ships-two-months

Organization, World Health. (2020). Coronavirus disease (COVID-19) pandemic.

Schaal, D. (2020, March 18). *Short-term rental firms face backlash over sharply different coronavirus cancellation policies*. Skift. https://skift.com/2020/03/20/short-term-rental-firms-face-backlash-over-sharply-different-coronavirus-cancellation-policies/

Tourism Alert and Action Forum. (2020, March 20). *Statement on Covid-19 pandemic crisis*. Facebook. https://www.facebook.com/groups/TourismAlertAndActionForum/

Travelzoo. (2020, March 11). *Travelzoo U.S. Survey Reveals Flexible Travellers Find Opportunity in Current Crisis Climate.* http://ir.travelzoo.com/news-releases/news-release-details/travelzoo-us-survey-reveals-flexible-travelers-find-opportunity

Weaver, D. (2007). Towards sustainable mass tourism: paradigm shift or paradigm nudge? *Tourism Recreation Research, 32*(3), 65–69.

World Health Organization. (2020). *Coronavirus disease (COVID-19) Pandemic.* https://www.who.int/emergencies/diseases/novel-coronavirus-2019.

Reset redux: possible evolutionary pathways towards the transformation of tourism in a COVID-19 world

Patrick Brouder

ABSTRACT

With international arrivals surpassing 1.5 billion for the first time in 2019 the long-term evolution of tourism demonstrates prolific path dependence with a decade of growth since the global financial crisis. This latest period of unfettered international tourism development has come to an abrupt end as the impact of COVID-19 has brought the sector to a near standstill. As the world grapples with the realities of the global pandemic there is an opportunity to rethink exactly what tourism will look like for the decades ahead. Key concepts in evolutionary economic geography, especially path dependence/creation and institutional inertia/innovation, show variations in pathways for travel and tourism in a COVID-19 world. A path that leads to transformation in tourism can be realized if sufficient institutional innovation occurs on both the demand and supply side of tourism that can foster the emergence of new paths. COVID-19 presents a once in a generation opportunity where the institutional pump is primed for transformation. Whether that leads to a radical transformation of the tourism sector remains to be seen, but the imprint it will leave on both the demand and supply of tourism will have long-term, incremental impacts for years to come and ultimately move us closer towards the transformation of tourism.

摘要

历经全球金融危机以来的10年增长后, 国际游客人次数在2019年首次超过15亿, 旅游业演化表现出明显的路径依赖。 近期国际旅游业务的自由发展突然终止, 这是由于新型冠状病毒疾病的冲击使整个行业近乎停滞。全世界正努力应对这个全球性流行病所带来的现实问题, 也让我们有机会重新思考旅游业在未来几十年会是什么样子。演化经济地理学的核心概念尤其是路径依赖/创造和制度惯性/创新, 为旅行和旅游业在新冠病毒疫情影响下的发展提供了路径变量。 如果旅游需求和旅游供给都有足够的制度创新培育出新路径, 旅游转型就可以实现。 新冠病毒疫情为在制度层面上推动转型提供了一次千载难逢的机会。制度创新是否会引起旅游业发生根本性变化还有待观察, 但未来几年旅游业的需求和供给所受到的影响将是长期性、渐进性的, 旅游业最终会逐步走向转型。

Introduction

With international arrivals surpassing 1.5 billion for the first time in 2019 (UNWTO, 2020) the long-term evolution of tourism demonstrates prolific path dependence with a decade of growth since the global financial crisis. This latest period of unfettered international tourism development has come to an abrupt end as the impact of COVID-19 has brought the sector to a near standstill. Tourism now faces a reset just as it did after the terrorist attacks of 11 September 2001 and the global financial crisis of 2008. This time, however, the reset has the potential to be transformative. As the world grapples with the realities of the global pandemic there is an opportunity to rethink exactly what tourism will look like for the decades ahead. While some are assessing exactly how rapidly tourism will rebound to the heady heights of 2019, others are planning for a tourism transformation inspired by the esprit de corps of a global populace fixed in place. In this paper we explore the possible evolutionary pathways through which a tourism reset could arise by drawing on key lessons learned from recent studies of evolutionary economic geography in tourism. As we find ourselves once again at a point of global reset it behoves us to think beyond when tourism will recover to how tourism will recover and evolve going forward.

Evolutionary economic geography (EEG) has been of interest to tourism geographers for a decade now and has proven its utility within tourism studies (Brouder & Eriksson, 2013a; Brouder et al., 2017a; Sanz-Ibáñez & Anton Clavé, 2014). Besides being a useful lens through which to view destination change over time (Brouder & Eriksson, 2013b), EEG also has 'important implications in terms of the dynamics of economic variety, environmental (in)equity and social justice' (Brouder et al., 2017b, p.9). Perhaps the most under-researched theme in evolutionary studies of tourism is how sustainable tourism paths emerge, grow, and manage to survive (Brouder, 2017). What makes the present moment unique is the potential for global tourism to return from zero, a return which could span anywhere from 'business as usual' right the way through to 'the end of tourism' (Brouder, 2018). The zeitgeist would strongly suggest that business as usual is not an option but the tangled web that is the global production network of tourism, with multiple actors embedded in a plethora of territories (Farmaki, 2015; Niewiadomski, 2014), is on standby with a pent up desire to 'bounce back' at the earliest possible opportunity. Economic institutions can be defined as 'mutual expectations and correlated interaction' (Bathelt & Glückler, 2014, p.341) and the state of any given region or sector can be simplified as exhibiting institutional inertia or institutional innovation (Brouder & Fullerton, 2017). Exactly which form the return takes remains to be seen and examining the possible evolutionary pathways it may take can elucidate the spaces of contestation and confluence going forward (Brouder, 2014a, 2014b; Ioannides & Brouder, 2016). Such examinations call for scholarly approaches which can progress our understanding of the evolution of the spatialities of capitalism (Brouder, 2019) as well as alternate courses that tourism can take (Brouder, 2018).

Evolutionary pathways

Sanz-Ibáñez et al. (2017) wrote of the heuristic potential of 'moments' as a way of understanding destination change. While the COVID-19 pandemic and related travel

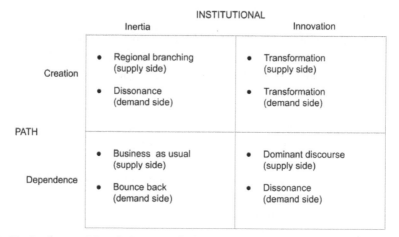

Figure 1. Matrix of potential evolutionary pathways towards tourism transformation.

restrictions are a massive system shock it is the series of 'moments' from now until the reset is complete that will reveal whether and how any real transformation has occurred in tourism. If, for instance, destination management/marketing organizations start to take a regional approach (i.e. those which were previously reliant on international travel from origin regions thousands of kilometres away now turning their attention to the often downplayed domestic and nearest neighbour markets) at the same time as there is unprecedented turbulence in tourism entrepreneurship (i.e. many long standing businesses disappearing and new ones with a new focus emerging) we may begin to see destinations re-emerge with an altogether different focus.

Such a supply-side change of focus would only have a slight chance of occurring after a 'regular' system shock. As evidenced by both the terrorist attacks of 11 September 2001 and the global financial crisis of 2008, tourism has proven its long-term resilience (Brouder & Saarinen, 2019). Notwithstanding the changes to travel security (after 2001) and airline restructuring (after 2008), the long-term development of international tourism has continued without any real evidence of systemic change (i.e. more people continue to travel and spend more money than ever before). Elsewhere, the affective aspects of the Anthropocene have made headlines in some regions such as northern Europe where environmental activist Greta Thunberg has inspired a notable number of travellers to opt out of greenhouse gas intensive modes of transport. While the COVID-19 pandemic has put the climate crisis on the back-burner of the global consciousness there is a kernel of hope for transformation in tourism in the fact that change is possible – the modest change in air travel in northern Europe infers a sea-change in post-COVID-19 tourism behaviour. In other words, there may be an institutional reckoning on the demand side of tourism as we emerge from the COVID-19 pandemic – as people's changed behaviours create new norms the tourism sector may need to come to terms with more local-oriented, environmentally-conscious tourists. Thus, the reset that was hoped for with eco-tourism, sustainable tourism, etc., and is before us once again may finally have the institutional alignment it needs to succeed globally.

It is important to note that the likelihood of a transformation of tourism is low and there is evidence of past moves towards sustainable tourism being ultimately undone by the dominant development path coming back after a few years of sustainable success (Gill & Williams, 2014, 2017). However, the current confluence of destinations grappling with starting from scratch, the growing global desire for sustainable development, and the cathartic chrysalis in which most potential tourists now find themselves means the elements needed for a transformation of tourism are in alignment (Niewiadomski, 2020). Thus, an evolutionary pathway towards the transformation of tourism exists alongside (and ultimately in competition with) other potential development pathways.

Towards the transformation of tourism?

Figure 1 presents an analytic matrix of potential evolutionary pathways towards tourism transformation. It can be applied broadly when considering change in tourism with two caveats: first, it is simplified with both 'PATH' development and 'INSTITUTIONAL' change being divided dichotomously (note: other paths and institutions are always present); and second, it is focussed on a regional (read: destination) scale but also incorporates the demand side of the institutional equation (note: tourism demand is ex-regional). The matrix implies that transformation in tourism is possible (top-right quadrant) when there is institutional innovation on both the demand and supply side which will see the emergence of new path creation in the region. This is why true transformation is so rare – near-simultaneous institutional evolution on both the supply side (in a given destination) and the demand side (which is outside the destination) is needed. The pervasive nature of COVID-19 on both economic and quotidian life across much of the globe affords us a rare alignment where the window of opportunity for a reset is there and a global transformation of tourism is possible.

Of course, while such a transformation is possible it remains unlikely. In reality, neither demand for nor supply of global tourism is uniform and thus the top-left and bottom-right quadrants of the matrix come into play. There is likely to be some notable elements of dissonance on the demand side of tourism in either of these scenarios – either the tourist sentiment is out of sync with the regional supply as path creation through regional branching for a more sustainable form of tourism is out of line with traditional markets (top-left quadrant) or the path dependent nature of tourism economies continues to push the dominant discourse (read: growth focussed) to a changed market that is no longer interested in the tourism of the past (bottom-right quadrant). The most likely scenario going forward is a patchwork of pathways based on these two quadrants as some destinations endeavour to reimagine their travel sector and some consumers reassess their priorities for life and leisure. The final pathway sees institutional inertia on the demand and supply side and a continuation of the path dependent processes that were in play previously (bottom-left quadrant). At first glance for the reader, this seems to be either the most likely scenario (i.e. we have bounced back before after crises) or the most egregious (i.e. we cannot just go back to the way things were). One of the great challenges for the tourism economy is that it is a people first sector – so many lives and livelihoods depend on it that getting back to 'business as usual' is both understandable as a reaction and seemingly necessary for the survival of many destination regions. The reality of the post-COVID-19 world is that few in the academy or the industry believe in a complete return to normal so we are left with an evolving picture which is clearly moving away from 'business as usual' and towards 'transformation' but whether the tourism sector can seize the moment afforded by the present crisis remains to be seen.

Conclusion

The COVID-19 crisis raises the question of whether we are in some form of 'reset redux' (just as we were after the terrorist attacks of 11 September 2001 and the global financial crisis of 2008) or if there is something unique about the present situation which opens the door to transformative change in tourism. Without a doubt, the present situation offers a unique opportunity for, first, the global tourism community to realign its raison d'être in a world with COVID-19; and second, for tourism scholars to examine exactly how any realignment manifests going forward.

The matrix of potential evolutionary pathways towards tourism transformation presented above shows there is a potential path that leads us to transformation in tourism if sufficient institutional innovation occurs on both the demand and supply side of tourism and if new paths also emerge. This would require a huge leap of faith on the part of destination regions as they prepare to come out of the crisis and it would also require a change in collective tourist behaviour unlike anything we have seen before. That is not to suggest that a vigorous bounce back will see a return to business as usual in short order. The more likely pathways involve some form of dissonance on the demand side as destination regions either begin to transform for a tourism market that is not interested or tourism markets are ready for transformative experiences while the destination regions are set in their old ways of doing things. In reality, each pathway will be part of the future at some level and the evolutionary trajectory of even one destination region may well have more than one pathway emerging. This is nothing new. However, while tourism evolution has always been piecemeal (e.g. ecotourism succeeds in many places alongside mass tourism), COVID-19 presents a once in a generation opportunity where the institutional pump is primed for transformation. Whether that leads to a radical transformation of the tourism sector remains to be seen but the imprint it will leave on both the demand and supply of tourism will have long-term, incremental impacts for years to come and ultimately move us closer towards the transformation of tourism.

Acknowledgements

The Vancouver Island University community acknowledges and thanks the Snuneymuxw, Quw'utsun, Tla'Amin, Snaw-naw-as and Qualicum First Nation on whose traditional lands we teach, learn, research, live and share knowledge.

Disclosure statement

No potential conflict of interest was reported by the author.

References

Bathelt, H., & Glückler, J. (2014). Institutional change in economic geography. *Progress in Human Geography*, *38*(3), 340–363. https://doi.org/10.1177/0309132513507823

Brouder, P. (2014a). Evolutionary economic geography: A new path for tourism studies? *Tourism Geographies*, *16*(1), 2–7. https://doi.org/10.1080/14616688.2013.864323

Brouder, P. (2014b). Evolutionary economic geography and tourism studies: Extant studies and future research directions. *Tourism Geographies*, *16*(4), 540–545. https://doi.org/10.1080/14616688.2014.947314

Brouder, P. (2017). Evolutionary economic geography: Reflections from a sustainable tourism perspective. *Tourism Geographies*, *19*(3), 438–447. https://doi.org/10.1080/14616688.2016.1274774

Brouder, P. (2018). The end of tourism? A Gibson-Graham inspired reflection on the tourism economy. *Tourism Geographies*, *20*(5), 916–918. https://doi.org/10.1080/14616688.2018.1519721

Brouder, P. (2019). Towards a geographical political economy of tourism. In D. K. Müller (Ed.), *A research agenda for tourism geographies* (pp. 71–78). Routledge.

Brouder, P., Anton Clavé, S., Gill, A., & Ioannides, D. (Eds.). (2017a). *Tourism destination evolution*. Routledge.

Brouder, P., Anton Clavé, S., Gill, A., & Ioannides, D. (2017b). Why is tourism not an evolutionary science? Understanding the past, present and future of destination evolution. In P. Brouder, S. Anton Clavé, A. Gill, & D. Ioannides (Eds.), *Tourism destination evolution* (pp. 13–30). Routledge.

Brouder, P., & Eriksson, R. H. (2013a). Tourism evolution: On the synergies of tourism studies and evolutionary economic geography. *Annals of Tourism Research*, *43*, 370–389. https://doi.org/10.1016/j.annals.2013.07.001

Brouder, P., & Eriksson, R. H. (2013b). Staying power: What influences micro-firm survival in tourism? *Tourism Geographies*, *15*(1), 125–144. https://doi.org/10.1080/14616688.2011.647326

Brouder, P., & Fullerton, C. (2017). Co-evolution and sustainable tourism development: From old institutional inertia to new institutional imperatives in Niagara. In P. Brouder, S. Anton Clavé, A. Gill, & D. Ioannides (Eds.), *Tourism destination evolution* (pp. 149–164). Routledge.

Brouder, P., & Saarinen, J. (2019). Co-evolution and resilient regions: Moving towards sustainable tourism development. In J. Saarinen & A. M. Gill (Eds.), *Resilient destinations and tourism* (pp. 67–76). Routledge.

Farmaki, A. (2015). Regional network governance and sustainable tourism. *Tourism Geographies*, *17*(3), 385–407. https://doi.org/10.1080/14616688.2015.1036915

Gill, A. M., & Williams, P. W. (2014). Mindful deviation in creating a governance path towards sustainability in resort destinations. *Tourism Geographies*, *16*(4), 546–562. https://doi.org/10.1080/14616688.2014.925964

Gill, A., & Williams, P. W. (2017). Contested pathways towards tourism-destination sustainability in Whistler, British Columbia: An evolutionary governance model. In P. Brouder, S. Anton Clavé, A. Gill, & D. Ioannides (Eds.), *Tourism destination evolution* (pp. 161–176). Routledge.

Ioannides, D., & Brouder, P. (2016). Tourism and economic geography redux: evolutionary economic geography's role in scholarship bridge construction. In *Tourism destination evolution* (pp. 195–205). Routledge.

Niewiadomski, P. (2014). Towards an economic-geographical approach to the globalisation of the hotel industry. *Tourism Geographies*, *16*(1), 48–67. https://doi.org/10.1080/14616688.2013.867528

Niewiadomski, P. (2020). COVID-19: from temporary de-globalisation to a re-discovery of tourism?. *Tourism Geographies*. http://doi.org/10.1080/14616688.2020.1757749

Sanz-Ibáñez, C., & Anton Clavé, S. (2014). The evolution of destinations: Towards an evolutionary and relational economic geography approach. *Tourism Geographies*, *16*(4), 563–579. https://doi.org/10.1080/14616688.2014.925965

Sanz-Ibáñez, C., Wilson, J., & Anton Clavé, S. (2017). Moments as catalysts for change in the evolutionary paths of tourism destinations. In P. Brouder, S. Anton Clavé, A. Gill, & D. Ioannides (Eds.), *Tourism destination evolution* (pp. 93–114). Routledge.

UNWTO. (2020, January 20). *International tourism growth continues to outpace the global economy*. United Nations World Tourism Organization. https://www.unwto.org/international-tourism-growth-continues-to-outpace-the-economy

COVID-19, indigenous peoples and tourism: a view from New Zealand

Anna Carr

ABSTRACT

The COVID-19 pandemic's impact is predicted to be long-lasting with intergenerational impacts for both Indigenous and non-Indigenous peoples. Indigenous peoples offer untapped potential for understanding how we are shaping resilient solutions to COVID-19 and similar threats in the future. In New Zealand, the Māori people occupy diverse leadership and occupational roles throughout society. As a result of the 1840 Treaty of Waitangi (*Te Tiriti o Waitangi*) they are recognised, through Acts of Parliament, as government partners who work in governance and planning processes, including the COVID-19 response. Such recognition can result in the inclusion of Māori values such as *whanaungatanga* (kinship and belonging), *kaitiakitanga* (environmental guardianship and responsibility) and *manaakitanga* (respect, care, and hospitality) within policy and Acts of Parliament. Māori leaders and spokespeople are stressing that environmental and social welfare needs of all communities should be prioritised as part of the COVID-19 solution and that tourism responses cannot be separated from social needs. Government responses and planning efforts that incorporate diverse cultural values ensure more equitable futures and positive experiences for tourism providers, travellers and the hosts. In this way Indigenous-informed approaches would positively contribute to transforming business, health and education for a more positive global society.

摘要

根据预测，新型冠状病毒肺炎（COVID-19）疫情的影响是长期的，将对原住民和非原住民都产生代际影响。在如何制定弹性解决方案以应对新冠疫情和今后类似威胁方面，原住民提供了尚未开发的潜力。在新西兰，毛利人在全社会中发挥着不同的领导和职业作用。根据1840年《威坦哲条约》（Te Tiriti），通过《议会法案》，他们被确认为政府的合作伙伴而参与治理和规划进程，包括应对新冠疫情。这种认可将使得毛利人的价值观被纳入议会的政策和法案之中，如whanaungatanga（亲属关系与归属感）、kaitiaki-tanga（环境监护与责任）和manaakitanga（尊重，关怀及好客）等。毛利人的领导者和发言人强调，作为新冠疫情应对方案的一部分，需优先考虑所有社区的环境和社会福利需求，旅游业的应对措施也不能脱离社会需要。在政府的应对措施和规划工作中应纳入多元文化价值观，以确保旅游供应商、游客和东道主有更加公平的未来和积极的体验。由此，通过原住民知情方法，可以积极促进商业、卫生和教育的转型，以建立一个更加积极的国际社会。

Introduction

COVID-19 has negatively democratized health risks and the financial wellbeing of people worldwide - not just the oppressed, the Indigenous nor the poverty stricken are affected by the inequity of COVID-19 which does not recognize how powerful or wealthy or poor a person is. When future historians look back on this significant pandemic event, lessons could be learnt from focussing on the experiences of Indigenous peoples during this time. Contemporary Indigenous peoples are diverse; many are westernised having been colonised, others live on or close to their ancestral lands according to traditional practices. There will need to be many flexible, nimble and socially responsive approaches to the COVID-19 recovery. Balancing the future industry so that tourism activities directly enhance the health and education of Indigenous peoples and communities is essential. Slow Tourism or degrowth that is locally focussed and grass roots driven are compatible ways forward for Indigenous Small and Medium Tourism Enterprises (ISMTEs), Indigenous and non-Indigenous communities.

New Zealand (NZ) provides the cultural context for this commentary. International tourism markets disappeared overnight resulting in many tourism businesses ceasing operations. When tourism activities that revitalised Māori economies ceased during the COVID-19 pandemic some alternative economic and social activities arose. New Zealand government interventions have included offering stimulus packages and wage supplements for staff so businesses would survive the financial strain of 'Lockdown'. Māori tourism operators' responses to COVID-19 have varied. Some have redeployed staff, others have diversified into alternative income sources whilst others have had no choice but to make staff redundant, either temporarily or permanently closing their tourism businesses.

As an Indigenous researcher the author presents an Indigenous Māori voice and most of the examples informing the commentary are from Māori tourism ventures. This commentary adopts a reflexive approach, underpinned by critical thinking, to ascertain positive responses to the pandemic and opportunities for Indigenous tourism. Academic literature, media accounts, field work, industry observations and insider knowledge arising from the researcher's conversations and interactions with Indigenous tourism practitioners globally enable further reflections to be drawn from an 'entanglement' of experiences (Ateljevic et al., 2005; Reissner, 2018). The paper will explore the negative realities and then positive responses of Indigenous tourism operators reacting to the loss of tourism activities and income.

Before COVID-19 many Indigenous peoples were struggling – even those within successful tourism ventures often have recurrent financial, marketing or visitor management challenges. Being isolated in rural areas peripheral to key tourism destinations or urban areas is common. In December 2019 I undertook field work in Murupara, visiting local tourism operators Karl and Nadine Toe Toe from Kohutapu Lodge and Tribal Tours. They have a sobering lack of domestic visitor demand owing to negative perceptions of a region associated with unemployment and poverty. In contrast their business was popular with inbound operators and international visitors (Carson, 2019). Karl and Nadine are positive about their future - Murupara has a strong community that values positive outcomes for youth – and are committed to mentoring and training Māori *rangatahi* (youth) in interpretation and hospitality skills, thus using tourism as a vehicle for change. They were the 2019 National Tourism Award recipients of the Community Engagement award (Rotorua Daily Post, 2019). Losing their international market overnight, as a result of NZ borders closing to stop the spread of COVID-19, Karl and Nadine continue to work but instead of tourism they are providing meals for community members and offering accommodation for those in need. Such community-based approaches by Māori tourism operators, their employees and/or local *marae* (meeting places) are strongly rooted in cultural values enabling hopeful and positive solutions to the detrimental impacts of climate change, natural disasters, ecological degradation and now the COVID-19 pandemic.

The 'new normal'?

As many academics and media commentators have noted, the scale of COVID-19 has shocked the global tourism industry with a force similar to the Great Depression or World Wars I and II (Bisby, 2020; Hall et al., 2020; Higgins-Desbiolles, 2020; Hollingsworth, 2020). Academic, journalistand social media commentators propose a 'new normal' (Ateljevic, 2020; Berentson-Shaw, 2020; Degarege, 2020), whilst the pandemic continues to evolve.

For many Indigenous communities worldwide the pandemic is a historical turning point as many are small scale, remotely located (so isolated from the virus unless outsiders arrive) and without health support needed to manage the pandemic should the virus reach their communities. Those with tourism ventures are experiencing business down-turns and many owner-operator or family businesses are unable to relocate or retrain easily without leaving their homelands. Undoubtedly there will be no singular Indigenous experience of the COVID-19 pandemic – instead the many experiences will be diverse and unsettling depending on each countries' government response to the health and socioeconomic needs arising from the pandemic. As Bisby (2020) noted, even in Canada with its strong economy, 'By June, ITAC estimates that a quarter of the country's 1,900 Indigenous tourism businesses will close, with more than a quarter of the subsector's employees – 12,000 people – losing their jobs'.

COVID-19, the new coloniser

The globalisation of travel which enabled access to Indigenous tourism experiences in remote regions of the world has spread the transmission of the virus. As racism has inhibited Indigenous tourism development (Ruhanen & Whitford, 2018), so has the pandemic brought a halt to Indigenous tourism with impacts similar to neo-colonialism (Spillane, 2005). COVID-19 disrupts livelihoods, accentuating the cumulative impacts from mass tourism, overtourism, and colonialism on Indigenous peoples. Considering the lack of pre-pandemic baseline data within health systems and Indigenous tourism sectors at national levels worldwide it may be difficult to estimate the true cost of the pandemic for many Indigenous peoples.

Ferrante and Fearnside (2020) plea for reduced visitor interactions with remote Indigenous communities globally as it is a viral form of colonialism – the new smallpox or measles in areas where health care systems have been non-existent or strain to deliver necessary medical care. Even communities with flourishing tourism developments often failed to deliver primary health care for local peoples before COVID-19, particularly in tropical or developing countries (Navarro et al., 2020). The virus, like colonialism, extends a legacy beyond this generation to future generations. Control measures such as self-isolation or social distancing affect the social fabric of Indigenous families and communities worldwide preventing emotional connections at funerals, births and other significant life events. Many Indigenous cultures, for instance Pasifika, expect employed persons to support extended family members. Employers' decisions to temporarily suspend employment, or make staff redundant, have a social ripple-effect that devastates such families.

The pandemic has strained Māori tourism businesses leaders and corporations. Internationally renowned, Ngāi Tahu Tourism (NTT) is an *iwi* (tribe) business corporation that is collectively owned by over 63,000 tribal members. NTT downsized their staff numbers from 348 to 39 people, including the Chief Executive Officer, and temporarily ceased or 'hibernated' operations at ten of the eleven tourism businesses nationwide as a result of the pandemic (https://ngaitahu.iwi.nz/ngai-tahu-tourism-update/). The action could be viewed as a westernised, corporate-style approach to the crisis that fundamentally detracts from core narratives of the Māori value of *manaakitanga* (caring for people respectfully and hospitably). For every unemployed staff member the consequences mean families have diminished finances for food, health, household power, sports and arts attendances. Thus the impact of unemployment for one can lowerstandards of living for many. Media reports about the NTT closures provided limited insights into the process behind the decision but suggested financial priorities, raising the question of whether businesses based on Indigenous (Māori) values differ from non-Indigenous businesses when faced with a crisis? The expectation of Ngāi Tahu Tourism decision-making would be that it was guided by *tikanga Māori* (ways of doing things), informed by *mātauranga Māori* (knowledge) and values of *kaitiakitanga* (environmental care or stewardship) and *manaakitanga* to protect the welfare of staff and local communities where the NTT businesses are located. Small and large scale, *iwi* and non-*iwi* owned businesses have made similar decisions with redundancies at Air New Zealand, Skyline Enterprises, Whakarewarewa Living Māori Village and Te Puia in Rotorua (Cropp, 2020). Alternatively there are pockets of hope as small scale, *whanau* (family) businesses pause, take a breath, "sit tight" as a family and wait the COVID-19 crisis out, for example Horizon Tours (https://www.horizontours.co.nz/) and Kapiti Island Nature Tours (https://www.kapitiisland.com/).

With COVID-19 the ongoing common aspirations for the 'new normal' will include empowerment and improvement of Indigenous peoples and their livelihoods – a state that does not differ greatly from the observations made in early tourism studies publications by academics such as De Kadt (1979), Macnaught (1982) and Hall et al. (1993). Publications pre-2020 continually reveal similar themes and issues reflecting the ongoing realities of Indigenous peoples worldwide seeking improved living, health and education standards. The challenge for many is that COVID-19's impact is cumulative alongside downward spiralling environmental conditions arising from global climate change, inequality arising from neoliberal business policies and the exploitation of natural resources. Indigenous communities and peoples provide a magnified example of the negative impact of COVID-19 on humanity. Yet the human drive to improve lifestyles may enable a hopeful response and solutions to the crisis by embracing indigenous values.

Informing positive futures

In New Zealand all landscapes and marinescapes have significance for Māori *iwi* (tribes), *hapu* (subtribes) and *whanau*. Indigenous values have increasingly been included in tourism planning practices, for example *manaakitanga* and *kaitiakitanga* are expressed within national tourism strategies (https://www.mbie.govt.nz/dmsdocument/5482-2019-new-zealand-aotearoa-government-tourism-strategy-pdf).

In 2018 the Tiaki Promise was launched. Informed by Māori values and developed in consultation with Māori Tourism NZ it encourages commitment to caring for the environment for present and future generations (https://tiakinewzealand.com/). Similar pledges exist elsewhere, i.e. the *Island of Hawaii Pono Pledge* which is expressed in the Hawaiian language and translated into English to encourage visitors and locals to behave in a way that is 'pono' (righteous) (https://www.ponopledge.com/).

Thus, just as Indigenous cultures can be revitalised by tourism (Idang, 2014; Lynch et al., 2010; Prasetyo et al., 2020; Whitney-Gould et al., 2018) there is the reverse potential for Indigenous cultures and individuals to revitalise communities and new ways of thinking or doing (pledges) that challenge and re-imagine the norms of western planning. The focus is no longer one of growth at all costs. Rather than reactionary management approaches to the negative impacts from tourism on nature and communities, positive change would be achieved by proactively incorporating indigenous values in post-COVID management approaches.

Involving Indigenous communities in planning processes, or enabling self-governance, can enhance resilience in health, recreation, leisure, education and business settings. New Zealand Māori are at an advantage to other Indigenous groups worldwide as a result of the strong *Te Tiriti* relationship with the government. *Iwi* are involved in planning processes throughout the country and do not hesitate to voice their concerns about environmental threats (e.g. Littlewood, 2010). As with any group in society, Indigenous peoples are not perfect and have been scrutinised for poor environmental practices, nevertheless indigenous values can lead to thoughtful, nature-centric solutions.

Reconnecting with nature

Indigenous values systems have influenced western environmental movements that counter neoliberal business, for instance permaculture or Brown's (2001) call for an Eco-Economy (Botezat, 2016; Brown, 2001; Holmgren, 2002; Kitchen & Marsden, 2009). Norwegian philosopher Arne Naess drew on Sami environmental values about the need for natural balance when he developed his philosophy of Deep Ecology, hoping to transform wider society and prevent ecological collapse. Naess and Rothenberg (1989, p. 129) observed *'humans' gross interference in nature mirrors our economic activity. Protection of what is left of free nature depends largely on the way humans are willing and able to change their ways of production and consumption'.*

Globally, Indigenous peoples are active as environmentalists, business people, policy makers, legislators and parliamentarians influencing the management of natural resources and protected areas. Prior to the COVID-19 pandemic New Zealand recognised indigenous place names and values, for instance the Whanganui River is a legal entity with the same rights as a human being. The former Urewera National Park was also recognised as a legal entity by the Te Urewera Act 2014, returning the ancestral landscape to the *Tuhoe* people as *kaitiaki* (guardians) represented by Te Urewera Board (https://www.ngaituhoe.iwi.nz/te-urewera). *Iwi* representatives serve on conservation boards (appointed by the Minister of Conservation) or as representatives on international organisations such as the PIPC (Permanent Indigenous Peoples' Committee of the Forest Stewardship Council).

Overseas the recognition of cultural values for natural areas can be contentious, for instance the ban on climbing Uluru/Ayers Rock to respect the cultural landscape of the Yankunytjatjara and Pitjantjatjara people (Altman & Finlayson, 2018). Normally, planners and managers realise the need to consider Indigenous values and this parallels an increased public desire to reconnect with nature, including Indigenous *'spiritual and material relationships with the lands'* (United Nations, 2020). Worldwide there is growing support for employing Indigenous protected area staff or integrating Traditional Ecological Knowledge (TEK) principles in conservation (Berkes, 1993; Paudel, 2016; Rotarangi & Russell, 2009).

National parks and protected natural resources can consequently be inseparable from broader societal issues such as food sovereignty and food security for Indigenous peoples (Degarege, 2019). Recreational activities including hunting and fishing have been positive sources of income but also, at times, a source of conflict within local Indigenous communities particularly when commercialised (Berkes, 1993; Boulé & Mason, 2019). Indigenous communities could further develop ecocultural interpretation for post-COVID visitor markets seeking reconnection with nature through foraging, permaculture, community gardening and similar cultural landscape experiences, when international and domestic travel networks return (Carr, 2004; Sidali et al., 2016; Thompson-Carr, 2016). Tourism operators have already successfully diversified into food production, for example the Barrett family of Kapiti Island Nature Tours developed a second business producing Manuka honey products from hives located on family owned lands, thus improving financial security from a second income stream not reliant on tourism during the pandemic (https://www.kapitiislandhoney.co.nz/).

Indigenous entrepreneurial responses

Kapiti Island's honey is an excellent example of an Indigenous family planning not just for a five or ten-year timeframe, but instead considering the resilience and welfare of descendants spanning decades or centuries into the future. Just as indigenous values have informed environmental management, so have western technologies furthered their indigenous business and enabled diversification and access (using the internet) to market their businesses online and via social media platforms such as Instagram.

Hybridisation of indigenous and non-indigenous approaches to managing the environment and businesses is an entrepreneurial way forward. Tretiakov et al. (2020, p.1) commented that *'Family is the source of Indigenous culture, while the mainstream culture is centered on global Western business culture ... Indigenous entrepreneurs integrate the values of the two cultures in managing their enterprises, thus acting as n-Cultural ... integrating the values of Indigenous culture and the mainstream culture'*.

The future for successful economies within Indigenous spaces therefore necessitates access to western technologies, especially the digital world with internet connectivity, technological capability and affordable hardware and software (Henry et al., 2017). Government agencies and the NZ Māori Tourism Council advocated for broadband, internet and telecommunications connectivity in many regions where such connectivity is weak - noting of course that many Māori and Pacifica households have limited or no access to internet or hardware. Multiple government and NGO agencies have coordinated together to develop a Māori Business Support Line "COVID-19 Support: Need expert business advice? Call 0800 4 POUTAMA".

Secure internet services and broadband coverage were essential for Māori communities to communicate with other 'bubbles', access health advice and participate in online learning during the NZ COVID-19 Alert Level 4. Strategically, tourism businesses connected over webinars and share advice. Digital spaces provided social support, information exchange and planning. ISMTEs rely on internet connectivity, affirming the observations of Henry et al. (2017) about the vital role that the digital economy plays in enhancing the power of Indigenous entrepreneurs. Those online were the adaptable, tech-savvy "n-Culturals" identified by Tretiakov et al. (2020) who continued to have a voice regarding how resources were managed. From the perspective of tourism, internet connectivity is essential for marketing to and informing domestic or international travel markets (virtual tourism experiences anyone?), vital for businesses to thrive, participate and possibly diversify into other digital economies.

Indigenous values re-configuring the tourist 'bubble'

Indigenous communities have histories where preceding populations have suffered depopulations from introduced viruses and diseases the most notorious being measles, mumps, smallpox, polio, tuberculosis and Spanish Influenza. Academic theories have cast the tourist bubble in a negative light. The pandemic has changed travel behaviours and until a vaccine is found countries' or communities' management responses include isolation, quarantine, social distancing, transmission tracing and tracking. The 'tourist bubble' has transformed into community or household bubbles. The tourist 'bubble' may work to a community's advantage as they separate from visitors or ensure interactions are controlled. Māori communities have instigated road blocks to keep non-locals away during the New Zealand lockdown – a move that was controversial but often assisted by Police (De Graaf, 2020). 'Keep away from our community is the strong message from Indigenous peoples to outsiders who may convey the virus, triggered by memories of the diseases of colonisation (Borges & Branford, 2020).

The recent phenomena of visitor or tourism pledges are perhaps a more hospitable way of creating a behavioural version of the 'tourist bubble' (Sampson, 2019). Pledges are a timely move towards implementing culturally and environmentally appropriate behaviour guidelines at national levels. As regions and countries become COVID-free there is discussion of forming regional or national bubbles. Trade or tourism bubbles may merge countries, i.e. an ANZAC-inspired 'Trans-Tasman bubble' between the New Zealand and Australia (Hollingsworth, 2020). Such 'bubbles' would revitalise the travel trade, for instance the potential for collaborations between Indigenous tourism operators envisaging a post-COVID future through marketing alliances with networks such as WINTA (the World Indigenous Tourism Alliance).

How academia can contribute

Academic theories may not make a difference to businesses and communities in times of crisis – theory does not pay the bills and feed hungry mouths. However academics researching indigenous tourism development alongside or with Indigenous communities and researchers do have a role to play alongside all of the diverse actors in global tourism by contributing the research informed skills and reflections necessary for critical thinking. Informed, socially-centred tourism policies and business/destination planning that work alongside and in communication with health, education and IT providers will enable all of us to enhance the long-term social and environmental well-being of our communities.

Decolonising Methodologies proposed that indigenous tourism research should ideally be indigenous-driven, i.e. with Indigenous peoples managing and critiquing the entire research process (Tuhiwai Smith, 2012). This aspiration can be extended to a call for more indigenous tourism educators and planners with insider knowledge critiquing indigenous tourism planning and development.

Tourism academics have been reviewing their roles as decades of academic publications arising from research and visitors' studies appear meaningless with COVID-19 bringing a halt to international travel. Papers that have posited planning approaches and critical theories about Indigenous and non-Indigenous communities provide insights that should be revisited and re-explored in the face of such a pandemic. Indigenous researchers tackling significant issues are emerging for instance Degarege's (2019) dissertation on food security in Ethiopia. Approaches such as participatory action research, mentoring young Indigenous students or scholars, supporting indigenous educational establishments, such as *Whare Wananga* in NZ, developing Indigenous journals or recommending Indigenous publications within course readings are all approaches that academia might adopt to benefit indigenous scholarship and education in a post-COVID world.

Conclusion

Justin Francis, the founder of travel firm Responsible Travel, echoed the thoughts of many when he stated '... *the democratisation of travel will take an uncomfortable backward step ... If we are to rebuild tourism better than before, and parts of the industry were well on the way to being pariahs in the eyes of both local residents and environ-mentalists, then I believe we must act and behave like we are "all in this together".'* (Francis, 2020).

Indigenous tourism operators can contribute to adaptations and planning for the future welfare of their businesses, local environment and affected communities. Government support and resourcing is needed at local, regional and national levels to ensure legislative and policy allow such interactions with Indigenous communities in their transition to a post-COVID future. The tourism future can be one encapsulating the indigenous social, environmental and cultural values that underpin ways of being and undertaking business – opposite to neoliberal, corporate models pre-COVID-19. Indigenous cultural landscapes are evocative of wellbeing, health, environmental guardianship, traditional ecological knowledge. Such landscapes are the future of cultural sustainability and their wise management should be of equal importance to economic development.

Finally, academics, tourism operators, planners and managers all have a role in re-visioning (or reimagining) how society 'does' business, through embracing indigenous environmental values and Indigenous ways of thinking to enable solutions for the way forward. This commentary calls for government agencies at national and local levels to advocate for and resource community and environment-centred tourism planning approaches that incorporate local or indigenous values; thus resilient and involved communities can directly influence the post-COVID response. Indigenous values and aspirations would underpin a renewed, resilient and caring global tourism industry for future generations and ecosystems world-wide.

Disclosure statement

No potential conflict of interest was reported by the author(s).

References

Altman, J., & Finlayson, J. (2018). *Aborigines, tourism and sustainable development*. Centre for Aboriginal Economic Policy Research.

Ateljevic, I. (2020). Transforming the (tourism) world for good and (re)generating the potential 'new normal. *Tourism Geographies*, doi: 10.1080/14616688.2020.1759134

Ateljevic, I., Harris, C., Wilson, E., & Collins, F. (2005). Getting 'entangled': reflexivity and the 'critical turn' in tourism studies. *Tourism Recreation Research*, 30(2), 9–21. doi: 10.1080/02508281.2005.11081469

Berentson-Shaw, J. (2020, May 2). *Covid-19: Understanding the New Normal*. Radio New Zealand. https://www.rnz.co.nz/news/on-the-inside/414216/covid-19-understanding-the-new-normal

Berkes, F. (1993). Traditional ecological knowledge in perspective. In J. T. Inglis (Ed), *Traditional ecological knowledge: Concepts and cases* (pp. 1–9). International Program on Traditional Ecological Knowledge International Development Research Centre.

Bisby, A. (2020, April 14). *Canada's Indigenous tourism operators call for more accessible federal assistance amid COVID-19 pandemic.* The Globe and Mail. https://www.theglobeandmail.com/life/travel/article-canadas-indigenous-tourism-operators-call-for-more-accessible-federal/?fbclid=IwAR2BtZ20gdMPoqt1Bfllxc_pd_g99x769ZoqSrxYbtUZT6pAi4SripOJdLg

Borges, T., Branford, S. (2020, April 2). *First COVID-19 case among indigenous people confirmed in Brazilian Amazon.* Mongabay News. https://news.mongabay.com/2020/03/first-possible-covid-19-indigenous-cases-detected-near-key-amazon-reserve/

Botezat, E. A. (2016). Fusing Economy, Ecology and Ethics in Tourism Management. *Annals of Faculty of Economics, 1*(2), 545–555.

Boulé, K. L., & Mason, C. W. (2019). Local perspectives on sport hunting and tourism economies: Stereotypes, sustainability, and inclusion in British Columbia's hunting industries. *Sport History Review, 50*(1), 93–115. doi: 10.1123/shr.2018-0023

Brown, L. R. (2001). *Eco-Economy: Building an economy for the earth.* Norton & Company Publications.

Carr, A. M. (2004). Mountain places, cultural spaces – interpretation and sustainable visitor management of culturally significant landscapes: a case study of Aoraki/Mount Cook National Park. *Journal of Sustainable Tourism, 12*(5), 432–459. doi: 10.1080/09669580408667248

Carson, J. (2019, May 11). *There was no just transition for Murupara & Minginui, but hopefully there will be for Taranaki.* LinkedIn. https://www.linkedin.com/pulse/meet-uncle-bronco-weng%C4%81ti-whare-just-transition-murupara-carson/

Cropp, A. (2020, April 24). *Coronovirus: Tourism companies plan to lay off more than 13,000 workers.* Stuff News. https://www.stuff.co.nz/business/121206357/coronavirus-tourism-companies-plan-to-lay-off-more-than-13000-workers

De Graaf, P. (2020, April 22). COVID19 Coronovirus: Ngāpuhi defends checkpoints after MP's shutdown calls. *The Northern Advocate,* https://www.nzherald.co.nz/northern-advocate/news/article.cfm?c_id=1503450&objectid=12326049

De Kadt, E. (1979). Social planning for tourism in the developing countries. *Annals of Tourism Research, 6*(1), 36–48. doi: 10.1016/0160-7383(79)90093-8

Degarege, G. A. (2019). *Tourism, Livelihood Diversification and Food Security in Ethiopia* [Doctoral dissertation, University of Otago]. University of Otago Library, Our Archive. http://hdl.handle.net/10523/9193

Degarege, G. A. (2020, May 3). Ethiopia's triumphant return: Finding the 'New Normal' in Tourism Post COVID-19. *The Capital.* https://www.capitalethiopia.com/society/ethiopias-triumphant-return-finding-the-new-normal-in-tourism-post-covid-19/?fbclid=IwAR0UQkci4al1MrU3Byezcdpw84eFkIlzI3WUVX4hQ_vvdOvufDrY3IqUAdg

Ferrante, L., & Fearnside, P. M. (2020). Protect Indigenous peoples from COVID-19. *Science (New York, N.Y.), 368*(6488), 251–251. https://science.sciencemag.org/content/368/6488/251.1 doi: 10.1126/science.abc0073

Francis, J. (2020). *The Future of Travel and Tourism: Post Covid-19,* Responsible Travel, https://www.responsibletravel.com/holidays/responsible-tourism/travel-guide/the-future-of-travel-and-tourism

Hall, C. M., Mitchell, I., & Keelan, N. (1993). The Implications of Māori perspectives for the management and promotion of heritage tourism in New Zealand. *GeoJournal, 29*(3), 315–322. https://link.springer.com/article/10.1007/BF00807051 doi: 10.1007/BF00807051

Hall, C. M., Scott, D., & Gössling, S. (2020). Pandemics, transformations and tourism: be careful what you wish for. *Tourism Geographies,* doi: 10.1080/14616688.2020.1759131

Henry, E., Newth, J., & Spiller, C. (2017). Emancipatory Indigenous social innovation: Shifting power through culture and technology. *Journal of Management & Organization, 23*(6), 786–802. doi: 10.1017/jmo.2017.64

Higgins-Desbiolles, F. (2020). Socialising tourism for social and ecological justice after COVID-19. *Tourism Geographies,* 1–14. doi: 10.1080/14616688.2020.1757748

Hollingsworth, J. (2020, May 4). *A "travel bubble" between New Zealand and Australia could be a model for the future.* CNN. https://edition.cnn.com/travel/article/new-zealand-australia-travel-bubble-intl-hnk/index.html

Holmgren, D. (2002). *Permaculture: Principles & pathways beyond sustainability.* Holmgren Design Services.

Idang, G. E. (2014). Revitalization of indigenous culture as instrument for attaining a virile multi-ethnic Africa. *International Journal of Development and Sustainability, 3*(2), 315–322.

Kitchen, L., & Marsden, T. (2009). Creating sustainable rural development through stimulating the eco-economy: beyond the eco-economic paradox? *Sociologia Ruralis, 49*(3), 273–294. doi: 10.1111/j.1467-9523.2009.00489.x

Littlewood, M. (2010, January 20). Ngāi Tahu Alarmed at Plans. *The Timaru Herald*, 1.

Lynch, M., Duinker, P., Sheehan, L., & Chute, J. (2010). Sustainable Mi'kmaw cultural tourism development in Nova Scotia, Canada: Examining cultural tourists and Mi'kmaw perspectives. *Journal of Sustainable Tourism, 18*(4), 539–556. doi: 10.1080/09669580903406605

Macnaught, T. J. (1982). Mass tourism and the dilemmas of modernization in Pacific Island communities. *Annals of Tourism Research, 9*(3), 359–381. doi: 10.1016/0160-7383(82)90019-6

Naess, A., & Rothenberg, D. (1989). *Ecology, community and lifestyle.* Cambridge University Press.

Navarro, J. C., Arrivillaga-Henríquez, J., Salazar-Loor, J., & Rodriguez-Morales, A. J. (2020). COVID-19 and dengue, co-epidemics in Ecuador and other countries in Latin America: Pushing strained health care systems over the edge. *Travel Medicine and Infectious Disease*, 101656. doi: 10.1016/j.tmaid.2020.101656

Paudel, R. P. (2016). Protected areas, people and tourism: Political ecology of conservation in Nepal. *Journal of Forest and Livelihood, 14*(1), 13–27. doi: 10.3126/jfl.v14i1.23159

Prasetyo, N., Carr, A., & Filep, S. (2020). Indigenous knowledge in marine ecotourism development: The case of Sasi Laut, Misool, Indonesia. *Tourism Planning & Development, 17*(1), 46–61. doi: 10.1080/21568316.2019.1604424

Reissner, S. C. (2018). Interactional challenges and researcher reflexivity: Mapping and analysing conversational space. *European Management Review, 15*(2), 205–219. doi: 10.1111/emre.12111

Rotarangi, S., & Russell, D. (2009). Social-ecological resilience thinking: Can indigenous culture guide environmental management? *Journal of the Royal Society of New Zealand, 39*(4), 209–213. doi: 10.1080/03014220909510582

Rotorua Daily Post. (2019, November 11). *Murupara Accommodation Venture Wins National Award.* https://www.nzherald.co.nz/rotorua-daily-post/news/article.cfm?c_id=1503438&objectid=12284258

Ruhanen, L., & Whitford, M. (2018). Racism as an inhibitor to the organisational legitimacy of Indigenous tourism businesses in Australia. *Current Issues in Tourism, 21*(15), 1728–1742. doi: 10.1080/13683500.2016.1225698

Sampson, H. (2019, October 25). Can tourism 'pledges' help keep visitors on their best behaviour. *The Washington Post* https://www.stuff.co.nz/travel/news/116924593/can-tourism-pledges-help-keep-visitors-on-their-best-behavior

Sidali, K. L., Morocho, P. Y., & Garrido-Pérez, E. I. (2016). Food tourism in indigenous settings as a strategy of sustainable development: The case of *Ilex guayusa* Loes in the Ecuadorian Amazon. *Sustainability, 8*(10), 967–984. doi: 10.3390/su8100967

Spillane, J. J. (2005). Tourism in developing countries: Neocolonialism or nation builder. *Management and Labour Studies, 30*(1), 7–37. doi: 10.1177/0258042X0503000101

Thompson-Carr, A. (2016). Indigenous food experiences, traditional values and tourism product development. In M. Scerri & L. Hui (Eds), *The changing landscape of tourism and hospitality: The impact of emerging markets and emerging destinations* (pp. 1268–1274). Blue Mountains International Hotel Management School.

Tretiakov, A., Felzensztein, C., Zwerg, A. M., Mika, J. P., & Macpherson, W. G. (2020). Family, community, and globalization: Wayuu indigenous entrepreneurs as n-Culturals. *Cross Cultural & Strategic Management*, ahead-of-print(ahead-of-print). doi: 10.1108/CCSM-01-2019-0025

Tuhiwai Smith, L. (2012). *Decolonizing methodologies: Research and indigenous peoples.* Zed Books.

United Nations. (2020). *2007 UN Declaration on the Rights of Indigenous Peoples, Part Six, Article 25*. Retrieved April 20, 2020, from https://www.un.org/development/desa/Indigenouspeoples/declaration-on-the-rights-of-Indigenous-peoples.html.

Whitney-Gould, K., Wright, P., Alsop, J., & Carr, A. (2018). Community assessment of Indigenous language-based tourism projects in Haida Gwaii (British Columbia, Canada.) *Journal of Sustainable Tourism*, *26*(11), 1909–1927. doi: 10.1080/09669582.2018.1526292

Regenerative tourism needs diverse economic practices

Jenny Cave and Dianne Dredge

ABSTRACT

Calls for a new relationship between tourism and capitalism have intensified as a result of COVID-19. The pandemic has exposed massive vulnerabilities in the tourism operating system, the effects of which have fallen unevenly across different groups and subsectors of tourism. Critics have been quick to point out capitalism's emphasis on resource exploitation, growth and profit is to blame and that tourism destinations have never been encouraged to foster diverse economic practices which would enhance resilient communities and regenerative tourism. The diverse economies framework envisages the co-existence of capitalist, alternative capitalist and non-capitalist practices and provides a pathway to more resilient and regenerative tourism practices in tourism. Tourism industry cases are used to illustrate the innovation inherent in diverse economic practices (enterprise, exchange, labour, transactions, property etc.) and illustrate their natural resilience as a result. Post COVID-19, a regenerative tourism that incorporates diverse economic practices will guide tourism practices worldwide to withstand future exigencies.

摘要

由于新型冠状病毒肺炎（COVID-19）疫情爆发，人们呼吁在旅游业与资本主义经济体系之间建立新的关系。大量旅游运营体系中的薄弱环节在这次新冠疫情大流行中暴露，并不同程度的影响了旅游业中的各个群体和子部门。批评者迅速将暴露的问题归咎于以资本为主的旅游业过于重视资源开发和利润增长。这种模式从未鼓励旅游目的地培育多样化经济实践以增强社区恢复力和再生性旅游业。多样化的经济框架设想了资本主义，另类资本主义和非资本主义实践的共存，并为旅游业提供了更具恢复力和再生力的途径。旅游产业的案例说明了多样化经济实践中的内在创新（企业、交易、劳动力、所有权等）和其自然恢复力。总而言之，在新型冠状病毒肺炎（COVID-19）疫情之后，全球的再生性旅游业应该采用多样化的经济实践以应对未来的紧急情况。

Beyond business as usual

Who could have imagined how quickly tourism would come to such a grinding halt? COVID-19 measures including travel bans, border-crossing restrictions, lockdowns and physical distancing have created an inflexion, or a pivot point for social, economic and political life—and for the ecological wellbeing of the planet. In tourism, aviation, accommodation, travel companies and booking agents, attractions, retail, food and beverage outlets have been hit unevenly; supply chains have been severely disrupted; entire workforces have been stood down; and some businesses have managed to pivot to address emerging opportunities. At the time of writing, the Chinese economy is reportedly entering a revival stage. However, the ripple effects across Europe and the Americas are contributing to a perfect storm of public health concerns, unemployment and economic uncertainty. As the virus emerges on the African continent, a second wave looms large with the effects expected to reverberate for years to come.

Against this background, there have been growing calls for a new relationship with capitalism and new measures of success in tourism. Rising concerns about climate change, overtourism, declining employment and labour conditions and resource degradation have all highlighted the inadequacy of the current capitalist system in addressing the failures of mass tourism. Now, under COVID-19, there are calls for tourism to move beyond 'business as usual' and to find a pathway to regenerative tourism. The question of how to move beyond simply advocating a shift to articulating what that shift might look like in tourism has received little attention, yet prototypes and experiments are everywhere. Tourism researchers have tended to take these examples as anomalies, as unlinked case studies, and there have been few attempts to draw systematic insights informing how the tourism operating system might be recast. The special issue on Diverse Economies in *Tourism Planning and Development* (2018, Issue 5) addressed this gap by seeking to develop a more coordinated set of insights into the diverse economies of tourism and to provide a pathway to recasting tourism systems.

Towards a new operating system

Over 25 years ago, Gibson-Graham, (1996) saw a need for post-capitalist economic alternatives given the exploitative nature of capitalism and the need for social and environmental systems to regenerate, if they are to become sustainable. Gibson-Graham conceptualised alternative and hybrid social worlds where capital accumulation, growth and profit were not the only motivations for economic organisation. They envisaged diverse social and community-based relationships where diverse kinds of monetary and non-monetary transactions took place and diverse kinds of value (e.g. community value, social good, regenerating natural resources, etc) were produced (Gibson-Graham, 2006).

Initially, the alternative economies narrative encountered resistance from mainstream economic interests. 'Alternative' was perceived as oppositional to mainstream capitalism, which the authors had not intended, and this stymied widespread engagement with their ideas. However, over the years, new renderings of different kinds of economic exchange (e.g. the rise of collaborative and sharing economies) and alternative motivations for economic transactions (e.g. blended value, impact investing and the commons economy) have emerged. Gibson-Graham's ideas about diverse economies have proven to be a timeless inspiration for those seeking to examine the value and possibilities of alternative economic systems. Diversifying our economic practices can contribute to the uptake of regenerative practices and resilience.

In tourism, the dominant form of economic organisation—what we call the tourism operating system (TOS)—has followed a capitalist agenda, with an emphasis on growth and profit. The value produced from the TOS is almost always measured in dollar terms (e.g. expenditure or investment) but the non-monetary value produced, co-created and shared in tourism is less well understood and rarely measured. While we know that travel and tourism produce benefits beyond money, the alternative economies literature has been little explored and thinking about diverse economies of tourism remains underdeveloped (see Mosedale 2012 as an exception). The occurrence of COVID-19 and calls for new forms of tourism have exposed the deficit in thinking and the need for new imaginaries about the TOS and diverse economies.

The need to re-imagine economic organisation has resurfaced more recently in the contributions of sustainability scientists (e.g. Rockström et al., 2009) and economists (e.g. Raworth), feeding calls for regenerative economic operating systems. Critical issues in the current model of capitalism have been laid bare. Firstly, the accumulation of wealth in the top one percent, reduced labour rights and working conditions, a rise in casualisation of labour, a decline in the influence of organised labour, and a rise of the precariat class have created high levels of social and economic vulnerability among upper-middle, middle and lower working classes. Secondly, an emphasis on hyper-consumption as a driver of growth has led to exploitation of natural resources, a decline in the capacity of natural systems to regenerate, and impacts that have placed at risk the sustainability of natural systems. Raworth (2017) has argued that sustainable and regenerative economies require a decoupling of resource use from economic growth. The challenge in tourism, however, is that seven decades of growth have thwarted any appetite to imagine new and alternative economic models in tourism.

Now, COVID-19 has created an inflection point and post-covid predictions are already starting to emerge. Yet we see little evidence of concern for the detail of new tourism operating other than modified 'business as usual'. Predictions and claims must be read with caution. No one is an expert. There is no precedent and no robust foresight work to inform how to move forward. We can make educated predictions that international travel will take years to re-emerge; domestic, particularly local visitor economies, will be first to gain traction; and that major restructuring of aviation will increase cost, in turn affecting international travel. Beyond that, those who offer predictions write through the lens of hope: 'bounce back'; a 'new world order'; or hope that we have time to learn and choose the optimal pathway forward. Our work in diverse economies contributes to this later stream of writing and responds to the need to rethink the values underpinning tourism operating systems. In particular, the need to acknowledge the importance of moving beyond the economic determinism of growth and profit and measures of success that emphasise volume or consumption.

Alternative and diverse economies

Anticipating the need for post-capitalist alternatives, given the failure of capitalism to address sustainable development and the tendency to exceed our social and

Table 1. An alternative economies framework.

Enterprise	Labour	Property	Transactions	Finance
CAPITALIST Private firm. Public company. Multinational.	WAGE Salaried. Unionised. Part-time. Casual.	PRIVATE Individually owned. Collective	MARKET Free. Naturally protected. Artificially protected. Monopolised. Regulated. Niche.	MAINSTREAM FINANCE Private banks. Insurance firms. Financial services. Derivatives.
ALTERNATIVE-CAPITALIST State-owned enterprise. Social enterprise. B-Corp.	ALTERNATIVE PAID Self-employed. Cooperative. Indentured. Reciprocal labour. In-kind. Work for welfare/ other benefits.	ALTERNATIVE PRIVATE State-owned. Customary (clan) land. Community land trusts. Indigenous knowledge (IP).	ALTERNATIVE MARKET Sale of public goods. Ethical 'fair-trade'. Local trading systems. Alternative currencies. Underground market. Co-operatives. Barter, swap. Informal market.	ALTERNATIVE FINANCE Cooperative banks. Credit unions. Community-based lenders. Micro-finance. Impact investing.
NON-CAPITALIST Communal. Independent. Feudal. Slave.	UNPAID Housework. Family care. Neighborhood work. Volunteer. Self-provisioning labour. Slave labour.	OPEN ACCESS Atmosphere. International waters. Open source IP. Outer space.	NON-MARKET TRANSACTIONS Household flows. Gifting. Indigenous exchange. State allocations. State appropriations. Gleaning. Hunt, fish, gather. Theft, poaching, piracy.	NON-MARKET FINANCE Sweat equity. Family lending. Donations. Interest-free loans. Remittances.

After Gibson-Graham et al. (2013).

environmental limits Gibson-Graham, (2008) spent many years exploring economic identity and dynamics. Their work conceptualises social worlds in which capitalism is not the only model. They envisage diverse economies – broadly conceived as systems of coordinated exchange through which value is produced, consumed and accumulated – organised into types of economic practice (conceived as enterprise, labour, property in 2006, then transactions and finance were added). Each of these five practices can be divided into capitalist, alternative capitalist and non-capitalist modes. Table 1 captures Gibson-Graham's seminal thinking.

A key value of Gibson-Graham's framework is to highlight a range of economic practices that have been largely ignored by mainstream economic thinking. In placing these practices in a framework, they highlight the co-existence of different types of market, alternative market and non-capitalist practices that remain hidden in plain sight. In the context of tourism, this framework helps to recognise alternative and diverse economic practices that exist outside mainstream tourism operating systems and that are often obscured in frequent calls for "a new relationship with capitalism" (Fletcher, 2011).

Diverse economies in tourism

So, does the diverse economies framework, and in particular, the investigations undertaken as part of the *Diverse Economies in Tourism* special issue, offer any insights for tourism in the context of COVID-19? We from our 2018 call and the industry case studies below, we find that the diverse economies framework helps to deconstruct economic practices in tourism. The individual papers comprising the Special Issue shone a light on different economic practices in tourism, such as the nature of labour (e.g. paid, unpaid and alternative); types of transactions (e.g. monetary, sharing, gifting, favours, etc); and the types and sources of finance (impact investing, blended value). Such insights into the nature of tourism enterprise helped to highlight the different ways that responsibility was construed by public, private and other types of actors. Importantly, the special issue also helped to highlight the various ways that value was (co)created in both monetary and non-monetary forms. Put simply, by deconstructing these diverse economies of tourism, we see an opportunity to articulate and measure the diversity of tourism and visitor economies in more systematic and meaningful ways. This in turn would help move beyond simply advocating for a new relationship to capitalism, by acknowledging the presence and contribution of existing alternative economic practices.

The special issue also revealed that, in tourism, alternative economic practices were well established in the Global South and in indigenous communities in particular. The Global South, distanced by geography and attitudes from the largely industrial North, enacts alternative economic models with ease and has a long tradition of locally constituted enterprises that adapt to opportunities of global interaction but in the main, however are not dependent upon them. The growth of mass tourism sourced from bourgeoning middle classes (e.g. China and India) has exposed many destinations to the overreliance on narrow international markets. However, cultural resilience, alertness to change, capacity to adapt grounded social values, collective notions of value-creation, and alternative economic transactions (e.g. sharing and gifting) are demonstrated by case studies contained in the Diverse Economies volume (Cave & Dredge, 2018; 2020). Situational and cultural antecedents, new interpretations of opportunity, and the alternative values underpinning exchange reveal in these cases, how enterprises operate outside the 'profit and growth economy' and 'business as usual' norms.

Lessons: Diverse economic practices in tourism

Hybrid cultural/mainstream economy: Indigenous ecotourism, New Zealand (ALT-CAPITALIST): Wealth and 'well-th' are values that underpin the alternative economic ecotourism operation, Blue Penguins Pukekura. Collectively owned by a Māori community in Dunedin, Aotearoa-New Zealand, the collective operates a hybrid Alt-Capitalist and Non-Capitalist enterprise. The enterprise thrives within a market economy generally hostile to socio-ecological activities because it invests in capacity building, socio-cultural collaboration and stable relationships that bridge both mainstream 'European' and Indigenous worldviews. The organisation values both unpaid and paid labour within cultural mores at strategic, operational and governance decision-making levels, yet also functions within mainstream regulatory and taxation regimes. Labour allocations are made according to skill and to build capacity/succession. This regenerative enterprise mediates global (tourism markets) and local (Maori cultural) values and ideologies to create fiscal wealth as well as 'well-th', defined as social, physical and mindful wellbeing within the social structure of the tribe. Most importantly, the successful initiative enables economic resilience against exogenous shock, enhances cultural continuance, and resistance to further social predation by colonization (Amoamo et al., 2018).

Collaborative technology platforms: Danish walking trail (ALT- CAPITALIST)

The collaborative technology platform model of a walking trail in Southern Denmark is an example of bottom-up co-operative development within the alternative-capitalist economy. It leverages pre-existing conditions, i.e. unused public land, a resourceful migrant community, volunteer labour, a heritage museum with a regional mandate, and an iconic island bio-scape. Two female leisure entrepreneurs conceived, initiated and developed a coastal walking trail, using digital platform technologies to enable access to the trail and direct connections with locals to book experiences (e.g. dinners, birdwatching, berry picking). The collaborative business model is community-driven but needed a core agency to host the platform. The regional non-profit museum saw an opportunity beyond material collections and walls to redefine its role, connect with their communities, undertake large-scale heritage landscape interpretation and valorise local resources for visitors. An additional benefit was to extend its own revenue potential and residents' wellbeing and connectedness. Ideologically, the organisation is communitarian since it co-opts a public partner, public resources, volunteers and is supported by private philanthropic funding for micro-entrepreneurs. Thus, benefits are localised and not extracted by a global company (Gyimóthy & Meged, 2018)

Community value co-creation: Open monuments event, Sardinia (NON-CAPITALIST/ALT-FINANCE)

Collective co-creation of a cultural tourism event in Sardinia co-exists alongside dominant forms of capitalism. Imago Mundi, a not-for-profit organisation and member of Sardex, an alternative finance complementary currency community aimed at alleviating the impacts of the global financial crisis, initiated the Open Monuments event because of the need to generate employment in the severe economic downturn experienced by Sardinia. An experience that parallels the impact of COVID-19. Direct and indirect value co-creation is developed within the organisation and its broader network of suppliers and partners by generating social values such as trust, dialogue and reciprocity as collective benefits for the multiple actors involved. Actors, firms and customers adopt specific positions and roles within social structures, the strength of which depends on proximity of social ties. The event has become an annual festival, engaging over 50 local councils and local associations spread all over the island, attracting around 17,000 volunteers, and 300,000 yearly visitors, enabled largely by volunteer labour and public funds. Stakeholders thus co-create non-capitalist forms of place-based and community value, as well as develop social capital and local resilience through relational, networking activity and collaborative practices in cultural, economic and environmental domains (Cannas, 2018).

Local associations, family networks: Ecuadorian beaches (NON-CAPITALIST)

The informal sector in Latin America has a long tradition of solidarity. Tourism development in four fishing communities located on beaches attractive to tourists shows that economic behaviours can leverage alternative value producing opportunities linked to family survival and solidarity. However, they are affected by the micro-politics of local community networks and a disconnect with modern regulatory frameworks. Unincorporated associations, unregistered tourism establishments, and small and medium enterprises thrive here outside public tax and social health systems as self-employed entrepreneurs and family tourism enterprises. Typically, the males of the family dedicated their work to fishing and the women lead tourism-related activities which complement the family budget and call in an informal workforce of close relatives and family members. Here, capitalistic tourism enterprise is the exception not the norm.

However, the Ecuadorian State supports a capitalist form of 'doing business', enacted through legal and regulatory practices of professional registration, taxation, social security and industry association membership. Yet in reality, less than one third of Ecuadorian enterprises fulfil these legal requirements, are industry or tax registered, hold professional licenses or comply with the social security system. Most of these enterprises are affiliated to local industry associations, which are active in community development, such as improving physical infrastructure, and environmental care (e.g. beach cleaning). Further, they redistribute economic surpluses, seek social compromise and community unity to act as a genuine and alternative source of tourism planning and regulation but also actively resist the Ecuadorian state and local administrations. Such resistance creates a diverse range of non- and alt-capitalist forms that operate alongside each other, all serving the tourist market but operating outside officialdom in ways that enhance resilience but produce precarity in employment, equity and wage security (Pécot et al., 2018).

Alternative development: Corporate hotels and community priorities, Fiji (ALT-CAPITALIST, ALT-MARKET)

Modernity is not a worldwide norm. International agencies from the developed, industrial North usually frame development aid for small island states to address vulnerability and the need for 'new' skills. In the process this inadvertently de-prioritises local issues, systems and cultural knowledge. Such aid is often short–term, periodic and project focussed, leading to discontinuity, increased vulnerability and overreliance on outside, short-term provision projects and equipment.

In Fiji, despite encouragement by government for foreign investment in the resort sector, international hotels cannot own land, but lease it from the tribal landholder. Further, hotels and tourism operations are required to contribute to community development by preferential employment of local indigenous Fijians; fees for village tours and beach access, as well as scholarships and leasehold fees. However, the majority of corporate hotels rationalise the local leasehold agreements and 'sustainability' initiatives (reef remediation, beach cleaning) as specific community benefits and corporate social responsibility (CSR) initiatives that enhance their global brand standards. With some exceptions, hotels rarely consider communities as equal partners in development of goals or understand the socio-cultural realities of Fijian collective priorities, nor the direct linkage of hotels with village life. Indigenous values and belief systems privilege shared resources and communal land-ownership so that income from external sources such as leases, wages from employment in hotels, performance fees and handicrafts is pooled within the village to develop communal infrastructure or for community development, although high cost equipment might be purchased by an individual for their enterprise.

The Development First framework proposed in this case example is an effective mechanism to achieve meaningful outcomes for both communities and hotels. The framework responds to local human development needs (e.g. schools, health care) as well as to funding partner goals. Recognition in the framwework of existing culturally-based alternative market economies keeps the well-being of the wider community to the fore by strengthening bottom-up processes that align labour with ethics of self-reliance and obligation. Such reciprocity and awareness of customary exchange connects the tourism sector to the livelihood practices of ordinary people, as well as to indigenous philosophies and local interpretations of development (Hughes & Scheyvens, 2018).

Collaborative commons, moral incentives: Post-Castro Cuba (NON-CAPITALIST, ALT-PAID, ALT-MARKET)

Post-Castro reforms, introduced to open up trade with the United States have enabled economic alternatives to develop that both preserve the central heritage and values of local Cuban culture and respond to global forces of tourism. In this case, the analogy of pre-1962 American oldsmobile (an iconic image associated with Cuba) is used to unpack the idea that the original vehicle exterior can be preserved while contemporary locally-inspired interior adaptions are made for comfort and functionality. The everyday practices of tourism in Cuba are an example of adaptive resourcefulness in the face of social and ideological adaptation to economic conditions and limited investment. Cubans operate tourism within a system that is both highly regulated (i.e. formal socialist economy) but also involves significant levels of informality (i.e. informal economy) illustrating economic transactions that combine both monetary and non-monetary models of development and that balance livelihood and well-being.

The industry is tightly regulated through the ministries of Tourism, Labour and the Armed Forces resulting in close surveillance, which ironically limits development and extracts profits from tourism entrepreneurs. However, Cubans use social mechanisms to subvert the formal regulatory process. For example, they expand capacity through a collaborative commons economy where individual benefit it is not the aim. New self-employment opportunities enable entrepreneurs to open private operations (restaurants, *casas partículares* or rooms for rent). These operate in a horizontal and collaborative schema that integrates entrepreneurial collaboration, reciprocal exchange, and the State's requirements. Transactions occur as verbal agreements, referrals to trusted friends/family to expand capacity, loans of scarce equipment or as refusals of service if someone proves untrustworthy, as well as social rather than formal contracts of employment. Residents priorise the needs and livelihoods of others and subsume their own. Hence, in this case, political and economic forms of exchange are interwoven with the socialist ideology that are communal and relational, producing alternative forms of enterprises, types of transactions, and forms of labour not seen elsewhere in the industry (Balslev Clausen & Velázquez García, 2018).

Diverse economy perspective: Air New Zealand (CAPITALIST)

Alterative economies are often argued as local in scale, but major companies, such as airlines, can co-create diverse models of exchange by activating different stakeholder interests, even when globally regulated and focused on market capitalisation. In the case of airlines, in aircraft design, flight trajectories, fuels, etc. Air New Zealand is a capitalist model that nonetheless grounds its business and operations on socio-cultural dimensions related to its bi-cultural national context. Indigenous Maori have been the flag-bearers and face of the country's tourism industry since 1895, although many argue this as cultural appropriation. Suppliers to the airline at all levels: from governance to maintenance, operations and inventory as well as marketing, must demonstrate compliance with ethical procurement and the airline's business practices. The airline emphasises social capital development through a sustained deep commitment to women in leadership and female pilots, to cultural symbolism and materials, and to working with social enterprises and vulnerable communities (Tham & Evers-Swindell, 2018).

Discussion and conclusions

In sum, we return to the question of whether the diverse economies framework offers any useful insights and lessons for moving forward in a post-COVID-19 world. While a razor-sharp focus on dealing with the immediate public health challenges is essential, as the pandemic peaks, infection rates flatten and then rebound, questions are starting to emerge about how and when to restart local, regional and national economies. Three paths open up before us: hope of a 'bounce back'; hope to enter a new world order; or hope that we have time to learn and choose the optimal pathway forward.

It is clear that COVID-19 has brought to the fore a range of failures in the traditional TOS and has highlighted widespread vulnerabilities from workers and small and medium-sized enterprises to multi-national corporations and global tourism supply chains. Tourism researchers have often hurled rocks from the sidelines, calling for 'a new relationship with capitalism' or claiming 'tourism is dead', but they have done little to explore, understand or contribute much needed alternative renderings of the tourism operating system.

We believe the diverse economies framework provides a promising pathway forward by directing attention towards the diversity of economic practices of tourism. If we recognise that transformation of the tourism operating system is necessary in order to create more resilient and sustainable tourism and visitor economies, then surely nuanced renderings and systematic analyses of alternative and diverse tourism practices are a useful step forward. Such renderings of the different enterprises, types of labour, property, exchange and finance that make up the production of tourism goods, services and experiences are the first step in designing tourism economies for the future. The second step would be to value these diverse economic practices by instigating appropriate evaluation and measurement of alternative models and practices. The third step would be to develop policy support mechanisms that acknowledge and encourage diversified economic practices with the explicit intention to reduce the overreliance on the dominant capitalist practices. The present distinction between formal and informal economies is perhaps judgemental and unhelpful in imagining the potential contributions that diverse economies of tourism can play in building resilience, well-being and connectedness, while also reducing vulnerability.

Disclosure statement

No potential conflict of interest was reported by the author(s).

References

Amoamo, M., Ruckstuhl, K., & Ruwhiu, D. (2018). Balancing indigenous values through diverse economies: A case study of Māori Ecotourism. *Tourism Planning & Development*, *15*(5), 478–495. doi: 10.1080/21568316.2018.1481452

Balslev Clausen, H., & Velázquez García, M. A. (2018). The tourism model in Post-Castro Cuba: Tensions between ideology and economic realities. *Tourism Planning & Development*, *15*(5), 551–566. doi: 10.1080/21568316.2018.1504817

Cannas, R. (2018). Diverse economies of collective value co-creation: The open monuments event. *Tourism Planning & Development*, *15*(5), 535–550. doi: 10.1080/21568316.2018.1505651

Cave, J., & Dredge, D. (2018). Reworking tourism: Diverse economies in a changing world. *Tourism Planning & Development*, *15*(5), 473–477. doi: 10.1080/21568316.2018.1510659

Cave, J., & Dredge, D. Eds., (2020). *Reworking tourism: Diverse economies in a changing world*. Routledge.

Fletcher, R. (2011). Sustaining tourism, sustaining capitalism? The tourism industry's role in global capitalist expansion. *Tourism Geographies*, *13*(3), 443–461. doi: 10.1080/14616688.2011. 570372

Gibson-Graham, J. K. (1996). *The end of capitalism (as we knew it): a feminist critique of political economy*. Blackwell.

Gibson-Graham, J. K. (2006). *A postcapitalist politics*. University of Minnesota Press.

Gibson-Graham, J. K. (2008). Diverse economies: performative practices for "other worlds. *Progress in Human Geography*, *32*(5), 613–632. doi: 10.1177/0309132508090821

Gibson-Graham, J. K., Cameron, J., & Healy, S. (2013). *Take back the economy: an ethical guide for transforming our communities*. University of Minnesota Press.

Gyimóthy, S., & Meged, J. W. (2018). The Camøno: A communitarian walking trail in the sharing economy. *Tourism Planning & Development*, *15*(5), 496–515. doi: 10.1080/21568316.2018. 1504318

Healy, S. (2009). Alternative economies. In R. Kitchin, & N. Thrift (Eds.), *International encyclopaedia of human geography* (pp. 338–344). Elsevier.

Hughes, E., & Scheyvens, R. (2018). Development alternatives in the Pacific: How tourism corporates can work more effectively with local communities. *Tourism Planning & Development*, *15*(5), 516–534. doi: 10.1080/21568316.2018.1478881

Pécot, M., Gavilanes, J., & De Viteri, A. S. (2018). Tales of informality: Tourism development in four Ecuadorian beaches. *Tourism Planning & Development*, *15*(5), 584–599. doi: 10.1080/ 21568316.2018.1504319

Rockström, J., Steffen, W., Noone, K., Persson, A., Chapin, F. S., Lambin, E. F., Lenton, T. M., Scheffer, M., Folke, C., Schellnhuber, H. J., Nykvist, B., de Wit, C. A., Hughes, T., van der Leeuw, S., Rodhe, H., Sörlin, S., Snyder, P. K., Costanza, R., Svedin, U., ... Foley, J. A. (2009). A safe operating space for humanity. *Nature*, *461*(7263), 472–475. doi: 10.1038/461472a

Rowath. (2017). *Doughnut economics: Seven ways to think like a 21st-century economist*. Chelsea Green Publishing.

Tham, A., & Evers-Swindell, B. (2018). Stand up and be counted—A diverse economy perspective of air New Zealand. *Tourism Planning & Development*, *15*(5), 567–583. doi: 10.1080/21568316. 2018.1504816

Human flourishing, tourism transformation and COVID-19: a conceptual touchstone

Joseph M. Cheer ⓘD

ABSTRACT

As the planet remains in the grips of COVID-19 and amidst enforced lockdowns and restrictions, and possibly the most profound economic downturn since the Great Depression, the resounding enquiry asks—what will the new normal look like? And, in much the same way, tourism aficionados, policy makers and communities are asking a similar question—what will the tourism landscape, and indeed the world, look like after the pandemic? As casualties from the crisis continue to fall by the wayside, the rethinking about what an emergent tourism industry might resemble is on in earnest. Many are hopeful that this wake-up call event is an opportunity to reshape tourism into a model that is more sustainable, inclusive and caring of the many stakeholders that rely on it. And some indicators, though not all, point in that direction. In line with this, the concept of 'human flourishing' offers merits as an alternative touchstone for evaluating the impacts of tourism on host communities. Human flourishing has a long genesis and its contemporary manifestation, pushed by COVID-19 and applied to travel and tourism, further expands the bounds of its application. Human flourishing has the potential to offer more nuanced sets of approaches by which the impact of tourism on host communities might be measured. The challenge remaining is how to develop robust indices to calibrate human flourishing policy successes.

摘要

当我们的星球仍然被新型冠状病毒掌控着、被强制封锁和限制着，可能还要面对大萧条以来最严重的经济衰退时，我们不禁要问——新常态会是什么样子？同样地，旅游爱好者、政策制定者和社区也在问类似问题——在这次流感大流行之后，旅游景观乃至整个世界会变成什么样子。随着危机造成的损失不断减少，人们开始认真反思紧急救助旅游产业的模式。许多人希望这次唤醒事件是一个重塑旅游业使之成为更可持续、更包容、更能照顾众多旅游业利益相关者的机会。有些指标，尽管不是全部，指向了那个方向。与此相一致，"人类繁荣"这个概念为评价接待地社区的旅游影响时提供了另一种衡量标准。人类繁荣有着悠久的起源和当代表现形式，因新冠病毒疫情的推动而应用于旅行和旅游业，进一步拓展了它的应用范围。人类繁荣有可能提供更细致的成套方法，从而可以测量当地社区的旅游影响。持续的挑战是如何开发稳健的指数来校准人类繁荣政策的成功。

Introduction

The rapid emergence of COVID-19 has made the much vaunted tourism growth trajectories of the last decade fragile and redundant, and the howls of overtourism that rose to prominence from 2017 to 2019 have descended into deafening silence as tourist hordes have disappeared. In Spain, the question: ¿Cuál será el escenario post Coronavirus? (What will be the post Coronavirus scenario?) (Bonet, 2020), echoes and in much the same way, this has boomed across the globe. In the shadow of the pandemic, the scramble to recalibrate, regenerate, remake and rethink tourism has taken on intense urgency. Although, the clamber to redefine a new steady state for global tourism had been on in earnest, well before COVID-19 (Brouder, 2018; Burrai et al., 2019; Hoogendoorn & Hammett, 2020).

COVID-19's ascendency has seen the global travel supply chain and the myriad service industry groups allied to it reel with redundancies, closures, and furloughs (Curley et al., 2020). Assuming, a recovery is eventual, what might a post COVID-19 tourism future look like (Gössling et al., 2020; Jamal & Budke, 2020)? What is unassailable is that transformation should recast the place of host communities within the new normal (Cheer et al., 2019; Cheer & Lew, 2017; Lew & Cheer, 2017). After all, this is what provoked overtourism backlash in Barcelona, Venice and Amsterdam (Dodds & Butler, 2019; Fletcher et al., 2019; Milano, Cheer, et al., 2019). The new normal raises appeals to deconstruct entrenched ways and reset into modes more cognisant of planetary limitations (Cheer, 2020; Gössling et al., 2019; Hall, 2019; Lew, 2020; Mostafanezhad & Norum, 2019).

Following Smith (2017) who associates tourism transformation with positive, forward thinking change, I confront what a transformed tourism after COVID-19 might look like. The central concept appraised is the notion of flourishing—human flourishing to be more precise. Why human flourishing and how might it complement tourism research enquiries is the main thrust. As a heuristic and conceptual device, human flourishing is more nuanced then its everyday and wider metaphorical usage that simply means to thrive. I envision, that human flourishing can give researchers the means of examining how host communities fare in the post COVID-19 milieu. Human flourishing suggests a "deep shift in values" and that "the old ways of thinking no longer works" (Ehrenfeld & Hoffman, 2013, p. 4; p. 6). It concerns the pivot away from redundant modes of valuing and conceiving of the way we inhabit the planet and interrelate with humans and non-humans, and underline well-being. In the post pandemic environment, human flourishing is set to become a much bigger concern as communities come to grips with their new realities and how we track and measure their well-being will become ever more pressing.

Human flourishing as a touchstone

The genesis of flourishing as a general concept is tied to Aristotelian philosophical thought, and *eudaimonia* (εὐ δαιμονία) or happiness, as explained in the revered work, *Nikhomachean Ethics*. Generally speaking, Aristotle considers virtuousness tied to morality and how to live a good life with the resultant outcome to flourish (Kenny, 2016). While this serves as a foundation for the approach taken to employing human flourishing, engaging deeply with Aristotelian philosophy is beyond this endeavour. Additionally, flourishing as conceived in positive psychology most popularly by Martin Seligman (2012) is also outside the bounds of this analysis. Instead, focus is quarantined to human flourishing in tourism praxis that although utilitarian, advocates rather radical conceptualisations that depart from prominent modus operandi of tourism and toward regenerative transformations (Pollock, 2019).

Flourishing and its application to tourism has been sparse with the exception of positive tourism entreaties by Filep et al. (2016). Although, to limit the concept to uses of it in positive psychology terms, belies its wider connotations to the intersections between people, place and space. Rasmussen (1999, p. 2) argues that human flourishing has "come to be used to develop an alternative to consequentialistic and deontological conceptions of ethics." Similarly, the ethical dilemmas evident in travel advocate for transformation to the way relationships between people and places is conceived, operationalized and commodified. Rasmussen contends that human flourishing infers action and agency and in its conceptual diversity, it emphasizes inherently worthwhile outcomes.

Similarly, Kleinig and Evans (2013, p. 539), consider human flourishing to be an "aspirational framework for thinking about human development and obligations" and that it "is not confined primarily to matters of physical development and reproduction, but embraces intentionality, experience, and culture" (p. 542). When it comes to applying human flourishing to tourism, the inference is that tourism as an activity or mode of production should consider the extent to which the concept permeates policy, planning and praxis, and ultimately into mutual flourishing within the host-guest nexus. Human dignity, according to Kleinig and Evans (2013, p. 556) is tied to notions of human flourishing:

> The various ways in which humans can, over the course of their lives, develop and live well, and insofar as such flourishing is not to be construed atomistically but, for the most part, socially, it is likely to be achieved only if certain social norms are taken on board and observed.

The norms referred to, if related to tourism, value and elevate human flourishing as fundamental tenets of the social contract between host and guest. Although, considering human flourishing in pure tourism praxis-based terms, the balance between the extent to which hosts and guests draw dividends from the encounter varies, with much sustainable tourism research critiquing the limited extent to which hosts are favored. This is clearly seen in overtourism where the discordance laments the plight of locals and their inability to flourish, despite the bourgeoning production of tourism (Cheer et al., 2019; Milano, Cheer, et al., 2019; Milano, Novelli et al., 2019). Apropos, if tourism is considered an extractive industry, how does the mining of people and place result in boomerang effects that leave hosts in more favorable positions that infer human flourishing?

As Rasmussen (1999, p. 2) points out, "Human flourishing, however, remains a technical notion, and its exact meaning varies with different theories of the human good". The implications in applying human flourishing to tourism is that in present-day terms, it extends beyond the Aristotelian view, towards contemporary considerations of human development, well-being and life satisfaction or as Rasmussen (p. 4) encapsulates, it is "inclusive of knowledge, health, friendship, creative achievement, beauty, and pleasure; and such virtues as integrity, temperance, courage, and justice". On its own, human flourishing implies the reaching of one's potential through active agency and collusion of externalities and endogenous conditions. Indeed, "concretely speaking, no two cases of human flourishing are the same, and they are not interchangeable" (ibid, p. 6). How to reconcile the myriad contexts and establish empirical human flourishing benchmarks remains a constraint to praxis and scholarly development in tourism.

To attempt to pin human flourishing down to a neat category, is to ignore that the central idea "is broader than many other concepts that mark more specific such assessments—including those of pleasure, well-being, welfare, affluence, and virtue, as well as those denoting various excellences and accomplishments" (Pogge, 1999, p. 333). For example, Hannis (2015) associates freedom as a broad notion fundamental to human flourishing. Whether or not as individuals we contend that our ability to reject or accept the circumstances of our lives, offers one insight into the human flourishing continuum. This lends guidance to enquiries into the impacts of tourism on hosts where diminished agency over life circumstances where tourism takes on a bigger footprint gives ground for effects that de-flourish and de-humanize.

As Ehrenfeld (In Ehrenfeld & Hoffman, 2013, p. 10) reminds us, human flourishing is inherently tied to constant change, impinged by changing external and internal stimuli, though its relevance lies in how machinations unfold:

> First, flourishing is the realization of a sense of completeness, independent of our immediate material context. Flourishing is not some permanent state but must be continually generated. The world is always moving forward, and those domains of our lives that have been momentarily satisfied will require attention again and again.

According to Ehrenfeld (Ibid, p. 18), "Flourishing pertains to all natural systems that include both humans and other life" and if viewed in tourism terms, asserts that the cooption of human flourishing must acknowledge system dynamics and the myriad actors within, and not just simply prioritize visitation growth. In employing human flourishing as a heuristic tool to evaluate well-being, Roche et al. (2019, p. 573) found that "human flourishing offers a useful and insightful perspective that can inform communities, governments, proponents and researchers alike about the potential impacts" of development on local-level well-being. The implications for tourism are that novel insights into the way host community well-being can be understood may be established, beyond generalized economic contributions and typical dimensions such as community satisfaction. Douglass' (2016) articulation of the four pillars of human flourishing offers a neat and comprehensive contemporary articulation shaped around: (1) Inclusiveness in public life; (2) Planetary environmental flourishing; (3) Conviviality of social and cultural life and (4) Inclusion in public life. Unlike Aristotle's rendering centered largely on virtuousness as a conduit for happiness, Douglas' four pillars, if applied to host community well-being, pays homage to systems thinking and is inclusive of the human and non-human as key variables.

Human flourishing: tourism praxis-based applications

When it comes to human flourishing in tourism, practitioners and advocates have been far more embracing of human flourishing than scholars. There are probably many reasons for this, particularly the challenges of measuring human flourishing and the development of appropriate scales and indices. A case in point is the Bhutanese approach to Gross National Happiness (GNH), although with vital distinctions, parallels the focus on human flourishing, advocating that economic prosperity is not the be-all and end-all. Theoretically at least, GNH places "socio-cultural, political-economic and spiritual-ecological wellbeing" central to development policy (Verma, 2017, p. 476). Importantly, as Munro (2016, p. 71) describes, "the four pillars of GNH are sustainable economic development, good governance, preservation of the natural environment and preservation of the national culture". A far cry from usual measures of well-being usually centred on Gross Domestic Product (GDP).

While GNH accentuates wider notions of national happiness, the upshot is human flourishing by a more expansive name. Despite the widespread popularity of Bhutan's GNH regime, Munro (2016, p. 86) argues that it "has been deliberately transformed into the official ideology of a ruling elite in a realpolitik response to rapid and disruptive social and economic change". Likewise, McCarthy's (2018) critique of the 2015 nationwide survey of the people of Bhutan, questions the ebullience over GNH "with nearly half of the Bhutanese falling into the "narrowly happy" camp, that's a sizeable chunk who are well short of bliss." Furthermore, Teoh (2015) found that in practice, the government of Bhutan actively elevated tourism-led economic development above the integrity of social, cultural and environmental inheritances. Notwithstanding, the popularity of GNH underlines international lamentations of GDP as an imperfect measure of national well-being. Apropos to considering the utility of human flourishing in tourism, GNH highlights the challenges of 'touchy-feely' or tactile non-economic indicators that aspire to apply empirical measures.

One of the leading proponents contextualizing human flourishing to tourism, Anna Pollock (2019) posits that global tourism in its current manifestation exceeds planetary thresholds and is thereby undermining social and ecological inheritances. The paradigm shift Pollock (2019) calls for emphasizes regenerative growth, hinged on several key conceptual pillars: (1) Humans are a part of nature and apart from it; (2) Humans are not superior to other life forms; (3) All life is inter-connected and inter-dependent. In practical terms, Pollock defines this as follows:

> In commercial terms this will be expressed in a greater engagement and passion experienced by both guest and host; a commitment to stewarding the natural resources on which tourism depends; a closer match between what the community wants to share and what the visitor values; and greater involvement from across the community which leads to greater creativity, collaboration and resilience.

In taking up Pollock's exhortations, practitioners answering the call include Tourism Bay of Plenty (TBOP) in New Zealand. In their recent destination plan, *The Love of Tourism*, TBOP emphasizes "aspirations to flourish while balancing the needs of people, the environment, and the tourism industry" (Archer, 2019). One of their key questions asks: "How can we fundamentally leave our place better than we found it?"—an "elevation of Māori thinking and the values that have been displaced by colonization or industrialization" (ibid.). While such ambitions are unheard of in destination management praxis, that this has emerged in the wake of COVID-19 gives it greater pertinence. Another praxis-based employment of human flourishing is Tourism Flanders' *Travelling to Tomorrow* that emphasises net benefit for all (Visit Flanders, 2018). Narratives meditate on aggregating wishes of the wider stakeholder cohort and transcending economic concerns, placing a premium on sense of place, local amenity and viable partnerships. The shift to a new paradigm is underscored by positive and gradual transformations that acknowledge systems interconnectedness and where economic growth is not decoupled from social and ecological well-being but is a vital pillar.

Just how human flourishing can be parlayed in tourism beyond destination managers remains the challenge or risk veering into platitudes and motherhood statements that are tricky to action. To what extent can human flourishing influence the demand side of tourism, yet maintain a viable balance between purpose and profitability? Global leader, Intrepid Travel, the forerunner in pushing for a recasting of how tourism is conducted, espouses balancing purpose and profit as part of wider corporate social responsibility agenda (Skift, 2018). Emphasis is on ensuring destination communities are bequeathed with a net positive benefit in economic terms, but also ensuring harmony with myriad social and ecological concerns from gender empowerment to regeneration of marine ecosystems, as exemplars.

Another praxis-based attempt to address human flourishing is the *Planet Happiness* initiative whose aims are "to highlight and strengthen the relationship between tourism and the well-being of host communities" (Planet Happiness, 2020). *Planet Happiness* strives to establish knowledge based on happiness data that measures how individual residents and destination communities view well-being. While not novel in its intent and approach, it emphasises the momentum for 'beyond GDP' movements. Human flourishing is likely an overarching concept under which initiatives such as GNH and Planet Happiness hovers. After all, as Bates (2009, p. 3) argues, "happiness can only take into account rights, ideas of justice and decision-making processes insofar as such matters influence the perceived happiness of individuals". Human flourishing suggests a broader and more complex continuum (Ehrenfeld & Hoffman, 2013).

Notwithstanding, praxis-based approaches link human flourishing and tourism largely espouse decoupling of growth-oriented policies, with myriad prescriptions from de-growth, enhancement of community engagement and agency, preservation of sense of place, elevation of the worth of the nature and the wider non-human world, acknowledgement of spirituality and conscious consumption and production. This implies that contrary to the oft-used phrase associated with former US President Bill Clinton, "It's the economy, stupid", human flourishing cannot elide economic concerns completely but must align them with related non-economic variables. This is the central concern with proponents of degrowth—if upon the inadvertent realisation of degrowth scenarios, what are the solutions to the gaps created from economic degrowth that may in fact impinge on wider notions of happiness and human flourishing, especially if incomes of the most vulnerable are diminished?

Human flourishing and the tourism agenda

While tourism discourses regarding sustainability have pivoted on broader, defining notions embedded in the Brundtland Report, particularly intergenerational equity, the sustainability treatise, according to Ehrenfeld and Hoffman has been misused and abused. In lamenting the progression of thinking around sustainability, Ehrenfeld and Hoffman (2013, p. 16) argue:

> Sustainability means absolutely nothing in practice without naming the end being sought. This dissonance has serious consequences because it leads to a term that can mean different things to different people depending on the static outcome they seek. It has lost any real meaning.

Ehrenfeld and Hoffman (p.17) frame sustainability in sanguine terms suggesting "sustainability is the possibility that humans and other life will flourish on the Earth forever." Associated with this is the "central idea of sustainability-as-flourishing", that is, sustainability that leads to an unswaying understanding of interconnectedness between humans and nature and the "need to move away from purely objective, quantitative, and "rational" reasoning to consider the spiritual, experiential, and pragmatic" (ibid, p. 19). Further, human flourishing argues for transcending utilitarian and economic notions at the heart of sustainability discourses and leapfrog towards other ways of valuing the human-in-nature and allied planetary inheritances.

Huppert and So (2013, p. 838) frame human flourishing simply as 'feeling good and functioning effectively', ostensibly optimal well-being as a broad concept. This takes tourism into social psychology territory indicating that human flourishing extends beyond simply ensuring that present-day activities avoid compromising planetary integrity for the next generation and instead lean towards acceptance that the dimensions of sustainability, if contextualized with human flourishing, makes way for capturing more nuanced understandings that include harder to grapple with variables. This harks back to Aristotle's original intent that ties human flourishing to *eudaimonia* or happiness as overarching philosophy.

What then might the possible applications of human flourishing in tourism look like? Similarly, how can the constraints that prevent human flourishing from entering the tourism policy and planning vernacular be overcome? The answer to the first question lies in how human flourishing as a conceptual framework might be best applied. As a heuristic device, it parallels much thinking around community based tourism and sustainable tourism, more generally. In response to the latter query, the challenge is in outlining the dimensions of human flourishing that apply given its malleability and limitations. Practitioners have sought to frame human flourishing in regenerative terms advocating that destinations nurture inclusive development and that net-benefit be prioritized, yet whether human flourishing can be integrated by policy makers and industry strategists is perhaps too early to tell. But in the COVID-19 wash-up, when lockdowns and restrictions eventually ease, and when tourism recovery takes flight, the compulsion to lurch toward economic recovery should not gloss over the essential dimensions that emphasize human flourishing.

Conclusion

This exercise to appraise human flourishing and espouse its application to tourism research acknowledges that the concept has rarely been applied, if at all. Although, some of its dimensions have been integrated in the pursuit of understanding host community attitudes and satisfaction. If indeed a paradigm shift is imminent for tourism in the post pandemic scenario as many advocates are promoting, then a commensurate transformation in the way the impact of tourism is assessed and monitored in host communities might also be appropriate. Human flourishing therefore, might provide a fillip to typical approaches that strive to quantify and validate the extent to which host communities are experiencing tourism. It might be that human flourishing is the key that unlocks more nuanced insights into the sector's deeper and enduring impacts given that the emergent new normal will likely enforce considerable change and how host communities grapple with this change will underline the merits of tourism in the post pandemic era.

When it comes to human flourishing, the need to consider the economic realities of COVID-19 will probably become clearer as the new normal becomes entrenched. However, "crisis moments also present opportunity: more sophisticated and flexible use of technology, less polarization, a revived appreciation for the outdoors and life's other simple pleasures" (Politico magazine, 2020, n.p). What does this all mean for the impacts on human flourishing? Will the capacity to absorb ripple effects of the current crisis mean we will embrace the new normal, or will we pine for a return to former contexts, precisely because the new economic models detract from human flourishing? Will human flourishing be hard pressed, especially if the post COVID-19 context is underpinned by global recession?

Wider notions of host community impact in tourism policy and practice has increasingly become guided by praxis-based tourism indicators that strive to outline just how communities fare. For example United National World Tourism Organisation (UNWTO) and Global Sustainable Tourism Council (GSTC) indicators for sustainable tourism are a case in point. Although, as useful as the aforementioned approaches to mapping criteria for sustainable tourism is, the nuances that underline human flourishing remain elusive. If in the Post COVID19 milieu, economic expediency makes way for more concerted attempts to integrate social and ecological considerations in praxis and policy development, human flourishing might be the launching pad that cultivates deeper insights of host community effects. Although, the challenge will be in overcoming similar criticisms of GNH as a measure of happiness where indices lack robustness.

Trials associated with embracing human flourishing and linking its utility to practice lies in drawing straight lines between it and the business of tourism, because for all the advocacy about regenerative principles and net benefit for all, the ultimate determinant of its worth might be in how it fits neatly under the overarching economic frameworks that emerge. COVID-19 has revealed what a drastic degrowth scenario looks like—on the one hand, clear lagoons and skies and the emergence of nature have been celebrated, and the wake-up call so overdue is has finally come. Furthermore, the economic wreckage that the crisis has instigated has given more than a glimpse of what life might be like in economic contraction, and for many, economic dystopia. COVID-19 has driven aircraft from the skies and cruise ships from the ocean and the flight shame movement and overtourism agitators have got their wish and the hordes are now staying at home. But whether on balance, this whole episode bequeaths tourism communities with a stronger hand will remain unknown for the foreseeable future.

Disclosure statement

No potential conflict of interest was reported by the author.

ORCID

Joseph M. Cheer (iD) http://orcid.org/0000-0001-5927-2615

References

Archer, D. (2019). *The love of tourism: Bay of plenty plans a future of flourishing.* Retrieved April 22, 2019, from https://destinationthink.com/blog/the-love-of-tourism-bay-of-plenty/

Bates, W. (2009). Gross national happiness. *Asian-Pacific Economic Literature, 23*(2), 1–16. https://doi.org/10.1111/j.1467-8411.2009.01235.x

Bonet, D. R. (2020, 28 March). ¿Apostaremos por el turismo sostenible cuando el confinamiento finalice? La Van Guardia. Retrieved April 4, 2020, from https://www.lavanguardia.com/economia/20200328/48105019477/fin-confinamiento-apostar-turismo-sostenible-brl.html?

Brouder, P. (2018). The end of tourism? A Gibson-Graham inspired reflection on the tourism economy. *Tourism Geographies, 20*(5), 916–918. https://doi.org/10.1080/14616688.2018.1519721

Burrai, E., Buda, D. M., & Stanford, D. (2019). Rethinking the ideology of responsible tourism. *Journal of Sustainable Tourism, 27*(7), 992–1007. https://doi.org/10.1080/09669582.2019.1578365

Cheer, J. M. (2020, 22 April). Not drowning, waving: Where to for cruise tourism PostCOVID-19? Monash Lens. Retrieved April 26, 2020, from https://lens.monash.edu/@politics-society/2020/04/21/1380110/not-drowning-waving-where-to-for-cruise-tourism-post-covid-19

Cheer, J. M., Milano, C., & Novelli, M. (2019). Tourism and community resilience in the Anthropocene: accentuating temporal overtourism. *Journal of Sustainable Tourism, 27*(4), 554–572. https://doi.org/10.1080/09669582.2019.1578363

Cheer, J. M. & Lew, A. A. (Eds.). (2017). *Tourism, resilience and sustainability: Adapting to social, political and economic change.* Routledge.

Curley, A., Dichter, A., Krishnan, V., Riedel, R., & Saxon, S. (2020). *Coronavirus: Airlines brace for severe turbulence.* McKinsey & Co. Retrieved 26 April, 2020, from https://www.mckinsey.com/

industries/travel-transport-and-logistics/our-insights/coronavirus-airlines-brace-for-severe-turbulence?

Dodds, R., & Butler, R. (Eds.). (2019). *Overtourism: Issues, realities and solutions* (Vol. 1). De Gruyter Oldenbourg.

Douglass, M. (2016). From good city to progressive city: reclaiming the urban future in Asia. *Insurgencies and revolutions: Reflections on John Friedmann's contributions to planning theory and practice*. Routledge.

Ehrenfeld, J. R., & Hoffman, A. J. (2013). *Flourishing: A frank conversation about sustainability*. Stanford University Press.

Filep, S., Laing, J., & Csikszentmihalyi, M. (2016). Synthesising positive tourism. In *Positive tourism* (pp. 219–228). Routledge.

Fletcher, R., Murray Mas, I., Blanco-Romero, A., & Blázquez-Salom, M. (2019). Tourism and degrowth: an emerging agenda for research and praxis. *Journal of Sustainable Tourism, 27*(12), 1745–1763. https://doi.org/10.1080/09669582.2019.1679822

Gössling, S., Hanna, P., Higham, J., Cohen, S., & Hopkins, D. (2019). Can we fly less? Evaluating the 'necessity'of air travel. *Journal of Air Transport Management, 81*, 101722. https://doi.org/10.1016/j.jairtraman.2019.101722

Gössling, S., Scott, D., & Hall, C. M. (2020). Pandemics, tourism and global change: a rapid assessment of COVID-19. *Journal of Sustainable Tourism*, 1–20. https://doi.org/10.1080/09669582.2020.1758708

Hall, C. M. (2019). Constructing sustainable tourism development: The 2030 agenda and the managerial ecology of sustainable tourism. *Journal of Sustainable Tourism, 27*(7), 1044–1060. https://doi.org/10.1080/09669582.2018.1560456

Hannis, M. (2015). *Freedom and environment: autonomy, human flourishing and the political philosophy of sustainability*, Routledge.

Hoogendoorn, G., & Hammett, D. (2020). Resident tourists and the local'other. *Tourism Geographies*, 1–19. https://doi.org/10.1080/14616688.2020.1713882

Huppert, F. A., & So, T. T. C. (2013). Flourishing across Europe: Application of a new conceptual framework for defining well-being. *Social Indicators Research, 110*(3), 837–861. https://doi.org/10.1007/s11205-011-9966-7

Jamal, T., & Budke, C. (2020). Tourism in a world with pandemics: local-global responsibility and action. *Journal of Tourism Futures*, 1–8. https://doi.org/10.1108/JTF-02-2020-0014

Kenny, A. (2016). *The Aristotelian ethics: A study of the relationship between the Eudemian and Nicomachean ethics of Aristotle*. Oxford University Press.

Kleinig, J., & Evans, N. G. (2013). Human flourishing, human dignity, and human rights. *Law and Philosophy, 32*(5), 539–564. https://doi.org/10.1007/s10982-012-9153-2

Lew, A. A., & Cheer, J. M. (Eds.). (2017). *Tourism resilience and adaptation to environmental change: Definitions and frameworks*. Routledge.

Munro, L. T. (2016). Where did Bhutan's gross national happiness come from? The origins of an invented tradition. *Asian Affairs, 47*(1), 71–92. https://doi.org/10.1080/03068374.2015.1128681

Lew, A. A. (2020). The global consciousness path to sustainable tourism: a perspective paper. *Tourism Review, 75*(1), 69–75. https://doi.org/10.1108/TR-07-2019-0291

McCarthy, J. (2018, February 12). *The birthplace of 'gross national happiness' is growing a bit cynical*. Retrieved March 28, 2020, from https://www.npr.org/sections/parallels/2018/02/12/584481047/the-birthplace-of-gross-national-happiness-is-growing-a-bit-cynical

Milano, C., Novelli, M., & Cheer, J. M. (2019). Overtourism and degrowth: a social movements perspective. *Journal of Sustainable Tourism, 27*(12), 1857–1875. https://doi.org/10.1080/09669582.2019.1650054

Milano, C., Cheer, J. M. & Novelli, M. (Eds.). (2019). *Overtourism: Excesses, discontents and measures in travel and tourism*. CABI.

Mostafanezhad, M., & Norum, R. (2019). The anthropocenic imaginary: Political ecologies of tourism in a geological epoch. *Journal of Sustainable Tourism, 27*(4), 421–435. https://doi.org/10.1080/09669582.2018.1544252

Planet Happiness. (2020). *Tourism and sustainability*. Retrieved April 22, 2020, from https://www. ourheritageourhappiness.org/why.html

Pogge, T. W. (1999). Human flourishing and universal justice. *Social Philosophy and Policy*, *16*(1), 333–361. https://doi.org/10.1017/S0265052500002351

Rasmussen, D. B. (1999). Human flourishing and the appeal to human nature. *Social Philosophy and Policy*, *16*(1), 1–43. https://doi.org/10.1017/S0265052500002235

Roche, C., Walim, N., & Sindana, H. (2019). Human flourishing and extractive-led development: "The mine will give me whatever I like. *The Extractive Industries and Society*, *6*(2), 573–583. https://doi.org/10.1016/j.exis.2019.02.002

Pollock, A. (2019). Flourishing beyond sustainability the promise of a regenerative tourism, *Presentation to ETC Workshop in Krakow*, February 6th, 2019. Accessed 14 April, 2020 https:// etc-corporate.org/uploads/2019/02/06022019_Anna_Pollock_ETCKrakow_Keynote.pdf

Politico (2020). *Coronavirus will change the world permanently*, 19 March, 2020. Accessed on 14 April.   https://www.politico.com/news/magazine/2020/03/19/coronavirus-effect-economy-life-society-analysis-covid-135579

Seligman, M. E. (2012). *Flourish: A visionary new understanding of happiness and well-being*. Simon and Schuster.

Skift. (2018). *Balancing between purpose and profit*. Retrieved March 15, 2020, from https://skift. com/insight/skift-trend-report-balancing-purpose-and-profit/

Smith, J. (2017). *Transforming travel: Realising the potential of sustainable tourism*. CABI.

Teoh, S. (2015). Gross National Happiness (GNH) in Bhutan's GNH tourism model: An investigation using grounded theory methodology [Doctoral dissertation]. Murdoch University.

Verma, R. (2017). Gross national happiness: Meaning, measure and degrowth in a living development alternative. *Journal of Political Ecology*, *24*(1), 476. https://doi.org/10.2458/v24i1.20885

Visit Flanders. (2018). *Travel to tomorrow*. Retrieved April 14, 2020, from https://issuu.com/toeris-mevlaanderen/docs/2018_toertrans_mag_210x260mm_en_web

Cancelling March Madness exposes opportunities for a more sustainable sports tourism economy

J. A. Cooper 🆔 and Derek H. Alderman 🆔

ABSTRACT

One of the earliest signals of the severity of the spread of COVID-19 in the United States and other countries was the swift cancelation of many highly prominent amateur and professional sporting events and seasons like the NCAA Division I Men's Basketball Tournament, known as "March Madness." The loss of March Madness is treated as a moment of creative tension, when disruptions can facilitate reflection and lead to positive change. We discuss the economic, socio-cultural, and environmental effects of shuttering the tournament and suggest that an understanding of the impacts of COVID-19 offers an opportunity to bring about an alternative, more sustainable sports tourism economy. The cancellation of March Madness resulted in the loss of millions of dollars in tourism revenue for local economies and deprived traveler-fans of pilgrimages to arenas, important socio-cultural gathering spaces for American basketball fans. However, it also prevented the emission of a sizable quantity of greenhouse gasses based on our carbon footprint calculated from the previous year's tournament. Ultimately, from the disruptive closing down of sport and event tourism, a post-pandemic sports tourism landscape should emerge that takes more seriously the triple-bottom line notion of balancing a reduction of greenhouse gas emissions with the creation and maintenance of resilient local economies all while both acknowledging the important role sport plays in society and keeping tourism actors healthy.

摘要

美国及其他国家新冠肺炎扩散严重性的早期标志之一就是迅速取消了诸多重要的业余和职业体育赛事, 如全国大学体育联合会一级男子篮球联赛, 即有名的"疯狂三月"(March Madness)。 取消该赛事创造了一种紧张态势, 且可促使人们反思并产生积极的改变。本研究讨论了取消联赛产生的经济、社会文化和环境效应, 并提出一种新的理解, 即新冠肺炎为另类的和更具可持续性的体育旅游经济提供了机遇。取消联赛不但使本地损失数百万美元的旅游收入, 而且也剥夺了旅行爱好者们的赛场朝圣, 因为赛场是美国篮球迷们的社会文化集聚空间。而且根据我们对上一年联赛的碳足迹计算, 取消联赛还防止了大量温室气体排放。最后, 体育与事件旅游的中断性关闭会引致后疫情体育旅游格局(landscape), 此格局下的三重底线理念须被认真对待, 包括：平衡温室气体排放的

This article has been republished with minor changes. These changes do not impact the academic content of the article.

减少与创造和维持有弹性的地方经济，承认体育在社会中发挥重
要作用，以及保持旅游行动者们的健康。

Introduction

The ongoing global coronavirus pandemic has and continues to result in myriad impacts for the tourism industry, many of which are not yet fully understood. One of the earliest signals of the severity of the spread of COVID-19 in the United States and other countries was the swift cancelation of many highly prominent amateur and professional sporting events and seasons. Before many private businesses shuttered windows and governments issued stay-at-home orders, the coronavirus forced a wholesale "closing down" of sports in the US. While this stoppage was disappointingly felt across multiple sports and planned events (Ahmed & Memish, 2020), it hit especially hard the spring ritual of hosting, playing, and watching the NCAA Division I Men's Basketball Tournament, known by its devotees as "March Madness." We treat March Madness as a moment of creative tension, when disruptions can facilitate reflection and lead to positive change. We discuss and estimate some of the economic, socio-cultural, and environmental impacts of the loss of the tournament as a result of the coronavirus pandemic. Doing so is instructive of what sports tourism adds to social life but also what it costs us, thus giving us a space to call for greater discussions of sustainability in mass sports tourism. More importantly, we argue that COVID-19 offers an opportunity to bring about an alternative, more sustainable sports economy and identify what is required to make that transformation happen. Ultimately, we hope that from the disruptive closing down of sport and event tourism can emerge a post-pandemic sports tourism landscape that takes seriously the triple-bottom line notion of balancing a reduction of carbon emissions with the creation of resilient and robust local economies all while both acknowledging the important role that sport plays in society and keeping tourists, tourism workers, and sport participants healthy.

Economic impact: sports tourism as revenue

The profit loss to the US sports tourism industry due to coronavirus closures is likely to be staggering. Tourism contributes significantly to the total economy of the United States and the world as an employment provider and revenue generator (Hara & Naipaul, 2008; see Milne & Ateljevic, 2001; Ioannides & Zampoukos, 2018), and this remains true for forms of sport (Collins & Cooper, 2017; Daniels & Norman, 2003; Gumprecht, 2008) and event tourism (Collins & Potoglou, 2019). The NCAA Men's Basketball Tournament itself is a major catalyst of economic activity both in primary advertising and university-based markets (Shapiro et al., 2009) and in secondary markets (Rishe et al., 2014). While there is skepticism of the extent to which mega events and high-profile competitions like the NCAA Tournament enhance the overall economy of host-destinations when you factor in stadium construction costs and public subsidies (Baade et al., 2011; Daniels & Norman, 2003; Matheson & Baade, 2004), they undeniably lead to a direct injection of cash into the local economy of the host place (Collins & Cooper, 2017, p. 148).

The NCAA's decision just before "Selection Sunday," when the bracket of 68 teams to compete for the championship was to be set, to cancel the entire tournament undoubtedly took a toll on both national corporate and local economic stakeholders who were counting on dollars from tournament-related spending. Though no robust quantification of the economic effect of the closing-down of the tournament has yet been published, the financial website *WalletHub* posted an informative infographic ahead of the tournament in early March 2020 when play was presumed to occur like normal (Kiernan, 2020). *WalletHub* estimated the economic impact of the cancelled competition to be $1.32 billion in television advertising revenue for the whole tournament. The impacts on first-round host Albany, New York and Final-Four host Atlanta, Georgia were to be $2.8 million and $106 million, respectively. Atlanta was expecting 113 thousand fans and 2 thousand volunteers to contribute to the city's tourism traffic in early April 2020. Dayton, Ohio, a host city for the tournament's play-in games since 2001, will not get to add to the $85 million in revenue it has collected from nearly two decades of basketball tourism. Additionally, there was to be a spike in pizza, wings, beer, and conciliatory desserts during tournament time. While these estimates are not definitive, it allows us to contextualize the scale at which this singular basketball tournament will impact local tourism infrastructures (Note 1).

Socio-cultural impact: sports tourism as pilgrimage

Beyond the dollar figures, sports fans across the United States have lost a widely popular springtime tradition. *WalletHub* reports that the office-place interest in the tournament was to be in the millions with a positive effect on workplace camaraderie (Kiernan, 2020). The tournament is one of the United States' largest sporting events, and fans all across the country follow it intensely if not obsessively every year—both in person at games and virtually through mass media (Shapiro et al., 2009). Sports are important outside of just the context of March Madness too as they have been argued to be a "cultural universal" and "one of the best indicators or expressions of culture" (Sands, 1999, p. 3). Sports can be expressions of "symbolic and emotional power" (Besnier et al., 2018, p. 158) through which we as cultures and societies tell stories about ourselves through "deep play" (Geertz, 1972). The geographic connections of the play and following of sport have been well established (Bale, 2003) as they can help reinforce ideas of the nation (Harris, 2008), heritage (Koch, 2015), home (Baker, 2018), community (Mitchelson & Alderman, 2011), and region (Cooper & Davis, 2019).

Specifically, in the context of tourism, sport is important because gameday travels to "the spectate" are indeed tourism activities (Cooper, 2020), and these travels work to reinforce narratives of identity (Harris, 2008) and place attachment (Zhang et al., 2018). We would argue that traveling to sports games is more than simply a bodily movement from home to stadium or arena; it is both a physical and emotional journey (Bale, 2003, p. 120) that constitutes a socio-spatial process. Some annual events even become ritualized to a nearly religious level (Bain-Selbo, 2009), and the travel to sports competitions can be aptly likened to an ancient form of tourism: pilgrimage (Harris, 2008; Nelson, 2017). And just as COVID-19 limited the size of Seder dinners and churches sat empty on Easter in 2020, the 14 stadium cathedrals of hoops and hardwood across the country remained vacant as the parishioner-fans stayed home without an important touchstone, tradition, and expression of identity to observe.

Environmental impact: sports tourism as carbon footprint

In addition to the economic and social effects of the closing-down of the US sports industry, there are important opportunities to consider and estimate the environmental impact that COVID-19 induced closures are having on tourism. These environmental implications are being discussed much less often, if at all, in the media and everyday discourse. We have begun to examine these implications through a carbon footprinting of the NCAA Men's Basketball Tournament (Note 2). While one will never know which teams would have ultimately been selected to compete in March Madness in 2020, we used data from the 2019 tournament to contextualize what the tournament's relative environmental impact might be. Following the framework of Cooper's (2020) approximation of a carbon footprint for a season of American college football, we calculated a total carbon footprint in CO_2 equivalents (CO_2eq) by applying apposite values from relevant literature from five pertinent economic sectors that have greenhouse gas (GHG) emissions associated with tourism: transportation (Dolf & Teehan, 2015; Filimonau et al., 2014), lodging (Ricaurte & Jagarajan, 2019), food (Berners-Lee et al., 2012), waste (Cooper, 2020), and stadium operations (Hedayati et al., 2014).

The initial results of our model estimate that tourism activities from March Madness in 2019 resulted in a total carbon footprint of just under 210 million kg CO_2eq. The results when broken down by host city, teams competing, and emissions sector all show the importance of attendance and geographic distance traveled to contributing to the total quantity of GHGs emitted. The more people who attend these games and the greater the distance they have to travel to get there, the more GHGs that are emitted. This is clear in a number of areas: the greatest contributor to the total by emissions sector was tourist and team travel which accounted for about 80 percent of the total carbon footprint. This result is consistent with other studies that include motorized transport as a part of their models (Cooper, 2020; Edwards et al., 2016; El Hanandeh, 2013; Filimonau et al., 2014; Pereira et al., 2019) because in tourism, the transport of people to their destinations is the largest contributor to the total carbon footprint (Dwyer et al., 2010; Lenzen et al., 2018; Kitamura et al., 2020; see Gössling & Schumacher, 2010; Larsson et al., 2018; Debbage & Debbage, 2019; Graver et al., 2019).

Additionally, Minneapolis, the host city of the 2019 Final Four, tops the list of GHGs emitted per host site by a wide margin. This crowning jewel of the tournament accounts for about 18 percent of the tournament's total emissions because the sheer number of people who attend the last three games of the tournament, which usually are played in an American football stadium to accommodate large crowds of spectators and media. The results broken down by team also reinforce the suggestion that attendance and distance traveled play a heavy role in contributing to a carbon footprint of sport event travel. When normalizing GHG emissions per-capita, those teams with the highest emissions were those who had to travel across the country to play their games. This included both east-coast teams playing on the west coast and vice versa. The inverse held true too; those teams that did not have a large carbon footprint were those located close to their game location.

Re-thinking sustainability in sports tourism

How then can we re-imagine the idea of sustainable sports tourism and indeed sustainable tourism writ large in the post-pandemic world? What can comparing the GHG emissions of the 2019 NCAA basketball tournament to its cancelled 2020 counterpart contribute to that conversation? How can we reconcile these countervailing impacts— the loss of revenue, jobs, and society-defining rituals and expressions on one hand and, on the other hand, significant environmental savings due to stay-at-home mandates? An opportunity is afforded here to more centrally locate mass sports tourism within discussions of sustainability (as this has not happened as often as it should) and to ensure that we calibrate these discussions by taking into consideration all the ways in which sports affect people and places. Only by doing so can we ensure transforming the nature of sports and tourism in the post-pandemic era.

The stated goals for avoiding a "climate apartheid scenario" (UN Human Rights Council, 2019, p. 14) of irreversible damage to Earth (Steffen et al., 2018) caused by unchecked GHG emissions is a primary component of approaches to sustainable tourism, and this should remain the case. Because of the need to decrease these global emissions to curb the effects of anthropogenic climate change (Ripple et al., 2020), the pre-pandemic literature consistently focused on reducing GHG emissions associated with tourism. Research is only beginning to examine the environmental effects of the COVID-19 pandemic forcing governments and industries like tourism to halt polluting activities (see Isaifan, 2020). We can expect to see overall improvements in pollution levels during and in the wake of the pandemic due to reduced human-induced fossil-fuel burning activities like daily commutes and tourist mobility. For example, while the NCAA Tournament's carbon footprint of 210 million kg of GHGs was an unwelcome addition to the world's carbon budget in 2019, that figure was slashed to zero in 2020 when the entire tournament was forced into cancelation by the spread of COVID-19. From only the cancellation of this one event, we will see a drop of millions of kilograms of carbon dioxide from the year before. Under the often stated goal of sustainable tourism of cutting emissions, this is a wild success for the environment.

Yet, the results of the NCAA Tournament carbon footprinting, as only one in a conglomeration of canceled tourism events globally, also show that in the post-pandemic tourism economy, "sustainable tourism development needs to encompass a broader vision" that takes more seriously economic viability and resilience (Gibson et al., 2012, p. 161). There is a dearth of academic and industry studies that examine the carbon footprints of American amateur and professional sports spectacles and their related tourism, pointing to a clear need for a deeper accounting—literally and politically—of the environmental sustainability and responsibility of sports-related travel in the post-pandemic era. Beyond this though, the economic impacts of cancellations due to COVID-19 starkly show that cutting GHG emissions cannot and must not be the singular goal of sustainable tourism. Nonexistent tourism is not sustainable tourism. Rather, sustainability requires a broad scope in the midst of this pandemic, one that actively pursues a reduction in emissions while enhancing economic resilience, realizing the social and psychological value of sports events, and protecting and the health, well-being, and catastrophic readiness of tourists, tourism workers, and sports participants.

The outbreak of COVID-19 has shown that "a sustained flow of tourists cannot be taken for granted" (Liu, 2003), and solutions are needed to ensure that the small businesses that undergird and support not only these sport tourism events but the host cities in extra-event times are able to be resilient in weathering disaster in its many forms. This runs true too for independent workers in the emerging digitally-based "gig economy" (Burtch et al., 2018; de Stefano, 2016; Manyika et al., 2016) who are increasingly a part of modern tourism economic infrastructures (Gurran & Phibbs, 2017; Ioannides et al., 2019; Nieuwland & van Melik, 2020) and who assume more economic risk while being further removed from social safety nets available to more traditional employees in the United States (Friedman, 2014).

The time it will take for local businesses and gig economy workers to rebound from the effects of lost tourism dollars during the COVID-19 pandemic is unclear, but with an increasingly globalized world and a warming planet, we can expect more disease spread and natural disasters along with periodic political upheavals, armed conflicts, and economic downturns that have been consistent across recorded history. The ultimate goal is to simultaneously expand both tourist activity and environmental sustainability (Pulido-Fernández et al., 2019) while remaining economically resilient and socially responsible. To begin to do this, O'Brien and Chalip (2007, p. 319) propose a strategic leveraging of sport event tourism to "maximize … benefits for host communities" under the triple-bottom line framework (Elkington, 1994) but to do so proactively rather than reactively. Sustainable tourism going forward must be proactive in preparing for any downturn that may negatively impact or completely halt tourism demand.

One solution we propose is inspired by Anthony Flaccavento's (2016) ideas of robust local economies. Flaccavento argues within a framework of the triple-bottom line to increase investments in local capacity for communities, cities, and regions to be able to meet their own needs (p. 160). This is difficult to conceptualize for tourism economies that are often externally economically dependent, but perhaps there is a solution rooted in local resiliency. Imagine a grouping of geographically connected locally-owned businesses who collaborate in funding a co-owned cooperative sustainability fund. Each business contributes, and that money serves as an extra source of insurance. In times of economic stability, this fund could be used for other avenues of sustainability in business operations and in the community. But in disaster times, this fund could be an extra backstop along with individual businesses' creative solutions to prevent only those multinational and large, traded corporations from being able to weather hardship and pull through. There would need to be a well-designed power-sharing agreement that legally binds the governing of funds usage, perhaps with automatic economic triggers that make funding available and turn the flow of cash off again. Public policy and nonprofit research fields would be best suited to conceptualize and implement a program design that could enhance sustainable tourism in this way.

Flaccavento argues that networks of small businesses coming together to each enhance their own activities and resilience in a way they could otherwise not actualize is critically important because local economies are outgunned in the overall market despite the important work they do in fostering sustainability (2016, p. 170). This remains true in the tourism industry as well. Many of the economic analyses of lost revenue from the 2020 March Madness will focus on the television or corporate advertising losses rather than the effects on the local businesses of the host cities that will lose not only expected revenue from tournament tourists but consistent cash flows from their regular customers (Note 1). This is why a sustainability network for local businesses that buttress cities' tourism economies would be beneficial.

Local businesses are a powerful part of a local economy and community, and local communities have a powerful potential in the future of sustainable tourism (Scheyvens, 1999). Local resiliency can in turn help businesses' dependence on travel-based (and therefore GHG emitting) tourism activities and events (Lenzen et al., 2018, p. 526). This local resiliency must be fully committed to an equitable form of resiliency and regeneration that not only sustains local economies and benefits the environment but also works towards social equity with a critical, self-reflective eye (Walsh, 2018) because existing environmental inequities are already translating to COVID-19 health-related inequities (Wu et al., 2020). The form of local equitable resiliency we propose here should fully flow from a holistic triple-bottom line approach.

With this all in mind, we reaffirm the idea of reframing COVID-19 as a creative tension within which we can critically assess recently experienced losses (and gains) and allow those insights to fuel how we imagine and realize positive change in the future. There is a need to theorize and actualize a more sustainable post-pandemic sports tourism landscape that does not simply reproduce and reestablish pre-pandemic modes of industrial operation and management. The virus-induced closing down of the service industry, gig economies, and US sports tourism spectacles such as March Madness represents a here-and-now moment in which scholars and managers can and should reemphasize the notion of sustainability as balance by recognizing the need for both environmental protection and resilient, profitable economic activity in tourism. Recognizing this, we agree with Liu (2003) that "sustainable tourism requires … a sound understanding and proper management of tourism demand" but that these "issues have generally been ignored in the sustainable tourism debate" because perpetual demand for tourism is often assumed to be "a constant … given condition" (p. 462). The COVID-19 pandemic has shown this logic to be faulty, and no longer can "destinations … assume tourists will continue to visit" (Gibson et al., 2012, p. 161).

Thus, during this time in which players are not in the locker rooms, fans are not in the stands, and cameras are not tuned toward the action on the court, tourism leaders in industry and the academy should progressively fight to alter the nature and structure of sport, event, and global travel for meaningful, positive, and enduring transformation. Doing so is not incongruous with a love for the game; rather, it is critical to its survival as we continue to move into a time when uncertainty is the new normal. We advocate for a future post-pandemic path forward in tourism that takes seriously the triple-bottom line notion of balancing the beneficence of economic and environmental effects of travel; empowers and enhances local, bottom-up sustainable economies; and recognizes the important role sport and event tourism play in society writ large.

Notes

1. There have been a few good pieces of journalism highlighting local businesses in the wake of COVID-19 March Madness cancelations, even if some were written before the complete closing-down of the NCAA Tournament. Please see: <https://fivethirtyeight.com/features/the-coronaviruss-economic-effect-on-sports-could-be-staggering/>, <https://www.si.com/college/2020/03/20/march-madness-corona-virus-spokane-gonzaga>, and <https://www.usatoday.com/story/sports/ncaab/tourney/2020/03/12/march-madness-coronavirus-impact-ncaa-tournament-hurts-businesses/5030297002/>.
2. This project's carbon footprinting model was calculated in a PostgreSQL database using the PostGIS extension. A full open-source online repository of the postgres and python code used to run the calculations as well as the initial team and host city locational datasets can be found at <https://github.com/cooperjaXC/covid_marchmadness>.

Disclosure statement

No potential conflict of interest was reported by the author(s).

ORCID

J. A. Cooper   http://orcid.org/0000-0002-4334-4079
Derek H. Alderman   http://orcid.org/0000-0002-5192-8103

References

Ahmed, Q. A., & Memish, Z. A. (2020). The cancellation of mass gatherings (MGs)? Decision making in the time of COVID-19. *Travel Medicine and Infectious Disease* 101631. Advance online publication. https://doi.org/10.1016/j.tmaid.2020.101631

Baade, R. A., Baumann, R. W., & Matheson, V. A. (2011). Big men on campus: Estimating the economic impact of college sports on local economies. *Regional Studies, 45*(3), 371–380. https://doi.org/10.1080/00343400903241519

Bain-Selbo, E. (2009). From lost cause to third-and-long: College football and the civil religion of the South. *Journal of Southern Religion, 11*, 1908–1918.

Baker, T. A. (2018). Long-distance football fandom: emotional mobilities and fluid geographies of home. *Social & Cultural Geography*, 1–17. Advance online publication. https://doi.org/10.1080/14649365.2018.1563709

Bale, J. (2003). *Sports geography* (2nd ed.). Routledge.

Berners-Lee, M., Hoolohan, C., Cammack, H., & Hewitt, C. N. (2012). The relative greenhouse gas impacts of realistic dietary choices. *Energy Policy, 43*, 184–190. https://doi.org/10.1016/j.enpol.2011.12.054

Besnier, N., Brownell, S., & Carter, T. F. (2018). *The anthropology of sport - bodies, borders, biopolitics*. University of California Press.

Burtch, G., Carnahan, S., & Greenwood, B. N. (2018). Can you gig it? An empirical examination of the gig economy and entrepreneurial activity. *Management Science, 64*(12), 5497–5520. https://doi.org/10.1287/mnsc.2017.2916

Collins, A., & Cooper, C. (2017). Measuring and managing the environmental impact of festivals: The contribution of the ecological footprint. *Journal of Sustainable Tourism, 25*(1), 148–162. https://doi.org/10.1080/09669582.2016.1189922

Collins, A., & Potoglou, D. (2019). Factors influencing visitor travel to festivals: Challenges in encouraging sustainable travel. *Journal of Sustainable Tourism, 27*(5), 668–688. https://doi.org/10.1080/09669582.2019.1604718

Cooper, J. A. (2020). Making orange green? A critical carbon footprinting of Tennessee football gameday tourism. *Journal of Sport & Tourism, 24*(1), 31–51. https://doi.org/10.1080/14775085.2020.1726802

Cooper, J. A., & Davis, E. H. (2019). Fandom on the air: Updating the geography of collegiate football radio broadcasting. *Northeastern Geographer, 11*, 1–29.

Daniels, M. J., & Norman, W. C. (2003). Estimating the economic impacts of seven regular sport tourism events. *Journal of Sport & Tourism, 8*(4), 214–222. https://doi.org/10.1080/1477508032000161528

De Stefano, V. (2016). The rise of the "just-in-time workforce": on-demand work, crowdwork, and labor protection in the "gig-economy. *Comparative Labor Law & Policy Journal, 37*(3), 471–503.

Debbage, K. G., & Debbage, N. (2019). Aviation carbon emissions, route choice and tourist destinations: Are non-stop routes a remedy? *Annals of Tourism Research, 79*, 102765. https://doi.org/10.1016/j.annals.2019.102765

Dolf, M., & Teehan, P. (2015). Reducing the carbon footprint of spectator and team travel at the University of British Columbia's varsity sports events. *Sport Management Review, 18*(2), 244–255. https://doi.org/10.1016/j.smr.2014.06.003

Dwyer, L., Forsyth, P., Spurr, R., & Hoque, S. (2010). Estimating the carbon footprint of Australian tourism. *Journal of Sustainable Tourism, 18*(3), 355–376. https://doi.org/10.1080/09669580903513061

Edwards, L., Knight, J., Handler, R., Abraham, J., & Blowers, P. (2016). The methodology and results of using life cycle assessment to measure and reduce the greenhouse gas emissions footprint of "Major Events" at the University of Arizona. *The International Journal of Life Cycle Assessment, 21*(4), 536–554. https://doi.org/10.1007/s11367-016-1038-4

El Hanandeh, A. (2013). Quantifying the carbon footprint of religious tourism: the case of Hajj. *Journal of Cleaner Production, 52*, 53–60. https://doi.org/10.1016/j.jclepro.2013.03.009

Elkington, J. (1994). Towards the sustainable corporation: Win-win-win business strategies for sustainable development. *California Management Review, 36*(2), 90–100. https://doi.org/10.2307/41165746

Filimonau, V., Dickinson, J., & Robbins, D. (2014). The carbon impact of short-haul tourism: A case study of UK travel to Southern France using life cycle analysis. *Journal of Cleaner Production, 64*, 628–638. https://doi.org/10.1016/j.jclepro.2013.07.052

Flaccavento, A. (2016). *Building a healthy economy from the bottom up: Harnessing real-world experience for transformative change.* The University Press of Kentucky.

Friedman, G. (2014). Workers without employers: shadow corporations and the rise of the gig economy. *Review of Keynesian Economics, 2*(2), 171–188. https://doi.org/10.4337/roke.2014.02.03

Geertz, C. (1972). Deep play: Notes on the Balinese cockfight. *Daedalus, 101*(1), 1–37.

Gibson, H. J., Kaplanidou, K., & Kang, S. J. (2012). Small-scale event sport tourism: A case study in sustainable tourism. *Sport Management Review, 15*(2), 160–170. https://doi.org/10.1016/j.smr.2011.08.013

Gössling, S., & Schumacher, K. P. (2010). Implementing carbon neutral destination policies: issues from the Seychelles. *Journal of Sustainable Tourism, 18*(3), 377–391. https://doi.org/10.1080/09669580903147944

Graver, B., Zhang, K., & Rutherford, D. (2019). *CO2 emissions from commercial aviation, 2018* (Working Paper). International Council on Clean Transportation.

Gumprecht, B. (2008). *The American CollegeTown.* University of Massachusetts Press.

Gurran, N., & Phibbs, P. (2017). When tourists move in: how should urban planners respond to Airbnb? *Journal of the American Planning Association, 83*(1), 80–92. https://doi.org/10.1080/01944363.2016.1249011

Hara, T., & Naipaul, S. (2008). Agritourism as a catalyst for improving the quality of the life in rural regions: a study from a developed country. *Journal of Quality Assurance in Hospitality & Tourism, 9*(1), 1–33. https://doi.org/10.1080/15280080802108226

Harris, J. (2008). Match day in Cardiff:(Re) imaging and (re) imagining the nation. *Journal of Sport & Tourism, 13*(4), 297–313. https://doi.org/10.1080/14775080802577219

Hedayati, M., Iyer-Raniga, U., & Crossin, E. (2014). A greenhouse gas assessment of a stadium in Australia. *Building Research & Information, 42*(5), 602–615. https://doi.org/10.1080/09613218.2014.896141

Ioannides, D., Röslmaier, M., & van der Zee, E. (2019). Airbnb as an instigator of 'tourism bubble' expansion in Utrecht's Lombok neighbourhood. *Tourism Geographies, 21*(5), 822–840. https://doi.org/10.1080/14616688.2018.1454505

Ioannides, D., & Zampoukos, K. (2018). Tourism's labour geographies: Bringing tourism into work and work into tourism. *Tourism Geographies, 20*(1), 1–10. https://doi.org/10.1080/14616688.2017.1409261

Isaifan, R. J. (2020). The dramatic impact of Coronavirus outbreak on air quality: Has it saved as much as it has killed so far? *Global Journal of Environmental Science and Management, 6*(3), 275–288. https://doi.org/10.22034/gjesm.2020.03.01

Kiernan, J. S. (2020, March 11). 2020 March Madness Stats & Facts. *Wallethub.* https://wallethub.com/blog/march-madness-statistics/11016/

Kitamura, Y., Ichisugi, Y., Karkour, S., & Itsubo, N. (2020). Carbon Footprint Evaluation based on Tourist Consumption toward Sustainable Tourism in Japan. *Sustainability, 12*(6), 2219. https://doi.org/10.3390/su12062219

Koch, N. (2015). Gulf Nationalism and the Geopolitics of Constructing Falconry as a 'Heritage Sport. *Studies in Ethnicity and Nationalism, 15*(3), 522–539. https://doi.org/10.1111/sena.12160

Larsson, J., Kamb, A., Nässén, J., & Åkerman, J. (2018). Measuring greenhouse gas emissions from international air travel of a country's residents methodological development and application for Sweden. *Environmental Impact Assessment Review, 72*, 137–144. https://doi.org/10.1016/j.eiar.2018.05.013

Lenzen, M., Sun, Y. Y., Faturay, F., Ting, Y. P., Geschke, A., & Malik, A. (2018). The carbon footprint of global tourism. *Nature Climate Change, 8*(6), 522–528. https://doi.org/10.1038/s41558-018-0141-x

Liu, Z. (2003). Sustainable tourism development: A critique. *Journal of Sustainable Tourism, 11*(6), 459–475. https://doi.org/10.1080/09669580308667216

Manyika, J., Lund, S., Bughin, J., Robinson, K., Mischke, J., & Mahajan, D. (2016). Independent work: Choice, necessity, and the gig economy. *McKinsey Global Institute, 2016*, 1–16.

Matheson, V. A., & Baade, R. (2004). An economic slam dunk or march madness? Assessing the economic impact of the NCAA basketball tournament. In J. Fizel &, R. Fort (Eds.), *The Economics of College Sports* (pp. 111–133). Praeger Publishers.

Milne, S., & Ateljevic, I. (2001). Tourism, economic development and the global-local nexus: Theory embracing complexity. *Tourism Geographies, 3*(4), 369–393. https://doi.org/10.1080/146166800110070478

Mitchelson, R. L., & Alderman, D. H. (2011). Mapping NASCAR valley: Charlotte as a knowledge community. *Southeastern Geographer, 51*(1), 31–48. https://doi.org/10.1353/sgo.2011.0001

Nelson, V. (2017). *An introduction to the geography of tourism* (2nd ed.). Rowman & Littlefield.

Nieuwland, S., & van Melik, R. (2020). Regulating Airbnb: how cities deal with perceived negative externalities of short-term rentals. *Current Issues in Tourism, 23*(7), 811–825. https://doi.org/10.1080/13683500.2018.1504899

O'Brien, D., & Chalip, L. (2007). Sport events and strategic leveraging: pushing towards the triple bottom line. In A. G. Woodside & D. Martin (Eds.), *Tourism management: Analysis, behaviour, and strategy* (pp. 318–338). Cabi.

Pereira, R. P. T., Filimonau, V., & Ribeiro, G. M. (2019). Score a goal for climate: Assessing the carbon footprint of travel patterns of the English Premier League clubs. *Journal of Cleaner Production, 227*, 167–177. https://doi.org/10.1016/j.jclepro.2019.04.138

Pulido-Fernández, J. I., Cárdenas-García, P. J., & Espinosa-Pulido, J. A. (2019). Does environmental sustainability contribute to tourism growth? An analysis at the country level. *Journal of Cleaner Production, 213*, 309–319. https://doi.org/10.1016/j.jclepro.2018.12.151

Ricaurte, E., & Jagarajan, R. (2019). Benchmarking index 2019: Carbon, energy, and water. *Cornell Hospitality Report, 19*(4), 1–23.

Ripple, W. J., Wolf, C., Newsome, T. M., Barnard, P., & Moomaw, W. R. (2020). World scientists' warning of a climate emergency. *BioScience, 70*(1), 100–112. https://doi.org/10.1093/biosci/biz152

Rishe, P. J., Mondello, M., & Boyle, B. (2014). How event significance, team quality, and school proximity affect secondary market behavior at March Madness. *Sport Marketing Quarterly, 23*(4), 212–224.

Sands, R. R. (1999). *Anthropology, sport, and culture*. Bergin & Garvey.

Scheyvens, R. (1999). Ecotourism and the empowerment of local communities. *Tourism Management, 20*(2), 245–249. https://doi.org/10.1016/S0261-5177(98)00069-7

Shapiro, S. L., Drayer, J., Dwyer, B., & Morse, A. L. (2009). Punching a ticket to the big dance: A critical analysis of at-large selection into the NCAA division I men's basketball tournament. *Journal of Issues in Intercollegiate Athletics, 2*, 46–63.

Steffen, W., Rockström, J., Richardson, K., Lenton, T. M., Folke, C., Liverman, D., Summerhayes, C. P., Barnosky, A. D., Cornell, S. E., Crucifix, M., Donges, J. F., Fetzer, I., Lade, S. J., Scheffer, M., Winkelmann, R., & Schellnhuber, H. J. (2018). Trajectories of the earth system in the anthropocene. *Proceedings of the National Academy of Sciences, 115*(33), 8252–8259. https://doi.org/10.1073/pnas.1810141115

United Nations Human Rights Council. (2019). *Climate change and poverty: Report of the Special Rapporteur on extreme poverty and human rights*. Session 41: June 2019.

Walsh, E. A. (2018). White fragility as an obstacle to anti-racist resilience planning: Opportunities for equity-conscious partnerships. *Journal of Urban Management, 7*(3), 181–189. https://doi.org/10.1016/j.jum.2018.12.005

Wu, X., Nethery, R. C., Sabath, B. M., Braun, D., & Dominici, F. (2020). Exposure to air pollution and COVID-19 mortality in the United States. *medRxiv*. Manuscript submitted for publication. https://doi.org/10.1101/2020.04.05.20054502.

Zhang, H., Huang, Z., Green, B. C., & Qiu, S. (2018). Place attachment and attendees' experiences of homecoming event. *Journal of Sport & Tourism, 22*(3), 227–246. https://doi.org/10.1080/14775085.2018.1480404

Ecological grief generates desire for environmental healing in tourism after COVID-19

Émilie Crossley

ABSTRACT

Tourism research is starting to take interest in the psychology of environmental distress, particularly as it relates to climate change. For both the COVID-19 pandemic of 2020 and the climate change movement that dominated international media in 2019, psychological parallels exist in terms of our experience of loss. As the world grapples with the pandemic and tourism grinds to a halt, stories on social media are surfacing that claim wildlife is returning to quarantined cities and that the Earth is healing itself. Much of the implicit critique of these stories is directed at the tourism industry, with two viral posts in particular supposedly documenting the 'rewilding' of Venice, that infamous icon of overtourism. While the popular media have been concerned primarily with the factual accuracy of these claims, what has gone largely unexplored is the apparent desire for environmental reparation that they express. The fixation on environmental healing evidenced in tourist social media can be interpreted as a response to widely-felt 'ecological grief', triggered by the events of COVID-19. In this context, animal reclamation of urban spaces can be identified as a motif of environmental hope that symbolises life, regeneration and resilience, the understanding of which may contribute to the project of hopeful tourism in the post-COVID-19 era.

摘要

旅游研究开始关注环境灾难心理学, 特别是与气候变化有关的心理学。无论是2020年的COVID-19全球大流行, 还是2019年霸占国际媒体的气候变化运动, 我们的损失体验在心理上都存在相似之处。随着世界与这一大流行病的斗争, 旅游业陷入停滞, 社交媒体上有报道称野生动物正在返回被隔离的城市, 地球正在自我修复。对这些报道的许多含蓄批评是针对旅游业的, 特别有两个热帖, 记录了据说是声名狼藉的"过度旅游标志"威尼斯的"回归自然"。尽管大众媒体已经关注了报道事实的准确性, 但尚未充分探究它们表达的环境补偿渴望。旅游社交媒体对环境修复的关注, 可以解释为是对COVID-19事件引发的普遍的"生态悲伤"的反应。由此而论, 城市空间的动物回归可以被视为环境的希望, 象征着生命、再生和复原力。认识这一问题, 对后COVID-19时代的希望旅游有所裨益。

This article has been republished with minor changes. These changes do not impact the academic content of the article.

Introduction

A catastrophe of unimaginable proportions is unfolding before our eyes. In the wake of the COVID-19 pandemic, the global tourism industry has all but ground to a halt, as have many other aspects of everyday life as the populations of whole countries go into lockdown to contain and slow the spread of the virus. Millions are facing the prospect of unemployment, a global economic depression is on the cards, healthcare systems are being overloaded as infections grow exponentially, and epidemiologists warn that, potentially, millions of people could die. And yet, amid all of this calamity, a glimpse of something positive has appeared. In a series of viral social media posts, images from Italy – the epicentre of the crisis at the time of writing – have showed Venice's canals running clear and undisturbed, shoals of fish visible in the turquoise shallows, swans gliding by and dolphins re-entering the city. As the author of one social media post put it, 'Nature just hit the reset button on us' (Daly, 2020). From a city besieged by tourists and labelled as an 'overtourism icon' (Seraphin et al., 2018; Visentin & Bertocchi, 2019) to a tranquil, utopian haven for wildlife, the transformation of Venice seems incredible and has provided much-needed hope that the pandemic might at least bring welcome relief to our pressured ecosystems.

A debate regarding the veracity of these social media posts has ensued. National Geographic was quick to publish an article debunking the claims of 'wild animals flourishing in quarantined cities' (Daly, 2020). Although the waters of Venice's canals were indeed clearer, due to reduced boat activity, we were informed that swans are in fact common visitors to the canals of Burano in the Venetian Lagoon and that the dolphins had been filmed off the coast of Sardinia, hundreds of kilometres away. While the article accused the posters of 'greed for virality' and 'spreading false hope in times of crisis', a Guardian News video and article released on the same date revealed that the original social media posts may have contained a kernel of truth (Guardian News, 2020; Brunton, 2020). The waterways were indeed clearer and shoals of fish were now visible; the dolphins, while not in Venice, were seen swimming at more than one empty Italian port, devoid of ships in the lockdown. In other parts of the world, animals have been documented returning to urban areas not out of curiosity but necessity. Animal populations artificially sustained through tourism have been forced to search elsewhere for food as the tourists they depend on have disappeared (Bisby, 2020; Davidson, 2020; Roth, 2020; Singh, 2020). Herds of sika deer in Nara, Japan have left the confines of the park where tourists usually feed them 'deer crackers', roaming the city streets supposedly in search of food. While in Lopburi, Thailand, macaques were filmed brawling over what is thought to have been a pot of yogurt.

While the appearance of wild animals in cities around the world has prompted some online commentators to declare that the Earth is undergoing a process of 'healing', conservationists have indicated that the influx is not the start of any significant rewilding event but merely the result of a temporary lull in human activity (Davidson, 2020). Popular media have been concerned primarily with the factual accuracy of these declarations but what has gone largely unexplored is the apparent desire for environmental reparation that they express. The current fixation on environmental healing evidenced in tourist social media can be interpreted as a response to widely-felt 'ecological grief', which denote feelings of loss and distress in relation to experiences of climate change and environmental degradation (Cunsolo & Ellis, 2018; Head, 2016; Heglar, 2020; Lertzman, 2013, 2015; Randall, 2009; Willox, 2012). This paper explores the intersection between the COVID-19 pandemic and the climate change movement that dominated international media last year, arguing that psychological parallels exist in terms of our experience of loss. In the context of ecological grief, animal reclamation of urban spaces can be identified as a motif of environmental hope that symbolises life, regeneration and resilience, which has resonated with millions of people across the world. The understanding of this motif may contribute to the project of hopeful tourism in the post-COVID-19 era (Pritchard et al., 2011).

Ecological grief, climate change and COVID-19

In 2019, climate change was rarely out of the media spotlight as the global climate movement mobilised unprecedented support and governments around the world declared climate emergencies. Climate strikes took places in thousands of locations and involved millions of people, including many school children rallied by Swedish climate activist Greta Thunberg (Hockenos, 2020; Weston, 2019). However, the sense of urgency felt by the climate justice activists, and shared by the international scientific community, was not reflected in resolute, ambitious action by governments and industries. As the protests took place, bushfires in Australia blazed with punishing tenacity, scorching an estimated 186,000 square kilometres of land and killing an estimated one billion animals, pushing some species to the brink of extinction (Baldwin & Ross, 2020; Harvey, 2020). Here in Te Waipounamu, the South Island of New Zealand, we awoke on New Year's Day to ash-filled skies that glowed orange and brought rain smelling of smoke from across the Tasman Sea. That day, I experienced a powerful sense of foreboding and I am sure that others will have felt it too. It was a surreal and visceral reminder of the precarity of our existence, and that of all life on Earth.

The need to balance action on climate change with consideration for the economy has frequently been cited by political and industry leaders for their slow response to the impending climate crisis. Now, just a few months after the last global climate strike of 2019, planes are grounded, consumption is slowing, the tourism industry is all but dead, and carbon emissions are dropping (Stone, 2020). Some authors and activists have heralded the cessation of human movement across the planet as proof that we can indeed act decisively on climate change, noting that both crises threaten a staggering loss of life (Galbraith & Otto, 2020; Trembath & Wang, 2020). Cohen (2020, p. 1) characterises the COVID-19 pandemic as 'simultaneously a public health emergency and a real-time experiment in downsizing the consumer economy' and is optimistic that it could act as a catalyst for social change towards more sustainable consumption as people acclimatise to the 'new normal'. However, Trembath and Wang (2020) warn that while the current lockdown period may well enlighten consumers to the fact that they can live without certain luxuries, such as holidays, we could equally see a resurgence in consumption, including tourism, once restrictions are lifted as countries strive to rebuild their economies and individuals reclaim their mobility.

Trembath and Wang (2020) acknowledge surface-level similarities between the current pandemic and the climate crisis: 'A global emergency. Wartime mobilization. Calls to "listen to the scientists." Demands for radical shifts in policy and human behavior. Tradeoffs between sacrifices today and larger suffering in the future.' However, they warn that COVID-19 should not be held up as a model for solving climate change; yes, global emissions are dropping, but at what cost to human life and the economy? Applauding environmental gains in the midst of so much death seems disturbingly eco-fascistic (Garcia, 2020). What we are seeing are short-term, emergency measures, not the birth of a long-term, viable solution to the climate crisis. Hockenos (2020) argues that the climate movement could actually be in worse shape once COVID-19 has passed. The prohibition of mass gatherings in many countries has sapped the movement of its momentum and it is uncertain whether emergent forms of 'cyber-activism' will be as effective at swaying public and political opinion as the iconic scenes of thousands flooding the streets in solidarity. The Earth Day 2020 Climate Strike, which was due to take place in April, has now gone online but it is hard to imagine what striking will look like while millions are either working from home, cannot work, or have been made redundant (Earth Day Strikes, 2020; Hockenos, 2020). We may be facing the prospect of the climate movement taking a back seat to more pressing health and economic concerns presented by this novel coronavirus.

There is clearly contestation regarding the extent to which COVID-19 and the climate crisis can be compared in terms of the potential for consumer adaptation and political or industry responses. Parallels that have been drawn between the crises have, to date, focused largely on pragmatic concerns such as the global movement of people or goods and their impacts on carbon emissions. What has received less attention is the affective dimension of each crisis and the implications of our collective emotional responses for future action. In an interview with the *Harvard Business Review*, grief expert David Kessler characterises current psychological responses to the pandemic as a form of collective grief: 'The loss of normalcy; the fear of economic toll; the loss of connection. This is hitting us and we're grieving' (Berinato, 2020). He says that we are likely experiencing a combination of grief for that which is already lost together with 'anticipatory grief' for an imagined future that will bring further loss of life, health, prosperity and normality. Climate justice essayist Mary Annaïse Heglar (2020) notes the 'devastating' similarities between her feelings of grief relating to COVID-19 and climate change: 'Both crises represent tectonic shifts in the way the world works. Both bring a sense of finality, that "nothing will ever be the same again." Both force me to accept the end of something big and precious and irreplaceable.'

While our vocabulary for describing the experience of shock and loss associated with the unfolding pandemic is still being formed, there is a far more mature psychological language related to environmental distress. Indeed, the connections between climate change and mental health have been explored for over a decade (Berry et al., 2010; Fritze et al., 2008). 'Eco-anxiety' or 'eco-fatigue' are terms that have gained currency in recent years in reference to environmental distress, and which have started to appear within the tourism literature (Mkono, 2020; Moscardo & Pearce, 2019; Pihkala, 2018), while 'climate anxiety' is a newer, more specific variant (Lewis, 2018; Pihkala, 2019). Another neologism is 'solastalgia', which can be conceptualised as a 'psychoterratic' (psycho: mental; terratic: Earth) state of distress induced by environmental change (Albrecht et al., 2007). Referring to 'the pain or distress caused by the loss of, or inability to derive, solace connected to the negatively perceived state of one's home environment. Solastalgia exists when there is the lived experience of the physical desolation of home' and it is likely that climate change is an emerging cause (Albrecht et al., 2007, pp. 96–98). However, the concept that seems to have resonated most strongly within academic and therapeutic communities looking to articulate the psychological distress associated with the Anthropocene is, returning to Heglar, ecological or climate 'grief' (Cunsolo & Ellis, 2018; Head, 2016; Lertzman, 2013, 2015; Randall, 2009; Willox, 2012).

Ecological grief can be defined as 'grief felt in relation to experienced or anticipated ecological losses, including the loss of species, ecosystems and meaningful landscapes due to acute or chronic environmental change' (Cunsolo & Ellis, 2018, p. 275). This conceptualisation of grief 'extends the concept of a mournable body beyond the human in order to frame climate change as the work of mourning' (Willox, 2012). It is perhaps this extension beyond the human frame of loss that has led to a lack of public acknowledgement, or 'disenfranchisement', of this process of grieving (Cunsolo & Ellis, 2018; Head, 2016). This lack of acknowledgement has consequences. Lertzman (2015) argues that when loss is not properly mourned and left unresolved, people can develop what she refers to as 'environmental melancholia', leaving them psychologically unable to translate their deep environmental concern into positive action. Early writing on the subject identified a bifurcation in public discourse on climate change, with loss appearing in relation to climate problems but not climate solutions (Randall, 2009). However, there is now greater acceptance that feelings of loss relate not only to the environment but also to the potential 'loss of the conditions that underpin contemporary Western prosperity' (Head, 2016, p. 2).

It is my prediction that the immediacy of the COVID-19 pandemic will, for many people, bring hitherto unresolved feelings relating to ecological grief out into the open. The escalation of climate consciousness, agitation and anxiety that we saw last year has, in a way, reached a bewildering and unexpected climax in the form of this pandemic. Action on carbon emissions has come, just not in response to pressure from the climate movement. The tourism industry finds itself at the centre of this historic confluence. Mounting climate-related concerns about the ethics of flying to holiday destinations have been answered by COVID-19's abrupt cessation of almost all non-essential air travel. Environmentally destructive cruise ships, once the height of glamour, are now shunned from the shores of many countries, their clients treated as pariahs. Tourism hotspots, overburdened for years and emblematic of the human pressure on our natural world, emptied practically overnight. It is against a backdrop of unresolved ecological grief, and the convergence of mounting environmental concerns with dramatic pandemic-related actions, that we can interpret the current fascination with possibilities of rewilding and environmental reparation. Far from a hollow 'greed for virality' (Daly, 2020), the images of swans and dolphins shared on social media may represent a surfacing of deep, collective desires that are only now starting to find expression.

In the context of ecological grief, animal reclamation of urban spaces can be identified as a motif of environmental hope that is rich with meaning and symbolism.

Indeed, we have seen this narrative before in relation to wildlife reclaiming Chernobyl, where one can now enjoy nature tours (Geddo, 2019). Wildlife has brought fecundity back to our empty, barren streets, which are a painful reminder of death. In a sense, we have framed these animals as the agents of environmental hope that we long to be; their agency abounds while we isolate helplessly in our homes. That stories of animals reclaiming human spaces have come from all over the world also provides a desired sense of connection – to the natural world and to one another – at a time of profound disconnection. The notion that nature has been able to 'hit the reset button on us' imparts a comforting reassurance that our planet's resilience is greater than the damage we have done to it and carries hope for a fresh start. This motif expresses desire for environmental reparation and, from a psychodynamic perspective, 'reparation – the desire to repair, make right, restore – arises out of experiences of guilt, loss and ambivalence' (Lertzman, 2013, p. 127). Expressions of hope for environmental reparation might thus rightly be connected to feelings of loss and guilt associated with ecological grief.

Environmental hope for hopeful tourism

Tourism academics are starting to turn their attention to how the psychology of environmental distress is impacting tourist decision-making and experience, particularly in relation to sustainable tourism. Moscardo and Pearce (2019) examine eco-fatigue in relation to demand for, and responses to, sustainable tourism. They argue that while tourists may be supportive of sustainability initiatives, their psychological exhaustion from continued media exposure may also result in a negative backlash to tourism products marketed with too explicit a focus on eco-consciousness. Higham et al. (2016) found climate anxiety to be a prominent theme in interviews on discretionary air travel with Australian tourists; while feelings of anxiety and guilt were not enough to eliminate the notorious 'attitude-behaviour' gap in this context, it did lead to some consumer mitigation behaviours such as carbon-offsetting for flights. Similarly, Mkono (2020) argues that growing eco-anxiety and eco-guilt are factors in the flight-shaming (flygskam) movement that has emerged in Sweden and has called for further research into the 'psychological and socio-cultural dynamics of climate change discourse'.

As evidenced by the empirical studies above, a deeper understanding of environmental distress has implications for research on the consumer 'attitude-behaviour' gap in which tourists who hold pro-environmental attitudes have been found to act sustainably at 'home' but not always when 'away' (Cohen et al., 2013; Hibbert et al., 2013; Higham et al., 2016; Juvan & Dolnicar, 2014). Explanations for the existence of the attitude-behaviour gap have focused on social cognition, identity, and spatialised behavioural norms, but less attention has been devoted to emotional factors. Lertzman (2013, 2015) argues that the attitude-behaviour gap is only perplexing in models of environmental subjectivity founded upon a unitary, rational subject. A psychodynamic perspective, on the other hand, views the subject as intrinsically conflicted, contradictory and ambivalent; 'we are able simultaneously to hold conflicting desires, thoughts and impulses, even those that appear diametrically opposed' (Lertzman, 2013, p. 120). According to this position, full integration of our competing desires is a psychological impossibility, but it may be possible to work through feelings of loss and grief that account for some barriers to environmental action.

What might a clearer understanding of ecological grief and environmental hope have to offer the project of hopeful tourism in the world that emerges post-COVID-19? Hopeful tourism presents a transformative vision of tourism scholarship founded upon a values-led humanist perspective, co-transformative learning, and critical emancipatory methodologies (Pritchard et al., 2011). Hope has started to be explored and debated within tourism research as well as gaining popularity across other parts of the social sciences, notably human geography (Anderson, 2006; Ateljevic et al., 2012; Bianchi, 2009; Brosnan et al., 2015; Cameron & Hicks, 2014; Everingham, 2016; Higgins-Desbiolles & Whyte, 2013; Pritchard et al., 2011; Swain, 2009). An ethos of hope embraces the indeterminacy of the future, for 'as long as the reality has not become a completely determined one, as long as it possesses still unclosed possibilities the shape of new shoots and new spaces of development, then no absolute objection to utopia can be raised by merely factual reality' (Bloch, 1986, p. 197, cited in Everingham, 2016, p. 521).

Pritchard et al. (2011, p. 952) argue, as part of their advocacy for hopeful tourism, that 'suppression of the emotional in tourism enquiry has produced a relatively sterile scholarship which marginalizes and excludes many of the complex emotional and passionate geographies from the knowledge worlds created in the field: worlds of pain-pleasure, fear-comfort, hate-love and despair-hope'. Everingham (2016, p. 536) also calls for a foregrounding of 'intangible affective registers and embodied relationships and connections' in our quest for hopeful tourism possibilities. I suggest that now is a time of critical importance to reflexively attune ourselves to such affects and emotions surfacing through the COVID-19 crisis (Crossley, 2019). It is possible that the timing and qualities of the current pandemic will trigger, or exacerbate, forms of psychoterratic distress such as ecological grief (Albrecht et al., 2007; Cunsolo & Ellis, 2018; Head, 2016; Heglar, 2020; Willox, 2012). While such distress could deepen emotional vulnerability for many at an already difficult time, it may also catalyse action for environmental reparation both within and beyond the tourism sector.

Whether or not the 'Venetian' swans and dolphins that went viral on social media are an example of the spread of false hope (Daly, 2020), what is clear is that they are an expression of environmental hope, and that the message of hope those images carry has resonated with millions of people across the world. There is growing recognition of how online spaces are being used by tourists to perform personal and collective moral reflexivity (Mkono, 2016; Mkono & Holder, 2019). Attending to social media may therefore enable us to comprehend how tourists are reflexively processing changes to the tourism landscape resulting from COVID-19, while also potentially allowing us to trace an emergent zeitgeist. The chances of a major voluntary shift in tourists' consumer behaviour may seem slim given the empirical evidence underscoring the persistent attitude-behaviour gap in sustainable tourism (Cohen et al., 2013; Hibbert et al., 2013; Higham et al., 2016; Juvan & Dolnicar, 2014). Indeed, as I write, news is breaking that the embattled cruise ship industry is already well on its way to recovery, with bookings for 2021 up despite multiple outbreaks of COVID-19 having caused chaos to the industry this year (Panetta, 2020). However, until the psychology of environmental distress has been investigated within tourism contexts, we will not know our individual and collective capacities to heal and to harness the power of environmental hope.

Conclusion

In this paper, I have explored intersections between the COVID-19 crisis and climate change. Building on existing tourism research on the psychology of environmental distress, I have shown how expressions of hope for environmental reparation can be connected to ecological grief. Understanding these psychological and emotional dynamics may help to advance our understanding of tourist consumer behaviour, including the persistent attitude-behaviour gap in relation to sustainable tourism. Widely shared social media stories of wildlife reclaiming urban spaces emptied by the coronavirus lockdowns, including famous tourist destinations, form part of a motif of environmental hope that symbolises life, regeneration and resilience. The notion that the Earth can heal itself in the absence of human interference has clearly resonated and brought comfort to millions of people. Our challenge now is to design for tourism futures by harnessing and channelling environmental hope in a way that truly does heal the natural world and, in the process, heals our ecological grief. While we may not reach utopia, a better version of the tourism industry we currently know is surely not beyond our grasp if we work collectively, imaginatively, and hopefully.

Disclosure statement

No potential conflict of interest was reported by the author.

References

Albrecht, G., Sartore, G. M., Connor, L., Higginbotham, N., Freeman, S., Kelly, B., Stain, H., Tonna, A., & Pollard, G. (2007). Solastalgia: The distress caused by environmental change. *Australasian Psychiatry*, *15*(1_suppl), S95–S98. https://doi.org/10.1080/10398560701701288

Anderson, B. (2006). Transcending without transcendence': Utopianism and an ethos of hope. *Antipode*, *38*(4), 691–710. https://doi.org/10.1111/j.1467-8330.2006.00472.x

Ateljevic, I., Morgan, N., & Pritchard, A. (Eds.). (2012). *The critical turn in tourism studies: Creating an academy of hope*. Routledge.

Baldwin, C., & Ross, H. (2020). Beyond a tragic fire season: A window of opportunity to address climate change?. *Australasian Journal of Environmental Management*, *27*(1), 1–5. https://doi.org/10.1080/14486563.2020.1730572

Berinato, S. (2020, March 23). That discomfort you're feeling is grief. *Harvard Business Review*. https://hbr.org/2020/03/that-discomfort-youre-feeling-is-grief

Berry, H. L., Bowen, K., & Kjellstrom, T. (2010). Climate change and mental health: A causal pathways framework. *International Journal of Public Health*, *55*(2), 123–132. https://doi.org/10.1007/s00038-009-0112-0

Bianchi, R. V. (2009). The 'critical turn' in tourism studies: A radical critique. *Tourism Geographies*, *11*(4), 484–504. https://doi.org/10.1080/14616680903262653

Brosnan, T., Filep, S., & Rock, J. (2015). Exploring synergies: Hopeful tourism and citizen science. *Annals of Tourism Research*, *53*, 96–98. http://doi.org/10.1016/j.annals.2015.05.002

Brunton, J. (2020, March 20). 'Nature is taking back Venice': Wildlife returns to tourist-free city. *The Guardian*. https://www.theguardian.com/environment/2020/mar/20/nature-is-taking-back-venice-wildlife-returns-to-tourist-free-city

Cameron, J., & Hicks, J. (2014). Performative research for a climate politics of hope: Rethinking geographic scale, "impact" scale, and markets. *Antipode*, *46*(1), 53–71. https://doi.org/10.1111/anti.12035

Cohen, M. J. (2020). Does the COVID-19 outbreak mark the onset of a sustainable consumption transition?. *Sustainability: Science, Practice and Policy*, *16*(1), 1–3. https://doi.org/10.1080/15487733.2020.1740472

Cohen, S. A., Higham, J. E. S., & Reis, A. (2013). Sociological barriers to sustainable tourism air travel behaviour. *Journal of Sustainable Tourism*, *21*(7), 298–982. https://doi.org/10.1080/09669582.2013.809092

Crossley, É. (2019). Deep reflexivity in tourism research. *Tourism Geographies*, 1–22. Advance online publication. https://doi.org/10.1080/14616688.2019.1571098

Cunsolo, A., & Ellis, N. R. (2018). Ecological grief as a mental health response to climate change-related loss. *Nature Climate Change*, *8*(4), 275–281. https://doi.org/10.1038/s41558-018-0092-2

Daly, N. (2020, March 20). Fake animal news abounds on social media as coronavirus upends life. *National Geographic*.https://www.nationalgeographic.com/animals/2020/03/coronavirus-pandemic-fake-animal-viral-social-media-posts/

Davidson, J. (2020, March 26). How COVID-19 shutdowns have affected the animal kingdom. *CBC News*. https://www.cbc.ca/news/technology/what-on-earth-newsletter-covid-19-animal-kingdom-1.5511266

Earth Day Strikes. (2020). *Earth Day Live: Strike, divest, and vote to save humanity and our planet.* https://strikewithus.org/

Everingham, P. (2016). Hopeful possibilities in spaces of 'the-not-yet-become': Relational encounters in volunteer tourism. *Tourism Geographies*, *18*(5), 520–538. https://doi.org/10.1080/14616688.2016.1220974

Fritze, J. G., Blashki, G. A., Burke, S., & Wiseman, J. (2008). Hope, despair and transformation: Climate change and the promotion of mental health and wellbeing. *International Journal of Mental Health Systems*, *2*(1), 10–13. https://doi.org/10.1186/1752-4458-2-13

Galbraith, E., Otto, R. (2020, March 20). Coronavirus response proves the world can act on climate change. *The Conversation*. https://theconversation.com/coronavirus-response-proves-the-world-can-act-on-climate-change-133999

Garcia, S. (2020, March 30). 'We're the virus': The pandemic is bringing out environmentalism's dark side. *Grist*. https://grist.org/climate/were-the-virus-the-pandemic-is-bringing-out-environmentalisms-dark-side/

Geddo, B. (2019, June 20). Take an eco-tour around Chernobyl and see how wildlife and nature has rebounded. *Lonely Planet*. https://www.lonelyplanet.com/articles/chernobyl-reserve-tours

Guardian News (2020, March 20). *Dolphins and fish: Nature moves into spaces left empty by Italian coronavirus quarantine* [Video]. YouTube. https://www.youtube.com/watch?v=jv0DLTVfwlc

Harvey, J. (2020, January 6). Number of animals feared dead in Australia's wildfires soars to over 1 billion. *The Huffington Post*. https://www.huffpost.com/entry/billion-animals-australia-fires_n_5e13be43e4b0843d361778a6

Head, L. (2016). *Hope and grief in the Anthropocene: Re-conceptualising human–nature relations.* Routledge.

Heglar, M. A. (2020, March 26). What climate grief taught me about the coronavirus. *The New Republic*. https://newrepublic.com/article/157059/climate-grief-taught-coronavirus

Hibbert, J. F., Dickinson, J. E., Gössling, S., & Curtin, S. (2013). Identity and tourism mobility: an exploration of the attitude–behaviour gap. *Journal of Sustainable Tourism, 21*(7), 999–1016. https://doi.org/10.1080/09669582.2013.826232

Higgins-Desbiolles, F., & Whyte, K. P. (2013). No high hopes for hopeful tourism: A critical comment. *Annals of Tourism Research, 40*, 428–433. https://doi.org/10.1016/j.annals.2012.07.005

Higham, J., Reis, A., & Cohen, S. A. (2016). Australian climate concern and the 'attitude–behaviour gap. *Current Issues in Tourism, 19*(4), 338–354. https://doi.org/10.1080/13683500.2014.1002456

Hockenos, P. (2020, March 26). Shifting gears: The climate protest movement in the age of coronavirus. *Yale Environment, 360* https://e360.yale.edu/features/shifting-gears-the-climate-protest-movement-in-the-age-of-coronavirus

Juvan, E., & Dolnicar, S. (2014). The attitude–behaviour gap in sustainable tourism. *Annals of Tourism Research, 48*, 76–95. https://doi.org/10.1016/j.annals.2014.05.012

Lertzman, R. (2013). The myth of apathy. In S. Weintrobe (Ed.) *Engaging with climate change: Psychoanalytic and interdisciplinary perspectives* (pp. 117–133). Routledge.

Lertzman, R. (2015). *Environmental melancholia: Psychoanalytic dimensions of engagement*. Routledge.

Lewis, J. (2018). In the room with climate anxiety. *Psychiatric Times, 35*(11), 1–2.

Mkono, M. (2016). The reflexive tourist. *Annals of Tourism Research, 57*, 206–219. https://doi.org/10.1016/j.annals.2016.01.004

Mkono, M. (2020). Eco-anxiety and the flight shaming movement: Implications for tourism. *Journal of Tourism Futures*, Advance online publication. https://doi.org/10.1108/JTF-10-2019-0093

Mkono, M., & Holder, A. (2019). The future of animals in tourism recreation: Social media as spaces of collective moral reflexivity. *Tourism Management Perspectives, 29*, 1–8. https://doi.org/10.1016/j.tmp.2018.10.002

Moscardo, G., & Pearce, J. (2019). Eco-fatigue and its potential impact on sustainable tourist experiences. In J. Pearce (Ed.) *BEST EN Think Tank XIX Conference Proceedings: Creating Sustainable Tourist Experiences* (pp. 140–164). James Cook University.

Panetta, G. (2020, April 13). Cruise ship bookings for 2021 are already on the rise despite multiple COVID-19 outbreaks. *Business Insider Australia*. https://www.businessinsider.com.au/cruise-ship-bookings-are-increasing-for-2021-despite-coronavirus-2020-4?r=US&IR=T

Pihkala, P. (2018). Eco-anxiety, tragedy, and hope: Psychological and spiritual dimensions of climate change. *Zygon®, 53*(2), 545–569. https://doi.org/10.1111/zygo.12407

Pihkala, P. (2019). *Climate anxiety*. MIELI Mental Health Finland.

Pritchard, A., Morgan, N., & Ateljevic, I. (2011). Hopeful tourism: A new transformative perspective. *Annals of Tourism Research, 38*(3), 941–963. https://doi.org/10.1016/j.annals.2011.01.004

Randall, R. (2009). Loss and climate change: The cost of parallel narratives. *Ecopsychology, 1*(3), 118–129. https://doi.org/10.1089/eco.2009.0034

Roth, A. (2020, March 16). Brawling monkeys. Wandering deer. Blame coronavirus. *The New York Times*. https://www.nytimes.com/2020/03/16/science/hungry-monkeys-deer-coronavirus.html

Seraphin, H., Sheeran, P., & Pilato, M. (2018). Over-tourism and the fall of Venice as a destination. *Journal of Destination Marketing & Management, 9*, 374–376. https://doi.org/10.1016/j.jdmm.2018.01.011

Singh, M. (2020, March 22). Emboldened wild animals venture into locked-down cities worldwide. *The Guardian*. https://www.theguardian.com/world/2020/mar/22/animals-cities-coronavirus-lockdowns-deer-raccoons

Stone, M. (2020, April 3). Carbon emissions are falling sharply due to coronavirus. But not for long. *National Geographic*. https://www.nationalgeographic.com/science/2020/04/coronavirus-causing-carbon-emissions-to-fall-but-not-for-long/

Swain, M. B. (2009). The cosmopolitan hope of tourism: Critical action and worldmaking vistas. *Tourism Geographies, 11*(4), 505–525. https://doi.org/10.1080/14616680903262695

Trembath, A., Wang, S. (2020, March 20). Why the COVID-19 response in no model for climate action. *The Breakthrough*. https://thebreakthrough.org/issues/energy/covid-19-climate

Visentin, F., & Bertocchi, D. (2019). Venice: An analysis of tourism excesses in an overtourism icon. In Milano, C., Cheer, J. M., & M. Novelli (Eds.). *Overtourism: Excesses, discontents and measures in travel and tourism* (pp. 18–38). CABI.

Weston, P. (2019, September 20). Climate strike: Key stats from protests as more than 4,600 events are held in 150 countries. *The Independent*. https://www.independent.co.uk/environment/climate-protests-greta-thunberg-strikes-global-warming-number-countries-a9113976.html

Willox, A. C. (2012). Climate change as the work of mourning. *Ethics & the Environment*, *17*(2), 137–164. https://doi.org/10.2979/ethicsenviro.17.2.137

How should tourism education values be transformed after 2020?

Johan Edelheim (iD)

ABSTRACT

Values and axiology are necessary components for successful and meaningful tourism education and research. They especially need to be revisited in considering the future of higher education in a COVID-19 world. If transformation means to bring about a substantial change in a positive direction, then the COVID-19 pandemic might be a blessing in disguise for tourism higher education, as a substantial change has been due for quite some time. The transformative powers that education offers are seen in the individual through the internal and external transformations of learners. Higher education holds the promise of transforming society, but it is widely criticized for being too enmeshed in neoliberal values, which weakens it ability to productively equip students with capacities to transform the society they are entering. Education, both generally and more specifically tied to tourism higher education, requires a stronger awareness of lived values and aspirational values to transform how education is carried out. These include, for example, an emphasis on wellbeing indicators over revenue and tourist arrival numbers. All humans act and plan for their futures according to their lived values, but such values are hardly ever overtly acknowledged in research or in daily parlance. The COVID-19 pandemic is stirring up a new search for these lived values in a context where past formulas are failing on a global scale.

摘要

价值观和价值论是成功且有意义的旅游教育和研究的必要组成部分。在考虑新型冠状病毒肺炎（COVID-19）疫情背景下高等教育的未来时，尤其需要重新审视这些问题。如果转型意味着在一个积极的方向上带来实质性的变化，那么新冠（COVID-19）疫情大流行可能是旅游高等教育的福音，因为实质性的变化已经出现了相当长的一段时间。教育所提供的变革力量是通过学习者内在和外在的转变在其身上看到的。高等教育有着改造社会的希望，但它被广泛批评为过于沉浸在新自由主义价值观中，而新自由主义价值观削弱了学生有效地具备改造他们正在进入的社会的能力。教育，无论是一般的还是更具体地与旅游高等教育联系在一起，都需要对生活价值观和理想价值观有更强烈的认识，以改变教育的实施方式。例如，这些措施包括强调幸福指数，而非收入和游客抵达人数。所有的人类都根据他们的生活价值观采取行动并计划他们的未来，但这些价值观在研究或日常用语中几乎从未得到公开承认。当过去的方法在全球范围内逐渐失去影响力的背景下，新

冠（COVID-19）疫情流行病引发了人们对这些生存价值的新探
索。

Education – where transformation should happen

Education has the opportunity to be one of the most transformative experiences any person can go through. By receiving education, be it at any level (skills, concepts, competencies, you name it), or of any type (formal, informal, life-long, coaching), the person who participates in it should by definition change (in a positive direction), that is the whole point with the exercise. If the change is really transformative depends on a range of issues, some of which are internal to the person being educated, and those around that person (including the people providing the education), other issues are external, and/or contextual.

I was privileged to work as a primary school teacher for two years some decades ago. The first year of teaching was first graders (approximately 6–7 years old in Finland, where I worked), the other year teaching fifth graders (10–11 years old). I experienced some amazing moments of transformation, such as students who 'broke the code' and learned to read and write, students who learned abstract thinking through mathematics, and students who learned ice-skating, and then went on to become professional ice-hockey players. My role in this varied, in some cases it was bigger, in other cases the students transformed probably despite being taught by me, my ice-skating skills are, for example, nothing to celebrate.

Societies invest a lot of money and effort in education, it is a way of creating national pride, inclusion, and equality. It is also a way of socializing young people into their future roles in society, initially by teaching about rules, expected behaviors, and naturally data that has been termed necessary for successful participation in any one society. Later, education might be a means to prepare students to become productive members of society as tax-paying employees or entrepreneurs, playing their given roles in a socially agreed upon reality (Lawson, 2019).

Transformative educational experiences are during the formative stages of students' educational career (i.e. during their primary and secondary education) mainly internal and personal, and only in a few cases external and societal. I count in vocational training and schooling in this formative stage, as it ultimately is meant to prepare students for an existing reality, and to reproduce successful practices as efficiently as possible. Tertiary education, so called higher education, is meant to be research-led, -oriented, -tutored, or -based (Healey, 2005), meaning that there should be an intimate link between what and how students learn, and relevant research that has been, or is conducted on that topic.

Truly transformative practices in higher education are unfortunately not the norm, higher education has in many cases morphed into an extension of a meritocratic society, obsessed by ranking-tables, metrics, and neoliberal efficiency measurements where students are regarded as input and output in a system, rather than individuals who have the potential to transform the realities we all inhabit. There are naturally exceptions, innovations take place, and there are programs for students to become successful practicing scientists, or entrepreneurs, but this is not how higher education degrees are generally structured.

THE higher education, built on shaky premises?

Education, teaching and learning, in the travel, tourism, hospitality, and events sector (for short THE from here onward) has often been a secondary thought behind something else. For the sectors of societies that lobby/lobbied for THE to be included in higher education, the reasons are/were often utilitarian – to fill skill shortages in existing systems Lo (2005). This is natural, people do live in present tense, and are informed in their decisions for the future by the past, and the needs of yesterday and today are always more pressing than any uncertainties of the future.

The gradual growth of THE, as a sector with significant economic implications in many societies, has also led to a need for higher professionalism in the workforce, and in the administration and management of enterprises within the sector. Higher education has, for the sectors depending on the workforce, often just been seen as a continuation of secondary education schooling, more skills and data to drum into young minds, in order to fill gaps in the workforce, albeit now at a higher level. Catrett has done an excellent historical analysis of how hospitality higher education has developed. In this he shows the meeting of two schools of thought; industry-created management training institutes' incorporation into universities on the one hand, and university program specializations stemming from geography, sociology or a similar related field, on the other hand (Catrett, 2018).

However, for THE to be accepted as 'serious' academic disciplines, on par with established sciences, academic research needs to be created, published in accepted channels, and surrounded with an apparatus of competitive grants, impact factor calculations, and the like. The whole game of gaining tenure, or other kinds of full-time employment in universities, is imbued with metrics, jargon, and an own reality that at times seems to be existing in parallel, rather than in symbiosis, with the fields it is supposed to be examining.

There are many THE academics who have never worked full-time, for a longer period of time, or at all, in the fields they are higher education specialists in. This does not have to be a problem, if they are able to connect with that other reality in fruitful ways, but it can be a problem, if they never see the reason for that connection to be made, and to continue living in that parallel existence. The whole academic reality is so strongly connected to measurable output through funding models and grants that education again receives a secondary role. There are some systems where teaching portfolios are parts of promotion processes, but they are seldom seen in the same light as publications. This secondary role of education is even built into the language of many academics when they refer to their professional roles being a mixture of duties to teach, but freedom to conduct research.

Examined in union, firstly, the misconception held by many that THE higher education is a continuation of schooling for existing roles, secondly, the divide between THE academia and the sectors that these academics are focusing on, and finally, the division between research and teaching, makes for quite a problematic mix. Like I said above, the past and the present shapes the ways we plan for the future. Thus, the current impetus on COVID-19, as it has reduced the past and the present's capacity to inform us in any way for what the future will be like. This is a time when true transformation of THE higher education could take place, so that it would lead to students being equipped for transformative practices as an outcome of their studies.

Explicit lived values and aspirational values

If the aim is not to go back to the same practices and realities that created overtourism, gentrification of city centers, communities and even nations with tourism dependence, natural resources unequally used by visitors rather than hosts, and a range of other challenges that the current model of tourism has created, then the curricula of THE higher education needs to be substantially overhauled, and the teaching practices needs to be radically changed. TEFI – Tourism Education Futures Initiative, has since its foundation urged for THE higher education to become values-based. There are five *universal* values that the founders instilled (*professionalism, knowledge, ethics, mutuality*, and *stewardship*), and these have been implemented in different settings (Schott et al., 2013).

However, education is always already values-based, and this is also important to highlight now. There are *lived* values that relate to how each and every one of us make sense of the lives we are living, and that we act by. Some of these lived values are *cultural* values and *social* values, that form the way we act properly in our respective communities, and in interactions with one another. There are *political* values that determine how we vote, how we create policies, and how we decide on boycotting or giving a 'thumbs up' for issues on social media. There are *ecological* values, that we turn to in our realization that nature is not only a resource, or a place of living, but also an experience (Suopajärvi, 2001). There are also *economic* values, that for long have dominated the way success and progress have been measured, and that now should be questioned for their relevance. These are not the values that the founders of TEFI referred to when they urged for values-based education, their universal values are *aspirational*, but in order to reach those aspirational values we need to first acknowledge the ones we live by.

Why COVID-19 might be the impetus THE higher education needed to change

COVID-19 can be a blessing in disguise, because it has created a shock to the system which has stopped all activity without a tangible pre-warning. Yes, there have been studies suggesting that a viral infection of pandemic scales is imminent, but there are also studies showing that a catastrophic collapse of the earth's ecological system is imminent, and neither of these types of studies have been heard loudly enough for a majority of the population to react to. Gradual change, like the one we all know is happening in the anthropocene, is hard to react to.

The destruction of the earth is not happening overnight, and it is not directly threatening the lives of most of those taking part in activities contributing to the change, like the pandemic is. However, WHO estimates that ambient air pollution is already now killing more than four million people on earth <u>yearly</u> (WHO, 2020a), and natural disasters, that are becoming more frequent due to climate change, are killing 90,000 people, whilst affecting a further 160 million people <u>annually</u> (WHO, 2020b). These are combined figures that the pandemic of 2020 probably will not even come near to, and still, COVID-19 has stopped most kinds of non-essential mobility, both internationally, and domestically. It has closed down factories, it has created national lockdowns where distance work and education keep roads and public transport empty, and it has cleared the air in polluted regions so that people have been able to see blue skies, or surrounding mountains, for the first time in decades.

At the same time, we read daily reports of the estimated billions of dollars the standstill will cost different sectors of society, with THE being amongst the worst hit. Wealthy countries have decided to give financial incentives to companies to furlough workers, poorer nations are reporting how those dependent on the tourism trade are in dire straits. When COVID-19 would allow all stakeholders time to reflect on the rationale in trying to keep sectors going in order to restart them 'as soon as it is over', ominously little reflection seems to take place.

One factor that has not been reported much on in media yet, but that has at least briefly been mentioned in Trinet postings, is what COVID-19 will do to student enroll-ment in THE degrees in the future. With current employees being laid-off, furloughed, or working minimal shifts, new graduates are heading out into a work life that prob-ably never will look the same again. There will now be many parents wondering if their children should rather focus their education on those fields that have been deemed 'essential', rather than one that for the most time is distinctly non-essential and built on leisure time, discretionary money, and unlimited mobility (Leiper, 2004).

A casual glance at which faculties THE are mostly connected to in higher education will also illustrate what lived values the sector is perceived to be related to. Economics, business and management dominate, and social sciences, arts, humanities, or natural sciences, to name some, are only in a few institutions the home for these studies. This will naturally shape the thoughts created, the research conducted, and the educational goals that are set for future THE professionals.

For example, each time we read an article or book about tourism that starts with the words 'Tourism is the XX largest sector in the world, and employs XX% of the workforce' or similar, then we know that the mindset the text is written in has eco-nomic values at the forefront, and that will ultimately shape the whole argument. It is naturally near impossible to expect all THE academics to stop researching whatever it is that they have specialized themselves in, or change their specialization, because that is what all our professional identities are based upon. But that is not the point here. Transformation is needed on many levels, and for that we need the expertise of colleagues that live by different values.

It is also evident that all schools, faculties, and independent institutions focusing on THE will not go unscathed through the events of 2020. The moment enrollment num-bers start to drop, there will also be flow-on effects in THE academia. Whereas this is a worrying thought as many of us, me naturally included, might not have a job in the future doing exactly what we are doing now, it is simultaneously a chance for COVID-19 to lead to a better form of THE higher education.

How axiology and values-based education might be part of a future path

One way to transform THE higher education is by instilling a stronger sense of all three of the foundational philosophies that all research is built upon. Epistemology, and a modernist focus on truth, credibility and knowledge, has long been the front-runner in our field, just like in academia generally. It is the philosophical norm by which much research is measured, regardless of what paradigm the education takes place in, or research is created in (e.g. Belhassen & Caton, 2009; Tribe & Liburd, 2016).

There is some THE research focusing on ontology, but mainly connected to research training, seldom investigating the actual being or meaning of THE, albeit such studies exist too (e.g. Franklin, 2008; Veijola et al., 2014). A real paucity is however to be found in the third foundational philosophy; axiology. Again, it has mainly been publications related to research methodologies that have even acknowledged this (e.g. Jennings, 2010; Killion & Fisher, 2018), research that discuss values are otherwise scattered between lived and universal values, often without explicitly grounding itself in what axiological assumptions the research is created by.

When 'values' enter the educational arena, they are almost always connected to ethics, as if this would be the only way values can be examined (Arnaud, 2014). Alternatively, when the 'value of' is investigated, the eyes turn to economic values. Neither of these are necessary, if axiology, and values would be considered a primary consideration in higher education (McDonald, 2004). Imagine how different both education and research would be, if the articles we read would spend as much effort on describing the values by which they are created, as the current attempts at showing their credibility or truth claims.

Transformation of THE higher education is only possible if we start to question how and what it is that we value in concepts such as 'growth', 'greed', 'development', 'globalization', or 'climate change'. None of these concepts are value-free, quite the opposite, they are value-laden, and they shape the way we go about our daily lives, or how we create our professional identities.

COVID-19 might be a blessing in disguise again here, as transformation of THE as a sector in the longer term is only possible if we equip our students, through the education we provide them, with tools not only to transform themselves, but also to transform the realities they will inhabit. The wonderful concept of worldmaking (Hollinshead et al., 2009), should be taken seriously. Each time we make a decision we are making the world that we are dwellers of.

What stands in the way of transformation happening, and what are alternatives?

The resistance to these transformations will mainly come from the economic lived values of our societies. Because we currently imagine reality through economic terms that circle around GDP, inflation, taxation, salaries, and all the other numerical functions, we are blinded from alternatives. There is so much sunk cost in societies, airplanes and cruise ships are made and sold, hotels and amusement parks are built and staffed, and so are countless universities, all invested in the belief that the current way of living is unchangeable, and that ends will always justify means.

We have for years learned that we are consuming close to two earth's worth of resources per year, and that human created changes affects the climate in harmful ways, and still, we carry on doing it. For all the economic stimulus that takes place right now across the world in the face of COVID-19, hardly any is invested in changing the path taken. When politicians discuss the implications of the pandemic, they are commonly referring to the economic ramifications before any health-related ones.

The protracted economic downturn that is forecasted for the years to come from 2020 onwards, coupled with the fear of contracting diseases in unfamiliar environments, or onboard closed settings, such as cruise ships, will most likely lead to a stronger demand in tourism that is local, national, and based on activities that can be done in relative safety. There will be economic hardship along the way to any kind of recuperation, but that is probably the only way for actual transformation to happen. Politicians have an urge to keep the 'economies' (as they so tellingly call the constituencies they are elected to govern, rather than societies or communities) healthy by keeping them open 'for business' as long as possible. They are thereby disregarding medical advice and international warnings, and they are thereby creating environments where people are put in harm's way. However, if the virus is not under control, many businesses will be forced to close for good.

THE higher education will have to adapt to a different reality, and words that have been added to degrees in the past, such as 'international' or 'global', will no longer have the same ring to them. Courses planned and executed for years using textbooks and readings that highlight the 'need' for growth will look dated, and rather pathetic. Attention will need to be directed at safety and security, health issues, and microenterprises that serve the THE sector whilst simultaneously being engaged in other fields that can secure an income in case of another lockdown. The whole sector of financial forecasting will need to be rewritten, as no forecasts hold in the current situation, and the same is true for both macro- and micro-finance after the debt burden of nations, organisations, and companies will reach levels never experienced on a global scale before. For any higher education provider who is currently planning their next semester's material a close examination is needed in order not to serve up a dated view of reality.

Finally

By taking a step back, by thinking of what is valuable for us, for its own sake – not for what it potentially will do, we take the first step towards transformation. Realizing the importance of both lived and aspirational values for how we live, act, and make sense of the world, gives us the key to become the positive worldmakers that we all have within us. It is worthwhile remembering that we live our lives in communities and societies, not in economies.

Disclosure statement

No potential conflict of interest was reported by the author.

ORCID

Johan Edelheim (iD) https://orcid.org/0000-0002-4183-5931

References

Arnaud, C. (2014). *Axiology 4.0: Proposal for a new axiology*. https://www.axiology.org.uk/

Belhassen, Y., & Caton, K. (2009). Advancing understandings - A linguistic approach to tourism epistemology. *Annals of Tourism Research*, *36*(2), 335–352. https://doi.org/10.1016/j.annals. 2009.01.006

Catrett, J. B. (2018). Hospitality education: A third paradigm. In J. Oskam, D. M. Dekker, & K. Wiegerink (Eds.), *Innovation in hospitality education: Anticipating the educational needs of a changing profession* (pp. 15–32). Springer.

Franklin, A. (2008). The tourism ordering - Taking tourism more seriously as a globalising ordering. *Civilisations, LVII. 1-2 - Tourisme, mobilités et altérités contemporaines*, 25–39.

Healey, M. (2005). Linking research and teaching: Exploring disciplinary spaces and the role of inquiry-based learning. In R. Barnett (Ed.), *Reshaping the university: New relationships between research, scholarship and teaching* (pp. 67–78). McGraw-Hill Education.

Hollinshead, K., Ateljevic, I., & Ali, N. (2009). Worldmaking agency – Worldmaking authority: The sovereign constitutive role of tourism. *Tourism Geographies* , *11*(4), 427–443. https://doi.org/ 10.1080/14616680903262562

Jennings, G. R. (2010). *Tourism research* (2nd ed.). John Wiley & Sons Australia.

Killion, L., & Fisher, R. (2018). Ontology, epistemology: Paradigms and parameters for qualitative approaches in tourism research. In W. Hillman & K. Radel (Eds.), *Qualitative methods in tourism research: Theory and practice*. Channel View Publications.

Lawson, T. (2019). *The nature of social reality - Issues in social ontology*. Routledge.

Leiper, N. (2004). *Tourism management* (3rd ed.). Pearson Education.

Lo, A. (2005). The past, present, and future of hospitality and tourism higher education in Hong Kong. In C. Hsu (Ed.), *Global* tourism higher education: *Past,* present, and future (pp. 137–166). Routledge. https://doi.org/10.1300/J172v05n01_07

McDonald, H. P. (2004). *Radical axiology: A first philosophy of values*, Rodopi.

Schott, C., Feng, C., & Fesenmaier, D. R. (Eds.). (2013). *Tourism education for global citizenship: Educating for lives of consequence* (Vol. 2). Oxford Brookes University.

Suopajärvi, L. (2001). *Vuotos- ja Ounasjoki-kamppailujen kentät ja merkitykset Lapissa*. [Doctoral dissertation University of Lapland, Rovaniemi]. http://urn.fi/URN:NBN:fi:ula-20111131020(270)

Tribe, J., & Liburd, J. J. (2016). The tourism knowledge system. *Annals of Tourism Research*, *57*(2), 44–61. doi:http://dx.doi.org/10.1016/j.annals.2015.11.011 https://doi.org/10.1016/j.annals.2015. 11.011

Veijola, S., Germann Molz, J., Pyyhtinen, O., Höckert, E., & Grit, A. (2014). *Disruptive* tourism *and* its untidy guests. Alternative ontologies for future hospitalities. Palgrave Macmillan.

WHO. (2020a). Air pollution. http://www9.who.int/airpollution/en/

WHO. (2020b). Environmental health in emergencies. https://www.who.int/environmental_ health_emergencies/natural_events/en/

Post COVID-19 ecological and social reset: moving away from capitalist growth models towards tourism as Buen Vivir

Phoebe Everingham and Natasha Chassagne

ABSTRACT

Tourism has been one of the industries most highly affected by COVID-19. The COVID-19 global pandemic is an 'unprecedented crisis' and has exposed the pitfalls of a hyper consumption model of economic growth and development. The scale of immediate economic impacts of the COVID-19 pandemic has shattered the myth of 'catch up development' and 'perpetual growth'. The Crisis has brought unintended degrowth, presenting opportunities for an economic and social 'reset'. In terms of long-term thinking post COVID-19, it is time to change the parameters of how we imagine a trajectory going forward, to prefigure possibilities for contesting capitalist imperatives that 'there is no alternative'. In relation to tourism, the pandemic provides an opportunity for reimaging tourism otherwise, away from exploitative models that disregard people, places, and the natural environment, and towards a tourism that has positive impacts. Non-western alternatives to neo-colonial and neoliberal capitalism, such the South American concept of 'Buen Vivir', can help us to shift priorities away from economic growth, towards greater social and environmental wellbeing, and meaningful human connections. Taking a Buen Vivir approach to tourism will continue the degrowth momentum, for transformative change in society within the earth's physical limits. Yet Buen Vivir also redefines the parameters of how we understand 'limits'. In limiting unsustainable practices in development and tourism, a focus on Buen Vivir actually creates growth in other areas, such as social and environmental wellbeing, and meaningful human connection. Buen Vivir can reorient the tourism industry towards localised tourism, and slow tourism because the principles of Buen Vivir require these alternatives to be small-scale, local and benefiting host communities as well as tourists to increase the wellbeing for all.

摘要

旅游产业是受到新冠状病毒严重影响的产业之一。新冠状病毒全球性危机是一场"前所未有的危机",暴露了过度消费型经济增长与发展模式的陷阱。新冠状病毒全球性危机对经济的直接影响程度已经打破了"追赶发展"、"永久增长"的神话。这次危机带来了意想不到的退增长,在一定程度上为经济和社会的重构提供了机会。关于后疫情时代的长期思考,是时候改变我们对未来轨迹设想了,

是时候预测挑战资本主义"无替代品"原则的可能性。对于旅游业
而言，这次流行病为重塑旅游业提供了机会，使其摆脱以往无视人
、空间和自然环境的剥削模式，转向了具有积极影响的旅游业。
新殖民主义和新自由资本主义的非西方替代品，例如南美洲"美好
生活"的概念，可以帮助我们将发展重点从经济增长转移到更大的
社会和环境福祉，以及更有意义的人际关系上。采用追求美好生
活的方式发展旅游业将继续保持退增长动力，以实现在地球的物
理极限范围内的社会变革。与此同时，美好生活也重新定义了我
们对"极限"的解析参数。在限制经济社会发展和旅游业的不可持
续行为时，对美好生活的关注实际上促进了其他领域的增长，如社
会和环境福祉，以及有意义的人际关系。美好生活可以将旅游业
重新定位为本土化旅游、慢速旅游业，因为美好生活原则要求这
些替代品必须是小规模的、本土的，以及有助于社区居民和游客
增加福祉的。

Introduction

The COVID-19 global pandemic is an 'unprecedented crisis', not only in terms of human health, but also because of its impact on the global economy. Hyper globalisation has meant that humans are more connected than ever before. The inequalities that underpin globalisation and neo-colonial, neo-liberal capitalism has thus far disproportionately affected those in the 'Global South'. The scale of immediate economic impacts of the COVID-19 pandemic is perhaps being felt more strongly now by the 'Global North' precisely because the myth of 'catch – up development' and perpetual growth is being shattered. Indeed, many communities across the globe have long experienced the negative consequences of hyper globalisation, bearing the brunt of externalised costs in the name of development (Mies, 1993). As Arundhati Roy (2020) says, "The tragedy is immediate, real, epic and unfolding before our eyes. But it isn't new". Certainly not for Indigenous and marginalised communities. The destructive environmental activities that underpin capitalist development and a culture of mass consumption, exposes humans to such novel viruses such as COVID-19 and is the "hidden cost of human economic development" (Jones, Patel and Dasak, cited in Vidal, 2020).

Neoliberal globalisation's stronghold has largely persisted in its power not only through the neocolonial legacies which structure our societies, economies and political systems, but through the colonisation of the mind – that there is no alternative to the current neoliberal capitalist global system. As an Indigenous action zine published by Indigenous Indigenous.action.org (Anonymous, 2020) so aptly puts it "Why can we imagine the ending of the world, yet not the ending of colonialism"? There has been much social commentary around the possibilities that Covid -19 presents in terms of a 'reset button' - to reset our economic, social and political realities towards a more equitable world. While cities all over the world have gone into lockdown some have argued that the natural world is taking a much needed 'breather' from less carbon dioxide in the atmosphere, clearer water in Venice canals (Clarke, 2020) and pandas in a Hong Kong zoo mating for the first time in 10 years (Linder, 2020). Is this a chance then, to rethink the hyper consumption endless growth model based on exploitation and a culture of 'death' (Shiva, 2010)? In going forward, economic alternatives to a growth economy that employs alternative economic activities will be crucial in ensuring the wellbeing of both collective society and the environment that supports it. There has already been an unintended degrowth of the most damaging sectors of the global economy. There is an opportunity to use this as an economic and social 'reset' (Chassagne, 2020). The most destructive decision that could be made in a post-COVID economic policy decision-making would be to ramp up production in extractive sectors to boost the economy in the short-term. The consequences would be catastrophic. What is needed now is to use this opportunity for long-term thinking towards the sustainable degrowth of the global economy; capitalising on innovation in technology and in mindsets to diffuse alternative economic activities that support what really matters.

In terms of long-term thinking it is time to change the parameters of how we imagine a trajectory going forward. In this article we propose a prefigurative politics of possibility to contest the capitalist imperative that there 'is no alternative' (Amsler, 2016). Prefigurative politics refers to actions "guided by values rather than instrumental efficiency" (Leach, 2013, p.1004). In the context of the COVID–19 pandemic providing a possibility to 'reset', it is time to choose, embody and 'prefigure' the kind of future we want for our human community and the planet. Capitalist accumulation has been based on the exploitation and suffering of the less privileged, and the natural environment, and the COVID-19 crisis has highlighted that that the system is also failing those who have thus far benefited from it. A prefigurative approach is based on the principles of "directly implementing the changes one seeks" by "developing counterhegemonic institutions and modes of interaction that embody the desired transformation" (Leach, 2013, p. 1004).

While we wish to prefiguratively work through alternative possibilities that counter hyper mass-consumption we also want to acknowledge that around the world Indigenous and anticolonailst movements have, for a long time, already been enacting alternatives to capitalist globalisation and neo-liberal power. We want to also push these narratives to the foreground of how we can mainstream this counter-hegemonic thinking and practice, not just for social change but "for the immanent creation of a radically other reality" (Amsler, 2016, p.20). Buen Vivir is one such alternative to neo-colonial, neo-liberal economic growth models. Buen Vivir represents a post development alternative, a way of life that prefigures an alternative to capitalist development models.

Buen Vivir has its roots in Latin American Indigenous cosmology, and approximately translates to 'Good Living', or as Vázquez (2012) defines it "living in plenitude". It offers a radical critique of the atomised individualistic culture of high mass consumption by taking a "a communitarian view of wellbeing based on reciprocity and complementarity that valorises indigenous identity and culture, and involves not only human beings but also the natural environment" (Giovannini, 2014, p.71). It has become a prominent concept in constitutional debates and transformations particularly in Bolivia and Ecuador (Vázquez, 2012).

The concept of Buen Vivir has been explored by some scholars in relation to tourism. For example Fischer discusses the way that Buen Vivir has been utilised in a 'post-neoliberal' context for tourism development in Nicaragua, with a national development campaign "Live Clean, Live Healthy, Live Beautiful, Live Well" (called Vivir

Bonito, Vivir Bien) (Fischer, 2019, p. 452). Karst (2017) has explored the notion of Buen Vivir in relation to indigenous perceptions of ecotourism and wellbeing in Bhutan, and considered the implications for tourism that engages with the values of Indigenous cultures. Chassagne and Everingham (2019) and Renkert (2019) have explored how Buen Vivir can enable localised degrowth tourism in communities in the highlands of Ecuador.

In this article we explore the prefiguration of a 'reset' underlined by the principles of degrowth through Buen Vivir. We define degrowth firstly as economic growth that must not surpass the biophysical limits of the planet, and secondly, that human well-being takes precedence over the pursuit of wealth (Whitehead, 2013, p. 142). We draw on LaTouche's (2012) premise that *decroissance* (degrowth) does not equal negative growth, but a degrowth of overconsumption and a growth of sectors that are about community wellbeing such as education and sanitation (Acosta, 2012). In the context of tourism, we wish to explore the opportunities might such a reset have on destructive forms of travel that neither benefit local natural environments nor host communities themselves.

Problems with catch-up notions of development, mass consumption and its effects on tourism inequalities

While sustainable tourism has offered a critique of these growth models of tourism, the term is too often greenwashed into sustaining tourism and thus sustaining growth (Higgins-Desbiolles, 2018). As Higgins-Desbiolles (2010, p. 125) makes clear; sustainable tourism needs to engage seriously with "the notion of limits that the current culture of consumerism and pro-growth ideology precludes". Even within the language of growth itself, tourism development underpinned by neo-liberal capitalist models often fails to live up to its promise (Chambers & Buzinde, 2015).

Measurements regarding the costs and benefits of tourism have tended to focus on 'objective' measures and indicators that do not question the ways in which they are embedded within capitalist models that privilege growth – much less consider the realities on the ground (Miller & Twing-Ward, 2005). Such measurements also reinforce universalist and positivist models of understanding the diverse and nuanced needs and desires of communities involved in tourism. These top-down approaches to sustainable tourism privilege Western epistemologies which foreground Western culture, while "concomitantly negating and denying legitimacy to the knowledge's and cosmologies of those in and from the South" (Chambers & Buzinde, 2015, p. 3).

It is the silencing of other ways of knowing and being that "provided the fundamental logic which informed the colonial project and which ignored the systems of knowledge built over centuries" by Indigenous groups and other colonised communities in the Global South (Chambers & Buzinde, 2015, p. 3). Drawing on Escobar, Higgins-Desbiolles (2010, p. 125) argues that sustainable approaches to tourism then, need to be unravelled from 'the universalising tendencies of current economic discourse' and instead 'make visible practices of cultural and ecological difference which could serve as the basis of alternatives'.

As Higgins-Desbiolles (2020) points out, the COVID-19 pandemic presents the tourism industry with an opportunity. Human activities will need to change to avoid the worst effects of human-induced climate change. Rather than try to return to 'business as usual as soon as possible' COVID-19 presents us with an opportunity to think about our consumption patterns and the unsustainability of the travel industry. Whitzman (2020), discusses the ways that "great pandemics often bring about social reform". The Black Death from 1347–1351 resulted in improved living conditions for low income workers, and the 1854 cholera epidemic in London led to epidemiologist John Snow establishing the link between clean drinking water and the disease (Whitzman, 2020). What then, can this pandemic teach us about the unsustainability of the culture of high mass consumption, not only in terms of the environment but also human health. We can look to its unintended degrowth and its effects on wellbeing.

An opportunity for new economic thinking

The pandemic has already had a massive effect on the global economy and commodities output. Consequently, economic analyst Lauri Myllyvirta's (2020) found that the virus may have reduced global emissions by 200Mt CO_2 to date; and in China alone coal consumption fell by 36%, and oil refining capacity was reduced by 34%. Without precedence, the COVID-19 pandemic is unleashing uncertainty into the global economy, resulting an unintended 'degrowth' of the industrial and extractive sectors. With it, comes opportunity for other more sustainable sectors – alternative tourism being one.

We argue that adopting a Buen Vivir approach to not only tourism, but our everyday lives can lead to degrowth of extractive capitalist industries that promote a 'culture of death'. We are already seeing an unintended global degrowth from the global shut down of borders, industries and supply chains. It is time to consider other models of living. It is time to acknowledge that the dominance of Eurocentric thinking and systems is not working. Highlighting non-western worldviews and models can help refocus the wellbeing of both people and the environment, in turn influencing how we might not only live differently in our everyday life, but how we do tourism too.

As the COVID-19 pandemic is demonstrating, in times of crisis we focus on what really matters in life: health, social connection, our environment, identity (Chassagne, 2020) – all of these are core focal points of a Buen Vivir approach. Just like the French term décroissance, LaTouche's approach to degrowth, Buen Vivir is about plenitude and enhanced wellbeing, rather than the growth of the economy. Where Buen Vivir differs is that it considers environmental and human health and wellbeing equally. In the wake of COVID-19, this distinction will be pivotal in avoiding such widespread global impacts in times of crisis.

Degrowing the global neoliberal economy while growing wellbeing through Buen Vivir

While the notion of limits poses a fundamental irony for the tourism industry that is embedded within capitalist growth models (Higgins-Desbiolles, 2018), we argue that focusing on Buen Vivir redefines the parameters of how we understand 'limits'. In limiting unsustainable practices in development and tourism, a focus on Buen Vivir actually creates growth in other areas, such as social and environmental wellbeing, and meaningful human connection. We thereby argue that privileging the growth of social and environmental wellbeing under a Buen Vivir approach, results in degrowth, because of the way in which the economy is conceptualised and the shifting of priorities away from an economic growth mentality.

Privileging social and environmental wellbeing, tourism as an alternative economic practice under a Buen Vivir approach supports the degrowth of socially and environmentally damaging sectors (Chassagne & Everingham, 2019). This is vital in a recovering economy, if we are to use this opportunity and shift towards a post-extractive society. The economic aspects of Buen Vivir shift priorities away from economic growth, towards greater social and environmental wellbeing, and meaningful human connection. In other words, we can capitalise on a Buen Vivir approach to continue the degrowth momentum, albeit unintentional, for transformative change in society within the earth's physical limits.

Buen Vivir has been linked to 'hope movements' demonstrating how possibility can be reclaimed from the hopelessness of neoliberal capitalism (Dinerstein & Deneulin, 2012). Hope becomes possible when we move beyond negative critique and "unlearn hegemonic epistemologies, identities, relationships and practices and learning how to create new ones that do not yet exist" (Amsler,2017, p. 20). In the here and now, in terms of prefiguring global futures we need to decolonise our lives, bodies and spirits to heal each other and the planet (Motta, 2014).

Through crisis comes creativity and challenges to the 'atomised individualism' that underpins travel consumption. Staying closer to home for example, could awaken us to the value of travelling less, staying local and slowing down. (Higgins-Desbiolles, 2020). The COVID-19 crisis has required us to immediately scale down the way we travel and live, to connect more locally, shop locally, and limit consumption to what we need (Chassagne, 2020). As climate scientist Katharine Hayhoe (cited in Chassagne, 2020) said, "What really matters is the same for all of us. It's the health and safety of our friends, our family, our loved ones, our communities, our cities, and our country. That's what the coronavirus threatens … " There is this collective realisation that it can no longer be business-as-usual.

Degrowth and the implications for tourism

COVID-19 will change tourism for the long-term. People will have less disposable income, travel will once again become a luxury, and so the types of tourism not only will change as a consequence, but also as a necessity. There will be more people travelling locally, which will have a significant impact on travel-related environmental impacts. Longer stays at destinations with less frequent travel as opposed to travel as a consumerist activity can also help lessen public health risks in the face of threats from global epidemics or pandemics, as well as strengthen local communities severely impacted by COVID-19.

In helping to refine our understanding of degrowth, Hall (2009, pp. 55-56) citing the 2008 conference Declaration of the First International Conference on Economic Degrowth, reasserts that the process degrowth has certain characteristics, including:

- Quality of life rather than quantity of consumption;
- Basic human needs satisfaction;
- Societal change based individual and collective actions and policies;
- Increased self-sufficiency, free time, unremunerated activity, conviviality, sense of community, and individual and collective health;
- Self-reflection, balance, creativity, flexibility, diversity, good citizenship, generosity, and non-materialism;
- Equity, participatory democracy, respect for human rights, and respect for cultural differences.

In terms of global societal shifts, we have started to witness almost all these characteristics as a consequence of economic, lifestyle, and priority changes during COVID-19 isolation.

People are focusing on quality of life, and consumptions patterns have shifted dramatically since January. Similarly, we can see a focus on what it is we actually need for our wellbeing and survival. There has been greater social cohesion and a change from individual needs to the wellbeing of our collective society – both globally and locally, in that, much more conviviality has been demonstrated – bringing communities closer together by being further apart than ever. People are focused on increasing self-sufficiency. One example is the significant increase in the amount of people starting home gardens and bread baking. This is of course dependent on people having more free time, which leads to self-reflection, creativity and non-material needs.

Once the pandemic is over and normal activities return, societal priorities may never return to what they were: individualism, wealth creation, busyness, and high levels of unnecessary consumption. COVID-19 may have played a vital role in finally achieving the transformative change that sustainable development never could. Time will be the crucial factor here.

To that end, tourism can be an alternative economic activity that can help support economic recovery in a sustainable manner by supporting the continual decline or degrowth of the more damaging sectors like extractivism, as well as helping to sustain the societal changes like social cohesion and reduced consumption brought on during peak COVID-19 period. The types of tourism activities will be of importance here. This, of course, will require policies that support a continual, intentional sustainable degrowth post-COVID19.

Tourism as an alternative economic activity under Buen Vivir

In our paper linking Buen Vivir to degrowth and tourism, we highlight Gudynas (2011, p. 446) who conceptualises degrowth neither as a comparison concept to Buen Vivir, nor an objective of Buen Vivir, but rather as a consequence. Gudynas (2011, p. 446) states that while there are several similarities to both concepts, Buen Vivir is

Table 1. Tourism, Buen Vivir and degrowth parallels (Chassagne & Everingham, 2019).

Tourism Practices	Buen Vivir Principles	Degrowth Characteristics
Cultural and knowledge exchange Production and promotion of traditional handicrafts and arts Volunteer tourism	Decolonisation and culture	Quality of life, equity, respect for cultural differences, creativity, diversity, unremunerated activity
Eco and agri-tourism initiatives Community stays	Reciprocity, nature and community	Conviviality, non-materialism, sense of community
Participatory local government initiatives	Plurality, wellbeing and contextuality	Participatory democracy, good citizenship, respect for human rights.

intercultural, biocentric and considers spiritual positions. Considering the unintended degrowth as a result of economic activity during COVID19, a Buen Vivir approach can help support intentional sustainable degrowth going forward.

This approach prescribed by Buen Vivir is supported by Hall's (2009, p. 55) argument for degrowth in sustainable tourism, as degrowth particularly calls for an observation of the principles of equity, participatory democracy, respect for human rights, and respect for cultural differences. Table 1 below demonstrates the parallel between the tourism practices discussed above, the relevant buen vivir principles and the characteristics of degrowth as described by Hall (2009).

Taking a buen vivir approach to degrowth post-COVID degrowth can help extend transformative change to the tourism sector. It will mean rethinking ideals of tourism as means for social cohesion, inclusivity, and wellbeing (Higgins-Desbiolles, 2010), creating positive interactions with the environment (Chassagne & Everingham, 2019).

Tourism that is underpinned by buen vivir supporting a sustainable degrowth can have positive impacts for both local communities and tourists alike. Tourism's supporting role in a degrowth society opens possibilities for the growth of intercultural learning and exchange, deeper human connections, and greater sense of reciprocity with the natural environment. This includes slow tourism and forms of ethical tourism which are compatible with some of the principles of degrowth, such as denouncing certain forms of consumption and promoting the sustainable use of resources. However, these 'slow' forms of consumption also require co-operation from consumers, communities, and governments (Hall, 2009).

Possibilities for slow tourism

Life everywhere has slowed down, and this can be an opportunity to engage in slow tourism practices, conducive to the kind of tourism practices supported by the principles of Buen Vivir. For Hall (2009), the slow consumption of tourism can be linked to degrowth and links to the post-development notion of 'rightsizing' through providing economic alternatives to the growth model. Slow tourism is about experiencing a different kind of temporality to that of mass tourism. It is about immersion in a place that can evoke different ways of being in the world - a different kind of logic to hyper-capitalist consumption models, one that values "travel experience as a kind of lived knowledge" (Fullager et al., 2012 p. 4).

The principles of Buen Vivir require these alternatives to be small-scale, local and benefiting local communities to increase the wellbeing for all. Buen vivir necessitates plural cooperation on all levels to produce knowledge and capabilities that can enact long-term change. Therefore, buen vivir is a plural approach that moves away from 'reform' and 'status quo' towards 'transformation' (Dryzek, 1997, p. 12). Degrowth as a consequence of COVID-19 opens possibilities of transformation that a Buen Vivir approach can help support.

Adopting the principles of Buen Vivir to guide tourism as an alternative economic activity in the wake of COVID-19 could also ensure that host communities receive equitable redistributive socio-economic effects from tourism through strategies that come from slow, informal, and bartered exchanges.

Conclusion

The tourism Alert and Action Forum Statement on COVID-19 Pandemic Crisis clearly articulates that the global tourism industry creates economic dependencies that are not sustainable. Instead diverse economies are needed that are structured around long term community well-being (TAAF, 2020). In this article we have argued that we need to escape from the logic of capital accumulation and decision making as always embedded with the logic of profit. We have drawn on the notion of degrowth as a way to respond to the ecological and social crisis. In prefiguring how tourism can be otherwise we have outlined how concept such as Buen Vivir can help us build the foundations for degrowth. .

We see the Covid-19 pandemic as a time to rethink the tourism as a hyper-consumption model. International and domestic travel has been severely impacted by COVID-19 because of isolation and quarantine policies, job losses and public health concerns. This opens opportunities for doing tourism differently in the future. In a post-COVID-19 degrowth society, tourism as an alternative economic practice, that is guided by the principles of buen vivir can help support a continual but intentional degrowth of the socially and environmentally damaging sectors of the economy that are damaging to the wellbeing of local communities. Slow tourism that is supported by the principles of Buen Vivir for example, is the kind of tourism we propose as an alternative economic practice to the dominant paradigm of capitalism and mass-consumerism.

We have drawn on the concept of Buen Vivir as a way of introducing the notion of 'limits', connection to the environment, and being sensitive to the social and environmental context in which tourism is practiced (Chassagne & Everingham, 2019). We have situated Buen Vivir within the context of much needed degrowth and argue that rather than focusing on degrowth as a 'lack' - linked to 'sacrifice', a focus on Buen Vivir as the growth of planetary well-being can reframe the parameters of how we imagine alternative futures. As Escobar (2004, p. 217) argues, to counter imperial globality, heightened marginalization and the suppression of knowledge and culture of non-western 'others', new logics are needed; 'another world is possible'. What is needed is alternative and dissenting imaginations.

In relation to tourism, the COVID-19 pandemic provides us with an opportunity to reimagine the future of tourism. As the Tourism Action Network COVID-19 statement (TAAF, 2020) so aptly sums up "The movements for social justice have long declared that 'another world is possible' and we have also declared 'another tourism is possible'. But the world we want to see won't be given to us; we have to act collectively for it". The COVID-19 crisis affords us   opportunities for working towards a world otherwise. Tourism scholars have a part to play in prefiguring alternative tourism trajectories. With falling consumption patterns and support for economic alternatives, there is an opportunity both politically and publicly to change our lifestyle and the failing economic model that supports it - to shift the focus and create innovation for wellbeing and the environment, over economic growth. COVID-19 has demonstrated that we need to change our priorities, for the sake of humanity. What we have here, is an open door for change.

Disclsoure statement

No potential conflict of interest was reported by the author(s).

References

Acosta, A. (2012). The Buen Vivir: An opportunity to imagine another world. Berlin, Germany. http://www.br.boell.org/downloads/Democracy_Inside_A_Champion.pdf#page=194

Amsler, S. (2016). Learning hope. An epistemology of possibility for advanced capitalist society. In A. C. Dinerstein (Eds.), *Social Science for an Other Politics: Women theorising without parachutes* (pp. 19–33). Palgrave Macmillan.

Anonymous. (2020, 9 March) Rethinking the apocalypse: An indigenous anti-futurist manifesto. Retrieved 28 March, from http://www.indigenousaction.org/rethinking-the-apocalypse-an-indigenous-anti-futurist-manifesto/?fbclid=IwAR0rRYg_deNzB7zwGvHZh1M6SDUTzFoSQHSz_trrPsxRaXccAY8w_AP1XkQ

Chambers, D., & Buzinde, C. (2015). Tourism and decolonisation: Locating research and self. *Annals of Tourism Research, 51*(1), 1–16. https://doi.org/10.1016/j.annals.2014.12.002

Chassagne, N. (2020, 27 March), Here's what the coronavirus pandemic can teach us about tackling climate change. *The Conversation*. Retrieved 28 March, from https://theconversation.com/heres-what-the-coronavirus-pandemic-can-teach-us-about-tackling-climate-change-134399

Chassagne, N., & Everingham, P. (2019). Buen Vivir: Degrowing extractivism and growing wellbeing through tourism. *Journal of Sustainable Tourism, 27*(12), 1909–1925. https://doi.org/10.1080/09669582.2019.1660668

Clarke, R. (2020, 26 March). Is Covid-19 the reset button we need towards a sustainable future of design? *Forbes*. Retrieved 28 March, from https://www.forbes.com/sites/roddyclarke/2020/03/26/is-covid-19-the-reset-button-we-need-towards-a-sustainable-future-of-design/#2dbf472f782a

Dinerstein, A. C., & Deneulin, S. (2012). Hope movements: Naming mobilisation in a post-development world. *Development and Change*, *43*(2), 585–602. https://doi.org/10.1111/j.1467-7660.2012.01765.x

Dryzek, J. S. (1997). *The Politics of the Earth: environmental discourses*. Oxford University Press.

Escobar, A. (2004). Beyond the third world: Imperial globality, global coloniality, and anti-globalisation social movements. *Third World Quarterly*, *25*(1), 207–230. https://doi.org/10.1080/0143659042000185417

Fisher, J. (2019). Nicaragua's Buen Vivir: A strategy for tourism development? *Journal of Sustainable Tourism*, *27*(4), 452–471. https://doi.org/10.1080/09669582.2018.1457035

Fullager, S., Markell, K., & Wilson, E. (2012). Starting slow: Thinking through slow motilities and experiences. In *Slow tourism: Experiences and mobilities*. E. Wilson and K. Markwell (Eds). (pp. 1–11). Channel View Publications.

Giovannini, M. (2014). Indigenous people and self-determined development: the case of community enterprises in Chiapas (University of Trento). *Global Vision for a social solidarity economy: Convergences and differences in concepts, definitions and frameworks*. http://www.ripess.org/wp-content/uploads/2017/08/RIPESS_Vision-Global_EN.pdf

Gudynas, E. (2011). Buen vivir: Today's tomorrow. *Development*, *54*(4), 441–447. https://doi.org/10.1057/dev.2011.86

Hall, C. M. (2009). Degrowing tourism: Decroissance, sustainable consumption and steady-state tourism. *Anatolia*, *20*(1), 46–61. https://doi.org/10.1080/13032917.2009.10518894

Higgins-Desbiolles, F. (2010). The elusiveness of sustainability in tourism: The culture-ideology of consumerism and its implications. *Tourism and Hospitality Research*, *10*(2), 116–129. https://doi.org/10.1057/thr.2009.31

Higgins-Desbiolles, F. (2020, 18 March). The end of global travel as we know it: An opportunity for sustainable tourism. Retrieved 28 March, from https://theconversation.com/the-end-of-global-travel-as-we-know-it-an-opportunity-for-sustainable-tourism-133783

Higgins-Desbiolles, F. (2018). Sustainable tourism: sustaining tourism or something more? *Tourism Management Perspectives*, *25*, 157–160. https://doi.org/10.1016/j.tmp.2017.11.017

Higgins-Desbiolles, F., Carnicelli, S., Krolikowski, C., Wijesinghe, G., & Boluk, K. (2019). Degrowing tourism: Rethinking tourism. *Journal of Sustainable Tourism*, *27*(12), 1926–1944. https://doi.org/10.1080/09669582.2019.1601732

Karst, H. (2017). This is a holy place of Ama Jomo": Buen Vivir, indigenous voices and ecotourism development in a protected area of Bhutan. *Journal of Sustainable Tourism*, *25*(6), 746–762. https://doi.org/10.1080/09669582

Latouche, S. (2012). Degrowth. *Journal* of Cleaner Production, *18*(6), 519–522. https://doi.org/10.1016/j.jclepro.2010.02.003

Leach, D. K. (2013). Prefigurative politics. . In *The Wiley-Blackwell Encyclopedia of Social and Political Movements*, David A. Snow, Donatella della Porta, Bert Klandermans, and Doug McAdam (Eds.). Blackwell Publishing Ltd.

Linder, A. (2020, 7 April). *With zoos closed to visitors pandas finally bang after 10 years*. Shanghaiist. https://shanghai.ist/2020/04/07/with-zoo-closed-to-visitors-pandas-finally-bang-after-10-years/

Mies, M. (1993). The Myth of Catching-up Development. In M. Mies & V. Shiva (Eds.), *Ecofeminism*. Zed Books.

Miller, G., & Twing-Ward, L. (2005). *Monitoring for a Sustainable Tourism Transition: The Challenge of Developing and Using indicators*. CABI Publishing. OxfordShore.

Motta, S. C. (2014). Constructing Twenty-First Century Socialism: The Role of Radical Education. In: *Constructing Twenty-First Century Socialism in Latin America. Marxism and Education*. Palgrave Macmillan.

Myllyvirta, L. (2020, 19 February). Analysis: Coronavirus temporarily reduced China's $CO2$ emissions by a quarter. *Carbon Brief*. Retrieved March 25, 2020, from https://www.carbonbrief.org/analysis-coronavirus-has-temporarily-reduced-chinas-co2-emissions-by-a-quarter.

Renkert, S. R. (2019). Community-owned tourism and degrowth: a case study in the Kichwa. *Journal* of Sustainable Tourism, *27*(12), 1893–1908.   https://doi.org/10.1080/09669582.2019. 1660669

Roy, A. (2020, 4 April). The pandemic is a portal. *The Financial times*. Retrieved April 4–5, 2020, from https://www.ft.com/content/10d8f5e8-74eb-11ea-95fe-fcd274e920ca

Shiva, V. (2010). Earth democracy: Beyond dead democracy and killing economies. *Capitalism Nature Socialism*, *21*(1), 83–95.   https://doi.org/10.1080/10455751003655922

Tourism Alert and Action Forum. (2020). Tourism alert and action forum statement on Covid-19 pandemic crisis - 30 March 2020. (In the possession of the author).

Vidal, J. (2020, 18 March) Tip of the iceberg': Is our destruction of nature responsible for Covid-19? *The Guardian*. Retrieved March 19, from https://www.theguardian.com/environment/2020/mar/18/tip-of-the-iceberg-is-our-destruction-of-nature-responsible-for-covid-19-aoe

Vázquez, R. (2012). Towards a decolonial critique of modernity. *Buen Vivir. Relationality and the Task of Listening*. In Raúl Fornet-Betancourt (Ed.), *Capital, Poverty, Development, Denktraditionen im Dialog:Studien zur Befreiung und interkulturalität* (Vol. 33, pp. 241–252). Aachen.

Whitzman, C. (2020, 25 March). Silver lining: Could COVID-19 lead to a better future? *The Conversation*. Retrieved 28 March, from https://theconversation.com/silver-lining-could-covid-19-lead-to-a-better-future-134204

COVID-19 is expanding global consciousness and the sustainability of travel and tourism

Adriana Galvani (iD), Alan A. Lew (iD) and Maria Sotelo Perez

ABSTRACT

The sustainable development model has largely failed to address the social and environmental challenges of the 21st century. True sustainability will only occur when it is valued as a part of the taken-for-granted daily life of individuals and cultures across the globe. This has not yet happened because humanity has not evolved a global consciousness quickly enough to match the global advances in telecommunications and transportation technologies that have created a socially and economically ever-shrinking planet. Travel and tourism contributes to the expansion of global consciousness, although only in a haphazard and unintentional manner. The COVID-19 pandemic is a result of planetary time-space compression and is forcing an expansion in human consciousness that will make humankind better able to address global problems. There will still be considerable diversity on the planet, as now, but the pandemic will stimulate growing numbers of people, businesses and governments to adopt new ways of thinking, behaving and operating that are more closely aligned with the goals of sustainable development. This could be further enhanced if travel and tourism were to adopt the expansion and awakening of global conscious as a fundamental and transformational value in the products and experiences that it offers.

摘要

可持续发展模式在很大程度上未能解决21世纪的社会环境挑战。只有当全世界不同的个体和文化都高度重视并将其视为日常生活的一部分时，真正的可持续发展才能得以实现。这一切尚未发生的原因是人类全球意识的形成速度还不够快，未能与全世界范围内通讯和交通技术的快速发展同步，而后者已经创造了一个社会和经济意义上不断缩小的地球。尽管是以偶然和无意的方式，旅行和旅游业的确促进了全球意识的扩展。新型冠状病毒肺炎（COVID-19）的全球蔓延是地球时空压缩的结果，正迫使人类意识发生全球性的转向，这将有助于人类更好地解决全球问题。虽然世界上仍将存在相当的多样性，但就总体而言，此次疫情将促使足够多的个人、企业和政府采取与可持续发展目标更加一致的全新的思维方式、行为方式及运营方式。假如旅行和旅游业能够将全球意识的扩展与激发作为其所提供的产品和体验的重要价值，那么这一点应得以强化。

The COVID-19 pandemic is a once-in-a-lifetime experience for everyone on planet Earth. There has never been an event in the recorded history modern humankind, that has affected everyone on the planet to the same degree as COVID-19. That is because the COVID-19 pandemic is the apex of a series of evolutionary changes that have brought together elements that did not exist prior to this moment in time.

As others have pointed out (Higgins-Desbiolles, 2020), COVID-19 can be seen as a result of neoliberal globalization and time-space compression (Harvey, 1990), with economic policies supported by advancements in telecommunications and transportation technologies that have unified humankind across borders and encompassed almost the entire habitable land surface of the planet. Transportation technologies, combined with porous political borders, have enabled people and money to reach increasingly more distant and remote corners of the planet. Telecommunication technologies have made information and knowledge sharing, along with financial transactions, instantaneous across the world (whether the information is accurate or not). These have contributed to advances in the global economic well-being, enabling the massive expansion of a wealthy-enough, leisure seeking middle class. Socially and economically, the planet is now smaller than it has ever been in a way that enables the outbreak of socially transmitted diseases, like the COVID-19 coronavirus, to be transmitted faster and across a broader geographic area than has been seen before.

The COVID-19 pandemic is, in this way, a direct result of time-space compression. It is the most recent manifestation of the modernization and globalization process that has been evolving and advancing on the planet since the Enlightenment and Industrial Revolution in the late 1700s. Time-space compression/modernization/globalization has had both positive and negative impact on the planet. As noted above, it has made the planet more integrated and accessible to more people. On the other hand, it has also contributed to the exploitation of vulnerable populations and environments, resulting in growing income inequalities, biodiversity losses, and, so far, an unrelenting drive toward global warming. Travel and tourism have been an integral component in both the positive and negative impacts of the globalization processes, and it is therefore not too surprising that it has possibly been the most impacted by the COVID-19 pandemic.

Creating a global mind

One of the most significant challenges in the world today has been how to address the damage caused by the overexploitation of natural and human resources. A major reason why these problems have emerged is because modern human culture has not evolved quickly enough to match the rapid advances of its transportation and telecommunications technologies so that these could be managed to avoid their negative impacts. Lew (2018; 2019) has suggested that travel and tourism could be a good thing if it intentionally and directly addressed the goal of enabling people to become more aware of, and sensitive to, the planet as a whole entity. He suggested that the more people travel, the more they experience and come to know other places, which expands their global consciousness, even without programs that specifically aim to achieve that transformational goal (Sheldon, 2020). Crises and distasters, such as the COVID-19 experience, also expand global awareness and consciousness.

There are other ways than travel and crises to expand the global consciousness of humankind, some of which are more effective than others. As humans, we come to know our world through a variety of direct and intermediary sources and experiences, from which we make decisions about what is true and what is false. Among these influences are: our education systems, which includes schools, intellectuals, and thought leaders; the media in all its different forms, but especially news outlets and entertainment; and various forms of public opinion, including our friends and word-of-mouth social media sources (Hsiao & Tseng 2011). These conscious ways of knowing our world, however, are limited because they only give us fragments of the full complexity of the planet.

According to Jung (1976, p. 157), expanding one's true awareness beyond these limitations requires a reawakening of the "unconscious within the mind and the integration of the ego with the unconscious, to forge the self". Accomplishing this is approached through a wide range of "technologies of consciousness" (Gangadean, 2010) that seek to take us beyond the thinking mind. In western allopathic medical traditions, this has primarily taken place in the realm of psychoanalysis and psychiatry (Skavronskaya et al., 2017). However, alternative experiential and embodied ways of world knowing also abound, including spirituality and psychic abilities (Dhiman & Marques, 2016), various forms of meditation (Heaton, 2016), recreational and religious uses of psychoactive substances (Tuper, 2006), and the direct experience of other people and places through travel and tourism (Lew, 2018; Sheldon, 2020). Like these, the experience of a pandemic can also be put into this category of being an altered, subconscious experience of the world.

Lew (2019) suggests that all these technologies of consciousness have the potential to move the human mind and body toward greater understandings of the non-duality or oneness of all that exists, and an acceptance that we are all essentially global beings. They enable individuals to gain critical intelligence that is beyond self-centered rationality, by increasing their capacity for moral compassion, integral cognition, and a global identity. Indeed, it is becoming increasingly more evident that the survival of the human species depends on the individual and collective transformation of humanism into global transhumanism, substantiated by a personal ethic that extends beyond personal self-interest (Ferdig, 2007).

Sustainable development

For over three decades, sustainable development has offered a widely endorsed model to address the challenges of modern globalization (WCED, 1987). However, it has largely failed because it has not been effectively adopted as the taken-for-granted *modus operandi* by cultures and peoples across the globe (Butler, 1999; Zimmermann, 2018). Sustainable development can only be realized when it is understood, perceived, and embodied in the identity and daily life of individuals. Political actions that force sustainability will not bring about a sustainable global culture without such an evolution of global consciousness and understanding at the individual level. Because of this, Lew (2019) suggests that a global consciousness, sustained through the *collective unconscious,* should form the basis and vision of sustainability, and as such, global consciousness should be added to the UN Sustainable Development Goals (SDGs), with tourism being one of the major means of its implementation.

Building on somewhat narrow interpretations, it is often believed that a change in global understanding can only come through the evolution of new forms of economic thinking that overcome the neoliberal tendency of people to focus on personal gains over social cooperation. This seems obvious, as almost all the major social crises that we are familiar with (e.g., wars, economic downturns, and political upheavals) seem to be based in a form of globalization that is driven by neoliberalism and its associated excesses of human competition and consumption.

To change our economic system, however, requires that humans change the way they think, and move towards the goal of a "mature self" (Fox & Alldred, 2020) who rejects the concept of innate human superiority. Many authors (e.g., Sharpley, 2000; Steiner & Reisinger 2006; Swanson & DeVereaux, 2017) have suggested that a post-mature modernity is emerging, driven by an epistemic crisis in which we do not know what is true and not true, nor even how to determine truth. For example, how we determine when something is 'sustainable' can be hotly debated by experts. Efforts to address our epistemic crisis are gradually shaping new paradigms for defining what sustainability is, and how we could recognize 'sustainable tourism' when we see it. Post-mature modernity and a focus on consciousness are, for example, suggestions for such a new paradigm. The resolution of this crisis has implications for "personal and place identities, moral, social, and cultural identity and sustainable development" (Steiner & Reisinger, 2006, p. 301). In other words, it would be the emergence of a new global culture.

To bring a new global culture into reality, the world needs people with an enhanced global consciousness who can address issues that are global in scale, such as climate change and the COVID-19 pandemic. The admittedly utopian assumption here is that people who have an expanded global consciousness would behave, make decisions, and contribute better to debates with the whole planet in mind, rather than their narrower personal or national interests. This would indeed bring about a new global culture that possibly would, naturally and without any legal requirements, be ingrained with values and behaviors that are more along the lines of sustainable development.

The planet is, obviously, far from such a global culture at the present time, although some places are more respectful of the natural environment and others are more sensitive to income and power inequalities than others. Thus, we propose that post COVID-19 travel and tourism has the potential to significantly enhance the expansion global consciousness, if that were made a clear and specific intention. Without such an intention, whether through tourism or elsewhere, the necessary change in global culture could be a very long process. In terms of tourism, for example, only a fraction of all the people on the planet experience international travel, and those that do mostly experience its more exploitative forms. At the same time, people everywhere are constantly exposed to ideologies that foster resentment and division against other peoples and places, rather than those that support mutual understanding across the planet.

Enter COVID-19

As noted above, COVID-19 is a direct result of globalization. Epidemiologists have predicted that a disease pandemic like this would eventually happen, although nobody really knew exactly how it might develop and evolve. Now it has happened and it is changing the planet. It is changing the people on the planet and is changing how the cultures on the planet will evolve moving forward, possibly redefining travel and tourism to align it more with the goals of global consciousness. Some news items as of early 2020 that have suggested such impacts of the pandemic include:

- Social distance may be here to stay, with periodic "suppress and lift" enforcements to control various disease outbreaks, along with an increased awareness of cleanliness and sanitation
- A form of tourism 'degrowth' may emerge in which travel will be smaller and more costly, fostering fewer, but more meaningful and less hedonisitc trips for most people, along with an increased appreciation of the 'right to travel'
- There may be an increased awareness of 'space', including global geographic space (what is happening on the opposite side of the world) and individual personal space (between people); related to this will be an increased appreciation for meaningful social interactions
- There will likely be a major increase in the use of technologies and robotics to monitor people and products to ensure health and security for both, and to enhance communication and enable more work from home, educational opportunities, and other social interactions
- There will likely be an increased appreciation and respect for the natural environment as the source of pandemic diseases and nature-based disasters, if it is not properly cared for
- Where possible, people will increase their home gardening, home cooking, and other home and self-care skills
- Social enterprising will become more common as companies show more concern for workers and community than for investor profits
- There will be a general increase in awareness of, and support for, vulnerable populations, such as the homeless, informal economy workers, and refugees, as well as for front-line services workers, such as grocery store employees
- Female political leaders will receive greater acknowledgement and respect following their apparent greater success in managing the COVID-19 pandemic

Some of these impacts will be around for a long time, while others may prove to be fleeting, or may resurface through future pandemic experiences. Either way, as a global phenomenon, COVID-19 is contributing to the expansion of global consciousness. While it may not be a welcome experience, it is a liminal and transformative one that is being forced on humankind in a shared manner. Everyone on the planet is experiencing this same pandemic, although its manifestations and timing varies geographically. Everyone on the planet, to some degree, is experiencing a similar discussions and response by their governments (their collective leadership) to manage this disease and to try to minimize incidents of illness and death, and to keep their hospitals from overflowing with patients.

Everyone on the planet, again to varying degrees, is experiencing lockdown and quarantine-in-place conditions, which is essentially a 'retreat' from worldly activities. By dangling the spectre of death, the pandemic is forcing people to think introspectively about home, about safety, about their relationship to other people, about their place in the world, and about the meaning of life. Robinson (2012, p. 370) in his work, *The emotional tourist,* suggests that different 'cultures of sustainability' emerge from self-critical explorations, which require a continuous re-actualization of reflexive competencies. Travel and tourism experiences are especially well suited to encourage such liminal and transformative experiences (Bristow & Jenkins, 2020). And so, too, is the COVID-19 experience.

Through social distancing, the pandemic is separating people; it is keeping them apart. But it is also bringing people together at a more subtle, and mostly subconscious, level. It is bringing people together because they recognize that each of them has the same responsibility and power to safeguard the larger society from illness, and to actually change the world through a shared focus. They see this in themselves, they see it in their neighbors, they see it in people they have no contact with it all. Those who have a home are forced to think about the safety of the homeless, as well, because the pandemic is just as easily spread through those without a home as through those with a home. Everyone in their community, everyone across the planet, has this potential to spread the COVID-19 disease and to catch the disease. And suddenly everyone is on an equal plane. And everyone is cooperating, to some degree.

Global consciousness was first conceptualized in a manner by Carl Gustav Jung (1933) in *Modern man in search of a soul.* Later Jung (1963) argued that the human subconscious mind has the propensity to produce and appreciate behaviors, symbols, and images that are biologically inherited from our ancestors, and thus collectively shared by social groups. According to Jung (1976), the most powerful emotions and their associated behaviors, from romantic love to nationalism, derive their intensity and shape from these subconscious *archetypes,* which form a universal collective unconscious, or collective memory.

In this sense, COVID-19 has emerged as a new collective archetype, with deep emotional significance due to the global reach of its impacts. Thus, even if its long-term impacts on human behavior and related planetary outcomes may be challenging to predict and identify on a superficial conscious level, it is likely that its deeper, unconscious significances will be profound for generations to come. Charles Eisenstein (2020) suggests that the COVID-19 experience "follows the template of initiation: separation from normality, followed by a dilemma, breakdown, or ordeal, followed (if it is to be complete) by reintegration and celebration."

The longer the pandemic remains problematic, the stronger its impact will likely be, and the more people will be both separating themselves from one another and cooperating through that separation — and possibly complaining about it the whole way. And by the same token, however, they will be expanding their global consciousness by expanding their awareness that this is a single planet. The smallest thing can affect the largest number of people, and what affects one can affect all. This is the lesson of the COVID-19 pandemic. This lesson could not have been taught if it were not for the level of globalization (the time-space compression) that existed on the Earth when this particular coronavirus emerged.

Outlook

Many scholars have recognized the need for a shift in human development, as the prevalent economic culture, with all of its challenges, cannot be sustainable for much longer (Hall et al., 2020). Gangadean (2006, p. 73) articulated this by stating:

> As we enter the 21st century, it is unmistakably clear that we are in the midst of an unprecedented shift in the human condition, a global renaissance that affects every aspect of our cultural lives, our self-understanding, and, of course, our rational enterprise. It is a global awakening of reason, scientific knowing, and the holistic worldview.

The world will not change completely, and not everyone will have a fully developed sense of global consciousness, once the COVID-19 pandemic settles down. But there will be a significant transformation in the direction of a global cultural worldview and a global consciousness that is more respectful of the planet, of home, and of others. This is because new, deeper and more inclusive knowledge patterns will emerge to bring about new ways of thinking across the sciences, philosophy, psychology, and education. COVID-19 is making us re-think how we conceive of ourselves as human beings, realizing that being human means caring about and attending to the physical–emotional–mental–spiritual world (Vogiatzakis et al., 2018; Vargas-Madraz, 2018; Yeoman & Postma, 2014).

The maturation of our human form is often difficult to see when our global and individual systems are overwhelmed by the cacophony of the new global information system and other aspects of our rapidly shrinking time-space reality. There are, however, indications that a sustainable development empathy is emerging that will enhance our emotional and subconscious connections with peoples and environments (Font et al., 2016).

And tourism will still be with us. Tourism is a quintessential symbol of modernity and an archetype of paradise and the good life (Veblen, 1965). After the pandemic, tourists will still overwhelm the world's most popular destinations, but perhaps not quite as much as before, if only due to social distancing demands. The hedonic benefits that were so strongly associated with tourism marketing (Kirillova et al., 2014) may be toned down some, along with related tourist consumption and behavior patterns, as quality experiences are sought over quantity.

Tourism has often been accused of causing negative environmental, social and mental impacts, the loss of traditional lifestyles and values, and the expansion of technology and consumption into previously untouched places (Galvani, 2014; Hall & Lew, 2009). However, tourism is really a symptom of a larger global culture, and as that culture changes, through a shift in the consciousness of a significant enough number of individuals, so too will tourism change. Tourism will them be primarily for:

1. expanding the traveler's knowledge and awareness of other places and the world;
2. providing opportunities for tourists to engage with other people and appreciate their lived experiences; and
3. offering a liminal space in which self-reflexivity and identity formation are natural outcomes.

Most people seek travel and tourism experiences precisely for these reasons, whether or not these are consciously understood or stated. As such, travel and tourism may be the single most effective and sought-after way for individuals to change their global consciousness, and, in turn, change the consciousness of the entire planet. The all-encompassing impact of the COVID-19 pandemic on travel and tourism worldwide can only hasten the evolution toward a more transformative form of tourism.

The degree of shift in mind and consciousness today is nothing less than an evolutionary expansion in awareness that promotes our maturation as a human species, or as Fox and Alldred (2020) suggest, the evolution towards being a "post-human" who finally understands one's self to be only a small part of the universe, not more important than other parts, living or not living, but embedded between nature and culture. We all are part of an evolutionary process (Brouder, 2017; Buttimer, 1990; Li, 2000; Lowenthal, 1961; Tuan, 1993).

Conclusions

The goals of sustainability might be incrementally achieved over time through the integration of economics with biology, philosophy, and neurology. It might also be realized by enhancing our knowledge of the world, our sense and appreciation of environmental beauty, and by qualitative and authentic improvements of places. In the end, changes in the physical world only come through changes in the human mind and consciousness. In recent decades, the human mind has been producing exponential changes in its knowledge and experiences, though some of these have been delivered in perhaps less than desirable directions. A deeper understanding of the less than rational and less than physical ways that we know and create our world experience is needed to move the planet in a more positive direction.

Sustainability, in this sense, is an unending process of moving toward positive outcomes, defined by shifting human beliefs, desires, knowledge, experiences, and consciousness. The COVID-19 pandemic is one of the more significant human experiences of the 21st century. It is not likely to be the last of such an experience, as the time-space compression origin of this crisis is likely to only increase with time. Sustainability as a concept has been evolving in tandem with societal change, and as humankind evolves, the vision and quality of sustainable development will also evolve, and most likely in ways that, like the COVID-19 pandemic, are as yet unpredictable.

Disclosure statement

No potential conflict of interest was reported by the author(s).

ORCID

Adriana Galvani   http://orcid.org/0000-0002-3640-5865
Alan A. Lew   http://orcid.org/0000-0001-8177-5972

References

Bristow, R. S., & Jenkins, I. S. (2020). Spatial and temporal tourism considerations in liminal landscapes. *Tourism Geographies*, *22*(2), 219–228. https://doi.org/10.1080/14616688.2020.1725618
Brouder, P. (2017). Evolutionary economic geography: reflections from a sustainable tourism perspective. *Tourism Geographies*, *19*(3), 438–447. https://doi.org/10.1080/14616688.2016.1274774

Butler, R. W. (1999). Sustainable tourism: A state-of-the-art review. *Tourism Geographies*, *1*(1), 7–25. Volume Issue https://doi.org/10.1080/14616689908721291

Buttimer, A. (1990). Geography, Humanism, and Global Concern. *Annals of the Association of American Geographers*, *80*(1), 1–33. https://doi.org/10.1111/j.1467-8306.1990.tb00001.x

Dhiman, S. & Marques, J. (Eds). (2016). *Spirituality and Sustainability*. Springer.

Eisenstein, C. (2020). The coronation. Essays by Charles. (March). https://charleseisenstein.org/essays/the-coronation/

Ferdig, M. A. (2007). Sustainability Leadership: Co-creating a Sustainable Future. *Journal of Change Management*, *7*(1), 25–35. https://doi.org/10.1080/14697010701233809

Font, X., Garay, L., & Jones, S. (2016). A Social Cognitive Theory of sustainability Empathy. *Annals of Tourism Research*, *58*, 65–80. https://doi.org/10.1016/j.annals.2016.02.004

Fox, N. J., & Alldred, P. (2020). Sustainability, feminist posthumanism and the unusual capacities of (post) humans. *Environmental Sociology*, *6*(2), 121–131. https://doi.org/10.1080/23251042.2019.1704480

Galvani, A. (2014). *Turismo tra impatti e sostenibilità*. (Tourism between impacts and sustainability-Monography). Giraldi Editions. ISBN 978-88-6155-584-6.

Gangadean, A. (2010). Integral consciousness through the global lens: The great shift in the presiding technology of consciousness. *Futures*, *42*(10), 1049–1055. https://doi.org/10.1016/j.futures.2010.08.003

Gangadean, A. K. (2006). The Awakening of Global Reason. The Logical and Ontological Foundation of Integral Science. *World Futures*, *62*(1-2), 56–74. Vol Issue https://doi.org/10.1080/02604020500406297

Hall, C.M., Scott, D. & Gössling, S. (2020). Pandemics, transformations and tourism: be careful what you wish for. *Tourism Geographies*, https://doi.org/10.1080/14616688.2020.1759131

Hall, C. M., & Lew, A. A. (2009). *Understanding and Managing Tourism Impacts: An Integrated Approach*. Routledge.

Harvey, D. (1990). *The Condition of Postmodernity*. Blackwell.

Heaton, D. (2016). Higher consciousness for sustainability-as-flourishing. In S. Dhiman & J. Marques (Eds.), *Spirituality and Sustainability* (pp. 121–137). Springer.

Higgins-Desbiolles, F. (2020). Socialising tourism for social and ecological justice after COVID-19. *Tourism Geographies*, https://doi.org/10.1080/14616688.2020.1757748

Hsiao, H. H. M. & Tseng, H-P. (2011). The formation of environmental consciousness in Taiwan: Intellectuals, media, and the public mind, *Asian Geographer*, *18*(1–2), 99–109.

Jung, C. G. (1933). *Modern man in search of a soul*. Harcourt, Brace & World.

Jung, C. G. (1963). *Die Beziehungen zwischen dem Ich und dem Unbewussten (The relationships between the I and the unconscious)*. Rascher.

Jung, C. G. (1976). *Die Archetypen und das kollektive Unbewusste (the archetypes and the collective unconscious)*. Walter Verlag.

Kirillova, K., Fu, X., Lehto, X., & Cai, L. (2014). What makes a destination beautiful? Dimensions of tourist aesthetic judgment. *Tourism Management*, *42*, 282–293. https://doi.org/10.1016/j.tourman.2013.12.006

Lew, A. A. (2018). Why Travel? – Travel, Tourism and Global Consciousness. *Tourism Geographies*, *20*(4), 742–749. https://doi.org/10.1080/14616688.2018.1490343

Lew, A. A. (2019). Tourism's surprising importance in creating sustainability and global consciousness. *Tourism Review*, (forthcoming).

Li, Y. (2000). Geographical Consciousness and Tourism Experience. *Annals of Tourism Research*, *27*(4), 863–883. https://doi.org/10.1016/S0160-7383(99)00112-7

Lowenthal, D. (1961). Geography, Experience, and Imagination: Towards a Geographical Epistemology. *Annals of the Association of American Geographers*, *51*(3), 241–260. https://doi.org/10.1111/j.1467-8306.1961.tb00377.x

Robinson, M. (2012). The emotional tourist. In D. Picard & M. Robinson (Eds.), *Emotion in motion: Tourism, affect and transformation* (pp. 21–48). Ashgate Publishing Ltd.

Sharpley, R. (2000). Tourism and Sustainable Development: Exploring the Theoretical Divide. *Journal of Sustainable Tourism*, *8*(1), 1–19. https://doi.org/10.1080/09669580008667346

Sheldon, P. J. (2020). Designing tourism experiences for inner transformation. *Annals of Tourism Research, 83,* 102935. https://doi.org/10.1016/j.annals.2020.102935

Skavronskaya, L., Scott, N., Moyle, B., Le, D., Hadinejad, A., Zhang, R., Gardiner, S., Coghlan ... , A., Shakeela, A. (2017). Cognitive psychology and tourism research: state of the art. *Tourism Review, 72*(2), 221–237. https://doi.org/10.1108/TR-03-2017-0041

Steiner, C. J., & Reisinger, Y. (2006). Understanding existential authenticity. *Annals of Tourism Research, 33*(2), 299–318. https://doi.org/10.1016/j.annals.2005.08.002

Swanson, K., & DeVereaux, C. (2017). A theoretical framework for sustaining culture: Culturally sustainable entrepreneurship. *Annals of Tourism Research, 62,* 78–88. https://doi.org/10.1016/j.annals.2016.12.003

Tuan, Y. (1993). *Passing Strange and Wonderful: Aesthetics, Nature, and Culture.* Island Press.

Tuper, K. W. (2006). The globalization of ayahuasca: Harm reduction or benefit maximization?. *International Journal of Drug Policy, 194,* 297–303.

Vargas-Madrazo, E. (2018). Contemplative dialogue as the basis for a transdisciplinary attitude: Eco-literacy toward an education for human sustainability. *World Futures, 74*(4), 224–245. Vol Issue https://doi.org/10.1080/02604027.2018.1444833

Veblen, T. (1965). *The theory of the leisure class* (revised). A. M. Kelley.

Vogiatzakis, I., Terkenli, T., Trovato, M., & Abu-Jaber, N. (2018). Landscapes in the Eastern Mediterranean between the Future and the Past. *Editorial. Land. Land. 7*(4), 160. https://doi.org/10.3390/land7040160

WCED (World Commission on Environment and Development). (1987). *Our Common Future.* Oxford University Press.

Yeoman, I., & Postma, A. (2014). Developing an ontological framework for tourism futures. *Tourism Recreation Research, 39*(3), 299–304. https://doi.org/10.1080/02508281.2014.11087002

Zimmermann, F. M. (2018). Does sustainability (still) matter in tourism (geography). *Tourism Geographies, 20*(2), 333–336. https://doi.org/10.1080/14616688.2018.1434814

Pandemics, transformations and tourism: be careful what you wish for

C. Michael Hall ⓘ, Daniel Scott and Stefan Gössling

ABSTRACT

Disease outbreaks and pandemics have long played a role in societal and economic change. However, the nature of such change is selective, meaning that it is sometimes minimal and, at other times, and change or transformation may be unexpected, potentially even reinforcing contemporary paradigms. A comprehensive overview of pandemics and their effects is provided. This is used to help contextualise the COVID-19 pandemic, its impact on tourism and government, industry and consumer response. Drawing on the available literature, factors that will affect tourism and destination recovery are then identified. Some measures will continue or even expand present growth orientations in tourism while others may contribute to sustainability. It is concluded that that the selective nature of the effects of COVID-19 and the measures to contain it may lead to reorientation of tourism in some cases, but in others will contribute to policies reflecting the selfish nationalism of some countries. However, the response to planetary limits and sustainable tourism requires a global approach. Despite clear evidence of this necessity, the possibility for a comprehensive transformation of the tourism system remains extremely limited without a fundamental transformation of the entire planet.

摘要

疾病爆发和大流行病长期以来在社会和经济变革中发挥着作用。然而, 这种变化的性质是有选择性的, 这意味着它有时是最小的, 而在其他时候, 变化或转变可能是出乎意料的, 甚至有可能强化当代范式。全面回顾了大流行病及其影响, 这有助于将COVID-19大流行病、其对旅游业和政府影响、产业和消费者反应具体化。在现有文献的基础上, 确定了影响旅游业和目的地恢复的因素。一些措施将继续甚至扩大目前旅游业的增长方向, 而其他措施可能有助于可持续性。结论是, COVID-19效应的选择性和遏制措施在某些情况下可能会导致旅游业的重新定位, 但在另一些情况下, 会有助于制定反映一些国家民族利己主义的政策。然而, 要应对全球范围的限制和可持续的旅游业, 就必须采取全球性措施。尽管有明确的证据表明这一必要性, 但如果没有整个地球的根本性转变, 全面改变旅游系统的可能性仍然极其有限。

Introduction

Pandemics and new diseases have long had a transformational effect on environments and societies. Arguably one cannot understand, for example, the Europeanisation of the New World, as well as other colonial conquests, without considering the transfer of Old World diseases that killed many of the indigenous inhabitants of the Americas, Australasia, and the Pacific (Crosby, 2004; Diamond, 1998). In the same way the history of Europe has been shaped by the plagues and various disease outbreaks for millennia. Such pandemics were essentially transformative because of their enormous demographic impacts and the effects that this had on production systems and the capacities of societies to adapt to external change. To reinterpret Wolfe et al. (2007), infectious diseases, as a leading cause of human morbidity, mortality and societal apprehension, have long exerted important selective forces on politics, society, the economy, and human's attitudes to nature, as well as the human genome. Therefore, the transformational actions and possibilities of modern pandemics are nothing new, they perhaps just seem that way because it is affecting the developed world and generations who have either not been exposed to, or otherwise just forgotten given access to antibiotics and modern medicine, the impacts of pandemic and the essential role of mobility within them.

Pandemics – definitional and transformational opportunities?

There is no single accepted definition of the term pandemic (Morens et al., 2009). Nevertheless, they have several common components (Morens et al., 2009):

- Wide geographic extension – they are widely spatially distributed or are global;
- Disease movement or spread via transmission that can be traced from location to location;
- High attack rates and explosiveness, i.e., multiple cases appear within a short time;
- Minimal population immunity;
- Novelty, they are new, and/or associated with novel variants of existing organisms.

In addition, they may also be regarded as infectious, contagious and severe (Doshi, 2010; Morens et al., 2009). However, confusion still occurs as the notion of a pandemic may be sensationalised or misunderstood. For example, the prepandemic/pandemic stages model of the (WHO 2009) to address influenza outbreaks was designed to inform and communicate public health responses rather than indicate the seriousness or severity of a disease situation (Morens & Taubenberger, 2011; Watson, 2011).

Unfortunately, controversy over the definition of a pandemic and previous national and international responses and criticisms is arguably why there was possibly a delay in the World Health Organization (WHO) declaring COVID-19 as a pandemic (Buranyi, 2020). Indeed, WHO's previous pandemic responses, as in the case of COVID-19, have been subject to accusations of politicisation and lack of transparency. For example, Cohen and Carter (2010) argued that scientists advising WHO on planning for an influenza pandemic had done paid work for pharmaceutical firms that stood to gain from the guidance they were preparing. The significant point being that the declaration of a pandemic contributes to the political momentum to enact public health measures including, where available, the provision of vaccines (Bijl & Schellekens, 2011). Nevertheless, the comments by Nicoll and McKee (2010) following their review of the WHO and European response are particularly cogent: 'To now neglect preparation for pandemics and other emergencies would be like a town investing in a good fire brigade that can deal with a major blaze. If in the first few years, it only has to deal with some house fires would anyone advise retiring the firemen and selling off the fire engines?'. Yet while public health researchers extol the value of coordinated international health security approaches to effectively respond to both pandemics and contribute to sustainable development, the reality is that, in part because of the experience of previous pandemics, many governments have chosen to focus more on national interest rather than international solidarity. As Buranyi (2020) observed in relation to the COVID-19 response, 'Many wealthy nations have not only pursued their own national strategies for public health, but have also withdrawn from the globalised world of diplomacy and trade that they themselves set up'. Aggressive nationalism has become normalised, as Lawrence Gostin, director of the WHO Collaborating Center on National and Global Health Law, stated 'All the previous rules about global norms, public health and understanding of what's expected in terms of an outbreak has crumbled ... None of us know where this is leading' (quoted in Buranyi, 2020).

In such a situation, many commentators have argued that the COVID-19 pandemic presents a transformative moment or opportunity that will change the world (Davies, 2020; Gills, 2020; Mair, 2020; Politico, 2020). McKinsey and Company (2020:1) suggest that the pandemic is 'not only a health crisis of immense proportion' but that it is 'also an imminent restructuring of the global economic order' as a result of the economic impact of virus suppression, potentially including the nature of international tourism as an economic and social phenomenon. Nevertheless, that things will change for the better or that economic development, including tourism, will become more sustainable, is not a foregone conclusion (Kozul-Wright & Barbosa, 2020; Mair, 2020). This paper discusses the transformative possibilities of the COVID-19 pandemic for tourism and its sustainability by looking at the implications of recent pandemics for potential societal and economic transformations, particularly as they affect tourism.

Pandemic risk and impact

Despite medical and public health advances, the threat of pandemics has been gradually increasing since the latter half of the twentieth century. The main reasons for this lie in processes of globalisation and global change of which travel and tourism is an integral component (Burkle, 2006; Hall, 2020; Allen et al., 2017). Several processes have come together to increase pandemic risk. First, humanity is now more urbanised than it has ever been with over half of the world's population living in urban centres. The greater concentration of people has increased the potential for diseases to be spread by contact and proximity (Connolly et al., 2020). Second, these urban centres are now more interconnected than ever before as a result of transport connectivity via plane, train, shipping and road. A passenger, and therefore a disease, can now travel from one urban centre to another the other side of the world in a day. Third, growing consumer demand for meat and encroachment on wilderness and biodiversity loss is bringing humans into closer contact with animal pathogens which, once they enter urban populations, can then become rapidly dispersed (Devaux et al. (2019); Mossoun et al., 2015; Myers et al., 2013). For example, coronaviruses affect a number of different animal hosts. Four coronaviruses (HCoV-229E, HCoV-OC43, HCoV-NL63, HCoV-HKU1) are endemic in human populations and are mainly associated with mild, self-limiting respiratory illnesses. Three other corona-viruses, namely SARS-CoV, MERS-CoV and COVID-19, the outbreaks of which are regarded as zoonotic events, can cause severe respiratory problems (Berry et al., 2015; Greger, 2007; Rothan & Byrareddy, 2020). As (Wu et al., 2017, p.18) noted, 'High-risk areas for the emergence and spread of infectious disease are where these … trends intersect with predisposing socioecological conditions including the presence of wild disease reservoirs, agricultural practices that increase contact between wildlife and livestock, and cultural practices that increase contact between humans, wildlife, and livestock'. Critically, for the COVID-19 outbreak, the expansion of the interface of contact between humans, wildlife, and livestock has been a major outcome of urbanisation processes in China (Chmura, 2017; Wang et al., 2008; Wu et al., 2018), as well as in other countries (Allen et al., 2017; Connolly et al., 2020; Kogan et al., 2019). 'Urbanization and associated land-use changes, in conjunction with rising meat consumption, have brought reservoirs of wildlife diseases into closer contact with livestock and people' (Wu et al., 2017). However, it is important to note that the potential health impacts of zoonotic events and pandemic emergence is not isolated to China alone, but represents the intersection of broader processes of urbanisation, globalisation, environmental change, agribusiness and contemporary capit-alism (Allen et al., 2017; Wallace, 2016; Wallace et al., 2018).

Yet, coronaviruses are not the only pandemic threat with much concern being given to influenza as well as other diseases (Fauci & Morens, 2012; Jonas, 2014; Labonte et al., 2011). Table 1 illustrates some of the major pandemics and disease out-breaks of the twentieth and twenty-first centuries. Several of these pandemics have become "normalised", i.e. they are part of the global health business as usual, or to be more precise developing country business as usual, even though their annual impact can be enormous. For example, globally in 2013, there were an estimated 1.8 million new HIV infections, 29.2 million prevalent HIV cases, and 1.3 million HIV deaths (Murray et al., 2014). To these we could add malaria, which accounts for around a mil-lion deaths per year, the deaths from which, like HIV/AIDS, occurs mainly in Africa (Murray et al., 2012), as well as diseases such as measles, globally reported cases of which increased by 48.1% between 2017 and 2018, with 98 countries reporting more measles cases in 2018 compared to 2017 (Durrheim et al., 2019), and influenza. For example, Iuliano et al. (2018). estimates that between 291,000 – 646,000 seasonal influ-enza-associated respiratory deaths (4·0 - 8·8 per 100,000 individuals) occur annually, while the average annual total economic burden of influenza in the United States alone has been estimated at $11.2 billion ($6.3–$25.3 billion) (Putri et al., 2018). Such endemic diseases may also suggest a likely health future for COVID-19 responses given that, in the absence of a vaccine, we would see seasonal peaks of infection of the dis-ease as it becomes part of the "normal" disease exposure for humans (Chen et al., 2011). What is also perhaps significant in the list of pandemics and global diseases is the absence of significant transformations that rise from them. They clearly have economic,

Table 1. Major pandemics and pathogen outbreaks.

Year(s)	Pathogen	Cases/mortality	Comments
1918–1920	Spanish Flu (Influenza)	500 million cases and 21 to 100 million deaths	The Spanish flu affected one third of the world's population and claimed the lives of 1–5% of world's population, far exceeding the death toll of WWI.
1957–1958 Influenza	Asian flu (Influenza)	1 to 2 million deaths	The WHO (2009) estimate that between one to four million people died as a result of the pandemic with resultant change of -3.5% to 0.4% of global GDP. Accelerated development of a vaccine limiting the spread of the responsible strain.
1968–1969	Hong Kong flu (Influenza)	500,000 to 2 million deaths	The Hong Kong flu was the first virus to spread extensively due to air travel. The WHO (2009) estimated it contributed to a loss of between -0.4 to -1.5% of global GDP.
1960-present	Human immunodeficiency virus infection and acquired immune deficiency syndrome (HIV/AIDS)	70 million cases and 35 million deaths (primarily Africa)	First identified in 1983. The earliest known case was in 1959. The decreased life expectancy in many African countries as a result of HIV/AIDS is associated with an estimated lowering of economic growth rates by -0.3 to -1.5% and potentially higher.
1961- present	Cholera	1.4 to 4 million annual cases and 21,000 to 143,000 annual deaths	'Cholera outbreaks impact negatively on both domestic and international demand for tourism industry services of affected countries' (Kirigia et al., 2009). The seventh cholera pandemic began in South Asia in 1961. Recent notable outbreaks include those in Zimbabwe (2008–2009), Haiti (2010–present) and Yemen (2016–present).
2002–2003	SARS (coronavirus)	8,098 cases and 774 deaths	Estimated global economic cost of US$100 billion, and US$48 billion in China alone. Originated in China, International travel allowed the SARS virus to spread to 37 countries.
2009 Influenza	Swine flu (Influenza)	284,000 deaths	The economic impact of the pandemic outbreak in Mexico where the swine flu pandemic started was estimated as >$3.2 billion (0.3% of GNP) with estimated tourism losses of US$2.8 billion
2012-	Middle East respiratorysyndrome (MERS-CoV) (coronavirus)	Transmitted by camels and humans, case-fatality rate of 35%	No vaccine available. The MERS outbreak in Korea in 2015 resulted in an estimated $2.6 billion in tourism loss. MERS advisories continue for those taking hajj and umrah pilgrimage to Saudi Arabia.
2014-present	Ebola (Hemorrhagic fever) West Africa (Mainly Guinea, Liberia, Sierra Leone) and the Congo	28,600 cases and 11,325 deaths reported (likely underestimates)	Caused by virus transmitted from wild animals, with case-fatality rate of up to 90% (50% average). Ebola vaccine now available. Estimates of the economic burden of the West African outbreak range from $2.8 to $32.6 billion in lost GDP.

(continued)

Table 1. Continued.

Year(s)	Pathogen	Cases/mortality	Comments
2015-present	Zika (Americas, primarily Brazil; flavivirus primarily transmitted by *Aedes aegypti* mosquitoes)	Unknown number of cases. Few if any deaths, but can result in microcephaly in infants born by infected mothers and in Guillain-Barré syndrome.	No vaccine available. The World Bank estimates that the short-term impact of the ZIKV outbreak for 2016 in Latin America and the Caribbean was about US$3.5 billion primarily in countries where tourism is significant, especially given the hosting of major sporting events.
2016 (present)	Dengue fever	100 million cases and 38,000 deaths	'Dengue is the most important vector-borne viral disease of humans and likely more important than malaria globally in terms of morbidity and economic impact' (Gubler, 2012, p.743). The total annual global cost of dengue illness in 2013 was estimated at US$8·9 billion. Outbreaks occur periodically but 2016 outbreak was global in scale.
2019-present	COVID-19 (coronavirus)	As of 22 April, 2020, over 2.5 million cases and 180,000 deaths with significant underreporting	The World Travel & Tourism Council (WTTC, 2020), anticipate a tourism-related loss of up to US$ 2.1 trillion in 2020 and up to 75 million jobs

Sources: Aleeban & Mackey, 2016; Al-Tawfiq et al., 2014; Bell et al., 2003; Bloom & Cadarette, 2019; Girard et al., 2010; Gubler, 2012; Huber et al., 2018; Joo et al., 2019; Kirigia et al., 2009; Petersen et al., 2016; Rassy & Smith, 2013; Shepard et al., 2016; Siu & Wong, 2004; Taubenberger & Morens, 2006; WHO, 2009; World Bank, 2016; WTTC, 2020.

tourism and social impact but they have arguably not become significant transition events. New health concepts that have emerged in response to zoonotic diseases, especially "One Health" which sees human and biodiversity health as entwined, are clearly very significant in light of the role of global environmental change and human and biotic wellbeing. However, while they have generated research (Hinchliffe, 2015; Zinsstag et al., 2012) and institutional (World Bank, 2012) interest, they have had little policy impact, and even less on tourism, even though relevant literature recognises the health risks to animal and human populations arising from tourism activities in remote locations (Coker et al., 2011; Hall, 2007; Thompson, 2013); as well as long-recognised risks to human health posed by transport-related pollution which make individuals substantially more susceptible to respiratory diseases (Clay et al., 2018; Sterpetti, 2020; Wu et al., 2020). Unfortunately, the impacts of climate change, to which tourism is both a significant contributor and substantially affected by (Scott et al., 2019), are only expected to increase the frequency of pandemics and disease outbreaks (Ebi et al., 2017a, Ebi et al., 2017b; Kavanagh et al., 2019/2020).

Although travel and tourism are critical for carrying disease and disease vectors (Browne et al., 2016), and pandemics have major impacts on tourism given the role of nonpharmaceutical interventions (NPI), such as quarantine and border control (Ryu et al., 2020), there is a surprisingly limited literature on the interrelationships between pandemics and tourism, and its long term implications. Although students of tourism are not alone in this, for example, in reflecting on social science research on the 1918-1919 flu pandemic ("Spanish influenza"), Phillips and Killingray (2003) observed, with respect to professional historians 'Overlooking cataclysmic natural disasters, they have focussed, rather, on political, economic, and intellectual processes to explain change over time'. In the case of tourism, the health responses on travel during pandemics have remained essentially the same since the Spanish flu and earlier. 'The harsh reality is that we have no 21st century tools to fight COVID-19. There is no vaccine or treatment. All we have is the methods that were used to control epidemics in the early 20th century. Those, as we shall see, tend to be very economically disruptive' (Baldwin & Weder di Mauro, 2020, p.11). If COVID-19 was the equivalent to a severe pandemic such as the Spanish flu it has been estimated that the world's GDP would fall by between -4.8% and -6.7% (McKibbin & Fernando, 2020; McKibbin & Sidorenko, 2006).

Indeed, the Spanish flu potentially has a number of analogues with the COVID-19 pandemic. The 1918-19 flu pandemic was referred to as the "Spanish flu" because Spain was neutral in the first world war and therefore not subject to news censorship as the British, French or American media was. Issues of censorship and state surveillance have been associated with the original COVID-19 outbreak as well as reporting and research on the disease in some countries (Jian, 2020; Kirchgaessner et al., 2020; Safi, 2020). Furthermore, even the name "Spanish" flu, the first outbreak of which was almost certainly in the United States (Barry, 2004), reflects the racism and xenophobia that has also been associated with COVID-19 (Aratani, 2020; Davidson, 2020). As Phillips and Killingray (2003) presciently observed, 'In the popular mind calamities often need to have their origin and cause identified and other countries or peoples credited with blame. This xenophobic response has been common in Europe, that impulse to blame others or the silent places of the Asian heartlands for the source of the disease'. However, in a tourism context such measures may also have a further effect in that the association of a disease with place, even generally with respect to outbreaks, can then have substantial effects on destination image. For example, even though Ebola has been limited to a small number of African locations (Table 1), tourism to other parts of the continent has been negatively affected purely by them being "African" and associated with increased risk (Maphanga & Henama, 2019; Novelli et al., 2018; WTTC, 2018).

Some of the ways in which tourism is affected by COVID-19 is illustrated in Figure 1 which details a range of short and longer term responses to pandemics, such as COVID-19. The figure highlights the importance of transport networks and transit regions for connectivity within the tourism system. This is especially significant given the enormous reduction in flights as a result of COVID-19 as well as the impacts on specific travel modes, such as cruise ships. In a rapid assessment of the impacts of COVID-19, Gössling et al. (2020) reported that as of 31 March, 2020, over 90% of the world's population were in countries with some level of international travel restrictions and many of these countries also had some degree of restrictions on internal movement, including limited air travel and stay at home orders. Moreover, for some intercontinental tourism markets, the extent to which transit regions, such as major aviation hubs, are open to tourists is extremely important for destination access. When access and mobility is removed the effects are substantial. In terms of the accommodation sector for the week of 21 March, 2020, STR (2020) reported that in comparison to the same week in 2019, guest numbers had declined by 50% or more, in virtually

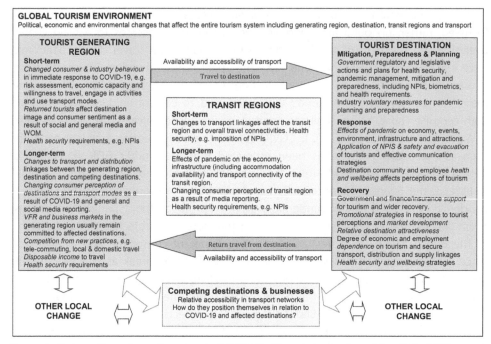

Figure 1. System dimensions of tourism in COVID-19 affected destinations (after Hall, 2005).

all countries. The IATA (14 April, 2020), scenario of the effects of COVID-19 was that full year air passenger revenues would be 55% below 2019, while traffic falls 48%.

The capacity for a destination to respond to pandemics has been framed in terms of the stages of a disaster, which also highlights the extent to which destinations and industry may learn from prior pandemic or other disaster experiences and adapt accordingly (Hall & Prayag, 2020). Significantly, the systems approach highlights that how destination and industry responds is also affected in the long-term by competing destinations and businesses. This may have implications for recovery trajectories as some destinations may deliberately position themselves in low cost terms, with little concern for externalities (e.g., introducing a second wave into the resident population), in order to try and increase visitor numbers and employment possibilities as soon as possible. Others, such as Hawaii (McAvoy, 2020), may continue to attempt to restrict arrivals and hotel reservations to reduce the potential of a second wave of infections or, like Singapore, introduce new third party audited cleaning standards to rebuild traveller trust (Singapore Tourism Board, 2020).

COVID-19 may provide an impetus for individuals to transform their travel behaviours, however transformation of the tourism system is extremely difficult. On one hand, resilience research in tourism highlights the need to consider biodiversity conservation and climate change imperatives in combination with destination models that seek to reduce leakage, enhance wellbeing, and better capture and distribute tourism value (Gössling et al., 2016). In contrast, there are strong business and political voices that the economy, including tourism, should be opened up as soon as possible so that it can return to "normal", and that affected businesses should receive substantial government financial support without necessarily having to meet any sustainability or climate change mitigation requirements (Harvey, 2020; Kaufman, 2020). For example, the International Air Transport Association (IATA) has called on the International Civil Aviation Organisation (ICAO) to amend the carbon offsetting and reduction scheme for international aviation (CORSIA), or risk airlines pulling out of the scheme (Topham & Harvey, 2020). Clearly, without appropriate regulatory and governance settings to ensure that government bailouts of the tourism industry, including the aviation and transport sector, come with environmental caveats, the prospects for an immediate major paradigm or third-order change with respect to more sustainable forms of tourism becomes all the more unlikely (Hall, 2011a). At time of writing, there is no evidence that sustainability is a consideration within massive economic stimulus package in the US, and some policy analysts fear the proposed US Green Deal will be scuttled by the pandemic (Williamson, 2020). In contrast, several European environment ministers have call for plans prepared for the European Green Deal to be central in rebuilding European economies (Vetter, 2020) and the New Zealand Climate Change Commission has written to the New Zealand government asking it to apply a "climate change lens" to their post-Covid-19 economic stimulation package noting that the wrong investments will make people and costly infrastructure more exposed to damage from climate change (Gibson, 2020). Nevertheless, the ongoing existential threats posed by climate change, biodiversity loss and exposure to zoonotic disease means that the demands for more sustainable forms of tourism will not fade away (Scott & Gössling, 2015; Scott et al., 2019).

So if not transformed what will the tourism recovery look like?

Pandemics are unlike many other disasters and crises that tourism has experienced. Although, as with any other disaster related tourism attention-issue cycle, consumer and industry confidence will rise and fall in relation to media reporting on the impacts of COVID-19 (Gössling et al., 2020) and government interventions to boost the economy, the capacity for recovery of the tourism system is fundamentally affected by the imposition of NPIs because of the extent to which they restrict mobility (Ryu et al., 2020). And without mobility there is no tourism. In addition to general disease and heath communication strategies and measures, e.g. hygiene measures, four broad areas of NPIs that affect tourism can be identified: a) social distancing; b) curbs on crowding; c) restrictions on domestic and international travel; and, d) quarantine requirements (Fong et al., 2020; Ryu et al., 2020). Social distancing requirements reduce the capacity of hospitality operations, such as restaurants, to be able to host guests while the most extreme measures require the closure of operations so as to prevent social contact. Bans on public gatherings and closure of public places, affect tourist activities but they also limit the hosting of events, meetings and conferences. Figure 2 provides an overview of the factors and interventions driving tourism change and recovery in relation to COVID-19.

Restrictions on travel have been widely enacted in response to COVID-19. In many countries, this has meant stay a home orders and domestic restrictions on moving between jurisdictions except for permanent residents and essential services and closure of international borders except to returning nationals and permanent residents/ visa holders (Wilson et al., 2020). Removal of such restrictions will be integral to

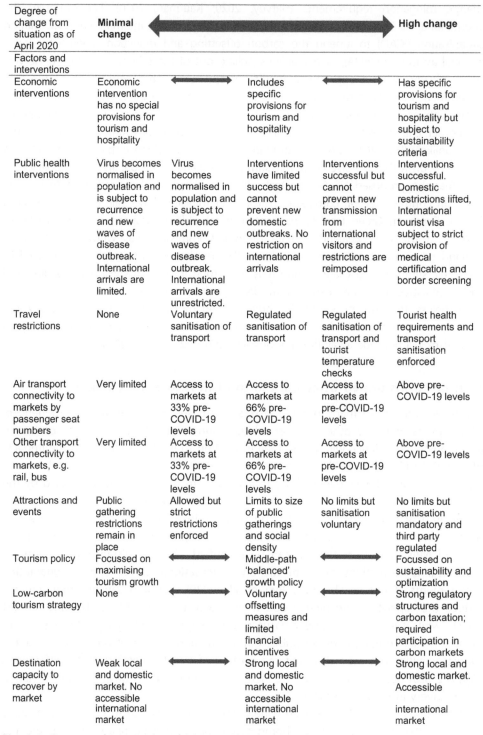

Degree of change from situation as of April 2020	Minimal change				High change
Factors and interventions					
Economic interventions	Economic intervention has no special provisions for tourism and hospitality	←→	Includes specific provisions for tourism and hospitality	←→	Has specific provisions for tourism and hospitality but subject to sustainability criteria
Public health interventions	Virus becomes normalised in population and is subject to recurrence and new waves of disease outbreak. International arrivals are limited.	Virus becomes normalised in population and is subject to recurrence and new waves of disease outbreak. International arrivals are unrestricted.	Interventions have limited success but cannot prevent new domestic outbreaks. No restriction on international arrivals	Interventions successful but cannot prevent new transmission from international visitors and restrictions are reimposed	Interventions successful. Domestic restrictions lifted, International tourist visa subject to strict provision of medical certification and border screening
Travel restrictions	None	Voluntary sanitisation of transport	Regulated sanitisation of transport	Regulated sanitisation of transport and tourist temperature checks	Tourist health requirements and transport sanitisation enforced
Air transport connectivity to markets by passenger seat numbers	Very limited	Access to markets at 33% pre-COVID-19 levels	Access to markets at 66% pre-COVID-19 levels	Access to markets at pre-COVID-19 levels	Above pre-COVID-19 levels
Other transport connectivity to markets, e.g. rail, bus	Very limited	Access to markets at 33% pre-COVID-19 levels	Access to markets at 66% pre-COVID-19 levels	Access to markets at pre-COVID-19 levels	Above pre-COVID-19 levels
Attractions and events	Public gathering restrictions remain in place	Allowed but strict restrictions enforced	Limits to size of public gatherings and social density	No limits but sanitisation voluntary	No limits but sanitisation mandatory and third party regulated
Tourism policy	Focussed on maximising tourism growth	←→	Middle-path 'balanced' growth policy	←→	Focussed on sustainability and optimization
Low-carbon tourism strategy	None	←→	Voluntary offsetting measures and limited financial incentives	←→	Strong regulatory structures and carbon taxation; required participation in carbon markets
Destination capacity to recover by market	Weak local and domestic market. No accessible international market	←→	Strong local and domestic market. No accessible international market	←→	Strong local and domestic market. Accessible international market

Figure 2. Factors and interventions driving tourism change and recovery.

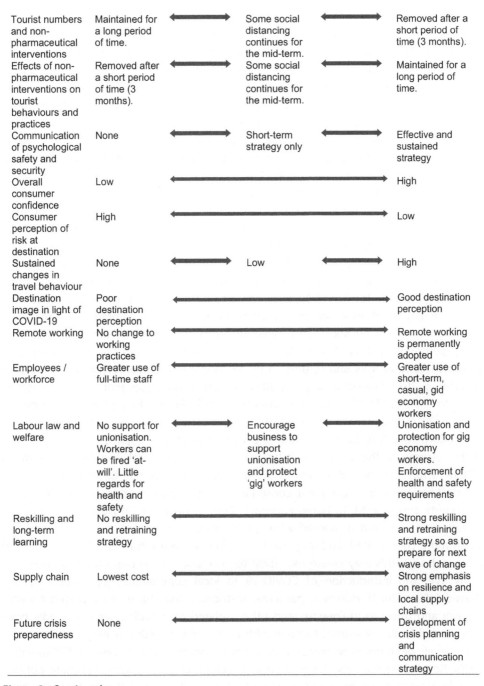

Tourist numbers and non-pharmaceutical interventions	Maintained for a long period of time.	⟷ Some social distancing continues for the mid-term.	⟷ Removed after a short period of time (3 months).
Effects of non-pharmaceutical interventions on tourist behaviours and practices	Removed after a short period of time (3 months).	⟷ Some social distancing continues for the mid-term.	⟷ Maintained for a long period of time.
Communication of psychological safety and security	None	⟷ Short-term strategy only	⟷ Effective and sustained strategy
Overall consumer confidence	Low	⟷	High
Consumer perception of risk at destination	High	⟷	Low
Sustained changes in travel behaviour	None	⟷ Low	⟷ High
Destination image in light of COVID-19	Poor destination perception	⟷	Good destination perception
Remote working	No change to working practices	⟷	Remote working is permanently adopted
Employees / workforce	Greater use of full-time staff	⟷	Greater use of short-term, casual, gid economy workers
Labour law and welfare	No support for unionisation. Workers can be fired 'at-will'. Little regards for health and safety	⟷ Encourage business to support unionisation and protect 'gig' workers	⟷ Unionisation and protection for gig economy workers. Enforcement of health and safety requirements
Reskilling and long-term learning	No reskilling and retraining strategy	⟷	Strong reskilling and retraining strategy so as to prepare for next wave of change
Supply chain	Lowest cost	⟷	Strong emphasis on resilience and local supply chains
Future crisis preparedness	None	⟷	Development of crisis planning and communication strategy

Figure 2. Continued.

tourism recovery. Initially, this will be at a domestic level, especially in locations in which new cases are no longer being recorded (Worthington, 2020). For most countries the tourism restart will occur domestically and likely include domestic tourism promotion campaigns to encourage people to travel locally and regionally to stimulate the economy and for continued Covid-19 surveillance and safety. There will be an uneven recovery as some markets will be aligned with early phases of restarting tourism. An emphasis on saving local restaurants, VFR tourism to reconnect with loved ones, essential business travel, and parks and nature tourism where physical distancing can be accomplished, will be the focus of initial tourism revival. Seniors tourism will continue to be discouraged or restricted because of vulnerability to Covid-19. Sports and events tourism will be restricted until a vaccine is developed and widely deployed, a timeline estimated to be 12-18 months (Liu et al., 2020). China, South Korea and other countries that were among the earliest to experience the pandemic are now entering this cautious restart phase, and their experience will be closely observed by the rest of the world (Koty, 2020).

International travel is more complicated in terms of restart, and for most countries will be dependent on the timing of vaccine development and mass deployment as well as uncertain traveller anxieties and the existence of at-risk market segments, such as senior tourists. Initially, we are likely see a scenario in which medical certificates (for either being clear of, or having had the disease), clearances and vaccination, when eventually available for COVID-19, may come to be required for entry and for tourists visas being granted, in a similar fashion to what is already commonplace for some destinations or for the short-term movement of natural persons for employment or study purposes (Hall, 2011b). Such a situation is not new, and has long been used with respect to arrivals and returns to many countries (Centers for Disease Control & Prevention, 2017; Freedman & Chen, 2019), including processes that have been developed to manage MERS and other disease threats among Hajj pilgrims (Aleeban & Mackey, 2016; Alqahtani et al., 2019). What will potentially be new is the inclusions of such information into biometric data and visa and passport applications. A significant likely outcome of this process will be that some international destinations in which COVID-19 has become naturalised in the general population will be identified as high risk destinations with subsequent consequences for risk perceptions, travel insurance, biosecurity and re-entry to home countries. Continuing to be an Australian, European or American snowbird or nomad who spends winters in warmer destinations will be much more complicated, and may not be feasible for senior travellers for a number of years, although this may create new local tourism and leisure opportunities once concerns over the introduction of COVID-19 to local communities by visitors can be allayed (Wales, 2020). However, particular restrictions may have to be placed on ecotourism and travel to indigenous and other isolated communities who not only have very limited health resources to cope with any new outbreak but may also have had lower levels of community exposure to previous waves of the disease (ABC Kimberley, 2020). Restrictions may also be needed to protect highly endangered primate populations from visitors in some cases (Dunay et al., 2018; Hall, 2007). Where countries have managed to restrict entry of COVID-19 via border control measures it is also possible that such countries may enter into bilateral and multilateral agreements to encourage and manage international tourism as part of broader biosecurity agreements and protocols.

A specific requirement of some countries NPIs with respect to international travel and COVID-19 has been a mandatory quarantine period for international arrivals

(Gong et al., 2020). Similar measures have been introduced in certain cases in previous pandemics (Caballero-Anthony, 2005; Hamre et al., 2003; Van Wagner, 2008). The presence of such measures will be a disincentive to all but the most determined traveller. However, there may also be longer term behavioural implications for those that experience quarantine as well as social isolation in their own homes (Brooks et al., 2020; Ho et al., 2020). Significantly, Brooks et al. (2020) report that quarantine experiences can lead some individuals to avoid public spaces and crowded public places for many months after quarantine has finished.

The overall recovery of tourist numbers will primarily be determined by the interplay of economic and health interventions that include travel restrictions. Individual country decisions cannot enable the restoration of international aviation and other transport services when other markets remain closed (IATA, 2020). As the pandemic wanes, the world will be poorer and more divided, which is not a recipe for a strong rebound in the tourism economy let alone a coordinated, strategic effort to transform it toward sustainability. There will be strong political and industry pressures to "restart" the economy as quickly as possible and generate employment in a period of major global economic recession (i.e., the International Monetary Fund (2020) projects the global economy to contract −3% in 2020, much worse than during the 2008–09 financial crisis). The mass unemployment caused by the unprecedented rapid shutdown of economies in many leading outbound tourism countries will work against international travel for cost, risks of a second wave, and likely patriotic messages to rebuild the domestic economy. The latter includes the promotion of domestic tourism as a tool by some governments to reduce leakage from the national economy and to bolster regional centres and rural economies. Such a policy focus may have the unintended outcome of creating new sustainable tourism trajectories with positive implications for lower emissions, place-based economic development and travel and tourism practices. Critically, the depth and length of the recession/depression will be the main driver of such socio-economic change. However, the domestic focus on tourism is likely to only be temporary while constraints on mobility remain in place.

The transformative possibilities are questionable under conditions when the focus of most governments will be to generate jobs, even lower paid, casual and part-time positions, in order to reduce unemployment rates. The optimistic take for those seeking the adoption of more sustainable, local, and environmentally friendly forms of tourism will be that COVID-19 and the economic effects of the measures to curb its spread will provide an exogenous shock that will change tourism related public policy. As (Greener, 2001, p.136) noted with respect to policy learning, 'The oil price and currency shocks of the early 1970s helped create hostile economic conditions which made it possible for advocates of monetarism to question the ability of Keynesians to run the economy". However, as he also went on to note, 'policy makers may well realise that existing policy is not working, but be afraid of the political implications of appearing to learn from the error' (Greener, 2001, p.140). Indeed, if existing policy instruments were substantially altered and new one's adopted, 'policymakers could then be accused of making a policy "U-turn" and abandoning their values' (Hall, 2011a, p.662). Instead, in a search for employment generation and government income to pay the costs of industry bail-outs the wealth inequalities associated with market-led neoliberalization, the emissions of the hyper-mobile and the rundown of natural capital may be set to continue and even enhanced. As Sparke and Anguelov (2012) commented, 'Like the systems that use biometrics to facilitate fast-track clearance at borders and airport checkpoints, the privatization and individualization of high-speed disease surveillance also represents an adaptation of state administration in the interests of ... a subset of privileged consumers who can afford the technological fast lanes and VIP services'.

Conclusion

Pandemics are clearly an important issue for society and tourism, even if many of their potential threats and the actions needed to manage them have either been ignored or forgotten by the public, industry and politicians at large. As noted in the introduction, infectious diseases and pandemics have long exerted important selective forces on politics, communities, the economy, and human's attitudes to nature (Wolfe et al., 2007). And to which we can now add the recovery of the tourism. Resilience research tells us that drivers for transformation and change can move up and down the different panarchical levels of the tourism system (Hall et al., 2018). This means that in some locations, individuals, businesses and communities will seek to transform and change the way in which tourism and hospitality is conducted (Nunn, 2020; Tourism From Zero, 2020). However, in others it may be business as usual or the deregulation, anti-unionisation, and commitment to carbon will get even worse. But the future of tourism on the planet is based on the absolute impact of tourism and tourists not the relative effects, meaning that even if there is greater efficiency at the level of the individual it makes not one jot of improvement to global sustainability if the focus remains on growth and that the level of growth is greater than efficiency gains (Gössling et al., 2016; Hall, 2015). At the global scale transforming tourism requires the commitment of global and international organisations and here the selective forces of the COVID-19 pandemic have become as much a justification for the selfish nationalism of some national leaders, and the racism associated with it, as it is for those who believe that sustainability solutions, including in relation to the tourism system, requires multilateral responses. For example, on the day that the official global death toll from COVID-19 passed 125,000 people, President Trump announced the withdrawal of funding to the World Health Organization (Smith, 2020).

Although there was substantial political and institutional interest, the global financial crisis of 2008-09 did not result in a new era of green growth and the global trajectories of tourism emissions and numbers only continued to increase. While the COVID-19 crisis has resulted in, quite literally, parked carbon assets in the form of cruise ships and aircraft, and a substantial drop in emissions, the possibilities of that being sustained, even at much more moderate levels, are doubtful. As Lauri Myllyvirta, lead analyst for the Centre for Research on Energy and Clean Air, said: 'The big question is whether government stimulus measures lead to pollution levels rebounding above the levels before the crisis, like happened after the 2008 financial crisis' (quoted in Ellis-Petersen et al., 2020). There is substantial concern in the renewable energy sector that the pandemic, low oil prices, and economic recovery packages will derail the economics for solar and wind projects needed to green the electricity grid (National Law Review, 2020; Maisch, 2020;

Fox-Penner, 2020), which is foundational to lowering emissions in accommodation and electrified ground transport. Furthermore, even if airlines and cruise ship companies are not bailed out the assets still exist and will provide opportunities for budget and low-cost ventures at a time of cheap capital and demands for employment generation and yet further deregulation. In such a situation, the rebound effects of tourism recovery may place the industry on an even more unsustainable trajectory, especially if aircraft and ship manufacturers keep adding capacity to the global tourism system on the basis of their very own projections of demand.

Changes to tourism as a result of COVID-19 will be uneven in space and time. While some destinations will undoubtedly reconsider the nature of their tourism industry and focus more on local and more sustainable forms of tourism, without substantial institutional and governmental interventions, which are currently overwhelmed with saving lives and creating conditions to restart domestic economies and education systems, the juggernaut that is international tourism will roll on. For many destinations and governments, especially those with authoritarian tendencies, the focus on tourism will be business-as-usual. Furthermore, there are not enough stakeholders in the tourism sector that question the sustainability of success defined by growth in visitor numbers or increases in material consumption to expect transformational change driven from within. The resilience of growth in international tourism numbers and the capacity of tourism to rebound from crisis has long been recognised. Given the likelihood that the recovery from COVID-19 may well eventually be more of the same, be careful what you wish for.

Disclsoure statement

No potential conflict of interest was reported by the author(s).

ORCID

C. Michael Hall http://orcid.org/0000-0002-7734-4587

References

ABC Kimberley. (2020, March 19). 'Stay home': Kimberley coronavirus tension prompts call to restrict 'unsafe' tourists. *ABC News*. https://www.abc.net.au/news/2020-03-19/coronavirus-call-to-protect-aboriginal-communities-from-tourists/12066254.

Aleeban, M., & Mackey, T. K. (2016). Global health and visa policy reform to address dangers of Hajj during summer seasons. *Frontiers in Public Health, 4*, 280. https://doi.org/10.3389/fpubh.2016.00280

Allen, T., Murray, K. A., Zambrana-Torrelio, C., Morse, S. S., Rondinini, C., Di Marco, M., Breit, N., Olival, K. J., & Daszak, P. (2017). Global hotspots and correlates of emerging zoonotic diseases. *Nature Communications, 8*(1), 1124. https://doi.org/10.1038/s41467-017-00923-8

Alqahtani, A. S., Tashani, M., Heywood, A. E., Booy, R., Rashid, H., & Wiley, K. E. (2019). Exploring Australian Hajj tour operators' knowledge and practices regarding pilgrims' health risks: A qualitative study. *JMIR Public Health and Surveillance, 5*(2), e10960. https://doi.org/10.2196/10960

Al-Tawfiq, J. A., Zumla, A., & Memish, Z. A. (2014). Travel implications of emerging coronaviruses: SARS and MERS-CoV. *Travel Medicine and Infectious Disease, 12*(5), 422–428. https://doi.org/10.1016/j.tmaid.2014.06.007

Aratani, L. (2020, March 24). Coughing while Asian': Living in fear as racism feeds off coronavirus panic. The Guardian. https://www.theguardian.com/world/2020/mar/24/coronavirus-us-asian-americans-racism

Baldwin, R., & Weder di Mauro, B. (2020). Introduction. In R. Baldwin & B. Weder di Mauro (Eds.), *Economics in the time of COVID-19* (pp. 1–30). CEPR Press.

Barry, J. M. (2004). The site of origin of the 1918 influenza pandemic and its public health implications. *Journal of Translational Medicine, 2*(1), 3.

Bell, C., Devarajan, S., & Gersbach, H. (2003). *The long-run economic costs of AIDS: Theory and an application to South Africa*. The World Bank.

Berry, M., Gamieldien, J., & Fielding, B. C. (2015). Identification of new respiratory viruses in the new millennium. *Viruses, 7*(3), 996–1019. https://doi.org/10.3390/v7030996

Bijl, D., & Schellekens, H. (2011). The sponsored pandemic of the Mexican flu? *International Journal of Risk & Safety in Medicine, 23*(2), 73–79. https://doi.org/10.3233/JRS-2011-0523

Bloom, D. E., & Cadarette, D. (2019). Infectious Disease Threats in the 21st Century: Strengthening the Global Response. Frontiers in immunology, 10, 549. doi:10.3389/fimmu.2019.00549

Brooks, S. K., Webster, R. K., Smith, L. E., Woodland, L., Wessely, S., Greenberg, N., & Rubin, G. J. (2020). The psychological impact of quarantine and how to reduce it: Rapid review of the evidence. *The Lancet, 395*(10227), 912–920. https://doi.org/10.1016/S0140-6736(20)30460-8

Browne, A., St-Onge Ahmad, S., Beck, C. R., & Nguyen-Van-Tam, J. S. (2016). The roles of transportation and transportation hubs in the propagation of influenza and coronaviruses: A systematic review. *Journal of Travel Medicine, 23*(1), tav002. https://doi.org/10.1093/jtm/tav002

Buranyi. (2020, April 10). The WHO v coronavirus: Why it can't handle the pandemic. The Guardian. https://www.theguardian.com/news/2020/apr/10/world-health-organization-who-v-coronavirus-why-it-cant-handle-pandemic

Burkle, F. M. Jr, (2006). Globalization and disasters: Issues of public health, state capacity and political action. *Journal of International Affairs, 59*(2), 231–265.

Caballero-Anthony, M. (2005). SARS in Asia: Crisis, vulnerabilities, and regional responses. *Asian Survey, 45*(3), 475–495. https://doi.org/10.1525/as.2005.45.3.475

Centers for Disease Control and Prevention. (2017). *CDC yellow book 2018: Health information for international travel*. Oxford University Press.

Chen, G. L., Lau, Y. F., Lamirande, E. W., McCall, A. W., & Subbarao, K. (2011). Seasonal influenza infection and live vaccine prime for a response to the 2009 pandemic H1N1 vaccine. *Proceedings of the National Academy of Sciences, 108*(3), 1140–1145. https://doi.org/10.1073/pnas.1009908108

Chmura, A. A. (2017). *Evaluating risks of paramyxovirus and coronavirus emergence in China* [PhD thesis]. Kingston University.

Clay, K., Lewis, J., & Severnini, E. (2018). Pollution, infectious disease, and mortality: Evidence from the 1918 Spanish influenza pandemic. *The Journal of Economic History, 78*(4), 1179–1209. https://doi.org/10.1017/S002205071800058X

Cohen, D., & Carter, P. (2010). WHO and the pandemic flu "conspiracies. *BMJ, 340*(jun03 4), c2912–c2912. https://doi.org/10.1136/bmj.c2912

Coker, R., Rushton, J., Mounier-Jack, S., Karimuribo, E., Lutumba, P., Kambarage, D., Pfeiffer, D. U., Stark, K., & Rweyemamu, M. (2011). Towards a conceptual framework to support one-health research for policy on emerging zoonoses. *The Lancet Infectious Diseases, 11*(4), 326–331. https://doi.org/10.1016/S1473-3099(10)70312-1

Connolly, C., Keil, R., & Ali, S. H. (2020). Extended urbanisation and the spatialities of infectious disease: Demographic change, infrastructure and governance. *Urban Studies,* https://doi.org/10.1177/0042098020910873.

Crosby, A. W. (2004). *Ecological imperialism: The biological expansion of Europe, 900-1900.* (2nd ed.). Cambridge University Press.

Davidson, H. (2020, April 13). Chinese official: Claims of racial targeting are 'reasonable concerns. The Guardian.https://www.theguardian.com/world/2020/apr/13/chinese-official-claims-racial-targeting-reasonable-concerns

Davies, W. (2020, March 24). The last global crisis didn't change the world. But this one could. The Guardian. https://www.theguardian.com/commentisfree/2020/mar/24/coronavirus-crisis-change-world-financial-global-capitalism

Devaux, C. A., Mediannikov, O., Medkour, H., & Raoult, D. (2019). Infectious disease risk across the growing human-non human primate interface: A review of the evidence. *Frontiers in Public Health, 7,* 305.

Diamond, J. M. (1998). *Guns, germs and steel: A short history of everybody for the last 13,000 years.* Random House.

Doshi, P. (2010). Pandemic influenza: Severity must be taken into account. *The Journal of Infectious Diseases, 201*(9), 1444–1445. https://doi.org/10.1086/651701

Dunay, E., Apakupakul, K., Leard, S., Palmer, J. L., & Deem, S. L. (2018). Pathogen transmission from humans to great apes is a growing threat to primate conservation. *EcoHealth, 15*(1), 148–162.

Durrheim, D. N., Crowcroft, N. S., & Blumberg, L. H. (2019). Is the global measles resurgence a "public health emergency of international concern"? *International Journal of Infectious Diseases, 83,* 95–97. https://doi.org/10.1016/j.ijid.2019.04.016

Ebi, K. L., Frumkin, H., & Hess, J. J. (2017a). Protecting and promoting population health in the context of climate and other global environmental changes. *Anthropocene, 19,* 1–12. https://doi.org/10.1016/j.ancene.2017.07.001

Ebi, K. L., Ogden, N. H., Semenza, J. C., & Woodward, A. (2017b). Detecting and attributing health burdens to climate change. *Environmental Health Perspectives, 125*(8), 085004. https://doi.org/10.1289/EHP1509

Ellis-Petersen, H., Ratcliffe, R., Cowie, S., Daniels, J. P., & Kuo, L. (2020, April 11). It's positively alpine!' Disbelief in big cities as air pollution falls. The Guardian. https://www.theguardian.com/environment/2020/apr/11/positively-alpine-disbelief-air-pollution-falls-lockdown-coronavirus.

Fauci, A. S., & Morens, D. M. (2012). The perpetual challenge of infectious diseases. *New England Journal of Medicine, 366*(5), 454–461. https://doi.org/10.1056/NEJMra1108296

Fong, M. W., Gao, H., Wong, J. Y., Xiao, J., Shiu, E. Y., Ryu, S., & Cowling, B. J. (2020). Nonpharmaceutical measures for pandemic influenza in nonhealthcare settings - social distancing measures. *Emerging Infectious Diseases, 26*(5), 976–984. https://doi.org/10.3201/eid2605.190995

Fox-Penner, P. (2020). COVID-19 will slow the global shift to renewable energy, but can't stop it. https://theconversation.com/covid-19-will-slow-the-global-shift-to-renewable-energy-but-cant-stop-it-133499

Freedman, D. O., & Chen, L. H. (2019). Vaccines for international travel. *Mayo Clinic Proceedings, 94*(11), 2314–2339. https://doi.org/10.1016/j.mayocp.2019.02.025

Gibson, E. (2020). Climate Commission warns high-emissions coronavirus spend-up will spark new crisis. https://www.stuff.co.nz/environment/climate-news/120969030/climate-change-commission-warns-dont-compound-covid19-with-climate-crisis

Gills, B. (2020). Deep restoration: From the great implosion to the great awakening. *Globalizations*. https://doi.org/10.1080/14747731.2020.1748364

Girard, M. P., Tam, J. S., Assossou, O. M., & Kieny, M. P. (2010). The 2009 A (H1N1) influenza virus pandemic: A review. *Vaccine*, *28*(31), 4895–4902. https://doi.org/10.1016/j.vaccine.2010.05.031

Gong, B., Zhang, S., Yuan, L., & Chen, K. Z. (2020). A balance act: Minimizing economic loss while controlling novel coronavirus pneumonia. *Journal of Chinese Governance*. https://doi.org/10.1080/23812346.2020.1741940.

Gössling, S., Ring, A., Dwyer, L., Andersson, A. C., & Hall, C. M. (2016). Optimizing or maximizing growth? A challenge for sustainable tourism. *Journal of Sustainable Tourism*, *24*(4), 527–548. https://doi.org/10.1080/09669582.2015.1085869

Gössling, S., Scott, D., & Hall, C. M. (2020). Pandemics, tourism and global change: A rapid assessment of COVID-19. *Journal of Sustainable Tourism*. 10.1080/09669582.2020.1758708

Greener, I. (2001). Social learning and macroeconomic policy in Britain. *Journal of Public Policy*, *21*(2), 133–152. https://doi.org/10.1017/S0143814X01001076

Greger, M. (2007). The human/animal interface: Emergence and resurgence of zoonotic infectious diseases. *Critical Reviews in Microbiology*, *33*(4), 243–299. https://doi.org/10.1080/10408410701647594

Gubler, D. J. (2012). The economic burden of dengue. *The American Journal of Tropical Medicine and Hygiene*, *86*(5), 743–744. https://doi.org/10.4269/ajtmh.2012.12-0157

Hall, C. M. (2005). *Tourism: Rethinking the social science of mobility*. Pearson.

Hall, C. M. (2007). Biosecurity and ecotourism. In J. Higham (Ed.), *Critical issues in ecotourism: Understanding a complex tourism phenomenon* (pp. 102–116). Elsevier.

Hall, C. M. (2011a). Policy learning and policy failure in sustainable tourism governance: From first-and second-order to third-order change? *Journal of Sustainable Tourism*, *19*(4-5), 649–671. https://doi.org/10.1080/09669582.2011.555555

Hall, C. M. (2011b). Biosecurity, tourism and mobility: Institutional arrangements for managing tourism-related biological invasions. *Journal of Policy Research in Tourism, Leisure and Events*, *3*(3), 256–280. https://doi.org/10.1080/19407963.2011.576868

Hall, C. M. (2015). Economic greenwash: On the absurdity of tourism and green growth. In M.V. Reddy & K. Wilkes (Eds.), *Tourism in the green economy* (pp. 361–380). Routledge.

Hall, C. M. (2020). Biological invasion, biosecurity, tourism, and globalisation. In D. Timothy (Ed.), *Handbook of globalisation and tourism* (pp.114–125). Edward Elgar.

Hall, C. M., & Prayag, G. (2020). Earthquakes and tourism: Impacts, responses and resilience – An introduction. In C.M. Hall & G. Prayag (Eds.), *Tourism and earthquakes*. Channel View.

Hall, C. M., Prayag, G., & Amore, A. (2018). *Tourism and resilience*. Channel View.

Hamre, J. J., Young, J. G., & Shurtleff, M. (2003). From smallpox to SARS: Is the past prologue? *The Journal of Law, Medicine & Ethics*, *31*(4_suppl), 13–20. https://doi.org/10.1111/j.1748-720X.2003.tb00740.x

Harvey, F. (2020, April 1). Financial help for airlines 'should come with strict climate conditions. *The Guardian*. https://www.theguardian.com/environment/2020/apr/01/financial-help-for-airlines-should-come-with-strict-climate-conditions

Hinchliffe, S. (2015). More than one world, more than one health: Re-configuring interspecies health. *Social Science & Medicine*, *129*, 28–35. https://doi.org/10.1016/j.socscimed.2014.07.007

Ho, C. S., Chee, C. Y., & Ho, R. C. (2020). Mental health strategies to combat the psychological impact of COVID-19 beyond paranoia and panic. *Annals of the Academy of Medicine, Singapore*, *49*(1), 1–6.

Huber, C., Finelli, L., & Stevens, W. (2018). The economic and social burden of the 2014 Ebola outbreak in West Africa. *The Journal of Infectious Diseases*, *218*(Supplement_5), S698–S704. https://doi.org/10.1093/infdis/jiy213

IATA. (2020). Remarks of Alexandre de Juniac at the IATA Media Briefing on COVID-19, 14 April 2020. *Pressroom*, https://www.iata.org/en/pressroom/speeches/2020-04-14-01/

International Monetary Fund. (2020). World Economic Outlook, April 2020 – The Great Lockdown. https://www.imf.org/en/Publications/WEO/Issues/2020/04/14/weo-april-2020

Iuliano, A. D., Roguski, K. M., Chang, H. H., Muscatello, D. J., Palekar, R., Tempia, S., Cohen, C., Gran, J. M., Schanzer, D., Cowling, B. J., Wu, P., Kyncl, J., Ang, L. W., Park, M., Redlberger-Fritz, M., Yu, H., Espenhain, L., Krishnan, A., Emukule, G., … Mustaquim, D. (2018). Estimates of global seasonal influenza-associated respiratory mortality: A modelling study. *The Lancet*, *391*(10127), 1285–1300.

Jian, M. (2020, February 26). Xi Jinping has buried the truth about coronavirus. The Guardian. https://www.theguardian.com/commentisfree/2020/feb/26/the-reaction-to-the-outbreak-has-revealed-the-unreceonstructed-despotism-of-the-chinese-state

Jonas, O. (2014). *Pandemic risk*. World Bank.

Joo, H., Maskery, B. A., Berro, A. D., Rotz, L. D., Lee, Y. K., & Brown, C. M. (2019). Economic impact of the 2015 MERS outbreak on the Republic of Korea's tourism-related industries. *Health Security*, *17*(2), 100–108. https://doi.org/10.1089/hs.2018.0115

Kaufman, A. C. (2020, March 24). If we bail out airlines, it better come with climate rules. *National Observer*. https://www.nationalobserver.com/2020/03/24/news/if-we-bail-out-airlines-it-better-come-climate-rules.

Kavanagh, M. M., Thirumurthy, H., Katz, R., Ebi, K. L., Beyrer, C., Headley, J., Holmes, C. B., Collins, C., & Gostin, L. O. (2019/2020). Ending pandemics: U.S. foreign policy to mitigate today's major killers, tomorrow's outbreaks, and the health impacts of climate change. *Journal of International Affairs*, *73*(1), 49–68.

Kirchgaessner, S., Graham-Harrison, E., & Kuo, L. (2020, April 11). China clamping down on coronavirus research, deleted pages suggest. The Observer. https://www.theguardian.com/world/2020/apr/11/china-clamping-down-on-coronavirus-research-deleted-pages-suggest

Kirigia, J. M., Sambo, L. G., Yokouide, A., Soumbey-Alley, E., Muthuri, L. K., & Kirigia, D. G. (2009). Economic burden of cholera in the WHO African region. *BMC International Health and Human Rights*, *9*(1), 8. https://doi.org/10.1186/1472-698X-9-8

Kogan, N. E., Bolon, I., Ray, N., Alcoba, G., Fernandez-Marquez, J. L., Müller, M. M., Mohanty, S. P., & Ruiz de Castañeda, R. (2019). Wet markets and food safety: TripAdvisor for improved global digital surveillance. *JMIR Public Health and Surveillance*, *5*(2), e11477. https://doi.org/10.2196/11477

Koty, A. C. (2020). Why China's COVID-19 stimulus will look different than in the past. https://www.china-briefing.com/news/chinas-stimulus-measures-after-covid-19-different-from-2008-financial-crisis/

Kozul-Wright, R., Barbosa, N. (2020). This crisis will change the world – for better, or worse. *Tribune Magazine*. https://tribunemag.co.uk/2020/03/coronavirus-will-change-the-world-for-better-or-worse.

Labonte, R., Mohindra, K., & Schrecker, T. (2011). The growing impact of globalization for health and public health practice. *Annual Review of Public Health*, *32*(1), 263–283. https://doi.org/10.1146/annurev-publhealth-031210-101225

Liu, C., Zhou, Q., Li, Y., Garner, L. V., Watkins, S. P., Carter, L. J., Smoot, J., Gregg, A. C., Daniels, A. D., Jervey, S., & Albaiu, D. (2020). Research and development on therapeutic agents and vaccines for COVID-19 and related human coronavirus diseases. *ACS Central Science*, *6*(3), 315–331. https://doi.org/10.1021/acscentsci.0c00272

Mair, S. (2020, March 30). What will the world be like after coronavirus? Four possible futures. *The Conversation*. https://theconversation.com/what-will-the-world-be-like-after-c … d=IwAR2wr9pzssSdBSxjaHaWba9-iHSF3fIYgZ9BVI1jAx_Y4YIXVAImcJcNdjM

Maisch, M. (2020). Covid-19 to wreck economics of new solar, wind projects. https://www.pv-magazine.com/2020/04/01/covid-19-to-wreck-economics-of-new-solar-wind-projects/

Maphanga, P. M., & Henama, U. S. (2019). The tourism impact of Ebola in Africa: Lessons on crisis management. *African Journal of Hospitality, Tourism and Leisure*, *8*(3). https://www.ajhtl.com/uploads/7/1/6/3/7163688/article_59_vol_8_3__2019.pdf

McAvoy, A. (2020). Hawaii looks to restrict lodging reservations to prevent visitor arrivals. *Associated Press*. https://skift.com/2020/04/14/hawaii-looks-to-restrict-lodging-reservations-to-prevent-visitor-arrivals/

McKibbin, W., & Fernando, R. (2020). The global macroeconomic impacts of COVID-19: Seven scenarios (CAMA Working paper 19/2020). Australian National University.

McKibbin, W. S., & Sidorenko, A. A. (2006). *Global macroeconomic consequences of pandemic influenza*. Crawford School of Public Policy, Centre for Applied Macroeconomic Analysis, Australian National University, and Lowy Institute for Foreign Policy.

McKinsey & Company. (2020). *Beyond coronavirus: The path to the next normal*. https://www.mckinsey.com/~/media/McKinsey/Industries/Healthcare%20Systems%20and%20Services/Our%20Insights/Beyond%20coronavirus%20The%20path%20to%20the%20next%20normal/Beyond-coronavirus-The-path-to-the-next-normal.ashx

Morens, D. M., Folkers, G. K., & Fauci, A. S. (2009). What is a pandemic? *The Journal of Infectious Diseases*, *200*(7), 1018–1021. https://doi.org/10.1086/644537

Morens, D. M., & Taubenberger, J. K. (2011). Pandemic influenza: Certain uncertainties. *Reviews in Medical Virology*, *21*(5), n/a–284. https://doi.org/10.1002/rmv.689

Mossoun, A., Pauly, M., Akoua-Koffi, C., Couacy-Hymann, E., Leendertz, S. A. J., Anoh, A. E., Gnoukpoho, A. H., Leendertz, F. H., & Schubert, G. (2015). Contact to non-human primates and risk factors for zoonotic disease emergence in the Taï region, Côte d'Ivoire. *EcoHealth*, *12*(4), 580–591. https://doi.org/10.1007/s10393-015-1056-x

Murray, C. J., Rosenfeld, L. C., Lim, S. S., Andrews, K. G., Foreman, K. J., Haring, D., Fullman, N., Naghavi, M., Lozano, R., & Lopez, A. D. (2012). Global malaria mortality between 1980 and 2010: A systematic analysis. *The Lancet*, *379*(9814), 413–431. https://doi.org/10.1016/S0140-6736(12)60034-8

Murray, C. J. L., Ortblad, K. F., Guinovart, C., Lim, S. S., Wolock, T. M., Roberts, D. A., Dansereau, E. A., Graetz, N., Barber, R. M., Brown, J. C., Wang, H., Duber, H. C., Naghavi, M., Dicker, D., Dandona, L., Salomon, J. A., Heuton, K. R., Foreman, K., Phillips, D. E., … Vos, T. (2014). Global, regional, and national incidence and mortality for HIV, tuberculosis, and malaria during 1990–2013: A systematic analysis for the Global Burden of Disease Study 2013. *The Lancet*, *384*(9947), 1005–1070.

Myers, S. S., Gaffikin, L., Golden, C. D., Ostfeld, R. S., Redford, K. H., Ricketts, T. H., Turner, W. R., & Osofsky, S. A. (2013). Human health impacts of ecosystem alteration. *Proceedings of the National Academy of Sciences of the United States of America.*, *110*(47), 18753–18760. https://doi.org/10.1073/pnas.1218656110

National Law Review. (2020). COVID-19 impact on US renewable energy projects. https://www.natlawreview.com/article/covid-19-impact-us-renewable-energy-projects.

Nicoll, A., & McKee, M. (2010). Moderate pandemic, not many dead—learning the right lessons in Europe from the 2009 pandemic. *European Journal of Public Health*, *20*(5), 486–488. https://doi.org/10.1093/eurpub/ckq114

Novelli, M., Burgess, L. G., Jones, A., Ritchie, B. W. (2018). No Ebola… still doomed'–The Ebola-induced tourism crisis. *Annals of Tourism Research*, *70*, 76–87. https://doi.org/10.1016/j.annals.2018.03.006

Nunn, J. (2020, April 14). Restaurants will never be the same after coronavirus – but that may be a good thing. The Guardian. https://www.theguardian.com/commentisfree/2020/apr/14/coronavirus-restaurants-pandemic-workers-communities-prices

Petersen, E., Wilson, M. E., Touch, S., McCloskey, B., Mwaba, P., Bates, M., Dar, O., Mattes, F., Kidd, M., Ippolito, G., Azhar, E. I., & Zumla, A. (2016). Rapid spread of Zika virus in the Americas – implications for public health preparedness for mass gatherings at the 2016 Brazil Olympic Games. *International Journal of Infectious Diseases*, *44*, 11–15. https://doi.org/10.1016/j.ijid.2016.02.001

Phillips, H., & Killingray, D. (2003). Introduction. In D. Killingray & H. Phillips (Eds.), *The Spanish influenza pandemic of 1918-1919: New perspectives*. Routledge.

Politico. (2020, March 19). Coronavirus will change the world permanently. Here's how. Politico Magazine. https://www.politico.com/news/magazine/2020/03/19/coronavirus-effect-economy-life-society-analysis-covid-135579

Putri, W. C., Muscatello, D. J., Stockwell, M. S., & Newall, A. T. (2018). Economic burden of seasonal influenza in the United States. *Vaccine, 36*(27), 3960–3966. https://doi.org/10.1016/j.vaccine.2018.05.057

Rothan, H. A., & Byrareddy, S. N. (2020). The epidemiology and pathogenesis of coronavirus disease (COVID-19) outbreak. *Journal of Autoimmunity, 109*, 102433. https://doi.org/10.1016/j.jaut.2020.102433

Rassy, D., & Smith, R. D. (2013). The economic impact of H1N1 on Mexico's tourist and pork sectors. *Health Economics, 22*(7), 824–834. https://doi.org/10.1002/hec.2862

Ryu, S., Gao, H., Wong, J. Y., Shiu, E. Y. C., Xiao, J., Fong, M. W., & Cowling, B. J. (2020). Nonpharmaceutical measures for pandemic influenza in nonhealthcare settings – international travel – related measures. *Emerging Infectious Diseases, 26*(5), 961–966. https://doi.org/10.3201/eid2605.190993

Safi, M. (2020, March 26). Egypt forces Guardian journalist to leave after coronavirus story. The Guardian. https://www.theguardian.com/world/2020/mar/26/egypt-forces-guardian-journalist-leave-coronavirus-story-ruth-michaelson

Scott, D., & Gössling, S. (2015). What could the next 40 years hold for global tourism? *Tourism Recreation Research, 40*(3), 269–285. https://doi.org/10.1080/02508281.2015.1075739

Scott, D., Hall, C. M., & Gössling, S. (2019). Global tourism vulnerability to climate change. *Annals of Tourism Research, 77*, 49–61. https://doi.org/10.1016/j.annals.2019.05.007

Shepard, D. S., Undurraga, E. A., Halasa, Y. A., & Stanaway, J. D. (2016). The global economic burden of dengue: A systematic analysis. *The Lancet Infectious Diseases, 16*(8), 935–941. https://doi.org/10.1016/S1473-3099(16)00146-8

Singapore Tourism Board. (2020). SG clean quality mark extended to tourism and lifestyle businesses as part of nationwide efforts to uplift sanitation and hygiene. https://www.stb.gov.sg/content/stb/en/media-centre/media-releases/sg-clean-qualitymarkextendedtotourismandlifestylebusinessesaspar.html.html

Siu, A., & Wong, Y. R. (2004). Economic impact of SARS: The case of Hong Kong. *Asian Economic Papers, 3*(1), 62–83. https://doi.org/10.1162/1535351041747996

Smith, D. (2020, April 15). Trump halts World Health Organization funding over coronavirus 'failure. The Guardian. https://www.theguardian.com/world/2020/apr/14/coronavirus-trump-halts-funding-to-world-health-organization

Sparke, M., & Anguelov, D. (2012). H1N1, globalization and the epidemiology of inequality. *Health & Place, 18*(4), 726–736. https://doi.org/10.1016/j.healthplace.2011.09.001

Sterpetti, A. V. (2020). Lessons learned during the COVID-19 virus pandemic. *Journal of the American College of Surgeons.* https://doi.org/10.1016/j.jamcollsurg.2020.03.018

STR. (2020). COVID-19: Hotel Industry Impact. https://str.com/data-insights-blog/coronavirus-hotel-industry-data-news

Taubenberger, J. K., & Morens, D. M. (2006). 1918 Influenza: The mother of all pandemics. *Emerging Infectious Diseases, 12*(1), 15–22. https://doi.org/10.3201/eid1209.05-0979

Thompson, R. A. (2013). Parasite zoonoses and wildlife: One health, spillover and human activity. *International Journal for Parasitology, 43*(12-13), 1079–1088. https://doi.org/10.1016/j.ijpara.2013.06.007

Topham, G., & Harvey, F. (2020, April 8). Airlines lobby to rewrite carbon deal in light of coronavirus. The Guardian. https://www.theguardian.com/business/2020/apr/08/airlines-lobby-to-rewrite-carbon-deal-due-to-coronavirus.

Tourism From Zero. (2020). #TourismFromZero Initiative. https://tourismfromzero.org/

Van Wagner, E. (2008). The practice of biosecurity in Canada: Public health legal preparedness and Toronto's SARS crisis. *Environment and Planning A: Economy and Space, 40*(7), 1647–1663. https://doi.org/10.1068/a40281

Vetter, D. (2020). Use lessons of COVID-19 to build a green recovery, say eu ministers. https://www.forbes.com/sites/davidrvetter/2020/04/13/use-lessons-of-covid-19-to-build-a-green-recovery-say-eu-ministers/#61c436b74335

Wales, S. (2020, March 25). Coronavirus border closures see thousands of grey nomads, travellers stuck in caravan parks. *ABC News.* https://www.abc.net.au/news/2020-03-25/coronavirus-sees-travellers-stuck-in-caravan-parks/12088742

Wallace, R. (2016). *Big farms make big flu: Dispatches on influenza, agribusiness, and the nature of science*. NYU Press.

Wallace, R., Chaves, L. F., Bergmann, L. R., Ayres, C., Hogerwerf, L., Kock, R., & Wallace, R. G. (2018). *Clear-cutting disease control: Capital-led deforestation, public health austerity, and vector-borne infection*. Springer.

Wang, L., Wang, Y., Jin, S., Wu, Z., Chin, D. P., Koplan, J. P., & Wilson, M. E. (2008). Emergence and control of infectious diseases in China. *The Lancet, 372*(9649), 1598–1605. https://doi.org/10.1016/S0140-6736(08)61365-3

Watson, R. (2011). European parliament criticises H1N1 pandemic response. *BMJ, 342*(feb01 1), d652–d652. https://doi.org/10.1136/bmj.d1639

Williamson, K. (2020). Goodbye, green new deal. *National Review*. https://www.nationalreview.com/2020/03/goodbye-green-new-deal/

Wilson, N., Barnard, L. T., & Baker, M. (2020). *Rationale for border control interventions and options to prevent or delay the arrival of Covid-19 in New Zealand: Final commissioned report for the New Zealand Ministry of Health*. Ministry of Health.

Wolfe, N. D., Dunavan, C. P., & Diamond, J. (2007). Origins of major human infectious diseases. *Nature, 447*(7142), 279–283. https://doi.org/10.1038/nature05775

World Health Organization (WHO). (2009). *Pandemic influenza preparedness and response: a WHO guidance document*. WHO

World Bank. (2012). *People, pathogens and our planet: Volume 2 – the economics of One Health*. World Bank.

World Bank. (2016). *The short-term economic costs of Zika in Latin America and the Caribbean (LCR)*. World Bank.

Worthington, B. (2020, April 13). The three tests Australia will need to pass before the coronavirus restrictions end. *ABC [Australian Broadcasting Corporation] News*. https://www.abc.net.au/news/2020-04-13/coronavirus-greg-hunt-lockdown-social-distancing-isolation/12144576

WTTC. (2018). *Impact of the Ebola epidemic on travel & tourism*. WTTC.

WTTC. (2020). Latest research from WTTC shows a 50% increase in jobs at risk in Travel & Tourism. https://www.wttc.org/about/media-centre/press-releases/press-releases/2020/latest-research-from-wttc-shows-an-increase-in-jobs-at-risk-in-travel-and-tourism

Wu, T., Perrings, C., Kinzig, A., Collins, J. P., Minteer, B. A., & Daszak, P. (2017). Economic growth, urbanization, globalization, and the risks of emerging infectious diseases in China: A review. *Ambio, 46*(1), 18–29. https://doi.org/10.1007/s13280-016-0809-2

Wu, X., Nethery, R. C., Sabath, B. M., Braun, D., & Dominici, F. (2020). Exposure to air pollution and COVID-19 mortality in the United States. *Preprint from medRxiv*. https://doi.org/10.1101/2020.04.05.20054502

Wu, Z., Lu, L., Du, J., Yang, L., Ren, X., Liu, B., Jiang, J., Yang, J., Dong, J., Sun, L., Zhu, Y., Li, Y., Zheng, D., Zhang, C., Su, H., Zheng, Y., Zhou, H., Zhu, G., Li, H., … Jin, Q. (2018). Comparative analysis of rodent and small mammal viromes to better understand the wildlife origin of emerging infectious diseases. *Microbiome, 6*(1), 1–14. https://doi.org/10.1186/s40168-018-0554-9

Zinsstag, J., Mackenzie, J. S., Jeggo, M., Heymann, D. L., Patz, J. A., & Daszak, P. (2012). Mainstreaming one health. *EcoHealth, 9*(2), 107–110. https://doi.org/10.1007/s10393-012-0772-8

A post COVID-19 future - tourism re-imagined and re-enabled

K. Michael Haywood

ABSTRACT

The urgent demands of the present necessitate an interrogation – a re-exploration and a re-envisioning of the future of tourism – of what has to change (and remain constant). Despite the crippling effects of COVID-19, new forms of solidarity are emerging that challenge the prevailing competitiveness ethic. While a transactional economic revival has to remain a top priority, progress will advance, so long as tourism becomes more transformational and transcendent. Discoveries of new methodologies for achieving the Sustainable Development Goals and versions of a Green New Deal, for example, are generating interest, notably 'mass flourishing' introduced in 'anti-fragile' ways. Utilizing a 'future-back' paradigm that demands deep-dive assessments and articulation of purpose, the gaps between 'what is' and 'what could or should be' are bound to close. Such undertakings represent a 'coming together' of all stakeholders, a role that academicians are urged to embrace, especially through action research, curriculum change and creation of 'daring classrooms'.

摘要

当前迫切需要对未来旅游的重新探索和再构想的审视——哪些一定会变化或不变化。尽管新冠肺炎引起"致残效应",但涌现的新式休戚与共挑战着主流的竞争性伦理。虽然交易经济的复苏仍为重中之重,但只要旅游变得更具变革性和超越性,其进步将会到来。例如发现实现可持续发展目标的新方法和各种"绿色新政"引起人们的兴趣,特别是以"抗脆弱"方式引入的"大众繁荣"。利用需要深度评估和明确目标的"未来-回溯"范式,"是什么"和"可能或应该是什么"之间的鸿沟必将弥合。这些工作表征所有利益相关者都聚合到一起,敦促学者们通过行动研究、课程改革和创建"大胆教室"纳入此角色。

The current reality – appreciated

The truth is that our finest moments are most likely to occur when we are feeling deeply uncomfortable, unhappy and unfulfilled. For it is only in such moments, propelled by our discomfort, that we are likely to step out of our ruts and start searching for different ways or truer answers. (M. Scott Peck)

This article has been republished with minor changes. These changes do not impact the academic content of the article.

In the wake of unfathomable carnage during the COVID-19 pandemic, a brutal decima-
tion in tourism-related employment became the new norm. Seventy-five million, and
counting, unemployed, many loaded with debt, unable to meet their financial obligations, thrust into poverty. Annual revenues for travel and tourism in excess of $2.1 tril-
lion lost forever (World Travel & Tourism Council, 2020), with hundreds of thousands
of small- to medium-sized enterprises worldwide ordered to close; thirty to forty percent never to be revived, with similar effects cascading throughout supply chains.

With movement of all kinds at a virtual standstill, aircraft parked, hotels shuttered,
it took a single month for the geography of a contagion to totally disrupt the geography of travel and tourism (Florida, 2020). Destinations reliant on tourism became
ghost towns. Cries of 'What's going on?' led to feelings of sheer hopelessness among
many, dramatized by 'Inner City Blues' (Marvin Gaye songs on YouTube).

WHY? An utter inability to learn from history. Ill-informed leaders. An unwillingness
to deputize knowledge. An asinine assault on, and denial of, facts and science. And, a
surfeit of procrastinated responses.

With no option but to capitulate, everyone pushed ‖ **PAUSE**, and took time to
comfort and care for each other, grieving, and sparing moments of time for sorrow
and expressions of sincere gratitude to those who unselfishly put their own lives in
harm's way.

Then came pensive reflection: Where do we go from here? What would, should, a
reset look like? Would disaster relief and corporate bailouts be enough, particularly for
hospitality and tourism workers? Would tightened borders and travel restrictions
remain, particularly as a deterrent to future climate- and food-related refugee migrations?

Forced to embrace current realities, everyone found themselves questioning priorities, how the trajectory of lifetime interests and pursuits would or should be altered,
including desires to travel, especially abroad. Amazing how catastrophic events suddenly alter perspectives and provide different outlooks on lives lived, and livelihoods
pursued. Current management practices, research projects, and curriculums somehow
seemed contextually irrelevant. Though some saw glimmers of hope: A Green New
Deal (Rifkin, 2019) conceivable; over-tourism receding; and, a global communitarian
spirit displacing a hyped-up ethic of competitiveness.

But, with competitiveness so deeply ingrained in human behaviour, would a sudden resurgence and pent-up demand for travel resurface? Were talks about an
emergence of stakeholder capitalism pre-mature (Govindarajan & Srivastava, 2020)?
In a frenzy to revive economies would governments and corporations act rashly
and irresponsibly? Suddenly it seemed as if the demand for more transformative
and conscious forms of travel and tourism (Pollock, 2020) might fall on deaf, or
tuned-out, ears. In fact, people like Geoffrey Lippman (SUN^X Malta) were becoming
increasingly apprehensive and adamant in their warnings about being sidetracked
in the collective quest to achieve the all-important Sustainable Development
Goals (SDGs).

Despite misgivings, there was hope: Futures don't have to be bleak, so long as
nations learn to act globally. While this cannot be predetermined, futures do allow for
aspirations; aspirations that can be coaxed into being, so long as 'can do' mindsets

prevail, conditions stabilize, and ready access to essential resources and vital community support systems remain.

Yet, with the prevalence of zoonotic viral threats remaining, scepticism seemed hard to quell. One thing became evident: COVID-19 ensured the irrelevance of assumptions once held in esteem. There were no other options but to follow Robert Frost down *'the road less travelled'*. Hoping it would make all the difference, and provide the gift of time, everyone sought to regroup and figure out how best to progress from mere surviving to thriving.

The current reality – breached

Civic pride provided the most heart-warming of responses to COVID-19, particularly in the way individuals and businesses came together to sing. Indeed one song, that could easily have come from the Beatles' playlist, *'Come together'* – signaled not just longing for family, friends and congenial gatherings, but for sociability and connectivity to people and places; and, more importantly, for a desire to reach out, support, and share – a desire to cooperate and bring the world back together again.

In this sense an over-arching theme emerged: *Survival is determined by those who adopt the path of solidarity, in comparison to those who continue to travel down the path of disunity* – solidarity, realized and recognized as both the inter-dependencies among communities, and the inter-dependencies among people and organizations within communities. Whereas in pre-COVID-19 times many communities-as-destinations demonstrated a love-hate relationship with tourism that was put into abeyance as they realized the importance of putting communities first.

While still a work-in-progress, it appears as if this reaffirmation actually represents a new beginning – a call for a moral form of capitalism (Young, 2003) that reinstates peoples' collective obligations to each other: Obligations companies, on one hand, have to communities and their citizens (Williams et al., 2007), though far above and beyond typical corporate social responsibilities (CSR); and, on the other hand, obligations that communities have to their citizens, including all forms of enterprises.

Pre-COVID, solidarity within communities-as-destinations had always been an uphill battle. Despite the prevalence of public/private partnerships in support of marketing and branding, the management of communities-as-destinations had remained an allusion, few destination marketing organizations (DMOs) saw fit to adopt a much-needed managerial focus of tourism, particularly as a cluster. According to the Destination Next Futures Study (Destinations International, 2019) there was the intention that this should change. Now, in a post-COVID world, many people are calling for a more profound reassessment.

Solidarity means pulling people out of the comfort of their fiefdoms, so they can act with the big picture in mind. And this applies to many tourism scholars and NGOs who, for example, continue to point to lack of progress on the sustainability front, while ignoring the degree of progress underway, and how well-advanced many enterprises are in their commitments and actions. A criticism that also applies to a general lack of understanding of hospitality and tourism-related businesses, and the progressive managerial practices that have been adopted.

Then again, ignorance manifests itself in all directions. Just as was learned from the collapse of the banks and other institutions during the 2007–8 financial crisis, the consequences of weak governance can be hard to spot until it's too late. Underpinning weak governance is ignorance – not knowing, not seeing, and not acting. Weak governance is not just about missed opportunities; it can leave in its wake a collapse of confidence throughout an entire industry or community, and chip away at public confidence – a lesson that a renewed sense of solidarity can help resolve and rebuild.

As a means of coming together on these and related issues, Steven Covey (2004) once said: To move from effectiveness to greatness (fulfillment, passionate execution, and significant contribution), it's essential we find our voice and inspire others to find theirs. Thanks to virtual community forums this is being accomplished today. Participating in these forums is essential if communities-as-destinations are to continue their journeys down the path of solidarity, so long as people recognize their commonalities while downplaying their differences – a frame of mind that reflects a willingness to have 'opposable minds' (Martin, 2009).

As is certain today: Everyone is in the same boat, staring down similar dilemmas and conundrums in an uncertain world. We are all in search of desirable, feasible and viable options, even though commerciality may not always win out when win-win outcomes are desirable but become contentious. Every business and every person is learning how to re-adapt on-the-fly; everyone working hard to achieve more solid financial footings, concerned about helping employees re-adjust, attempting to regain customers and visitors, many of whom remain skittish, hard-wired to physically distance themselves from infectious others.

With no one able to conceive of re-building to pre-COVID levels of demand (Bariso, 2020), and all visitor-serving enterprises knowing they have no other choice but to adapt to new gathering guidelines, business models are bound to change (Ritter & Pedersen, 2020). Domestic tourism seems destined to dominate, with the vast majority of customers or visitors likely to come from nearby catchment areas, everyone being told to be very selective about the number of trips they make.

With consumer habits and behaviors in flux, virtually everyone is in the midst of figuring out how tourism should be re-conceived, a process that will remain frustratingly complex due to a substantial lack of funds and extreme austerity measures. Though an agonizing present continues to consume everyday thoughts and actions, it's too early to assume that a clearer post-COVID vision is emerging. Yet, dreams and aspirations have a way of sneaking through. After all, people conquer despair through stories of hope. By looking for inspiration people find their imaginations (Reeves & Fuller, 2020).

With new start-ups (Blank, 2018) being re-imagined, the need for extreme creativity is becoming more notable, with renewed interest in 'design thinking' (Liedtka, 2018) coming to the fore. Of course, with the massive co-creation efforts to find suitable vaccines requiring mass immunization garnering the most attention and fascination, the more pressing issue is the resurrection of our global economies, our communities-as-destinations. Given the dire need for a financial or economic resurgence, 'mass flourishing' has become the other go-to requirement. As a consequence, growing interest is being given to Phelps' (2013) work on this topic that won him the Nobel Prize in economics.

The possibilities are exciting, except for the fact that many people have expressed caution and have conditions: The first being adoption of a sustainability platform, such as those proposed by Raworth (2020) and Rifkin (2019); and, the second being the need to inculcate 'anti-fragility' so as to avoid being blindsided again. This concept, proffered by Taleb (2013), reveals how companies, countries and communities can ameliorate the physical shocks (associated with both climate risk and pandemics, for example), while escalating ingenuity and entrepreneurial spirit.

While these references represent esoteric versions of what has to transpire in situ, what is still missing are echoes of Franklin D. Roosevelt's pleas during the Great Depression for 'bold, persistent experimentation' (to get his New Deal underway), and a refreshing call for Enlightenment Now (Pinker, 2018). As for 'do-ability' Rippley (2009), in 'Unthinkable – Lessons from Survivors', provides needed reassurance. Following unthinkable disasters, she reported that peoples' preparedness and frames-of-mind, in rebound situations, are not based simply on being 'stoic and resilient', but on ensuring that everyone has fact-driven knowledge about disasters, is fully aware of the warning signs and, in particular, knows how to respond effectively and urgently.

Indeed, if there is one thing that has been learned from the pandemic, it's preparedness and brutal honesty, even though these lessons are only gradually becoming self-evident. Even so, those communities-as-destinations likely to be quick off the mark will be those that have already placed a premium on travel and tourism, with government officials and business leaders recognizing them not as afterthoughts, or as a tertiary economic sector, but equivalent to a special kind of innovative and entrepreneurial cluster, even as a new form of a super-cluster (Brookfield Institute, 2017).

Without going into the special characteristics of tourism as a super-cluster, one stands out: The desire and ability to work collaboratively, as a collective unit. So far, the possibilities for recovery and getting on with the herculean task of reviving communities-as-destinations seems more plausible when coupled with a whole-of-government approach (OECD, 2017), particularly in regard to creating much needed functional, emotional, life-enhancing and social value (Almquist et al., 2016), with due consideration given to 'shared value' (Porter & Kramer, 2011).

Of course, as communities re-emerge from crisis situations, it's impossible to predict or forecast outcomes. Post-COVID scenarios may help re-imagine 'future-forward' worlds. But what's more useful is a 'future-back' approach (Johnson & Suskewicz, 2020). When efforts are made to articulate and achieve aspirations, a 'future-back' approach helps identify any capability gaps that need to be closed. Future-back protocols depend, therefore, on having clarity as to a journey's starting points, that is to say, clear knowledge as to the prevailing situation or state. Only then can strategies (Porter, 1996) be identified and used in order to close the gaps between 'what is' and 'what could or should be'. Future-back protocols are also useful when operational philosophes and values shift. While post-COVID renewal definitely calls for higher degrees of cooperativeness, changing the competitiveness ethic, promulgated by World Economic Forum (2019), is bound to remain a challenge, even though the WEF index factors in efforts to improve sustainability.

Despite this ethic, however, most individual communities-as-destinations rarely view themselves as being in a competitive game, the exception being in regard to attracting the M.I.C.E. markets. As unique entities offering different types of value to very different sets of visitors, the most astute remain content trying to be the very best they can be. The concept they are implicitly trying to master, is the art of 'presence', in the full meaning of the concept (Senge et al., 2004), with 'presence' activated through astonishing incremental improvements: First, to the design of public places, parks and streetscapes, exemplified through the efforts of organizations like Project for Public Places. Second, by encouraging and showing how every public-serving entity can become an enticing destination in and of themselves. Third, by individuals revitalizing and beautifying their neighborhoods and communities. And then, by relying on marketing, with its focus on segmentation and differentiation, to portray and promote their uniqueness.

What's most evident is that change has been afoot for a while. Having an industry persona, the 't' in tourism has always represented that which is transactional. Post-COVID, however, this emphasis is being down-played. In fact, more travelers, visitors, and residents are revealing their desires to have the 't' be reflective of that which is, or should be, transformational and transcendent. While such a call is intended to highlight that which is human, humane and hospitable, it's as if the 'our' in tourism is begging for fuller expression: Our communities, our lives, and the quality of our lives; our livelihoods, our cultures, our natural endowments and environments.

A revival of this emphasis will come as welcome news to those who have been extremely critical of travel and tourism's excesses and negative impacts, but a further coming together among all stakeholders is required if communities-as-destinations are to unlock the status quo, to re-shape, re-vitalize, re-strategize, and re-structure them in accord with renewed purpose.

As proponents of community-based tourism attest: When others are inspired to find their 'voice', a range of fresh perspectives emerge. Industry insiders, even academicians, may consider themselves to be the 'big picture' tourism experts, but they aren't. In fact, in their impulsiveness, they tend to overly generalize and jump to conclusions about what's right, wrong or misguided. As Greene (2018) reminds us: 'Your first impulse should always be to find the evidence that disconfirms your most cherished beliefs and those of others. That is true science.' If tourism is to become 'smarter', to be managed better, then everyone's contextual realities and versions of 'smarter', must be considered, and eventually realized in one way or another.

One cherished belief is the notion of 'mass tourism'. As a descriptor for scale, there can be no doubt: Tourism is a mass phenomenon. But when juxtaposed with tourism, it implies 'commodified', 'undifferentiated', 'uniform' and often leads to a conjunctive event bias (Parrish, 2020) that only presupposes either preferable or disastrous outcomes,

Travel and tourism are universal, but no two places, no two people, are alike. In fact, every community is a destination of sort. Every person who visits a destination does so for highly individualized, personal, business or leisure-related reasons, most often with no ill effects. Yet, so often, critics only dwell only on those places with concentrated numbers of vacationers, then chastise tourism for causing immeasurable harm, even though there are many ways to mitigate and manage over-capacity situations (Pullman & Rodgers, 2010).

In reality, the vast majority of communities-as-destinations suffer from under-tourism – a problem that is bound to become an even more serious as economies tank and poverty levels ratchet up. Just as many in the business world have been asked to better serve those at 'the Bottom of the Pyramid' (Simanis, 2012) – a stretch goal if there ever was one – it seems more astute if solutions to under-tourism issues could be found. By improving the worthiness of these destinations, the crowds would disperse; and, tourism could be called upon to revive livelihoods and economies.

Pre-COVID, far too little effort was made to clarify the role of tourism within communities. Rather than articulate tourism's purpose, which represents a higher-order calling (Sinek et al., 2017), the explicit desire was only to maximize arrivals, lengths-of-stay, and expenditures. Now, with greater interest being given to creating life-affirming and social value (Almquist et al., 2016), the opportunities to formulate tourism in more transformational and transcendent ways (in this instance, helping alleviate poverty) is far more likely to succeed.

As many enterprises have discovered, working toward purpose (Blount & Leinwand, 2020) takes time and involves a process requiring considerable contemplation and deliberation. Prompted by the song 'Imagine' and with examples drawn from the social side of innovation (Nicholls et al., 2015), it's amazing how many aspirational seeds can be planted, nurtured and germinated, so good work can begin and a readiness for transformation can be assessed.

This is why more and more community-as-destinations are starting to undertake deep-dive assessments (Horwath, 2009) – probes that really help determine what is happening, what isn't; what's flourishing, what isn't; what's possible, what isn't … why and why not. When invaluable first-hand strategic information is generated by those with 'skin-in-the-game' – people from the community, including those involved in, and affected by, travel and tourism activities – the essentiality of travel and tourism to communities-as-destinations can be determined, not simply as a driver of economic prosperity, but as a means to honor, strengthen, and celebrate the notion of what it means to be a community.

Looked at in another way, until COVID-19 struck, few people within communities ever realized how dependent they were on tourism, until it utterly ceased to exist. What a momentous realization that has been! No wonder everyone is now beside themselves, wondering how to become wiser, not just in advocacy for travel and tourism, but in their collective responsibility to re-imagine tourism's purpose, principles and transformative possibilities, especially when approached with curiosity and appreciation for the unbounded and unprejudiced aspirations of others.

In continuing to manage ahead, such an undertaking has to be a collaborative effort. Indeed, by working diligently for the betterment of communities and their worthiness as compelling destinations, everyone is engaged in wayfinding, figuring out how to co-create and capture greater value for the benefit of all; how to re-design and deliver delightful and singularly unique experiences as they begin again to legitimize and honor tourism as a flourishing super-cluster that has unlimited potential to contribute to everyone's social, cultural, and economic 'wellth'. Smarter tourism *by design* (Haywood, 2020)

The academic community – engaged

In staring down the *'road less travelled'* no one can afford to drift aimlessly along the *'path of disunity'*. Finding strength along the *'path of solidarity'* requires, if not demands, that the academic community work even harder in their collective efforts to inculcate *'anti-fragile'* properties into the operations of our communities-as-destinations, so that sustainable versions of *'mass flourishing'* can be achieved.

As every community struggles in their attempts to re-learn how to astonish and resonate as destinations, detailed attention has to be focused on determining exactly what it means, and what it will take, for communities to be compelling, for hospitality to be inspiring, for sustainability to be comprehensive, for shared value to be achieved, and for innovation to be collaborative. No mean feat.

To assist communities in these and other endeavors, the professoriate is obliged to re-evaluate their role during these times of crisis. Utilizing a 'future-back' approach, there is an urgent need to determine, and ask, how skills and knowledge can be put to better use:

- Beyond moving classes on-line, cancelling travel programs, and helping students adjust, colleges and universities have unparalleled opportunities, to help communities cope. Nothing is working as it once did; there is a scramble to adjust to new realities and rapidly changing circumstances. New and radical thinking, new and different approaches to problem-solving are required (Naidoo, 2020). Trust and confidence, knowledge, information, and research are in short-supply. Find out what's needed, and make it so.
- Universities have always played a leadership role in society. The role of leaders is to call people to reason. If this is lacking, so is trust. In another sense, leadership has to be seen as 'management practiced well' (Mintzberg, 2009). What this entails may surprise some in that managerial effectiveness, considered in context, is at once reflective, collaborative (analytic and worldly) and integrative – the very traits that everyone reveres and expects students to have upon graduation, though employers are also on the look-out for those who are energetic and proactive. Why is this worth mentioning? Simply to say, many colleges and universities are not doing a good enough job in being leaders, and in ensuring these managerial traits are being learned and applied. Herein lie opportunities to get students involved in community projects – destination assessments being but one form of action research. Far more can also be done to create 'daring classrooms', to update curriculums to meet current needs in a post-COVID world (Tufano, 2020), and to work hand-in-glove with organizations to create meaningful, project-based internships and job opportunities.
- Remaining on the topic of management, the purpose and mandates of DMOs have to be updated. The academic community, in conjunction with other professional groups, can play more formidable roles in informing mayors, municipal

governments, and city officials about the importance of managing communities-as-destinations: How to establish a purpose for communities-as-destinations; improve governance; formulate tourism strategies and make revisions to policies that reflect purpose and principles. Similarly for those who operate on the frontlines: Embroiled as they are in day-to-day operational demands, many welcome holistic perspectives in regard to visitor and resident (host) expectations; perfecting their understanding of comprehensive sustainability, inspired hospitality, and creation of more equitable shared value.

- Small- to medium-sized businesses are in desperate need of assistance, especially in regard to the development of reconfigured survival and entrepreneurial skills to meet new exigencies. Some universities offer consulting services to SMEs, but far more could be done in regard to tourism-related enterprises.

- Based on discussions, within various sectors of tourism, there is a high degree of interest in building cultures of experimentation, improving decision making in uncertain times, initiating conscious social change, applying social innovation to tourism, making public place and space improvements, and forming Tourism Innovation Hubs or Labs, some of which could be located at universities.

- Faculty need to be engaged in communities to help identify, study and resolve many critical issues. Not only does this refer to promoting and leading action research projects and destination assessments, but also to a need to disseminate needed information in easily accessible ways (notably on topics such as risk, finance, safety, employee relations). It might help if faculty read more widely in the field of management. Publications of merit include the Harvard Business Review, Strategy and Business, the blogs and newsletters from Destination Think, City Lab, McKinsey and the Boston Consulting Group, for example, particularly their coverage of COVID-19.

- 'Come together' will remain a rallying cry, but it's unlikely local communities-as-destinations are going to come to you. Faculty must initiate these relationships if you haven't already done so. The most successful university/industry partnerships have always been those in which there is mutual respect for each other's contributions, everyone encouraging each other to work for the common good. To be seen in this light, it helps when everyone gets involved in each other's realm of interest, participates in industry associations, attends 'real' gatherings/conferences, and goes out of their way to network, network, network.

Tourism becomes smarter *by design* when the revival and revitalization of all communities-as-destinations takes center stage and is taken seriously. Progress on this front is not just a matter of modernizing a rather moribund competitiveness ethic, though it helps to understand the interplay between competition and cooperation (Hoffmann et al., 2018). Rather what's essential is a better appreciation for tourism's transformative and transcendent possibilities that through a combination of economic, technological, scientific, cultural, and organizational advancement can continue to transform lives and raise standards of living for decades to come.

If there is an upside to crises like COVID-19, it's the on-going, intense scrutiny of the past, and exploration of more desirable futures. With communities-as-destinations now pulling together to better understand 'what is' through deep-dive destination assessments, so as to determine 'what could and should be', the whole process of figuring out how to transition toward transformation can proceed.

Other than what's already been mentioned, imagine faculty from all disciplines coming together to create a science of progress (Collison & Cowin, 2019) applied to tourism. The ramifications in regard to continuing development of all 'future back' initiatives could be immense. Imagine the progress that could be made in the efforts to engender 'anti-fragile' forms of mass flourishing and achievement of the all-important SDGs.

'Carpe diem', seize the day.

Disclosure statement

No potential conflict of interest was reported by the author(s).

References

Almquist, E., Senior, J., & Bloch, N. (2016, September). The elements of value. *Harvard Business Review*, 46–53. https://hbr.org/2016/09/the-elements-of-value

Bariso, J. (2020, April 13). Bill Gates says the coronavirus will change life forever. *Inc.* https://www.inc.com/justin-bariso/bill-gates-says-coronavirus-will-change-life-forever-heres-how-to-adapt.html

Blank, S. (2018, September 5). *Is the lean start-up dead?* https://steveblank.com/2018/09/05/is-the-lean-startup-dead/

Blount, S., & Leinwand, P. (2020, April 10). In a crisis, companies must know their purpose. *Strategy and Business.* https://www.strategy-business.com/article/In-a-crisis-companies-must-know-their-purpose?gko=5a4a1

Brookfield Institute. (2017, April 17). *Superclusters – Lessons and opportunities for Canada.* https://brookfieldinstitute.ca/wp-content/uploads/Superclusters-Lessons-Opportunities-for-Canada-BIIE-ICP.pdf

Collison, P., & Cowin, T. (2019, July). We need a new science of progress. *The Atlantic.* https://www.theatlantic.com/science/archive/2019/07/we-need-new-science-progress/594946/

Covey, S. (2004). *The 8th habit.* The Free Press.

Destinations International. (2019). *Destination next futures study.* https://destinationsinternational.org/sites/default/master/files/Destinations%20International%20DestinationNEXT%202019.2.pdf

Florida, R. (2020, April 3). The geography of the coronavirus. *City Lab.* https://www.citylab.com/equity/2020/04/coronavirus-spread-map-city-urban-density-suburbs-rural-data/609394/

Greene, R. (2018). *The laws of human nature.* Viking Press.

Govindarajan, V., & Srivastava, A. (2020, January 30). We are nowhere near stakeholder capitalism. *Harvard Business Review.* https://hbr.org/2020/01/we-are-nowhere-near-stakeholder-capitalism

Haywood, M. (2020). *Astonish! Smarter tourism by design* (Forthcoming).

Hoffmann, W., Lavie, D., Reuer, J. J., & Shipilov, A. (2018). The interplay of competition and cooperation. *Strategic Management Journal*, *39*(12), 3033–3052. https://doi.org/10.1002/smj.2965

Horwath, R. (2009). *Deep dive*. Greenleaf Press.

Johnson, M., & Suskewicz, J. (2020). *Lead from the future*. HBR Press.

Liedtka, J. (2018, October). Why design thinking works. *Harvard Business Review*. https://hbr.org/2018/09/why-design-thinking-works

Martin, R. (2009). *The opposable mind*. HBS Publications.

Mintzberg, H. (2009). *Managing*. Prentice Hall.

Naidoo, E. (2020, April 21). Successful battle strategies to beat COVID-19. *Harvard Business School, Working Knowledge*. https://hbswk.hbs.edu/item/7-winning-war-strategies-to-beat-covid-19

Nicholls, A., Simon, J., & Whelan, C. (Eds). (2015). *New frontiers in social innovation research*. Palgrave Macmillan.

Parrish, S. (2020, April). Unlikely optimism – Conjunctive events bias. *Farnham Street*. https://fs.blog/2020/04/conjunctive-events-bias/

Phelps, E. (2013). *Mass flourishing*. Princeton University Press.

Pinker, S. (2018). *Enlightenment Now – The case for reason, science, humanism and progress*. Penguin Books.

Pollock, A. (2020). *Conscious travel*. http://www.conscious.travel/

Porter, M. (1996, November/December). What is strategy? *Harvard Business Review*. https://hbr.org/1996/11/what-is-strategy

Porter, M., & Kramer, M. (2011, January/February). Creating shared value. *Harvard Business Review*. https://hbr.org/2011/01/the-big-idea-creating-shared-value

Pullman, M., & Rodgers, S. (2010). Capacity management for hospitality and tourism. *International Journal of Hospitality Management, 29*(1), 177–187.

OECD. (2017). *Fostering a whole of government approach to tourism*. https://www.oecd.org/cfe/tourism/Tourism-meeting-Issues-Paper-on-Fostering-a-Whole-of-Government-Approach-in-Tourism.pdf

Raworth, K. (2020). The Amsterdam city doughnut – A tool for transformative action. *Doughnut Economics Action Lab*. https://assets.website-files.com/5d26d80e8836af2d12ed1269/5e8d99c337b3af64c790372f_20200416-AMS-portrait-EN-Spread-web-420x210mm.pdf

Reeves, M., & Fuller, J. (2020, April 10). We need imagination more than ever. *Harvard Business Review*. https://hbr.org/2020/04/we-need-imagination-now-more-than-ever

Rifkin, J. (2019). *The green new deal*. St Martin's Press.

Rippley, A. (2009). *The unthinkable*. Random House.

Ritter, T., & Pedersen, C. (2020, April 15). Assessing coronavirus's impact on your business model. *Harvard Business Review*. https://hbr.org/2020/04/assessing-coronaviruss-impact-on-your-business-model

Senge, P., Scharmer, C., Jaworski, J., & Flowers, B. (2004). *Presence – Human purpose and the field of the future*. Doubleday.

Simanis, E. (2012, June). Reality check at the bottom of the pyramid. *Harvard Business Review*. https://hbr.org/2012/06/reality-check-at-the-bottom-of-the-pyramid

Sinek, P., Mead, D., & Docker, P. (2017). *Find your why*. Penguin.

Taleb, N. (2013). *Antifragile – Things that gain from disorder*. Random House.

Tufano, P. (2020, March 11). A bolder vision for business schools. *Harvard Business Review*. https://hbr.org/2020/03/a-bolder-vision-for-business-schools

Young, S. (2003). *Moral capitalism*. Berrett-Publishers.

Williams, P., Gill, A., & Ponsford, I. (2007). Corporate social responsibility at tourism destinations: Toward a social license to operate. *Tourism Review International, 11*(2), 133–144.

World Economic Forum. (2019). *The travel and tourism competiveness report*. http://www3.weforum.org/docs/WEF_TTCR_2019.pdf

World Travel and Tourism Council. (2020). *The domino effect of COVID-19*. https://wttc.org/News-Article/Latest-research-from-WTTC-shows-a-50-percentage-increase-in-jobs-at-risk-in-Travel-and-Tourism

Socialising tourism for social and ecological justice after COVID-19

Freya Higgins-Desbiolles

ABSTRACT

The COVID-19 pandemic of 2019–2020 has the potential to transform the tourism industry as well as the context in which it operates. This global crisis in which travel, tourism, hospitality and events have been shut down in many parts of the world, provides an opportunity to uncover the possibilities in this historic transformative moment. A critical tourism analysis of these events briefly uncovers the ways in which tourism has supported neoliberal injustices and exploitation. The COVID-19 pandemic crisis may offer a rare and invaluable opportunity to rethink and reset tourism toward a better pathway for the future. 'Responsible' approaches to tourism alone, however, will not offer sufficient capacity to enable such a reset. Instead, such a vision requires a community-centred tourism framework that redefines and reorients tourism based on the rights and interests of local communities and local peoples. Theoretically, such an approach includes a way tourism could be 'socialised' by being recentred on the public good. This is essential for tourism to be made accountable to social and ecological limits of the planet.

摘要

2019–2020年的新型冠状病毒肺炎（COVID-19）疫情有可能改变旅游业及其运营环境。这场使得全世界许多地方的旅游、旅行、接待和事件活动都被迫停止的全球危机，提供了一个在这历史性变革时刻发现各种可能性的机会。对这些情况的批判性旅游学分析简要地揭示了旅游业对新自由主义下的不公正和剥削的支持方式。新冠（COVID-19）疫情危机提供了一个难能可贵的契机，让大家可以进行反思，让旅游业重新走上更好的、面向未来的发展路径。然而，仅有"负责任"旅游方式这一种途径还不能为实现这种调整提供足够的能力。相反，这种愿景需要以社区为中心的旅游框架，即根据当地社区和当地人民的权益来对旅游业进行重新的定义和定位。理论上，这个框架包括了通过重新关注旅游的公益性而使其实现"社会化"的方式。对于让旅游业承担起对地球社会和生态极限的责任而言，这是至关重要的。

Introduction

The arrival of COVID-19 has been viewed as a watershed moment. In terms of tourism, the unthinkable has happened. While previously the industry was grappling with concerns of overtourism, we suddenly have been catapulted into a collapse of the entire sector. This is because the tourism, hospitality and events sectors have been crippled by government efforts to curtail and control the pandemic. Borders have been shut, travel has been banned, social activities have been curtailed, and people have been told to stay in their homes. In undertaking these actions, governments around the world are trying to strike a balance between keeping their economy going and preventing dangerous levels of unemployment and deprivation, while trying to respond to dire public health imperatives that are necessary to prevent collapse of health systems and mass deaths. In such difficult circumstances, it is clear that one era is passing, but it is too early to identify what will emerge. In a world where growing inequality has led to massive numbers of vulnerable populations, it is clear that the COVID-19 pandemic and actions to address its spread are impacting these vulnerable communities in disproportionate and deadly fashion (see, for instance, Evelyn, 2020; Kazmin, 2020).

While it might seem that the concerns of tourism are of secondary importance in the middle of such a global crisis, this may not necessarily be true due to the significant role tourism has come to play in the economic growth and development plans of many nations. International and domestic tourism have been effectively shut down as unfortunate casualties of the crisis. The World Tourism Organization (UNWTO, 2020a) claimed 'ours has been the sector hardest hit by the crisis' and has proposed an agenda for recovery. The rising unemployment, the economic damage and instability, and the unprecedented size of government interventions to address the economic crisis all point to travel, tourism and hospitality being pillars of many economies around the world.

Tourism and its affiliated industries have experienced numerous crises before, including the 2005 tsunami in the Indian Ocean region, the impacts of the '9/11' terrorist attacks on the USA in 2001 and previous pandemics such as the 2009 swine flu crisis. These experiences have seen the development of toolkits of risk management, risk mitigation and crisis recovery (e.g. Lynch, 2004) as well as a recent focus on resilience (Hall et al., 2018). However, the COVID-19 pandemic is of a much higher magnitude than previous crises because of its global scale and the widespread shutdown of travel, businesses and life activities.

It is predictable that industries such as tourism will be keen to get back to business as usual and are seeking shares of government stimulus packages and interventions. For example, one of the world's largest tourism multinational companies, Tui, is seeking aid from both the UK and German governments and has indicated it is slashing costs in its global operations (Hancock, 2020). Airlines around the world are presenting themselves as facets of critical transport infrastructures and also seeking government bailouts and packages. Qantas Airlines in Australia is one example that has been heavily criticized for harsh cuts to its staff while seeking government aid despite record profits in past years (Butler, 2020). An Organisation of Economic Cooperation and Development (OECD) report noted: 'The industry is now focussed on ensuring business continuity despite the crisis' (OECD, 2020, p. 6). The question this raises is: what balance will be struck between supporting tourism multinationals, tourism small business, vulnerable tourism workers and destination communities in an environment that challenges the very foundations of current economic systems?

Despite such efforts to enable a return to 'business as usual' as soon as possible, some have identified this as a transformational moment opening up possibilities for resetting tourism. The UNWTO has seized on this rhetoric:

> Tourism has the potential to recover and once again establish itself as a key part of national economies and of the wider sustainable development agenda.

> This crisis may also offer a unique opportunity to shape the sector to ensure it not only grows but it grows better, with inclusivity, sustainability and responsibility prioritized. Furthermore, to build for the future, special attention should be placed on building resilience and on promoting sustainability at all levels (UNWTO, 2020b, p. 33).

We should be critically aware of the purposes of such rhetoric from an industry that has resisted substantial change despite widespread criticism and even protests and unrest (Cassinger, 2019; Higgins-Desbiolles, 2008). This analysis addresses the problem of tourism in neoliberal contexts and offers a case study of the cruise tourism sector to illustrate how this results in ecological and social injustices. Following thinking that the crisis offers an opportunity to reset tourism, this article reveals the false promise of 'responsible' tourism solutions. Instead, this work builds on recent analysis of redefining and reorienting tourism and offers new insights for rethinking tourism by 'socialising' it. Such efforts are important in this moment when possibilities for transformative change are made possible through the pandemic's disruption to business as usual.

Methods

This work is a conceptual analysis that draws on the theory, methods and insights of critical tourism epistemologies. At such a moment as this, critical tourism approaches are vital. Tribe argued 'critical research is essential for setting an agenda for ethical management, governance and coexistence with the wider world' (Tribe, 2008, p. 245). Despite his influential leadership in the tourism academy and the expansion of critical, responsible and transformative approaches to tourism in both the academy and without, we are in fact little closer to placing tourism in a context of sustainable, ethical and just coexistence with the wider world. Before the COVID-19 induced shutdown, the relentless drive for growth, profits and expansion were evident in most parts of the world; overtourism was one well noted symptom (Higgins-Desbiolles, 2018b; Jover & Díaz-Parra, 2020). A critical question to consider is what opportunities does the COVID-19 interruption of business as usual offer to us to rethink tourism?

In her book on *Anti-crisis*, Roitman noted that Marin Luther King had planned a speech titled 'Normalcy-Never Again' for his Lincoln Memorial Speech of 28 August 1963 (Roitman, 2014, p. 1). He amended the speech at the last minute to the 'I have a dream' theme we have come to know well. This decision to emphasise the more positive narrative has inspired many in the decades that have followed. But from a critical perspective, the demand for 'normalcy-never again' may have had the emancipatory, anti-oppression and justice focus that was required to address profound injustices against the Black American community in that moment of civil rights action and continuing to this day (see Evelyn, 2020). This article draws inspiration from these words 'normalcy-never again' to make a key point that approaches of 'responsible tourism' that are increasingly being touted in this moment will not be sufficient to create the fundamental changes that are required to reorient tourism away from the injustices and oppressions it currently enacts and supports.

Roitman studied crisis narratives in her *Anti-crisis* work, arguing: '[...] Crisis is mobilized in narrative constructions to mark out or to designate "moments of truth"; it is taken to be a means to access historical truth, and even a means to think "history" itself' (Roitman, 2014, p.3). This article uses the COVID-19 pandemic crisis to search out the truth about tourism and to ask what is revealed in this history-making moment of crisis for travel and tourism. The taken as given notions of tourism as an industry (Higgins-Desbiolles, 2006), the push for commodification of peoples and places through tourism (e.g. Kirtsoglou & Theodossopoulos, 2004), the privatisation of commons for profit-making in tourism and the transformation of communities into destinations (Higgins-Desbiolles et al., 2019) are all now open to thoughtful rethinking. Using the anti-oppression and pro-justice theorisation of critical tourism approaches, we can not only sharpen the critique of the moment we find ourselves in but also imagine radical and emancipatory solutions.

The revelatory power of the COVID-19 crisis: neoliberalism undone

The revelatory power of this crisis is enormous. Ideas that are rocked by this pandemic and responses to it include:

- that globalisation is an unstoppable force;
- that we cannot unlink from the logics of continuous economic growth;
- that consumerism is the key to expressing our identity; and
- that neoliberal capitalism is the best system for organising and allocating resources.

Neoliberalism from the 1980s has promoted: reducing government roles and regulations; increasing marketisation and privatization; reducing tax on the wealthy and big businesses; a consumer-based ideology; and radical individualism (Harvey, 2007). As a result of this system, workers' rights and conditions have deteriorated, environmental protection regulations have been attacked, and social safety nets have been reduced or abandoned in many nations (Monbiot, 2016). Importantly, a key outcome from neoliberal transformations is the attempt to diminish society in favour of the economy; as former British Prime Minister Margaret Thatcher, one of the founders of neoliberal politics, once exclaimed 'there is no such thing as society'[1] (2013).

Accompanying this has been an ideology that 'there is no alternative' (TINA), such that opposition and protests have been often sidelined (Flanders, 2013). It is neoliberalism that has hollowed out societies and their resources, especially healthcare systems, making the pandemic even harder to address. The experience of the COVID-19 crisis has revealed that neoliberalism has embedded market values in social and welfare institutions that should have been dedicated to meeting the needs of people and society.

This crisis has also revealed the falsehood of TINA as neoliberal governments around the world are having to abandon their ideological positions. In response to the pandemic, these governments are: redeveloping social safety nets; calling on social solidarity in the action to get everyone to stay at home in the attempt to reduce COVID-19 transmission; and printing money and spending taxpayer funds in enormous amounts to maintain economic and social stability. With this crisis, we also can identify whose labour is needed to perpetuate society's wellbeing: the undervalued caring labour of nurses, grocery store workers, aged care, teachers, and gig economy delivery staff – many of whom are women and/or People of Colour.[2] It is neither the 'captains of industry' nor the celebrities that are seeing us through this crisis.

This also matters to the question of whether we return to neoliberal normalcy after the crisis passes, because these workers have been subject to poor pay and conditions, wage theft, job precarity and/or redundancy in the relentless drive to reduce costs and increase profits for the privatised entities that employ them. It is clear that profound change has been possible because of the unique challenges of this globalised crisis and it suggests that a systemic change is underway. Perhaps underscoring the way COVID-19 has caused a break with neoliberalism, the British Prime Minister Boris Johnson on the 30th March 2020 stated that 'there really is such a thing as society' in a message released while suffering with Covid-19 himself (Johnson, 2020).

An illustrative case study: the cruise tourism industry exposed

This article will take the example of the cruise ship as iconic of the conduct of neoliberalism and its failures in terms of human, social, economic and environmental well-being. In fact, the iconic image of the global COVID-19 pandemic and its abrupt shutdown of our hyper-mobile world have been those stranded cruise ships, full of passengers desperate to disembark and destination communities less than keen to receive them (see Cdanowicz, 2020).

The Cruise Lines International Association (CLIA) positions its membership in terms of 'responsibility': 'CLIA cruise lines are leaders and innovators in responsible tourism and offer the best way for travelers to experience the world' (CLIA, n.2020d.) However, many cruise ships sail under a 'Flag of Convenience' (FOC), which does not suggest a commitment to responsibility. FOC describes when some cruise companies register their ships in a country other than the country of ownership. Common FOC nations include Malta, Bermuda, Panama and the Bahamas. Cruise companies choose to use a FOC as part of their economic model, helping their business gain profits by helping them avoid stringent economic, social and environmental regulations (see Tourism Concern, 2016). The practice of using FOC makes the cruise tourism sector emblematic of neoliberal forms of tourism. As Segnini and Rojas (2015) demonstrated in an analysis of the American cruise sector: 'The multi-billion dollar cruise industry is one of the least regulated in the United States, and is shielded under the laws of the tax havens from which it operates.'

In March 2020, when the cruise sector sought access to the $2 trillion USD stimulus plan funds being rolled out in the USA to deal with the economic fallout from the COVID-19 pandemic, these unjust and unsustainable practices were highlighted by opponents. Marcie Keever, Oceans and Vessels Program Director at Friends of the Earth stated:

> The cruise ship industry should not be rewarded for polluting our oceans, breaking laws, harming communities and mistreating workers. Congress must hold the cruise industry accountable for its past abuses and not provide them a single dime before the American people are secure. We must make people and the environment the priority during this health crisis, not cruise industry profits (Friends of the Earth, 2020).

Cruise tourism has also been identified as one culprit in the overtourism crisis in places such as Venice, Barcelona and Dubrovnik (Street, 2019). In this COVID-19 crisis, the health and safety of the thousands of workers trapped on the cruise ships denied port entry was seldom discussed often with only maritime unions speaking out for them (see ABC News, 2020). At the time of writing this, many of them have been forced to stay on infected ships while these arguments raged on, with those falling sick being evacuated to hospitals. This stands in marked contrast to the repatriation of cruise passenger nationals on charter flights by their concerned governments.

This case study of the cruise tourism sector is one example of the injustices and exploitations of the tourism industry operating under neoliberalism. The COVID-19 crisis has revealed often ignored aspects of this system. As the cruise ships became stranded around the world as ports closed to them, the question of exactly where home for them was, as they operated under FOC, began to be discussed. Maritime union advocacy drew attention to the plight of the unfortunate crews, some of whom to date have not been afforded proper protections and care during the pandemic. The cruise sector has benefited from neoliberal ideology and practices and now hopes to benefit from the bonuses of disaster capitalism[3] (see Klein, 2008) to access unprecedented government stimulus funds on offer (see OCCRP, 2020).

In the 'The truth about tourism', Tribe argued: 'The job of critical theory is initially to identify which particular ideological influences are at work. Ideology critique then asks whose interests are being served by a particular ideology' (2006, p. 375). As noted by Tribe (2006, p. 375), Desmond explained how tourism is itself an ideology: 'tourism is not just an aggregate of commercial activities; it is also an ideological framing of history, nature and tradition; a framing that has the power to reshape culture and nature to its own needs' (Desmond, 1999: xiv). The critical questions to ask include: who defines the boundaries and operations of tourism; who benefits from these forms of tourism; how is power exercised; and how is power limited and controlled? With neoliberalism now arguably on the nose, we have an invaluable window of opportunity to overturn the received wisdom on tourism and reorient it in ways that better serve society.

Addressing the problem of tourism: responsible tourism is not the answer

Some will advocate more responsible forms of tourism as the answer to transforming tourism in these circumstances. Article one of the UNWTO's 'Global Code of Ethics for

Tourism' articulates responsible tourism effectively. Titled 'tourism's contribution to mutual understanding and respect between peoples and societies', it states: 'the understanding and promotion of the ethical values common to humanity, with an attitude of tolerance and respect for the diversity of religious, philosophical and moral beliefs, are both the foundation and the consequence of responsible tourism' (UNWTO, 1999). Responsible tourism approaches have been advocated as a way to address the negative social and environmental impacts of tourism. Recently, Jamal et al. (2013) argued that responsible tourism approaches, together with a micro-macro ethical framework, were superior to sustainable tourism approaches that have predominated in recent years.

However, others have disagreed that either 'sustainable' or 'responsible' approaches are sufficient:

> What has occurred has been investigations of inequality and tourism (Cole & Morgan, 2010) and justice tourism (Higgins-Desbiolles, 2008) which have sought to address questions of who benefits from tourism, how tourism can be made fairer and more just, what are the purposes of tourism and at the more extreme end, how tourism can be mobilised as a tool for securing justice (Higgins-Desbiolles, 2018a).

In work on justice issues in tourism, Higgins-Desbiolles (2008) explained how these kinds of efforts aimed at reforming tourism and can easily be co-opted and undermined. We see this co-option in the cruise tourism industry case study above, where CLIA couched the cruise sector clearly as a part of responsible tourism. Higgins-Desbiolles' work (2008) offered an analysis using a continuum to illustrate how various reformist interventions advanced changes to tourism processes, but were not sufficient to address ongoing exploitations and injustices that tourism enacts (see Figure 1).

The problem with responsible tourism approaches are that they merely admonish tourism actors to be a little more caring and responsible and to clean up the sharper edges of their poor practices. Responsible tourism advocates fail to recognise that these businesses are a part of a structure that is set up unjustly and extracts profits through exploitative practices. An illustrative example is offered in Whyte's (2010) analysis of Indigenous tourism. Using an environmental justice frame for analysis, he explains how Indigenous tourism can result in 'mutually beneficial exploitation' when Indigenous communities are compelled by poverty and structural injustices to engage with forms of tourism that often fail to recognise Indigenous sovereignty and lifeways. Responsible tourism proponents might unwittingly identify these forms of tourism as a 'win-win' because Indigenous peoples actively engage with the 'tourism opportunity'. However, Whyte shows how the structural injustices under which tourism operates undermines the possibility for Indigenous peoples' lifeways to thrive under such conditions, and ultimately undermines their sovereignty in the process.

This analysis of the limitations of responsible tourism as one possible tool in this COVID-19 transformative moment underscores the need to employ critical approaches. If this transformative moment is to be seized with the goal of attaining greater social and ecological justice, we must seek a radical break from what has come before, rather than a more simplistic reformist approach.

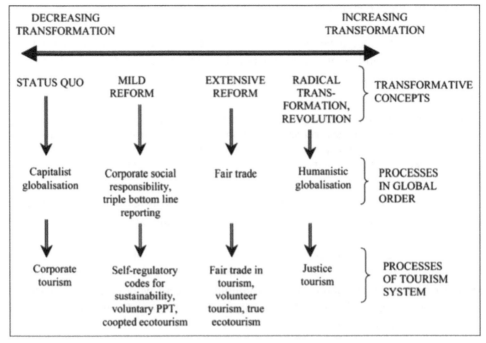

Figure 1. Continuum of transformation possible in global order and tourism system (from Higgins-Desbiolles, 2008, p. 359).

What is to be done: socialising tourism for social and ecological justice

The COVID-19 pandemic crisis has challenged the premises of neoliberalism that smaller government, individualism, and marketisation benefit people and society. Forms of government interventions, the redevelopment of social safety nets, and the significance of social caring and networks have been the primary responses to challenges of this crisis. After COVID-19, we could take up an agenda to properly socialise tourism. The word 'socialise' could hold multiple meanings including: following the principles of socialism; to act socially well in interactions with others; or to guide on proper ways of behaving with regards to society. In his discussion of 'socialising the stranger', Scott provides an insight into the way socialising tourism is meant here. Scott explained: 'Hospitality becomes an initiation of the process that would result in the socialisation and thus integration into the 'local' society' (Scott, 2006, p. 57). It is both tourists and tourism businesses that must be socialised into supporting the ways, needs and interests of the local societies in which they tour or offer tourism services.

Recent COVID-19 analysis has noted how neoliberal governments have willingly adopted 'socialised' policies in their response to the crisis, for instance by creating the health, social and educational measures they had previously white-anted with privatisation in an effort to avoid widespread social unrest. But I use this phrase 'socialise tourism' in a broader way, meaning to make tourism responsive and answerable to the society in which it occurs. The problem with tourism under neoliberal globalisation is that the power of society to manage, control and benefit from tourism businesses operating in their communities is undermined because the market is outside of their control.

It is well known that governments under neoliberal globalisation have ceded considerable freedom and rights to multinational corporations, which has had profound implications for societies. As Stiglitz reminded us, corporations are created to further society's goals:

> Corporations are legal entities governments create to enhance the well-being of their citizens by producing certain conditions that are conducive to investing and conducting business. Governments grant certain rights-limited liability-but we have argued that these are not 'natural rights' or 'human rights' but only instrumental rights, shaped to further societal goals (2007, p. 553).

Discourses from corporate social responsibility advocates have advocated an approach to business requiring their 'social licence to operate' (Wheeler, 2015; see also Campos et al., 2018).

However, the concept of socialising tourism advocated in this work is a call to place tourism in the context of the society in which it occurs and to harness it for the empowerment and wellbeing of local communities. Recent work by Higgins-Desbiolles et al. (2019, p. 1936) offering a Community-Centred Tourism Framework assists this radical rethinking of tourism:

> If we are to avoid violence, strategies for degrowth in tourism must be progressive, inclusive, just and equitable. This begins with the redefinition of tourism in order to place the rights of local communities above the rights of tourists for holidays and the rights of tourism corporates to make profits.

These authors offered an illustrative model to indicate how such an approach to tourism would radically transform the way tourism could be conducted (see Figure 2).

Key lessons of the COVID-19 crisis have been the vital importance of community, social connections and society; privatisation and marketisation have been shown to be damaging to public health and well-being. We also saw the way the corporate model of tourism was devastated by the efforts to address the pandemic; like global supply chains, global tourism has proved fragile and unreliable. Some commentators are drawing the lesson that a more localised form of tourism would be the way of the future. But that is not taking the thinking far enough. We need tourism in the service to the public and to be accountable to the public.

An agenda to socialise tourism would reorient it to the public good; including:

- States could choose to preference local corporations and businesses over multinational corporations (MNCs) (see Stiglitz, 2007). Too often MNCs are not answerable to local places; small to medium tourism enterprises are the ones that should be facilitated for a more just and sustainable future in tourism.
- Tourism corporations must pay a fair amount of taxes and must no longer use unjust practices such as tax havens to avoid taxes. These corporations should not be allowed to offload costs as market failures onto the public purse.
- If tourism businesses go bankrupt, workers should be the first prioritised debt holder of such businesses and they should be supported to takeover such

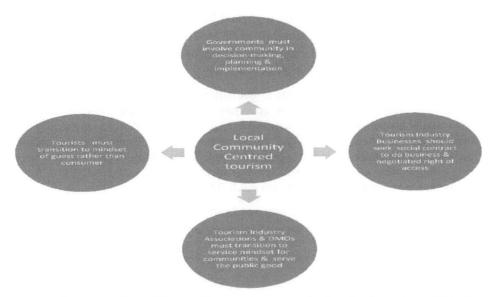

Figure 2. Community-Centred Tourism Framework as a mechanism for degrowing tourism (from Higgins-Desbiolles et al., 2019, p. 1937).

businesses if they desire this (see Higgins-Desbiolles, 2012 on the Hotel Bauen example).

- Alternative models including cooperatives, social enterprises, non-profits and forms of social businesses should be facilitated to support tourism for the public good (see Biddulph, 2018 for critical perspectives).
- State tourism commissions must return to their original mission of public service rather than continue down the path of statutory corporations. They must be restructured away from the marketing and public communications focus that has come to dominate under neoliberalism, and instead be comprised of people of diverse expertise that can facilitate a public good form of tourism.
- Public good forms of tourism should be facilitated and promoted, including educational tourism, citizen science, social tourism, community exchanges, etc. Informal sectors that facilitate local people's benefit from tourism should also be prioritised.
- The commons should be protected and no further privatisation of public assets such as national parks and protected areas should occur. Ecological protection of conservation environments must be a high priority under the threat of climate change
- The types of tourism developed should be decided by the local community. The public must be properly consulted on the forms of tourism that are developed in the community according to processes that they identify.
- A universal basic income is a basis on which precarious tourism and hospitality work can be made secure. Significant efforts must be made to secure workers' rights and good working conditions. It should no longer be tolerated that tourism workers do not receive a living wage and secure conditions for their labour in the industry.

This agenda needs more dedicated work and fleshing out to ensure we set tourism on different pathway so that it supports social and ecological justice. There is both possibility and danger in this transformative moment offered by the crisis of COVID-19. As the Tourism Alert and Action Forum warned:

> Industries such as tourism will be keen to get back to business as usual, grabbing on to the phrase undertourism to ramp it up again. Governments will be keen to take advantage of control and surveillance capacities that are being imposed on the excuse of the crisis and to extend these further. Whole segments of our communities are being dismissed as disposable, including workers in the informal sectors of tourism who will find that starvation and homelessness are their direct threat as well as COVID-19. It is foreseeable that an elite form of travel will result (TAAF, 2020).

This work on socialising tourism requires both thought and action to ensure that we do not fail at this moment to secure real transformation from the disaster that the COVID-19 crisis has brought.

Conclusion

'The old world is dying and the new world struggles to be born. Now is the time of monsters'- Antonio Gramsci (cited in Žižek, 2010) [4]

There is some hubris in trying to develop effective analysis on a global crisis when it has not yet fully unfolded. It would seem that we are in an era of major change of the equivalent of a world war or great depression. There are contrasting views on whether this should be a source of great optimism or fear. If correct that we are living through a major transition, this assessment of Gramsci cautions us to be alert to a possible time of monsters. In a world where growing inequality has led to massive numbers of vulnerable populations (Kearney, 2017), it is clear that the COVID-19 pandemic and actions to address its spread are likely to impact these vulnerable communities in disproportionate and deadly fashion (see, for instance, Evelyn, 2020; Kazmin, 2020). Thus, it matters how we support a transition for greater justice and well-being.

This article has offered an analysis using a critical theory lens to briefly uncover the ways in which tourism has supported neoliberal injustices and exploitation. Taking the assumption that the COVID-19 pandemic crisis offers a rare and invaluable opportunity to rethink and reset tourism, this article has explained why 'responsible' approaches to tourism do not offer sufficient means to break with these structures and processes of injustice, oppression and exploitation. Instead, this work has drawn on recent theorisation to redefine and reorient tourism based on the rights and interests of local communities and local peoples. It advances this work by further theorising a way tourism could be 'socialised' and made accountable to social and ecological limits.

In the neoliberal era, tourism facilitated and enacted serious inequities and injustices on people and wrought significant ecological damage, including contributions to global climate change. As we try to give birth a new era in the aftermath of COVID-19, it is our task as concerned scholars in tourism to offer our contributions to imagine ways tourism can be developed to enable human thriving and ecological recovery. Socialising tourism to such purposes would be a positive way forward.

Notes

1. Thatcher's full statement was: 'They are casting their problems at society. And, you know, there's no such thing as society. There are individual men and women and there are families. And no government can do anything except through people, and people must look after themselves first. It is our duty to look after ourselves and then, also, to look after our neighbours' (from an interview in *Women's Own* in 1987 as cited in Thatcher, 2013).
2. 'People of Colour' is not a satisfactory term but it is used to encompass the range of 'non-white' people who do not benefit from privileged positions of power (see Glover, 2016).
3. Klein used the term 'shock doctrine' to describe the strategy of using the public's disorientation following a collective shock – wars, coups, terrorist attacks, market crashes or natural disasters – to push through radical pro-corporate measures, often called 'shock therapy'. Corporations use this to advance their interests and ability to profit through what she called 'disaster capitalism' (2008).
4. This is from a liberal translation of Gramsci popularized by Slavoj Žižek (2010), which amends 'In this interregnum a great variety of morbid symptoms appear' to 'Now is the time of monsters'.

Disclosure statement

No potential conflict of interest was reported by the authors.

References

ABC News. (2020, April 2). Maritime Union urges Government to repatriate crew members on foreign cruise ships. https://www.msn.com/en-au/video/sport/maritime-union-urges-government-to-repatriate-crew-members-on-foreign-cruise-ships/vp-BB123SMr

Biddulph, R. (2018). Social enterprise and inclusive tourism. Five cases in Siem Reap. *Tourism Geographies, 20*(4), 610–629. doi:10.1080/14616688.2017.1417471

Butler, B. (2020). Outrageous': Qantas criticised for standing down 20,000 workers without pay. The Guardian, 19. March. Online. https://www.theguardian.com/business/2020/mar/19/coronavirus-qantas-and-jetstar-to-suspend-international-flights-and-stand-down-20000-workers.

Campos, M. J. Z., Hall, C. M., & Backlund, S. (2018). Can MNCs promote more inclusive tourism? Apollo tour operator's sustainability work. *Tourism Geographies, 20*(4), 630–652. doi:10.1080/14616688.2018.1457074

Cassinger, C. (2019). Communicating anti-tourism – movement, protest, phobia. *28th Nordic Symposium on Tourism and Hospitality Research*, 23-25 October 2019.

Cdanowicz, C. (2020, March 18). Multiple cruise ships are left stranded as coronavirus cases increase. CNN Travel, Online. https://edition.cnn.com/travel/article/cruise-ships-stranded-coronavirus-trnd/index.html.

CLIA. (n.d.). CLIA homepage. https://cruising.org/.

Cole, S. & Morgan, N. (eds.) (2010). *Tourism and inequality: Problems and prospects*, Wallingford: CABI. doi:10.1079/9781845936624.0000

Desmond, J. (1999). *Staging tourism: Bodies on Display from Waikiki to Sea World*. University of Chicago Press.

Evelyn, K. (2020, April 8). 'It's a racial justice issue': Black Americans are dying in greater numbers from Covid-19. *The Guardian Online*. https://www.theguardian.com/world/2020/apr/08/its-a-racial-justice-issue-black-americans-are-dying-in-greater-numbers-from-covid-19.

Flanders, L. (2013). At Thatcher's Funeral, Bury TINA, Too. The Nation, Online. https://www.thena-tion.com/article/archive/thatchers-funeral-bury-tina-too/.

Friends of the Earth. (2020, March 20). Green groups call on Congress to not bail our rule-break-ing cruise industry. https://foe.org/news/green-groups-call-congress-not-bail-rule-breaking-cruise-industry/.

Glover, C. (2016). 4 reasons 'People of Color' isn't always the best choice of words. Everyday Feminism Magazine. https://everydayfeminism.com/2016/08/poc-not-best-choice-of-words/

Hall, C. M., Prayag, G., & Amore, A. (2018). *Tourism and resilience: Individual, organisational and destination perspectives*. Channelview.

Hancock, A. (2020, March 20). Grounded flights force Tui to cut staff hours and wages. Financial Times. Online. https://www.ft.com/content/85a8d648-6a07-11ea-800d-da70cff6e4d3.

Harvey, D. (2007). *A brief history of neoliberalism*. Oxford University Press.

Higgins-Desbiolles, F. (2006). More than an Industry: Tourism as a social force. *Tourism Management, 27*(6), 1192–1208.

Higgins-Desbiolles, F. (2008). Justice tourism and alternative globalisation. *Journal of Sustainable Tourism, 16*(3), 345–364. doi:10.1080/09669580802154132

Higgins-Desbiolles, F. (2012). The Hotel Bauen's challenge to cannibalizing capitalism. *Annals of Tourism Research, 39*(2), 620–240. doi:10.1016/j.annals.2011.08.001

Higgins-Desbiolles, F. (2018a). The potential for justice through tourism. *Via Tourism Review*, (13), 13. https://journals.openedition.org/viatourism/2469. doi:10.4000/viatourism.2469

Higgins-Desbiolles, F. (2018b). Sustainable tourism: sustaining tourism or something more? *Tourism Management Perspectives, 25*, 157–160. doi:10.1016/j.tmp.2017.11.017

Higgins-Desbiolles, F., Carnicelli, S., Krolikowski, C., Wijesinghe, G., & Boluk, K. (2019). Degrowing tourism: Rethinking tourism. *Journal of Sustainable Tourism, 27*(12), 1926–1944. doi:10.1080/09669582.2019.1601732

Jamal, T., Camargo, B., & Wilson, E. (2013). Critical omissions and new directions for sustainable tourism: A situated macro–micro approach. *Sustainability, 5*(11), 4594–4613. doi:10.3390/su5114594

Johnson, B. (2020, March 30). Boris Johnson says 'there really is such a thing as society' in self-isolation update – video. The Guardian, Online. https://www.theguardian.com/global/video/2020/mar/29/boris-johnson-says-there-really-is-such-a-thing-as-society-in-self-isolation-update-video.

Jover, J., & Díaz-Parra, I. (2020). Who is the city for? Overtourism, lifestyle migration and social sustainability. *Tourism Geographies*. doi:10.1080/14616688.2020.1713878

Kazmin, A. (2020, March 25). India's migrant workers flee cities and threaten the countryside. The Financial Times, Online. https://www.ft.com/content/069d818c-6df9-11ea-89df-41bea055720b.

Kearney, M. (2017). How should governments address inequality? *Foreign Affairs, 96*(6), 133–138. https://www.foreignaffairs.com/reviews/review-essay/2017-10-16/how-should-governments-address-inequality.

Kirtsoglou, E., & Theodossopoulos, D. (2004). They are taking our culture away' tourism and cul-ture commodification in the garifuna community of Roatan. *Critique of Anthropology, 24*(2), 135–157. doi:10.1177/0308275X04042650

Klein, N. (2008). *The shock doctrine: The rise of disaster capitalism*. Picador.

Lynch, M. (2004). *Weathering the storm: A crisis management guide for tourism businesses*. Leicester: Matador.

Monbiot, G. (2016). Neoliberalism – the ideology at the root of all our problems. The Guardian, Online. https://www.theguardian.com/books/2016/apr/15/neoliberalism-ideology-problem-george-monbiot.

OCCRP. (2020). Critics argue that US government should not bail out cruise liners. Organised Crime and Corruption Reporting Project. https://www.occrp.org/en/daily/11907-critics-argue-that-us-government-should-not-bail-out-cruise-liners

OECD. (2020). COVID-19: Tourism policy responses. https://read.oecd-ilibrary.org/view/?ref=124_
124984-7uf8nm95se&title=Covid-19_Tourism_Policy_Responses

Roitman, J. (2014). *Anti-crisis*. Duke University Press.

Scott, D. G. (2006). *Socialising the stranger: Hospitality as a relational reality (Dissertation,* March).
http://hdl.handle.net/10523/1283.

Segnini, G., Rojas, R. (2015). Holidays in the waters of nobody. http://huelladigital.univisionnoti-
cias.com/cruceros-vacaciones-en-aguas-de-nadie/index.html

Stiglitz, J. E. (2007). Regulating multinational corporations: Towards principles of cross-border
legal frameworks in a globalized world balancing rights with responsibilities. *American
University International Law Review, 23*(3), 451–558.

Street, F. (2019). Is the cruise industry responsible for overtourism? CNN Travel, online. https://
edition.cnn.com/travel/article/overtourism-cruise-industry/index.html.

Thatcher, M. (2013). Margaret Thatcher: A life in quotes. The Guardian, Online. https://www.the-
guardian.com/politics/2013/apr/08/margaret-thatcher-quotes

Tourism Alert and Action Forum. (2020). Tourism Alert and Action Forum Statement on Covid-19
Pandemic Crisis - 30 March 2020. (In the possession of the author).

Tourism Concern. (2016). Cruise tourism – what's below the surface briefing paper. https://www.
tourismconcern.org.uk/cruise-tourism-whats-below-the-surface/.

Tribe, J. (2006). The truth about tourism. *Annals of Tourism Research, 33*(2), 360–381. doi:10.1016/
j.annals.2005.11.001

Tribe, J. (2008). Tourism: A critical business. *Journal of Travel Research, 46*(3), 245–255. doi:10.
1177/0047287507304051

UNWTO. (1999). The global code of ethics for tourism. https://www.unwto.org/global-code-of-
ethics-for-tourism.

UNWTO. (2020a, April 1). Message from Madrid: Tourism and Covid-19". https://www.unwto.org/
news/madrid-tourism-covid-19.

UNWTO. (2020b, April 1). Supporting jobs and economies through travel and tourism. https://
webunwto.s3.eu-west-1.amazonaws.com/s3fs-public/2020-04/COVID19_Recommendations_
English_1.pdf

Wheeler, S. (2015). Global production, CSR and human rights: the courts of public opinion and
the social licence to operate. *The International Journal of Human Rights, 19*(6), 757–778. doi:
10.1080/13642987.2015.1016712

Whyte, K. (2010). An environmental justice framework for Indigenous tourism. *Journal of
Environmental Philosophy, 7*(2), 75–92.

Žižek, S. (2010). A permanent economic emergency. New Left Review, 64. https://newleftreview.
org/issues/II64/articles/slavoj-zizek-a-permanent-economic-emergency.

The COVID-19 crisis as an opportunity for escaping the unsustainable global tourism path

Dimitri Ioannides ⓘ and Szilvia Gyimóthy

ABSTRACT

The COVID-19 pandemic has halted mobility globally on an unprecedented scale, causing the neoliberal market mechanisms of global tourism to be severely disrupted. In turn, this situation is leading to the decline of certain mainstream business formats and, simultaneously, the emergence of others. Based on a review of recent crisis recovery processes, the tourism sector is likely to rebound from this sudden market shock, primarily because of various forms of government interventions. Nevertheless, although policymakers seek to strengthen the resilience of post-pandemic tourism, their subsidies and other initiatives serve to maintain a fundamentally flawed market logic. The crisis has, therefore, brought us to a fork in the road – giving us the perfect opportunity to select a new direction and move forward by adopting a more sustainable path. Specifically, COVID-19 offers public, private, and academic actors a unique opportunity to design and consolidate the transition towards a greener and more balanced tourism. Tourism scholars, for example, can take a leading role in this by redesigning their curriculum to prepare future industry leaders for a more responsible travel and tourism experience.

摘要

COVID-19 大流行以前所未有的规模中止了全球的流动性, 严重破坏了世界旅游业的新自由主义市场机制, 继而导致某些主流商业模式的衰落, 同时也导致其他商业模式的兴起。根据对近期危机复苏进程的回顾, 旅游业可能会从这场突如其来的市场冲击中反弹, 主要原因是政府采取了各种形式的干预措施。 虽然政策制定者试图增强大流行后旅游业的复原力, 但他们的补贴和其他举措只能维持一个存在根本缺陷的市场。因此, 这场危机将我们带到了岔路口——给了我们选择新方向的绝佳机会, 并采取更加可持续的道路前进。具体而言, COVID-19为公众、个人和学术团体提供了独特的机会来布局和加强向更绿色、更平衡的旅游业过渡。例如, 旅游学者可以通过重新设计课程, 为未来的行业领导者提供更负责任的旅行和旅游体验, 从而在其中发挥主导作用。

Since its emergence in early 2020, the rapidly-spreading COVID-19 (also referred to as Corona) pandemic has wreaked global havoc. While numerous communities have been facing lockdowns of varying lengths the economic consequences of the virus have been devastating. The effects on the global tourism sector, not to mention thousands of destinations worldwide, have been particularly harmful as our normally hyper-mobile society has ground to a halt. It is not only the major players in the tourism supply chain (e.g., airlines, cruise companies, transnational hotel chains) who have suffered unfathomable damage, which is estimated to amount to €400bn (Goodwin, 2020; Nicolás, 2020). In thousands of localities, businesses of all sizes, which depend either directly or indirectly on the visitor economy, have suspended operations and indications are that many of these will likely never reopen. The impact on the sector's labour force has been devastating, especially considering the precarious nature of numerous tourism and hospitality-related jobs at the lower rungs of the occupational ladder (Chanel, 2020; see also, UNWTO., 2020).

Both the scope and consequences of global immobility induced by the Corona-crisis have seriously perplexed tourism practitioners, policymakers and researchers (Miles & Shipway, 2020). While, just a few years ago, Hall (2015) anticipated the possibility of a global pandemic playing out as the "perfect storm", the interlinked social, cultural, psychological and economic effects of a crisis of this magnitude are leading us along unforeseen trajectories. On the one hand, there is already growing speculation especially in the mass media that the pandemic might trigger an enduring shift in market behavior, which could radically transform global travel patterns (Irwin, 2020). On the other hand, we recognize that in the past, following a particular crisis, including the outbreak of epidemics, the tourism industry has usually bounced back, demonstrating the sector's remarkable resilience to mitigate sudden breakdowns in demand or supply (Novelli et al., 2018; Papatheodorou et al., 2010).

Indeed, evidence suggests that memories following crises and disasters tend to be short and sooner, rather than later, things return to the status quo (Kontogeorgopoulos, 1999). For instance, although the SARS epidemic in the early 2000s initially led to a drastic fall in visits to China, the destination rapidly rebounded (Zeng et al., 2005). Meanwhile, in an exercise of "disaster capitalism", powerful stakeholders in destinations like Thailand and Sri Lanka, which were devastated by the massive tsunami in the Indian Ocean in 2004 used the catastrophe as an opportunity to implement land grabs, leading to brand new large-scale developments that quickly enticed international visitors to return (Cohen, 2011). If a particular tourist destination is affected by an unforeseen sudden event such as a volcanic eruption or a terrorist attack, the major international travel suppliers (e.g., tour operators and airlines) substitute this with another one offering similar attractions and facilities (Ioannides, 1994). Obviously, this ability of footloose international players to shift their turf, aerospace or fairway around the globe is currently a moot point. Following the closure of international borders, almost all international passenger air traffic has been cancelled and transnational cruise-liners sailing underflags of convenience are refused entry into most ports.

The unprecedented circumstances that the travel and tourism sector currently faces as a result of the COVID-19 pandemic signify that in an evolutionary sense, we have reached a fork in the road where at least two general outcomes are possible. The first (based on extrapolations of past recovery history) is that the sector will gradually revert to the pre-crisis unsustainable growth-oriented trajectory. An alternative scenario entails a transition towards a radically different way of doing things (Loorbach et al., 2017). Arriving at this metaphorical fork in the road constitutes an opportunity for society at large to pause and ponder the way forward. After all, from an etymological aspect, the word "crisis" originates from the Ancient Greek 'κρίσις', which among its several definitions has to do with coming to a judgement or making a decision. Nowadays, a crisis implies that a turning point has been reached giving rise to the opportunity to institute varying degrees of change that may allow us to move away from the original trajectory and escape some of the problems associated with this (Miles & Petridou, 2015). As Thierry Breton, EU Commissioner of the internal market claims: "[…] there is an opportunity to take advantage of the current crisis to reinvent he tourism of tomorrow - towards a more sustainable, resilient and innovative sector" (Nicolás, 2020).

In the remainder of this commentary, we treat the disruption in global tourism as a prism through which we contemplate how broader transformations could play out in the aftermath of the COVID-19 crisis. We admit it is dangerous to make predictions with limited facts, nor do we possess a crystal ball as to how things might evolve in the aftermath of the present crisis. Instead, by adopting a far less ambitious stance, we discuss how the present catastrophic effects on the tourism sector present an opportunity for reconsidering certain practices. Below, we present out reflections by contrasting the potential decline of mainstream tourism practices, which are currently severely disrupted by COVID-19, with emergent niche activities, for which opportunities might arise from the very same disruptions. Thereafter, we discuss potential avenues that policymakers may wish to pursue. Because of space constraints, we focus on just two issues, namely *mobility* and *resilience*.

Mobility

Since the outbreak of COVID-19, the imposed mobility restrictions have been unprecedented on a local, regional and global scale. The shutdown of numerous communities and the implementation of major restrictions on border crossings has virtually eliminated the tourism economy in communities throughout the world (Goodwin, 2020). Places, which only a few months ago were suffering from extreme problems of overvisitation (Milano et al., 2019) are presently eerily quiet (Kimmelman, 2020). Museums, hotels and restaurants have closed, beaches and ski-slopes are empty and events of all sizes have been postponed or cancelled. Undoubtedly, the economic effects especially on localities or even countries depending heavily on tourism arrivals have been catastrophic.

Because at the time of writing it remains anyone's guess as to when the crisis will subside one can only ponder as to whether or not we shall see major shifts in the global tourism system or whether things will largely revert to what they were before the crisis occurred. Certainly, this unprecedented situation has made one thing clear. It has given us, at least momentarily, a glimpse of a world of slow-paced, which does not entail traveling large distances by cars, trains or planes. For many, trips have been confined to a few short blocks from home, while numerous middle and upper middle-class people can only reflect how privileged they have been to be able to travel to far-flung spots around the planet. Meanwhile, because of the significant reduction in both local and international travel but also the slowdown of manufacturing activities, there is mounting evidence that the air in several localities worldwide is far cleaner than it has been for decades since pollutants have dropped off (McGrath, 2020; Watts & Kommenda, 2020). This combination of facts opens up the possibility for people to view their immediate surroundings in a whole new way, especially when millions have been locked up for weeks within the confines of their homes. Newton (2020) discusses how the restrictions have created a surge of visitations to parks and forests.

Coupled with this, we can assume that the scope and depth of the crisis has challenged the economies of millions of households worldwide, effectively putting a major dent in their discretionary incomes. Thus, it could be a long while before leisure-oriented travel and especially long-haul flights reach their pre-COVID-19 levels. Further, companies in all sectors, which are facing massive losses due to fickle demand and reduced production might institute measures such as replacing most business travel with meetings on virtual platforms. The fact that over the last 2 months Zoom and Skype meetings have become the new norm for numerous public and private entities worldwide might accelerate a fundamental paradigm shift in the way of conducting business.

On a broader level, the current crisis could lead to shifts in the dominant logic of neoliberalism over the last few decades whereby numerous destinations around the world have persisted in pursuing growth-oriented strategies in a highly deregulated environment. For example, just a few months ago, despite rising accusations that tourists were loving them to death, European destinations were on a never-ending search for new strategic "emerging" markets (attracting long-haul travelers from China, India and Southeast Asia). Their growing middle class but also lower travel restrictions have been a major reason behind the massive increase in demand from these regions. With the advent COVID-19 and the imposition of draconian measures to restrict the virus' spread, one must wonder whether we are entering a new era where risk mitigation might prevail over the logic of unrestricted growth. Rising concerns about the threats associated with the unrestricted circulation of goods and people across the world might mean that these imposed controls might take time to disappear while nervous consumers may not wish to venture far from their comfort zone until they are reassured that the danger has lapsed. A recent survey conducted by the Tourism Crisis Management Initiative at the University of Florida reveals that, at least in the early days after things eventually return to normal, most Americans who are able to and choose to travel are likelier to venture close to home. Most likely, these trips will be car-based (Glusac, 2020). Meanwhile, others may pursue leisure activities that do not require much mobility, due to both economic and risk considerations.

From a philosophical standpoint, these circumstances lead us to contemplate the possibility of a post-COVID-19 era where tourists' mobility could be significantly transformed not only temporarily but over the long-run. Could we, for instance, envision a scenario where our endless neophilia and unquenching thirst for (often irresponsible) adventure in far-flung places are substituted by travel and leisure activities much closer to home? Media coverage of cruise passengers evacuated by their respective national governments may induce an enduring risk-avoidance consumer trend, in which exotic travel and places with high population concentration lose their appeal. Moreover, could we see the reemergence of patriotic consumption (similar to the kickstart of post-WW2 markets), where citizens support domestic destinations and local tourism businesses as an act of communitarian commitment?

A word about resilience

Resilience and the mobilization of adaptive capabilities have been addressed in organizational studies relating to sustainable transitions (Engle, 2011; Keskitalo, 2008, Tsao & Ni, 2016), which offer a glimpse of recovery responses. In the case of enterprises, a crisis may trigger the emergence of new business models and revenue strategies, which will ultimately define the survival chances of the firm. Innovative and adaptive capabilities play a key role in post-crisis recovery (Engle, 2011), yet numerous tourism businesses suffer from innovation deficiencies (Hjalager, 2002; Sundbo et al., 2007). Small operators, traditionally deemed as vulnerable market players, may prove to respond to the crisis in more flexible ways, especially due to their local embeddedness and community support. Previous research has shown local economies respond to crises with collaborative action and social bricolage (Di Domenico et al., 2010) while rural enterprises have better recovery outlooks than their urban counterparts (Johannisson & Olaison, 2007). This seems to be the case with Danish countryside inns and restaurants, which shifted to takeaway operations during the lockdown. Their revenues actually increased due to loyal guests from the local community (Skinbjerg, 2020).

What then, does the COVID-19 mean for various travel and hospitality firms? When it comes to larger-scale multinationals, these companies operate across long supply chains in order to minimize their production costs. As a consequence of the crisis, however, they may have to re-examine their practices and concentrate on shorter, regional or local supply chains. This may entail both contracting more local providers of food, raw materials and services, as well as instituting a shift in the labour force's composition (e.g., substituting low-waged migrants with domestic employees). Could such collaborative agreements be framed according to guidelines, which more closely adhere to the tenets of sustainable development such as green practices and fair labor conditions?

On another note, do current circumstances signify a reduction in the attractivity of certain growth hotspots such as large and densely inhabited urban centers, which traditionally have drawn major international investments and visitors because these places may now be considered as too risky? If this is the case, it would open up the opportunity for less attractive, more sparsely populated regions to enhance their competitiveness as tourism destinations. Accordingly, would this create a scenario where smaller-scale, locally controlled and operated niche companies can step up to the challenge by flexibly catering to market demands?

Policy implications: design opportunity for sustainable transitions?

To be sure, the tourism sector has traditionally shown considerable resilience in rebounding in the aftermath of crises and disasters, including previous regionally-based epidemics such as SARS. Commonly, this recovery has been assisted through the intervention of local, regional or national governments, which create an environment whereby, in the prevailing spirit of neoliberalism, they entice investors through a series of incentives (tax breaks, lifting of stringent land use regulations, etc.) (Brouder, 2020). Even at present, due to the huge negative effect of COVID-19 on the airlines, the US government has committed to provide the industry a rescue packet amounting to 25 billion dollars (BBC, 2020). Similarly, the European Union, which notoriously opposes state subsidies to air carriers, has endorsed the Danish government's aid of 137 million euro to SAS to deal with the effects of the Corona virus (TravelNews, 2020). As tourism is a strategic economic sector in all Mediterranean countries, it is expected that the European Union will earmark about one fifth of its COVID-19 funds for tourism, making the industry the largest beneficiary of its recovery plan (Nicolás, 2020).

It is important, however, to recognize that unlike previous events, the present Corona pandemic qualifies as a sudden shock, which occurs on multiple scales (Lew, 2014). This is because the pandemic-induced crisis overlaps with several other crises, including those on socio-political but also production/consumer demand levels. In the situation of a pandemic, which has clearly been exacerbated because of the mechanisms of globalization and the mass circulation of goods and people, it is becoming increasingly clear that it is not enough to offer quick band-aid fixes to deal with the consequences. By bailing out only the large-scale travel and tourism players (airlines, multinational hotel chains and tour operators) there is a real danger that existing power asymmetries in the sector will prevail. What about the locally-based small and medium-sized businesses, not to mention the millions of lowly-paid workers who depend so heavily on international visitors? We should question the logic of handing out bailouts to companies (e.g., airlines and cruise lines) that are notorious for their dubious and, sometimes outright unethical, business practices when it comes to complying with guidelines on issues such the environment or workers' rights.

Recently, Robert Reich (2020) who served as US Labor Secretary under the Clinton administration penned an opinion piece in *The Guardian* lamenting the bailout of major US-based corporations because of the COVID-19 crisis. He argues that under the Trump administration, these companies have benefitted massively from huge tax cuts, using these to pay out bonuses for executives while many of their workers struggle to survive. His point is that such incentives do nothing to support middle class, lower-middle class and working class families and, as such, are "morally intolerable."

On a global scale, interventions such as these aim at keeping a capitalist market logic alive (Fletcher, 2011) and yet, this logic thrives on unjustifiable value capture in situations where the externalities are absorbed by the environment, the precarious labor force, host communities, and mom-and-pop businesses. Thus, we argue that any intervention must come with plenty of strings attached. Indeed, the COVID-19 crisis opens up the unique opportunity whereby funders can request that recipient transnational companies must fix issues relating to resource and waste handling, labor exploitation and benefit redistribution.

Closing remarks

Sustainability, we have often said, will be achieved eventually – either by disaster or by design. As streets are emptied and planes are grounded, air pollution has gone down, and the global carbon footprint has decreased. (Hanscom, 20th March, 2020)

The beneficial effects of the crisis on global emissions and air quality are immediate and palpable. However, instead of cheering, the CEO of the Global Footprint Network acknowledges the gravity of the situation triggered by COVID-19 and stresses that present circumstances run contrary to one of GFN's fundamental goals that *everyone* will eventually be able to "thrive within the means of our planet." Nevertheless, despite her reservations, we believe that the present crisis has opened up an unprecedented situation, allowing us to grasp the opportunity and to rectify an otherwise defective global system.

While it is certainly not easy to shift path-dependent institutional mindsets, which are driven by the logic of capitalism's need to reinvent itself (Harvey, 2020), the pause we find ourselves in at this moment offers the possibility for sketching a new way forward in the years to come. We must, of course, caution that for us, the tourism scholars, this should not be limited only to intellectual reflections and scenario-building exercises. Rather, we should start taking responsibility by being active participants in enabling substantial changes to happen. As a beginning we must seriously think about redesigning our curricula and educational activities in order to train students to gain skills in complexity-thinking, knowledge of post-capitalist economies and collaborative business models.

Disclosure statement

No potential conflict of interest was reported by the author(s).

ORCID

Dimitri Ioannides ⓘ https://orcid.org/0000-0002-3549-750X

References

BBC. (2020, April 15). US airlines to receive $25bn rescue package. *BBC*. https://www.bbc.com/news/business-52288860

Brouder, P. (2020). Reset Redux: possible evolutionary pathways towards the transformation of tourism in a COVID-19 world. *Tourism Geographies*. https://doi:10.1080/14616688.2020. 1760928

Chanel, S. (2020, April 15). 'It's catastrophic': Fiji's colossal tourism sector devastated by coronavirus. *The Guardian*. https://www.theguardian.com/world/2020/apr/16/its-catastrophic-fijis-colossal-tourism-sector-devastated-by-coronavirus

Cohen, E. (2011). Tourism and land grab in the aftermath of the Indian Ocean tsunami. *Scandinavian Journal of Hospitality and Tourism*, *11*(3), 224–236. https://doi.org/10.1080/15022250.2011.593359

Di Domenico, M., Haugh, H., & Tracey, P. (2010). Social bricolage: Theorizing social value creation in social enterprises. *Entrepreneurship Theory and Practice*, *34*(4), 681–703. https://doi.org/10.1111/j.1540-6520.2010.00370.x

Engle, N. L. (2011). Adaptive capacity and its assessment. *Global Environmental Change*, *21*(2), 647–656. https://doi.org/10.1016/j.gloenvcha.2011.01.019

Fletcher, R. (2011). Sustaining Tourism, Sustaining Capitalism? The Tourism Industry's Role in Global Capitalist Expansion. *Tourism Geographies*, *13*(3), 443–461. https://doi.org/10.1080/14616688.2011.570372

Glusac, E. (2020, April 15). How will COVID-19 affect future travel behavior? A travel crisis expert explains. *New York Times*. https://www.nytimes.com/2020/04/15/travel/q-and-a-coronavirus-travel.html?action=click&module=Features&pgtype=Homepage

Goodwin, H. (2020, April 12). Latest developments in responsible tourism. *Responsible Tourism Partnership*. https://responsibletourismpartnership.org/2020/04/12/latest-developments-in-responsible-tourism-04-2020/

Hall, C. M. (2015). The coming perfect storm: Medical tourism as a biosecurity issue. In N. Lunt, D. Horsfall, & J. Hanefeld (Eds.), *Handbook on Medical Tourism and Patient Mobility* (pp. 193–204). Edward Elgar Publishing.

Hanscom, L. (2020, March 20). Letter from the CEO: Reflecting on the sudden shift in our global reality. *Global Footprint Network*.https://www.footprintnetwork.org/2020/03/20/letter-from-the-ceo-reflecting-on-the-sudden-shift-in-our-global-reality/

Harvey, D. (2020, March 19). Anti-capitalist politics in the time of COVID-19. *davidharvey.org*. http://davidharvey.org/2020/03/anti-capitalist-politics-in-the-time-of-covid-19/

Hjalager, A. M. (2002). Repairing innovation defectiveness in tourism. *Tourism Management*, *23*(5), 465–474. https://doi.org/10.1016/S0261-5177(02)00013-4

Ioannides, D. (1994). *The state, transnationals, and the dynamics of tourism evolution in small island nations* [Unpublished Ph.D. dissertation]. Rutgers University.

Irwin, N. (2020, April16). It's the end of the world economy as we know it. *New York Times*. www.nytimes.com/2020/04/16/upshot/world-economy-restructuring-coronavirus.html

Johannisson, B., & Olaison, L. (2007). The moment of truth—Reconstructing entrepreneurship and social capital in the eye of the storm. *Review of Social Economy*, *65*(1), 55–78. https://doi.org/10.1080/00346760601132188

Keskitalo, E. C. H. (2008). Vulnerability and adaptive capacity in forestry in northern Europe: a Swedish case study. *Climatic Change*, *87*(1-2), 219–234. https://doi.org/10.1007/s10584-007-9337-1

Kimmelman. (2020, March 23). The great empty: *New York Times*. https://www.nytimes.com/interactive/2020/03/23/world/coronavirus-great-empty.html

Kontogeorgopoulos, N. (1999). Sustainable tourism of sustainable development? Financial crisis, ecotourism, and the 'Amazing Thailand' campaign. *Current Issues in Tourism*, *2*(4), 316–332. https://doi.org/10.1080/13683509908667859

Lew, A. A. (2014). Scale, change and resilience in community tourism planning. *Tourism Geographies*, *16*(1), 14–22. https://doi.org/10.1080/14616688.2013.864325

Loorbach, D., Frantzeskaki, N., & Avelino, F. (2017). Sustainability transitions research: transformingscience and practice for societal change. *Annual Review of Environment and Resources*, *42*(1), 599–626. https://doi.org/10.1146/annurev-environ-102014-021340

McGrath, M. (2020, March 19). Coronavirus: Air pollution & CO_2 fall rapidly as virus spreads. *BBC*. https://www.bbc.com/news/science-environment-51944780

Milano, C., Cheer, J. M. & Novelli, M. (Eds.). (2019). *Overtourism: Excesses, discontents and measures in travel and tourism*. CABI.

Miles, L., & Petridou, E. (2015). Entrepreneurial resilience: Role of policy entrepreneurship in the political perspective of crisis management. In I. Aflaki, E. Petridou & L. Miles (Eds.), *Entrepreneurship in the Polis: Understanding Political Entrepreneurship* (pp. 67–81). Routledge.

Miles, L., & Shipway, R. (2020). Exploring the COVID-19 Pandemic as a Catalyst for Stimulating Future Research Agendas for Managing Crises and Disasters at International Sport Events. *Event Management*, https://doi.org/10.3727/152599519X15506259856688

Newton, C. (2020, April 3). Google uses location data to show which places are complying with stay-at-home orders – and which aren't. *The Verge*. https://www.theverge.com/2020/4/3/21206318/google-location-data-mobility-reports-covid-19-privacy

Nicolás, E. S. (2020, April 22). EU pledges help, as tourism faces €400bn hit. *EU Observer*. https://euobserver.com/coronavirus/148137

Novelli, M., Burgess, L. G., Jones, A., Ritchie, B. W. (2018). No Ebola ... still doomed"–The Ebola-induced tourism crisis. *Annals of Tourism Research*, *70*, 76–87. https://doi.org/10.1016/j.annals.2018.03.006

Papatheodorou, A., Rosselló, J., & Xiao, H. (2010). Global economic crisis and tourism: Consequences and perspectives. *Journal of Travel Research*, *49*(1), 39–45. https://doi.org/10.1177/0047287509355327

Reich, R. (2020, March 22). It's morally repulsive how corporations are exploiting the crisis. Workers will suffer. *New York Times*. https://www.nytimes.com/2020/04/15/travel/q-and-a-coronavirus-travel.html?action=click&module=Features&pgtype=Homepage

Skinbjerg, D. (2020). April 10). Wonderful Copenhagen: Turistbranchen taber milliarder. *Finans*. https://finans.dk/erhverv/ECE12012996/wonderful-copenhagen-turistbranchen-taber-milliarder/?ctxref=ext.

Sundbo, J., Orfila-Sintes, F., & Sørensen, F. (2007). The innovative behaviour of tourism firms-Comparative studies of Denmark and Spain. *Research Policy*, *36*(1), 88–106. https://doi.org/10.1016/j.respol.2006.08.004

TravelNews. (2020, April 16). EU godkänner danskt statsstöd till SAS. *TravelNews*. https://www.travelnews.se/flyg/eu-godkanner-danskt-statsstod-till-sas/

Tsao, C. Y., & Ni, C. C. (2016). Vulnerability, resilience, and the adaptive cycle in a crisis prone tourism community. *Tourism Geographies*, *18*(1), 80–105. https://doi.org/10.1080/14616688.2015.1116600

UNWTO. (2020, April 14). COVID-19: Putting people first. *UNWTO*. https://www.unwto.org/tourism-covid-19

Watts, J. & Kommenda, N. (2020, March 23). Coronavirus pandemic leading to huge drop in air pollution. *The Guardian*. https://www.theguardian.com/environment/2020/mar/23/coronavirus-pandemic-leading-to-huge-drop-in-air-pollution

Zeng, B., Carter, R. W., & De Lacy, T. (2005). Short-term perturbations and tourism effects: The case of SARS in China. *Current Issues in Tourism*, *8*(4), 306–322. https://doi.org/10.1080/13683500508668220

Reconnecting tourism after COVID-19: the paradox of alterity in tourism areas

Dominic Lapointe (iD)

ABSTRACT

One of the transformations induced by the almost complete halt of tourism due to the COVID-19 pandemic has been a turning of the tourism sectors to a greater orientation towards their host communities. The enclavic tendencies of tourism areas, along with a multilayered approach to alterity gives insight into ongoing changes in the Quebec, Canada, tourism industry that have been enhanced by the COVID-19 pandemic. These changes points to a relinking of tourism to the needs of the host communities as part of a survival strategy in a time when there are no tourists, and could become, in the long run, a resilience strategy. On the other hand, there is a possibility of a reinforcement of the alterity and a further delinking of tourism in a "6 foot-tourism world" where sanitary safety would be at the core of a closed and controlled tourism development.

摘要

由于新冠肺炎疫情在全球广泛传播，造成旅游业几乎完全停摆。它所带来的一个转变是，旅游部门转向更重视其所在社区。旅游区的飞地化倾向，以及对疫情变化的多层次研究，使我们能够洞察到加拿大魁北克省旅游业正在发生的变化，这些变化因新冠肺炎疫情大流行而加剧。这些变化表明，在一个没有游客的时代，旅游业需要重新适应当地社区的需求，这是旅游业生存战略的一部分，从长远来看，可能会成为一种弹性战略。另一方面，疫情有可能进一步切断旅游业的联系，并重建人们"6英尺旅游生活世界"，而公共卫生安全将是这种封闭和受控制旅游发展的核心。

As the COVID-19 pandemic unfolds, skyrocketing international tourism numbers have fallen like a stone with forecasted trends shifting dramatically from the predicted 3-4% annual growth to a 20-30% decline for 2020 (UNWTO, 2020). According to its April 14, 2020 brief, the World Travel & Tourism Council (WTTC) estimates that 75 million jobs are at risk globally with a potential Travel & Tourism GDP loss of up to $2.1 trillion this year (WTTC, 2020). As 166 countries restrict entry into their national territories, global mobilities have come to a near standstill leaving tourism destinations empty handed as their main resource, mobile tourists, are effectively absent. The smooth space of international tourism has suddenly become highly striated (Deleuze & Guattari, 1980). This situation is deeply paradoxical: everyday micro-mobilities have been constrained as a result of hedonistic macro-mobilities, i.e. international tourism, responsible for spreading the virus around the world. Moreover, social isolation and quarantine are exposing the reality that most organized tourism operations and revenue streams are not embedded within the essential economy of host communities, pointing to the enclavic tendencies of tourism (Saarinen, 2017; Judd, 1999) in creating physical and symbolic boundaries in the multiple layers of alterity (MIT, 2008). Of the transformations that tourism could undergo in response to the hardship of the COVID-19 pandemic, we may experience the re-embedding of some tourism businesses into essential local economies in an effort to overcome alterity while, paradoxically, health concerns and social distancing could lead to some tourism areas becoming even more enclavic. To explore this paradoxical transformation, we will quickly review the literature on enclave tourism, linking it to the process of alterity in tourism areas and their potential for territorialization and deterritorialization (Deleuze & Guattari, 1980; Lapointe, 2020).

The trend for tourism to tend towards the development of differentiated space is epitomized by Judd (1999) in *Constructing the tourists' bubbles*. In this exposé, he points out how American cities have been securing and homogenizing space for tourism activities. Through this process, tourism becomes an autonomous urban function providing entertainment, fantastical authenticity and safety to visitors, in disjunction with the resident populations. The latter are simultaneously part of the tourism product as they perform their own daily life and excluded from the performance (Minca & Oakes, 2006). This operates through the emergence of physical and symbolic boundaries (Manuel-Navarrete, 2016), negotiated through discourses of development and regionalism (Saarinen, 2004).

> Based on this approach, destinations tend to transform toward more standardized and homogenous tourist spaces mainly serving the needs of non-locals, i.e. visitors, and, at the same time, they are differentiated from their surrounding socio-cultural and economic environment, turning the local tourism development path toward enclavization. (Saarinen, 2017: 429)

Through the concept of economy of presence, this service economy for the non-locals has been tackled by the French territorial development tenet (Pecqueur & Tallandier, 2011). In this form of development, the economy of presence is not about producing value in place, as in traditional industrial development, but rather capturing the surplus from value created elsewhere through consumption by mobile subjects present in place, especially tourists, seasonal residents and commuters. Further, they point to the economy of absence, examining who these mobile subjects are replacing by using Paris as an interesting example, where tourism consumption barely replaces the residents' non-consumption while they are absent (Terrier, 2006). This articulation creates a double alterity whereby visitors encounter the alterity of the place visited, and locals exist in the co-presence of an industry catering to the needs of non-locals.

This double alterity must be addressed in order to look at the transformation of tourism due to the COVID-19 pandemic. Places can be the markers of alterity. Through boundaries geographically establishing differentiated space, the others' place is defined and rules of conduct, about who is in place and who is out of place, are formed (Cresswell, 1996). Tourism is part of the production of alterity in its discursive practices of otherness and social control, where it defines not only who is the other being visited but also what can and cannot be done, where, and by whom (Dann, 1996).

Tourism seeks these alterities as tourists crisscross the planet experiencing differences, sometimes subtle, from one place to another. Alterity is not always associated with distances (MIT, 2008). Sometimes, the experience of alterity is just around the corner, where differences and alterity may be located. It can thus become some form of place recoding (Hollinshead & Suleman, 2018). This recoding can accentuate alterity to satisfy tourist demand and needs by evacuating the dimension of their daily life through the spectacularization of space (Judd, 1999) or reducing alterity by touristifying daily life (Bélanger et al., 2020; Russo & Scarnato, 2018). This alterity between local residents and tourism can be important enough to actually reconceptualize them as local "others" and target them as potential "tourists" in their own city (Diaz-Soria, 2017).

We observe this situation acutely when encountering mono-industrial communities where tourism is the main, if not the only, economic activity. The situation in Tadoussac in Québec, Canada, is quite exemplary of this. While being successful as a tourism destination with annual visitation at around 300 000 tourists for a local population of 799 inhabitants, in 2016, there are major issues for the resident populations, expressing that reliance on tourism as their only industry puts them at risk (Lebon et al., 2018). High seasonality, external stakeholders and local political institutions lacking in agency over tourism development are ongoing challenges. As tourism numbers grow in Tadoussac, year-long services and resident populations decline. Limited access to basic commercial services, including food retailers, has become an issue during the low season. Local development is entirely based on tourism, with development, planning and public action being pushed along to satisfy the visitors' demand for alterity. These visitors are the main beneficiaries not only of the community amenities, but also of a prominent economic system tailored to capture their consumption at the expense of resident populations' needs. All development is based on this alterity and is constructing a disconnect between places of value production, places of consumption, and a whole system to capture value created elsewhere (a third alterity that isn't explored in this paper) (Pecqueur & Talandier, 2011). Now, COVID-19 has halted mobilities at the core of this double alterity, leaving places with an economic structure tailored to capture mobile consumer demand without mobile consumption to capture. This brutal crisis calls for a transformation of the tourism economy towards overcoming alterity and reconnecting tourism services to some of the local needs.

The restriction of nonessential services, movement and travel, and the closing down of sites where social distancing has not been possible during a time of mobilities, has made tourism a casualty of the COVID-19 pandemic. With the flow of international and domestic travelers stopped, a portion of businesses tailored to tourism services are left with few, if any, clients. Alternatively, in some places there may be a reconnection of some components of the tourism industry with the local community and their needs, in an attempt to overcome the alterity that has been created. The focus here remains on examples within Québec, Canada, with limitations imposed by the nature of the rapid and unpredictable progress of this situation, and initiatives taking place within a time of crisis management. In Abitibi-Témiscamingue, a region north of Montreal, the hospitality sector has collaborated with the public health authority to provide accommodation for its medical staff; employees and doctors who have not been able to return to their homes because family members are in isolation. With the characteristically long distances in and between areas of low population density, albeit an attractive feature for tourism, local accommodation has also allowed health workers to avoid driving back home during a period of long shifts and overtime work.

A second illustration relates to many restaurants, especially in Montreal and Québec City where tourism is an important part of the local economy, reframing their activities and discourses around providing meals for the local population. This is taking the form of meal pick-up, home deliveries and drive-through. Moreover, the regional association of restaurateurs has developed a public communications campaign: *Feeding people, feeding our people*, and is paired with a broader initiative by the provincial government focusing on incentives to support buying local. At this stage, it is still too early to know how some niche *terroir* producers, accustomed to selling luxury food items within agritourism schemes, will democratize their products and develop an economically viable and accessible solution for the localized, small scale production systems.

A final example being witnessed in Québec is the tendency for tourism sites to go online. While this can be seen as merely a marketing strategy – indeed it is, in part – some businesses have shifted focus towards creating educational materials available for parents in their communities, suddenly forced to homeschool their kids. Museums, zoos and science centers are cooperating with the school boards to develop home-teaching materials. Further, the tourist guidebook company Ulysse is also re-embedding its activities within the local economy, releasing a children's "Guide to Québec" which, during lockdown, can be used as material for learning about the social geography of the province. Although these various initiatives can be seen as strategies for survival, in the long term they could become initiatives of resilience in an effort to diversify the customer base and rely more on a local market, less subject to future mobility restrictions.

While we are seeing the transformation of several segments of the tourism industry towards a desenclavic movement to overcome the local/tourist alterity, paradoxically we are also witnessing a shift in the opposite direction as further enclavic tourism activities are justified by sanitary guidelines and restrictions, at least until a vaccine will be available. We could call these the 6 foot-tourism products. Following this tendency, alterity will be reinforced along class lines, based on who can and cannot afford leisure mobility, as well as immunity lines (which won't be addressed in this commentary), according to who has and has not been cured from the virus by having developed or acquired the antibodies. The class line will materialize in the form of rising prices for tourism products as they undergo demassification, to allow for the 6 ft space around clients. Planes flying with 6 ft between seats, resorts with fewer guests and larger dining rooms, restaurants and bars selling luxury goods to socially distanced customers – fewer clients; more space; more rent; costlier. These types of enclavic products will be even more disconnected from their local environment, with immunity tests for staff and protection from the outside environment secured due to sanitary risk, reinforced through development discourses based on sanitation and safety. In 6 ft-tourism, the enclave and therefore alterity is key because it is constructed as safe.

CODA

In the Post-COVID-19 era tourism will be transformed. As mobilities continue to be strongly impaired due to sanitation orders, some tourism businesses and areas will see their economy of presence shrink, forcing them to turn towards local consumers and their needs. Upon rising immunity, the tourist, other, will once again become part of the landscape while the local links built during the crisis period may remain, as diversification and resilience strategies. In contrast, if mobilities remain highly constrained for an extended period of time and the 6 ft-tourism era becomes the new normal, an even more enclavic alterity-building tourism industry may appear. In a much more striated space-world, there would be some smooth corridors of mobilities creating reterritorialization, following Deleuze and Guattari (1980), that is, the transformation of the tourism sector within the striated zones, and simultaneous deterritorializing movements in the smooth corridors of 6 ft-tourism products.

Deleuze and Guattari (1980) pointed at the hand as a deterritorialized paw. The enclavic double alterity tendencies of tourism that we exposed here echo this deterritorialization movement, with tourism being deterritorialized daily life (Lapointe, 2020). As the COVID-19 pandemic wrestles tourism down to earth, the deterritorialization movements of tourism could be reinforced and 6 ft-tourism may become the new normal for tourism. There will also have to be a reterritorializing movement of practices and performances anchored to local subjectivities, desires and needs – a reterritorializing movement to inhabit striated space that might call for a new and different name, other than tourism.

Disclosure statement

No potential conflict of interest was reported by the author(s).

ORCID

Dominic Lapointe ⓘ http://orcid.org/0000-0002-5696-1471

References

Bélanger, H., Lapointe, D., & Guillemard, A. (2020). Central neighbourhoods revitalization and tourists bubble: From gentrification to touristification of daily life in Montréal. In J. Bean (Ed.), *Critical practices in architecture: the unexamined* (pp. 71–94). Cambridge Scholars Publishing.

Cresswell, T. (1996). *In place/out of place: Geography, ideology, and transgression*. University of Minnesota Press.

Dann, G. (1996). *The language of tourism: A sociolinguistic perspective*. CABI

Deleuze, G., & Guattari, F. (1980). *Milles Plateaux*. Les éditions de minuits.

Diaz-Soria, I. (2017). Being a tourist as a chosen experience in a proximity destination. *Tourism Geographies, 19*(1), 96–117. https://doi.org/10.1080/14616688.2016.1214976

Hollinshead, K., & Suleman, R. (2018). The everyday instillations of worldmaking: New vistas of understanding on the declarative reach of tourism. *Tourism Analysis, 23*(2), 201–213. https://doi.org/10.3727/108354218X15210313504553

Judd, D. R. (1999). Constructing the tourist bubble. In D. R. Judd & S. S. Fainstein (Eds.), *The tourist city* (pp. 35–53). Yale University Press.

Lapointe, D. (2020). Tourism territory/territoire(s) touristique(s): when mobility challenges the concept. In M. Stock (Ed.), *Progress in Francophone tourism geographies. Inhabiting touristic worlds* (pp. 104–118). Springer.

Lebon, C., Lapointe, D., et al. (2018). Community well-being between climate risk and tourism development. In B.S.R. Grimwood (Ed.). *Tourism and wellness: Travel for the good of all?* Lexington Book.

Manuel-Navarrete, D. (2016). Boundary-work and sustainability in tourism enclaves. *Journal of Sustainable Tourism, 24*(4), 507–526. https://doi.org/10.1080/09669582.2015.1081599

Minca, C., & Oakes, T. (2006). Introduction: Travelling paradoxes. In C. Minca & T. Oakes (Eds.), *Travels in paradox* (pp. 1–32). Rowman & Littlefield.

MIT. (2008). *Tourismes 1: Lieux communs*. Belin

Pecqueur, B., & Talandier, M. (2011). *Les espaces de développement résidentiel et touristique–état des lieux et problématiques. Territoires 2040*. DATAR.

Russo, A. P., & Scarnato, A. (2018). Barcelona in common": A new urban regime for the 21st-century tourist city? *Journal of Urban Affairs, 40*(4), 455–474.

Saarinen, J. (2004). 'Destinations in change': The transformation process of tourist destinations. *Tourist Studies, 4*(2), 161–179. https://doi.org/10.1177/1468797604054381

Saarinen, J. (2017). Enclavic tourism spaces: Territorialization and bordering in tourism destination development and planning. *Tourism Geographies, 19*(3), 425–437. https://doi.org/10.1080/14616688.2016.1258433

Terrier, C. (2006). *Mobilité touristique et population présente*. Ministère du Tourisme.

UNWTO. (2020) *International tourism arrivals could fall by 20-30% in 2020*. https://www.unwto.org/news/international-tourism-arrivals-could-fall-in-2020?fbclid=IwAR1m54QtK-WGn3RoHIIALy6IsuYYquLsoHU-4Nr3stJFJMcIvXadvXdxEhg

WTTC. (2020). Corona Virus Brief: *April 14 2020*. https://wttc.org/Portals/0/Documents/WTTC%20Coronavirus%20Brief%20External%2014_04.pdf?ver=2020-04-15-081805-253

Covid-19 is an unnatural disaster: Hope in revelatory moments of crisis

Mary Mostafanezhad

ABSTRACT

The unfolding COVID-19 pandemic has closed borders, grounded planes, quarantined more than half of the world's population, triggered anxiety en masse, and shaken global capitalism to its core. Scholars of the political ecology of disasters have sought to denaturalize so-called "natural" disasters by demonstrating their uneven consequences. Work in the political ecology of health similarly accounts for how risk of illness and disease are socioeconomically mediated. While this scholarship has demonstrated the need to contextualize the unequal fallout from ecological and health disasters in ways that reveal the festering wounds of structural inequality, we know much less about how hope is cultivated in moments of crisis. The current revelatory moment of the COVID-19 pandemic offers an opportunity to find hope in the rubble through the deconstruction of framings of crisis as "error" and by homing in on the current and potential role of tourism to contribute to a more socially and environmentally just society. This reframing the pandemic as an "unnatural" disaster opens new debates at the intersection of tourism geographies and political ecologies of hope in revelatory moments of crisis.

摘要

不断扩散的新冠肺炎导致边境关闭、航班停飞,全世界半数以上的人口居家隔离,进而引发大范围的焦虑甚至动摇了资本主义的核心。灾难政治生态学学者研究发现所谓的天灾其实有相当大部分是起源于人祸,而健康政治生态学的相关成果也说明社会经济行为对于疾病感染与传播的风险有缓解作用。尽管此类成果已表明审时度势地采取措施应对灾难与疾病随机多变的后果很有必要,但在危机时刻有望解决的办法仍是寥寥无几。就像新冠病毒疫情暴露出愈益严重地结构性不公,而人们对这一未知事物也只是焦头烂额地疲于应对。不过,在此过程中我们认为可以从政治生态学的视角将危机事件解构为种种人为"错误",然后从旅游地理学的视角寻根溯源,进而依靠旅游业当前与潜在的影响力促进社会公平与环境可持续,这为解读危机中的转机开创出学科间新的对话渠道。

Introduction

The unfolding COVID-19 pandemic has closed borders, grounded planes, quarantined more than half of the world's population, triggered anxiety en masse, and shaken global capitalism to its core. Scholars of the political ecology of disasters have sought to denaturalize so-called "natural" disasters by demonstrating their disproportionate consequences, while work on the political ecology of health similarly accounts for how risk of illness and disease are socio-economically mediated. While this scholarship has demonstrated the need to contextualize the uneven consequences of disaster and health, we still know very little about how hope is cultivated in moments of crisis. This commentary integrates the aforementioned scholarship to not only account for how the unequal consequences of the COVID-19 disaster reveals the festering wounds of structural inequality, but also how, in this revelatory moment, we may find hope in the rubble. By deconstructing framings of crisis as "error" and homing in on the current and potential role of tourism to contribute to a more socially and environmentally just and sustainable society, this commentary opens new debates at the intersection of tourism geographies and political ecologies of hope in revelatory moments of crisis.

Crisis and the unnatural consequences of disaster

Crises, on one hand, are historical judgments that mark epochal transitions (Barrios, 2017: 151). Marshal Sahlins (1972) describes how crises may be revelatory in so far as they lay bare the structural contradictions of the modes of production that can no longer be ignored (Sahlins, 1972), while Janet Roitman (2013) highlights how crisis narratives also produce meaning and initiate critique of a given condition. Commentators on the COVID-19 crisis have addressed its potentially transformational role. Thomas Friedman, for instance, suggested that "There is the world B.C. — Before Corona — and the world A.C. — After Corona" (Friedman, 2020). Disaster, on the other hand, accounts for "the end result of historical processes by which human practices enhance the materially destructive and socially disruptive capacities of geophysical phenomena, technological malfunctions, and communicable diseases ... " (Barrios, 2017: 151). In his seminal text, `Man-made Disasters model", Turner describes the "disaster incubation period" by which he accounts for the how disasters rarely develop instantaneously, but rather are the result of an "accumulation over a period of time of a number of events which are at odds with the picture of the world and its hazards represented by existing norms and beliefs (Pidgeon & O'Leary, 2000: 16). Scholarship on the political ecology of disasters has built on these early observations, focusing on various forms of environmental degradation, most notably climate change (Barnes & Dove, 2015; McElwee, 2016; Orr et al., 2015; Nyaupane & Chhetri, 2009). Thus, the vulnerability and consequences that societies will bare from COVID-19, like other disasters, anthropogenic or otherwise, are not one of nature but a question of politics and economy (O'Keefe, 1976). Thus, as David Harvey writes, "There is ... no such thing as a truly natural disaster" (Harvey, 2020), because "Capital modifies the environmental conditions of its own reproduction but does so in a context of unintended consequences" (Harvey, 2020). In this way, the pandemic has the potential to reveal the structural inequalities through which differential health and economic outcomes materialize in, yet well beyond COVID-19.

The aftershocks of the Covid-19 pandemic will present us with an unprecedented opportunity to reimagine more resilient and equitable tourism forms (Lew et al., 2016). Yet, through the reframing of the COVID-19 pandemic as "error" or malfunction of current industry norms, it is also possible that this potential may be squandered. Those with the means to monopolize what will become the post- COVID-19 tourism industry will undoubtedly seek to do so. Smaller, locally owned tourist venues close daily while corporations that support tourism and are "too big to fail" receive state support to not only survive but thrive through consolidation with less fortunate competitors. Just as the top 1% of Americans captured 91% of the income growth after the Great Recession, we may find that the precarity of most tourism industry actors will follow suit. Indeed, as one *Forbes* commenter suggests, "this simply is the normal reaction of inequality to a recession. The rich lose the most in the recession and then gain the most in the aftermath and recovery. That second simply being a result of the first" (Worstall, 2020). The need for a new "normal" could not be more urgent and activists and academics around the world have sought for their audiences to heed this warning. As Edward Huijbens (2020) explains, "That is not tourism as business as usual. That is a completely different type of tourism that starts in our own backyards". As states prepare for the economic fallout of COVID-19, we may also witness how crisis is appropriated as a political tool to stabilize existing political-economic structures as well as bridle efforts towards collective mobilization (Masco, 2017).

These responses are familiar tricks in what Naomi Klein (2017) describes as the disaster capitalist playbook in which she describes with disturbing clarity how power profits from disaster. She explains, "Shock tactics follow a clear pattern: wait for a crisis …, declare a moment of what is sometimes called 'extraordinary politics', suspend some or all democratic norms – and then ram the corporate wish list through as quickly as possible" (Klein, 2017). While Klein first described these plays more than a decade ago, they resonate deeply with the current response to the COVID-19 disaster. With one out of 10 people in the world working in tourism and the industry accounting for 10% of the global GDP, the effect of this kind of socio-economic restructuring could echo the post-2004 Indian Ocean tsunami recovery efforts where, as Rob Fletcher recalls, there was a deepening of privatization and corporate consolidation (Fletcher et al., 2020).

Hope in revelatory moments of crisis

As a "world-making force" (Huijbens, 2020), tourism has the potential to play a pivotal role in the reshaping of society (Gibson, 2019). Yet, the story of how COVID-19 will restructure society is yet to be written and there is reason to believe that citizens around the world will push back against efforts to appropriate the crisis narrative in ways that consolidate power (Klein, 2020). Thus, finding hope in moments of crisis requires a recognition of the structural inequalities through which the uneven aftermath of disaster strikes. The tourism industry and progressive actors within it have begun contributing to this endeavor of finding hope in the rubble in creative ways.

"Pre-coronavirus travel and tourist industries," Andrew Evans warns us, "will not function in a post-coronavirus world" and everything including "our very concept of vacation may have to change" (2020). Tourism focused scholars have heeded these warnings and sought to identify the silver lining of the COVID-19 pandemic. Several have already offered points of departure for rebuilding a more sustainable and just tourism (e.g. Fletcher et al., 2020). In this vein, Alan Lew contends that "We need to take this opportunity to listen and learn what our larger planet-self is trying to tell us" (2020), while Pope Francis has suggested that COVID-19 may be nature's response to climate change (Wise, 2020). Indeed, reports (substantiated or otherwise) abound that describe how non-human earthly cohabitants are thriving as more than half the planet is quarantined behind walls (MacDonald, 2020): "Nature is taking back Venice" (Brunton, 2020), reads one headline. As air pollution plummets, globally, people have taken notice of the massive impact of human activity on the atmosphere. For instance, "In India, where air pollution is among the world's worst, 'people are reporting seeing the Himalayas for the first time from where they live,'" explained Lauri Myllyvirta, lead analyst at the Helsinki-based Centre for Research on Energy and Clean Air (Gardiner, 2020). Similar observations have been made from Beijing to Durban to Paris (Associated Press, 2020). Commenters are hopeful that the current respite from toxic air "may offer lessons for the kind of world we want to build after the pandemic" (Gardiner, 2020).

In a similar vein, calls for global unity among tourism actors have proliferated from the UNWTO (2020) global tourism crisis committee which calls for a collective response to not only recover, but "grow back better" to a range of INGO and NGOs around the world. As iconic tourism destinations that were once overwhelmed with tourists have witnessed the emptying of streets and cafes for perhaps the first time in decades, people have come to rethink what a middle path might be for the renewal of tourism. In many global tourism destinations, residents are leading the effort to respond to the wave of xenophobic rhetoric triggered by the outbreak. For instance, the French Asian community created the hashtag, #JeNeSuisPasUnVirus (#Iamnotavirus) that has since been translated into numerous languages around the world to fight racial prejudice. In a similar vein, Massimiliano Martigli Jiang, an Italian-Chinese citizen, produced a video of himself standing blindfolded in downtown Florence. He held a sign that read, "I am not a virus, I am a human being, free me from prejudice" as tourists and residents alike hugged him and photographed the encounter. The video has been viewed more than 300,000 times on YouTube and counting. In a similar vein, a Wuhan jiayou! (stay strong Wuhan) solidarity movement developed during the months long quarantine of Wuhan, where global audiences posted pictures of themselves holding signs expressing solidarity with its residents. In major tourism centers throughout Asia, restaurants, shops and markets shared a collective concern for China as it weathered its COVID-19 peak. In a shop window in Phuket, Thailand, a sign read: "The Thai people pray for China and hope China will recover soon. China and Thailand are family!" (Reuters, 2020).

Hope, in these and numerous other mundane and extraordinary ways, circulates widely in this time of crisis. As a powerful antidote to fear, hope has the potential to galvanize social action in ways that support social justice campaigns such as access to health care, livable wages, and affordable education (Pain & Smith, 2012: 209). Thus, as rather than a purely sentimental endeavor, in post-COVID-19 tourism, hope will also be creative practice of solidarity. As part of this practice, Evans (2020) asks tourists to ask themselves: "Who/What/Which resource am I exploiting? How can I make sure my adventure benefits the individuals, communities, cultures, and natural spaces I encounter? How can I support small and medium social enterprises? How can I help empower women around the world? How can I help protect the wildest bits of our planet and make sure they survive this century?"

In efforts to rebuild tourism around more socially and economically just relationships, we may adopt Arjun Appadurai's "ethics of possibility" in order to account for "those ways of thinking, feeling, and acting that increase the horizons of hope, that expand the field of the imagination, that produce greater equity" (Appadurai, 2013, p. 295). Yet, it is important to recognize that hope itself is unevenly distributed and Appadurai cautions us to not lose sight of the broader "ethics of probability" in our rebuilding of society. While it has been suggested that COVID-19 represents "the end of neoliberalism" (Jose, 2020), it is important to proceed cautiously and not let our guard down against efforts to exploit crisis as an accumulation practice or mold it into the latest commodity frontier.

In the context of international development, Bebbington highlights how "'[T]he question becomes not why are some people poor in society, by why some societies tolerate poverty as an outcome and for whom, and how this toleration becomes embedded within institutional norms and systems' (Bebbington, 2007: 806). In the current context, hope is enacted not through normalizing institutions of structural violence through which disease circulates, but rather paying close attention to the political economic accounting of the value of some lives over others. Thus, as Berlant has taught us, "Social optimism has costs when its conventional images involve enforcing normative project of orderliness or truth. This kind of bargaining demands scrutiny, in that desires for progress in some places are so often accompanied by comfort with other social wrongs" (Berlant, 2014, p. 5). If hope for a more socially and environmentally just post-COVID-19 tourism is to be realized and we are to harness the potential of the current crisis to help us rethink how we live, work and travel, we must first recognize the unnatural consequences of the COVID-19 disaster.

Conclusion

COVID-19 will reshape tourism as we previously knew it. Yet, while there are reasons to be hopeful, who will benefit from this restructuring is still an unsettled question. There are currently more than 10 special issues and five books currently being developed to address what COVID-19 means for tourism, many focused on the impacts of COVID-19 on the industry as well as how tourism can be reimagined and enacted in more sustainable and resilient ways. As we collectively seek a more equitable and socially just path forward it is important that we do not hide the forest in search of the trees; the consequences are too severe. We must denaturalize the political-economic drivers of disasters and their human and non-human consequences in ways that not only reveal the open wounds of structural inequality, but also offer more than a band-aid to heal them. This commentary advances scholarship on the political ecology of disasters by adding a hopeful framing to debates surrounding the role of tourism in coping with the current and future challenges posed by the COVID-19 pandemic.

Disclosure statement

No potential conflict of interest was reported by the author(s).

References

Appadurai, A. (2013). *The future as cultural fact: Essays on the global condition*. Verso.

Associated Press. (2020, April 22). As people stay home, earth turns wilder and cleaner. *VOA News, online*. https://www.voanews.com/covid-19-pandemic/people-stay-home-earth-turns-wilder-and-cleaner.

Barnes, J., & Dove, M. R. (2015). *Climate cultures: Anthropological perspectives on climate change*. Yale University Press.

Barrios, R. E. (2017). What does catastrophe reveal for whom? The anthropology of crises and disasters in a'post-truth'world. *Annual Review of Anthropology, 46*(1), 151–166. https://doi.org/10.1146/annurev-anthro-102116-041635

Bebbington, A. (2007). Social movements and the politicization of chronic poverty. *Development and Change, 38*(5), 793–818. https://doi.org/10.1111/j.1467-7660.2007.00434.x

Berlant, L. (Ed.). (2014). *Compassion: The culture and politics of an emotion*. Routledge.

Brunton, J. (2020, March 20). 'Nature is taking back Venice': wildlife returns to tourist-free city. *The Guardian, online*. https://www.theguardian.com/environment/2020/mar/20/nature-is-taking-back-venice-wildlife-returns-to-tourist-free-city.

Evans, A. (2020, April 19). The coronavirus will change how we travel. That will probably be good for us. *NBC News, online*. https://www.nbcnews.com/think/opinion/coronavirus-will-change-how-we-travel-will-probably-be-good-ncna1186681.

Fletcher, R., Murray, I. M., Blázquez-Salom, M., Asunción, B.-R. (2020, March 24). Tourism, Degrowth, and the COVID-19 Crisis. *POLLEN Ecology Network*. https://politicalecologynetwork.org/2020/03/24/tourism-degrowth-and-the-covid-19-crisis/.

Friedman, Thomas L. (2020). *We need herd immunity from trump and the coronavirus*. April 25, 2020. The New York Times. https://www.nytimes.com/2020/04/25/opinion/coronavirus-immunity-trump.html.

Gardiner, Beth. (2020). Pollution made COVID-19 worse. Now, lockdowns are clearing the air. April 8, 2020. *National Geographic*. https://www.nationalgeographic.com/science/2020/04/pollution-made-the-pandemic-worse-but-lockdowns-clean-the-sky/.

Gibson, C. (2019). Critical tourism studies: new directions for volatile times. *Tourism Geographies*, 1–19. https://doi.org/10.1080/14616688.2019.1647453

Huijbens, E. (2020, April 10). Future of tourism after the Corona crisis. https://centreforspaceplacesociety.com/2020/04/10/blog-future-of-tourism-after-the-corona-crisis-by-edward-huijbens/?fbclid=IwAR3j70471Qsj8zAtoeoGFJtofil7BNBVArcuxiQ9yi1lR0vv9Q5HGWfO2-M.

Jose, J. (2020, March 29). Covid-19: Is this the end of neo-liberalism? *The Hindu Business Line, online*. https://www.thehindubusinessline.com/opinion/covid-19-is-this-the-end-of-neo-liberalism/article31197779.ece.

Klein, N. (2017, July 6). Naomi Klein: How Power Profits from Disaster. *The Guardian, online.* https://www.theguardian.com/us-news/2017/jul/06/naomi-klein-how-power-profits-from-disaster.

Klein, N. (2020, March 16). Coronavirus Capitalism—How to Beat it. *The Intercept, online.* https://theintercept.com/2020/03/16/coronavirus-capitalism/.

Lew, A. A., Ng, P. T., Ni, C. C., & Wu, T. C. (2016). Community sustainability and resilience: Similarities, differences and indicators. *Tourism Geographies, 18*(1), 18–27. https://doi.org/10.1080/14616688.2015.1122664

MacDonald, M. (2020, April 15). Animals are rewilding our cities. On YouTube, at least. *The New York Times Magazine, online.* https://www.nytimes.com/2020/04/15/magazine/quarantine-animal-videos-coronavirus.html.

Masco, J. (2017). The crisis in crisis. *Current Anthropology, 58*(S15), S65–S76. https://doi.org/10.1086/688695

McElwee, P. D. (2016). *Forests are gold: Trees, people, and environmental rule in Vietnam.* University of Washington Press.

Nyaupane, G. P., & Chhetri, N. (2009). Vulnerability to climate change of nature-based tourism in the Nepalese Himalayas. *Tourism Geographies, 11*(1), 95–119. https://doi.org/10.1080/14616680802643359

O'Keefe, P. (1976). Taking the "Naturalness" out of Natural Disaster. *Nature (London), 260,* 566–567. https://doi.org/10.1038/260566a0.

Orr, Y., Lansing, J. S., & Dove, M. R. (2015). Environmental anthropology: systemic perspectives. *Annual Review of Anthropology, 44*(1), 153–168. https://doi.org/10.1146/annurev-anthro-102214-014159

Pain, R., & Smith, S. J. (2012). *Fear: critical geopolitics and everyday life.* Ashgate Publishing, Ltd.

Pidgeon, N., & O'Leary, M. (2000). Man-made disasters: why technology and organizations (sometimes) fail. *Safety Science, 34*(1–3), 15–30. https://doi.org/10.1016/S0925-7535(00)00004-7

Reuters. (2020, February 1). Coronavirus hits Thailand tourism as Chinese visitors desert Phuket. *The South China Morning Post, online.* https://www.scmp.com/news/asia/southeast-asia/article/3048543/coronavirus-hits-thailand-tourism-chinese-visitors-desert.

Sahlins, M. (1972). *Stone age economics.* Aldin Atherton.

Roitman, J. (2013). *Anti-crisis.* Duke University Press.

UNWTO. (2020, April 1). UNWTO Launches a Call for Action for Tourism's COVID-19 Mitigation and Recovery. *UNWTO, online* https://www.unwto.org/news/unwto-launches-a-call-for-action-for-tourisms-covid-19-mitigation-and-recovery.

Wise, J. (2020, April 22). Pope says coronavirus outbreak may be one of 'nature's responses' to climate change. *The Hill, online.* https://thehill.com/policy/energy-environment/491734-pope-says-coronavirus-outbreak-may-be-one-of-natures-responses-to.

Worstall, T. (2020, June 20). Of course the top 1% get the most of the recovery - they lost the most in the recession. *Forbes Magazine, online.* https://www.forbes.com/sites/timworstall/2016/06/20/of-course-the-top-1-get-the-most-of-the-recovery-they-lost-the-most-in-the-recession/#352807967d68.

Adventure travel and tourism after COVID-19 – business as usual or opportunity to reset?

Sanjay K. Nepal

Tom Friedman, one of the columnists from the New York Times, opined recently that the current generation will come to think of BC and AC as Before Corona and After Corona (Friedman, 2020) This got me thinking how the world of adventure travel and tourism will look like After Corona. The following commentary is focused on how adventure tourism may respond, after the extraordinary events of these past two months will be behind us.

On February 8, I was on my way to Kathmandu for a tourism-related workshop. China was coming to grips with the Coronavirus, Europe was still a safe destination to travel to, and North America was going about its business as usual, but was wary of what was happening in China, Hong Kong, Taiwan and South Korea. As I arrived at Toronto's Pearson International Airport for my flight to Kathmandu, I was almost shocked how empty the departure lounge was at noon, normally a busy time of the day at the airport. This had a dampening effect on my mood, and I thought about the likely effect on adventure tourism destinations in countries like Nepal which had declared 2020 as the Visit Nepal Year. We all know by now how things have turned out since January 1 of this year; tourism-dependent communities around the world have turned into communities in crisis (Tsao & Ni, 2016).

The tourism industry in Nepal has always worked under the assumption that things will be normal, and that tourists would continue to flock to Nepal, as long as there is growth in international travel. This is also the case for many other adventure tourism destinations around the world including Australia, New Zealand, Norway, Slovenia, Iceland, to name a few countries that capitalize on this sector. A recent news article on COVID-19 effects on Canada's Banff National Park suggests that adventure tourism destinations will have to rethink their business as usual approaches going into the future (Macdonald, 2020). Communities around the world that are heavily dependant on adventure tourism are particularly vulnerable as their livelihood is threatened in unprecedented ways.

This article has been republished with minor changes. These changes do not impact the academic content of the article.

Adventure tourism industries in countries like Nepal have always conducted businesses with their eyes focused on global tourism trends. Since the global economic recession that saw a decline of 40 million tourists between the year 2008 (920 million tourists) and 2009 (880 million tourists), international arrivals have rapidly expanded to 1.46 billion in 2019 (WTO, 2020). This is indeed a remarkable growth that the tourism industry in many countries are closely following. Then the Coronavirus pandemic happened, now, global tourism has come to a complete halt.

I will briefly focus on Nepal, where I have had almost three decades of research experience in high mountain tourism (see Mu et al., 2019; Nepal, 2005). To begin with, the Visit Nepal 2020 Year was not thought out well, especially considering Nepal's goal to attract two million tourists. As of 2019, there were 1.17 million tourists to Nepal (MoCTCA, 2020). I thought the goal of attracting two million tourists was simply crazy even to just think about it – Nepal does not have the infrastructure to support that number. On the contrary, roads that have been haphazardly dug out in the mountains have not only increased the frequency and intensity of landslides, they have simply ruined the aesthetic appeal of the mountains. Annapurna is no longer a classic trekking destination, its mountains that evoke a sense of adventure have been crisscrossed by hazard-prone and hazard-inducing roads. Khumbu (Everest) has become overly commercial, people trying to cash out tourism as if there is no tomorrow. It's as if the tourism industry in Nepal is going "all in", that is, it is thinking of increasing the number of tourists to Nepal no matter the type of tourists, their interests and motivations, and their stay too short to make any meaningful positive impact on the livelihoods of people engaged in tourism. The tourism industry is completely oblivious to the fact that Kathmandu's alarming pollution remains a major deterrent to vast majority of the tourists to Nepal, despite it being the host of several UNESCO heritage sites. Thamel, the hub of tourist services in Kathmandu's core area, has turned into a mini "sin city," unlike its image two decades ago as a gateway for adventure travel. As someone born and raised in Kathmandu, it is painful to see what Thamel has become. Instead of attracting tourists, it is now detracting tourism due to its hedonistic pleasures aimed at locals and tourists.

I think the COVID-19 has given the global adventure tourism industry an opportunity to reset. The adventure travel sector has the opportunity for turning its attention away from haphazard development to one that repositions itself as a major partner in contributing to sustainable and mindful travel. Also, the term adventure needs to be reconceptualized not just in its classical sense of hard adventure activities but also cultural activities that are part and parcels of the total adventure experience. I am interpreting adventure as the "all-inclusive" travel that blends natural and cultural experiences as one big adventure. We cannot go back in time, but we can certainly learn lessons from past mistakes of prioritizing quantity over quality, and destruction over sensible development that can positively influence quality of life and the environment for communities dependent on tourism. The kingdom of Bhutan has learned from Nepal's negative experience and is charting a very different course, though I admit Bhutan's tourism development has its own set of challenges (see Nepal & Karst, 2016). Adventure tourism destinations have to rethink their destination appeal – should they aim to attract adventure tourists of all kinds, or should they focus on specific types with a laser-like focus on quality tourists. A few important steps are needed if the global adventure tourism wants to pivot from an all-in "mass" to "class" tourism development practices. Mass tourism is not going to go away anytime soon, but that needs to be carefully planned, and not considered as "free for all."

1. Improving and reorienting adventure travel destinations' access to international tourism markets – we cannot put all eggs in one basket and need to make significant efforts in developing a diverse portfolio of tourism markets. The freefall of tourism in 2020 should be considered a lesson from overreliance on the Chinese market. Marketing efforts should also focus on the emerging "adventure tourists". These are city-based, below 40 people, increasingly orienting their lifestyle toward exploration and outdoor adventure.

2. Dramatically improving tourism infrastructure and service provisions, particularly at remotely located destinations. New Zealand appears to have done a very good job in this aspect, for example, there are well-placed tourist information centers and high-quality interpretive signs across the country. Hygiene, sanitation, access to quality health services, and trustworthy health and safety information are going to be critical for adventure tourists, particularly for those who are on extended travel. I remember a very unpleasant incident several years ago when one of my Canadian students desperately wanted to use the toilet during a field excursion in Kathmandu. Given the lack of public toilets in the city, I had to approach a resident and request permission to allow my student to use the toilet in his house. There also needs to be a system of regulating and monitoring quality in service provisions. The profusion of trekking and adventure travel agents is not sustainable as it leads to unhealthy competition and price undercutting. Same can be said about the profusion of homestays in rural areas of Nepal, northern Thailand and other rural tourism destinations. This unnecessary "democratization," or free for all type of tourism entrepreneurship, does not appear to align well with the goal in ensuring quality over quantity.

3. From a tourism development perspective, we cannot open every rural area via roads, or establish new tourist trails. Certain areas need to be totally off-limits to tourism development, while some areas should limit developments to maintain as highly attractive high-value tourism destinations. Tourism need not be developed everywhere!

4. Diversifying and extending the adventure tourism experience. Adventure travel to remote areas is often limited to highway and trail corridors. These highway and trail corridors have the capacity to function as important tourist traffic corridors that provide access to tourism attractions in the region. These attractions, if planned and developed carefully with specific theme-based itineraries, are able to facilitate adventure experience for all age groups. The case of pilgrimage to Muktinath (a holy site for the Hindus) in the Annapurna region of Nepal illustrates the lack of big-picture thinking in tourism planning and development. Tourists to Muktinath are currently focused on a very narrowly defined purpose of travel, i.e. it is focused on temple visits. This motivation needs to be expanded to include nature and culture experiences, in addition to religious and spiritual experiences. The primary idea here is to think of

tourism destinations in terms of *lines*, *circuits* and *clusters*, and develop areas and itineraries accordingly, and manage sustainably.

5. Building professionalism in sustainable tourism practices. Majority of the future tourists is most likely going to be mindful, sustainability-oriented tourists – this is already the trend in many countries in Western Europe, North America and East Asia. A positive impact of COVID-19 on future tourists, including those arriving in Australia, Nepal, India, New Zealand and similar other adventure travel-oriented countries, is a heightened sense of awareness of environmental health and well-being. Adventure travel destinations around the world should position themselves to capture this wave of the "new," mindful, sustainability-oriented tourists.

Of course, many more items can be added to this list. The point of this brief is to highlight that ways of doing tourism business in countries like Nepal needs to change if we want to be able to survive COVID-19 like crisis in the future. While one can be cynical of the morally bankrupt social-political order present in many countries in the developing world, where institutionalized corruption and crime rules the day, it is the sensible development and promotion of adventure tourism that has the ability to pull back these countries from the brink of economic and environmental collapse.

Given the widespread and long-lasting impact of this pandemic, we must ask: will the global tourism industry heed the call for changing its course, doing away with the ill-practices Before Corona, or will the industry go back to its "business as usual" model After Corona? If the past offers any lessons (e.g. the 2008–09 recession), it is likely that the latter will be the case. There is a fundamental disconnect between what the UNWTO preaches (sustainability), and what it practices (growth expansion). This disconnect must be fixed first before we can consider the future of tourism. I think tourism scholars also need to consider if their research should be community-responsive in order to have a meaningful impact on the society, for research for the sake of research only appears to take us nowhere.

Disclosure statement

No potential conflict of interest was reported by the author.

References

Friedman, T. L. (2020). Our new historical divide: B.C. and A.C. — the world before corona and the world after. The New York Times. https://www.nytimes.com/2020/03/17/opinion/corona-virus-trends.html

Macdonald, N. (2020). A ghost town': With tourist access cut off, Banff unemployment soars. The Globe and Mail. https://www.theglobeandmail.com/business/article-a-ghost-town-with-tourist-access-cut-off-banff-unemployment-soars/

MoCTCA. (2020). *Nepal Tourism Statistics 2019.* Government of Nepal, Ministry of Culture, Tourism, and Civil Aviation.

Mu, Y., Nepal, S. K., & Lai, P. (2019). Tourism and sacred landscape in Sagarmatha (Mt. Everest) National Park, Nepal. *Tourism Geographies, 21*(3), 442–459. https://doi.org/10.1080/14616688. 2018.1558454

Nepal, S. K. (2005). Tourism and remote mountain settlements: Spatial and temporal developments of tourist infrastructure in the Mt. Everest Region, Nepal. *Tourism Geographies, 7*(2), 205–227. https://doi.org/10.1080/14616680500072471

Nepal, S. K., & Karst, H. (2016). Tourism in Bhutan and Nepal. In C. M. Hall & S. Page (eds.), *Routledge Handbook of Tourism in Asia* (pp. 287–297). Routledge.

Tsao, C., & Ni, C. (2016). Vulnerability, resilience, and the adaptive cycle in a crisis-prone tourism community. *Tourism Geographies, 18*(1), 80–105. https://doi.org/10.1080/14616688.2015. 1116600

WTO (2020). World Tourism Barometer – January 2020. Vol *18*(1), 1–5, Madrid: UNWTO.

COVID-19: from temporary de-globalisation to a re-discovery of tourism?

Piotr Niewiadomski

ABSTRACT

The processes of globalisation and time-space compression, driven mainly by the neoliberal agenda and the advancement of various space-shrinking technologies, have markedly re-shaped the world over the last 75 years in an almost unchallenged manner. Amongst the most significant outcomes of these processes have been the popularisation of international travel and the accompanying global expansion of the tourism industry. As the first major force ever to effectively stop (or even reverse) globalisation and time-space compression, the COVID-19 outbreak has also put on hold the whole travel and tourism industry. In this respect, the tourism as we knew it just a few months ago has ceased to exist. Although the price the world is paying for this is enormous, the temporary processes of de-globalisation offer the tourism industry an unprecedented opportunity for a re-boot – an unrepeatable chance to re-develop in line with the tenets of sustainability and to do away with various 'dark sides' of tourism's growth such as environmental degradation, economic exploitation or overcrowding. However, the path of re-development and transformation which the global tourism production system will follow once the COVID-19 crisis has been resolved is yet to be determined.

摘要

新自由主义和各种空间压缩技术的发展推动了全球化与时空压缩的进程, 在过去75年中以一种无可挑战的方式明显地重塑了世界。在这些过程中最重要的结果之一是国际旅游的普及和旅游业的全球扩张。作为迄今为止首次有效阻止 (甚至逆转) 全球化和时空压缩的主要力量, COVID-19的爆发使整个旅游业陷入停滞状态。就在几个月前, 旅游活动也戛然而止。尽管全世界为此次危机付出了巨大的代价, 但由COVID-19引起的临时性去全球化过程却为旅游业带来了前所未有的重启机会。这是一个无法复制的机会, 借此去重新发展旅游的可持续性原则, 同时消除旅游发展的各种弊端, 例如环境恶化、经济剥削或过度拥挤。但COVID-19危机过后, 全球旅游生产体系将走怎样的再发展和转型之路还有待确定。

The processes of globalisation and time-space compression that accelerated after World War Two have significantly reshaped the world over the last 75 years. Relative distances between places have markedly shrunk, societies have been stretched across space and time, the pace of life has increased and the significance of spatial barriers to economic, social, cultural and political relations has largely diminished (Agnew, 2001, Dodgshon, 1999, Harvey, 1989, Warf, 2011).

Two major forces have been driving these changes – the neoliberal agenda rooted in the Bretton Woods system and the emergence and popularisation of advanced transportation and communication technologies – the so-called space-shrinking technologies (Agnew, 2001, Harvey, 1989). While the former fostered a gradual withdrawal of the state from economic activity, sparked an elimination of barriers to foreign direct investment and stimulated increased liberalisation of international trade, the latter intensified the exchange of information and knowledge and the cross-border movement of goods and people to unprecedented levels (Agnew, 2001, Dicken, 2011, Warf, 2011). The processes of de-colonisation from the 1950s onwards and the disintegration of the former communist bloc in 1989 facilitated all these processes further. As a result, the world has become more interconnected than even before (Dicken, 2011) and, although some disruptions to these tendencies did occur (e.g. the financial crisis of 2008-2009), no major force has effectively challenged or reversed globalisation. Until now.

While the COVID-19 outbreak in China in January 2020 was initially seen to be a local issue (albeit its worldwide economic effects were recognised very soon), the spread of the virus to other parts of the world in February and March 2020 started a major global crisis of an unprecedented scale and nature. As UN Secretary General António Guterres observed, the world is now facing the most serious global test since World War Two (BBC, 2020a). The various extra-ordinary measures which many national authorities have resorted to in order to stop the plague have changed the world in a way that would have been entirely unthought of a few months ago. National administrations quickly realised that the ease of travel – one of the comforts of modern life in the era of globalisation – is a main factor facilitating the outbreak. As a result, national borders have been closed, cross-border movement of people has been stopped and international transportation has been suspended. All these measures have been accompanied by adequate domestic efforts ranging from banning mass events and encouraging people to self-isolate to restrictive lockdowns imposed on entire countries. Since all these measures have inevitably led to putting many forms of economic activity (mainly services) on hold, national administrations have concomitantly faced a challenge of saving their respective economies.

As a consequence, the world is now experiencing a temporary de-globalisation. Due to heavy travel restrictions and the suspension of international travel, geographical barriers between places have re-emerged, relative distances have increased and remote places have again become truly remote. Even though advanced communication technologies still interlink places and communities virtually, thus helping numerous individuals to stay in touch with their families and friends in these difficult times, most of other processes of time-space compression have been stopped or partly reversed. Moreover, the COVID-19 outbreak has also largely undermined the neoliberal agenda. As the market seems incapable of resolving the crisis (at least on its own), the outbreak has led to a stronger revival of the nation state than during the financial crisis of 2008-2009 (Dicken, 2011). Indeed, national authorities are yet again proving to be a much more effective mechanism for implementing necessary life – and economy – saving solutions than what the market could offer. This is evident not only in reinstating border controls, but most importantly in developing far-reaching anti-crisis economic packages for firms and workers – even in those countries where governments are known to strongly favour free market ideals (see BBC, 2020b for the example of the UK).

The unquestionable importance of public health services in fighting the pandemic and the strategic role which other state-controlled industries play in mitigating its effects attest to the revived prominence of the nation state even further. For example, despite passenger aviation having been liberalised and deregulated, many national airlines have been called on by their respective governments to bring residents home from places where non-national carriers were no longer flying (see Spiegel International 2020 for the example of Lufthansa in Germany and Rudziński, 2020 for the example of LOT Polish Airlines in Poland). The COVID-19 crisis has exposed the limits of the neoliberal orthodoxy, thus effectively undermining another important force that has been driving globalisation and time-space compression to date.

One of the most significant manifestations of globalisation over the last half a century has been the popularisation of international tourism. While the revolutionary advancements in transport (mainly the development of the jet aircraft) fostered the increase in international tourist traffic from 25 million in 1950 to over 1.3 billion in 2017 (UNWTO, 2010, 2018), the cross-border expansion of capitalist relations and the dominant logic of capitalist accumulation allowed the tourism production system to gain a global extent (Mowforth & Munt, 2009, Williams, 2009). Not only have various tourism firms expanded internationally (mainly in transportation and in the hospitality sector), but also, at the same time, peripheral places previously unexplored by tourists have been increasingly drawn into the tourism nexus (Mowforth & Munt, 2009, Williams, 2009). Consequently, tourism developed to become one of the largest and most global industries, and, as Williams (2009) observed, this development seemed unstoppable, even by various tragic events such as wars, terrorist attacks, and natural disasters, or by major economic downturns such as the oil crisis in the 1970s.

The COVID-19 outbreak, however, seems to be a stronger force. Since all the important factors that made international travel easy and allowed the tourism industry to spread globally have now been stopped, the processes of de-globalisation have engulfed tourism almost entirely. The closure of hotels, restaurants, entertainment centres, and various tourist attractions has put on hold the whole tourism and travel industry. Simultaneously, with international travel largely suspended, and domestic travel also largely restricted, distances between 'home' and 'away' have grown to an extent that they are often impossible to overcome. As a result, tourism as we knew it just a few months ago has ceased to exist.

Tourism as we knew it, however, was a mixed bag. Despite bringing many positive economic effects for economies and communities (e.g., in 2017 tourism supported 10% of all jobs worldwide and accounted for 10% of the world's GDP; UNWTO, 2018) and providing societies with an opportunity to travel and experience other places more easily than ever before, the global development of tourism also proved to have various negative effects (Hall & Page, 2014, Mowforth & Munt, 2009, Niewiadomski,

2017, Sharpley & Telfer, 2002, Williams, 2009). Environmental degradation (e.g. Gössling & Hall, 2006, Gössling & Peeters, 2015), tourism as neo-colonialism (e.g. Hall & Tucker, 2004, Tucker & Akama, 2012), overcrowding and various other negative social impacts of tourism on host places (e.g. Popp, 2012, Santana-Jimenez & Hernandez, 2011, Tovar & Lockwood, 2008) are only selected 'dark sides' of tourism's growth. Although the idea of sustainable development, formulated by the World Commission on Environment and Development (WCED) in the 1980s (WCED, 1987), fostered a pursuit of more sustainable forms of tourism and sparked a vast number of ambitious initiatives and strategies (see e.g., UNWTO, 2003), the progress on the ground made on this front to date has been far from sufficient.

In this respect, it is conceivable to look at the current crisis with a degree of optimism. Although the price we are paying for this is enormous – measured in thousands of lives, millions of lost jobs, and a corresponding number of many other personal tragedies – the temporary processes of de-globalisation are giving the global tourism industry a unique chance for a re-boot – an unrepeatable opportunity to re-develop in line with the tenets of sustainability. To use the language of evolutionary economic geography (EEG), the world is experiencing a major shock – a true criticality that is likely to shift the existing system to a new configuration (Boschma & Martin, 2007, 2010). The key question that still remains is: What is this new configuration going to be? Or, in the words of Schumpeter (1942, in: Boschma & Martin, 2007): How 'creative' will this 'destruction' be? While we already know what is being 'destroyed', we are yet to see what will be 'created' to fill the void.

Once the crisis has been resolved, tourism and all of its sub-sectors will face unlimited path-shaping opportunities. If the opportunities are taken, we will see a meta-path-creation across the global tourism production system. The key point is to ensure that the changes will be for the better.

The very apt comment that "the world had to stop in order not to fall" (author unknown) is also fully pertinent to the case of tourism. There is a lot of evidence that in many respects tourism growth had gone too far and down a wrong path. Now that it has stopped, there is time for reflection. Indeed, the crisis has created an exceptional window of opportunity which all advocates of sustainable tourism could not even dream about a few months ago – an opportunity to make tourism more environmentally sustainable, less exploitative and greedy, more respectful to host communities and their cultures and traditions, and more mindful. Fortunately, the springboard for this in the form of the UN Sustainable Development Goals (see UNWTO, 2017) already exists, although undoubtedly more work needs to be done and a lot of good will is required to make it happen.

Perhaps there is a lot of wishful thinking here. Perhaps there are already corporations, governments and various other organisations lying in wait for all the opportunities to pursue their selfish political and economic interests which the current shock might create, even at the expense of those negatively affected by the pandemic the most. As Klein (2007) demonstrated, such risk is real and should not be ignored. The opportunity is still there, however, and it will be down to everyone involved (i.e., the tourism sector, policy-makers, tourists themselves, experts and academia) to inform the new path of growth as much as possible and make the post-COVID-19 tourism more economically equitable, more socially just, and more environmentally sustainable.

Disclosure statement

No potential conflict of interest was reported by the author(s).

References

Agnew, J. (2001). The new global economy: time-space compression, geopolitics, and global uneven development. *Journal of World-Systems Research*, 7(2), 133–154. doi:10.5195/jwsr.2001.167

BBC. (2020a). Coronavirus: Greatest test since World War Two, says UN chief. *BBC News*. Retrieved April 1, 2020, from http://:www.bbc.co.uk/news

BBC (2020b). Coronavirus: Government to pay up to 80% of workers' wages, BBC News, 20 March 2020, available at: http://:www.bbc.co.uk/news

Boschma, R., & Martin, R. (2007). Editorial: Constructing an evolutionary economic geography. *Journal of Economic Geography*, 7(5), 537–548. doi:10.1093/jeg/lbm021

Boschma, R., & Martin, M. (2010). The aims and scope of evolutionary economic geography. In R. Boschma, R. Martin (Eds.), *The handbook of evolutionary economic geography* (pp. 3–39). Edward Elgar.

Dicken, P. (2011). *Global shift: Mapping the changing contours of the world economy* (6th ed.). Sage.

Dodgshon, R. (1999). Human geography at the end of time? Some thoughts on the idea of time-space compression. *Environment and Planning D: Society and Space*, 17(5), 607–620. doi: 10.1068/d170607

Gössling, S., & Hall, C. (Eds.). (2006). *Tourism and global environmental change*. Routledge.

Gössling, S., & Peeters, P. (2015). Assessing tourism's global environmental impact 1900-2050. *Journal of Sustainable Tourism*, 23(5), 639–659.

Hall, C., & Page, S. (2014). *The geography of tourism & recreation: Environment, place and space* (4th ed.). Routledge.

Hall, C., & Tucker, H. (Eds.). (2004). *Tourism and postcolonialism: Contested discourses, identities and representations*. Routledge.

Harvey, D. (1989). *The condition of postmodernity*. Blackwell.

Klein, N. (2007). *The shock doctrine: The rise of disaster capitalism*. Picador.

Mowforth, M., & Munt, I. (2009). *Tourism and sustainability. Development, globalisation and new tourism in the third world* (3rd ed.). Routledge.

Niewiadomski, P. (2017). Economics of tourism. In L. Lowry (Ed.), *The SAGE international encyclopedia of travel and tourism* (pp. 392–396). SAGE Publications.

Popp, M. (2012). Positive and negative urban tourist crowding: Florence, Italy. *Tourism Geographies*, 14(1), 50–72. doi:10.1080/14616688.2011.597421

Rudziński, L. (2020). Koronawirus: Akcja "Lot do domu". Rząd sprowadza Polaków do kraju. Zobacz, jak wrócić do Polski. *Polska Times*. Retrieved March 15, 2020, from https://polska-times.pl

Santana-Jimenez, Y., & Hernandez, J. (2011). Estimating the effect of overcrowding on tourist attraction: the case of Canary Islands. *Tourism Management*, 32(2), 415–425.

Sharpley, R., & Telfer, D. (Eds.). (2002). *Tourism and development: Concepts and issues*. Channel View Publications.

Spiegel International. (2020). Lufthansa airlift: Transports planned for goods and stranded germans. *Spiegel International*. Retrieved March 17, 2020, from https://www.spiegel.de/international

Tovar, C., & Lockwood, M. (2008). Social impacts of tourism: An Australian regional case study. *International Journal of Tourism Research, 10*(4), 365–378. doi:10.1002/jtr.667

Tucker, H., & Akama, J. (2012). Tourism as postcolonialism. In T. Jamal and M. Robinson (Eds.). *The SAGE handbook of tourism studies* (pp. 504–520). Sage.

UNWTO. (2003). *Climate change and tourism*. UNWTO. https://www.e-unwto.org

UNWTO. (2010). Tourism highlights 2010 edition. United Nations World Tourist Organization. Retrieved April 2011, from, www.unwto.org

UNWTO. (2017). Tourism and *the sustainable development goals*. United Nations World Tourist Organization. Retrieved October 2014, from, www.unwto.org

UNWTO. (2018). Tourism *highlights 2018 edition*. United Nations World Tourist Organization. Retrieved October 2018, from, www.unwto.org

Warf, B. (2011). Teaching Time–Space Compression. *Journal of Geography in Higher Education, 35*(2), 143–161. doi:10.1080/03098265.2010.523681

Williams, S. (2009). *Tourism geography: A new synthesis* (2nd ed.). Routledge.

World Commission on Environment and Development (WCED). (1987). *Our common future*. Oxford University Press.

Critical tourism scholars: brokers of hope

Tomas Pernecky (iD)

ABSTRACT

The past four decades of tourism research have demonstrated that the field would be impoverished without recognising the human aspect of scientific inquiry. The contributions made through critical approaches, Indigenous perspectives, qualitative methods and morally instilled concepts such as 'sustainability' or 'community development' have accentuated that tourism scholars are not detached and value-free producers of knowledge. Rather, our gender, ethnicity, personal and political views enter research agendas and actively shape knowledge. Alarmed by a host of social, economic, environmental, political and ethical concerns, and motivated to end injustice, inequality, oppression and discrimination, we also circumnavigate hope. However, researchers' relationships with hope can be problematic, as evidenced by the recent tensions within critical tourism scholarship. In order to examine the extent to which hope ought to be part of tourism research, it is important to engage with the notion of hope seriously and methodically. By drawing on different varieties of hope, it is argued that these can underpin research projects to different degrees, including critical hope, hope-as-utopia, transformative hope, radical hope and pragmatic hope. It is emphasised that hope is connected to critical research in elementary ways and plays a vital role in envisioning a more just, inclusive, sustainable and equitable world. The acknowledgment of hope as part of critical research is particularly valuable amid the COVID-19 pandemic – an event with devastating consequences for communities worldwide. Through a hopeful lens, our momentary loss of tourism may bring with it a renewed appreciation and care, which has been eroded by rampant commodification and comatose consumerism. The hope driving post COVID-19 visions of tourism is argued to lie in more thoughtful and responsible engagement with tourism, and in our ability to positively transform it.

摘要

过去40年的旅游研究表明, 若忽视科学探究中的人文因素, 那么旅游研究将会陷入一种贫瘠状态。通过批判性方法、本土观点、质性方法和道德灌输的概念 (如"可持续性"或"社区发展") 所作的贡献, 凸显出旅游学者不是超然的、价值中立的知识生产者。相反, 旅游学者将自己的性别、种族、个人的政治观点带入研究议程中, 并能动地塑造了知识体系。我们对一系列社会、经济、环境、政治和道德问题保持警惕, 致力于去解决不公正、不平等、压迫和歧视的社会问题, 同时也怀抱希望。然而, 研究者与"希望"的关系可能是有问题的, 这一点可以从近期批判性旅游学术研究中的张力得到证明。希望应该成为旅游研究的一部分, 且有必要对其概念进行严肃、系统地探讨以检验其程度大小如何。本文通过借鉴不同类别的希望, 认为这些希望可以在不同程度上支撑研究项目, 其中包括批判式希望、乌托邦式希望、变革式希望、激进式希望和实用式希望。需要强调的是, 希望与批判性基础研究有关, 在构想一个更加公平公正、包容、可持续的世界过程中发挥着至关重要的作用。在对全人类社会产生毁灭性影响的新型冠状病毒肺炎(COVID-19) 蔓延期间, 希望在批判性研究中显得尤为重要。透过希望的镜头, 因商品化和麻木的消费主义造成旅游业的暂时损失可能会给我们带来新的理解和关注。后新冠 (post COVID-19) 时代旅游业发展的希望在于参与旅游业的严谨和责任以及积极变革旅游业的能力。

Introduction

The purpose of this *very* special issue is to respond, in hopeful ways, to the COVID-19 pandemic, and address 'how the events of 2020 will transform our planet in potentially positive ways, with travel and tourism being among the most significant areas to be impacted' (Lew, 2020, para. 2). Given that hope is the central theme of this collection of contributions, it seems appropriate, and perhaps necessary, to consider the extent to which hope ought to be part of tourism scholarship. This is particularly valuable within critical tourism studies (Ateljevic et al., 2007, 2011; Morgan et al., 2018; Ren et al., 2010), where tensions between the hopeful (Pritchard et al., 2011) and the not-so-hopeful adherents (Higgins-Desbiolles & Whyte, 2013) have highlighted that researchers' relationships with hope can be problematic.

The aim of this article, therefore, is to unpack some of the concerns about the compatibility of hope and critical inquiry. In order to do so, the paper first maps the issues raised by Higgins-Desbiolles and Whyte (2013) and concurs that some varieties of hopeful scholarship demand critical reflexivity. However, it is argued that the bond between hopefulness and criticality has been underestimated and misunderstood, and that tourism researchers can employ different varieties of hope. This leads to the next part, which concentrates on delineating the different kinds of hope academics have access to, including critical hope, hope-as-utopia, transformative hope, radical hope, patient hope, sound hope, resolute hope and pragmatic hope. The last section recognises tourism as a social construct whose fragility has been underlined by the COVID-19 pandemic and suggests that there is a hopeful silver lining in temporarily losing tourism.

The misunderstood link between hope and criticality

Hope as a concept and an attitude to be adopted by thinkers without the loss of academic dignity was radically undermined by the scientific method. Hope had no hope against Cartesian objectivity, because hope indicated attachment, and Descartes's rationalist philosophy championed detachment. The social sciences, in order to be objective, followed in the footsteps of the natural sciences and chiselled out a new model of the scientist by cutting away anything human that could jeopardise scientific inquiry. The past four decades of tourism research, however, have demonstrated abundantly that without qualitative approaches, Indigenous methods, and morally instilled notions of 'sustainability' or 'community development', tourism would be an impoverished science. Hope has become a close companion to a number of tourism scholars, as illustrated in this special issue which seeks to mobilise both the mind and the heart. Discounting hope is, of course, possible, but not always desirable. The lack of hope has been perhaps best articulated in the educational philosophy of Paulo Freire (1994), for whom hope was an ontological necessity:

> When it becomes a program, hopelessness paralyzes us, immobilizes us. We succumb to fatalism, and then it becomes impossible to muster the strength we absolutely need for a fierce struggle that will re-create the world. I am hopeful, not out of mere stubbornness, but out of an existential, concrete imperative. [...] One of the tasks of the progressive educator, through a serious, correct political analysis, is to unveil opportunities for hope, no matter what the obstacles may be. After all, without hope, there is little we can do. (pp. 2–3)

It is important to note that Freire was against naïve hoping; he understood that hope on its own was not enough and could lead to hopelessness and cynicism, and therefore had to be anchored in practice. The field of tourism studies has similarly embraced hopeful perspectives, with researchers – alarmed by a host of social, economic, environmental, political and ethical concerns – motivated to end injustice, inequality, oppression and discrimination and calling for radical actions. Nevertheless, hopefulness and criticality have not been reconciled in the tourism academy. The suggestion of critical scholars engaging in hopeful tourism led to tensions after the publication of *Hopeful Tourism: A New Transformative Perspective* (Pritchard et al., 2011) and the subsequent commentary by Higgins-Desbiolles and Whyte (2013). Hopeful tourism, described as 'a new perspective which combines co-transformative learning and action to offer a distinctive approach to tourism knowledge production' (Pritchard et al., 2011, p. 942), did not sit comfortably with the latter critics, who questioned the place for hope in the tourism critical movement. Specifically, Higgins-Desbiolles and Whyte (2013) pondered: 'why would Pritchard et al. discard criticalness for the sake of instilling hopefulness in the tourism academy and to what effect?' (p. 428) and raised whether Pritchard et al. are more focused on 'researchers' needs rather than the needs of those with whom the researcher should be in solidarity' (p. 429).

We would be wise to engage with Higgins-Desbiolles and Whyte's (2013) questions surrounding hope – questions that are at once philosophical, ethical, political and methodological. When the authors ponder 'what the hopeful are hoping for and why' (p. 429) and propose that others we hope for 'may not wish to be hoped for by those who have not suffered under the same or similar circumstances' (p. 429), they demand responsibility and critical reflexivity. Gergen puts it in similar terms when he asks: 'have you truly "helped someone in need" if the recipient detests your action?', and 'can you "help" another without his or her affirming that it is help and not hindrance?' (Gergen, 2009, p. 31). These are important critically reflexive and critico-relational matters, because hope approached naively can turn into an impediment – a form of arrogant hope, derailing critical scholarship. Higgins-Desbiolles and Whyte (2013) thus shine an interrogative spotlight on the critical academy, but they omit to recognise that hope and criticality are two sides of the same coin.

The debate between Pritchard et al. (2011) and Higgins-Desbiolles and Whyte (2013) is invaluable because it unmasks the problematic and difficult matters of academic identity, integrity and fragility that are seldom debated openly. What appears most curious about this interchange, however, is the binary treatment of hope and criticality. Critical tourism studies scholars are not a homogenous group; they range from activist champions and critical analysts, to theorists, to passionate igniters of hope – the last category representing those academics who are fully aware of the problems faced by the communities they study but choosing to focus on finding pragmatic solutions. Hence, we are better off conceiving a continuum that accommodates the radically critical members (Bianchi, 2009) as well as the hopeful fellows (Pritchard et al., 2011). When juxtaposed, criticality and hope are mistakenly presumed to be incompatible. Yet hope as resoluteness to address and remedy the wrongs in the world is fully compatible with critical thought. We may hope for less crime, less pollution, less carbon emissions, less conflict, more equality, equal human rights, and so forth, and it is this kind of hoping that fuels critical engagement and the drive to construct more equitable social realities. Of course, one can debate whether it is hope that is 'misplaced' (Higgins-Desbiolles & Whyte, 2013, p. 428) or the critique that is mislaid (Caton, 2016), yet it is far more productive to consider hope as many different states.

The plurality of hope

There are different varieties of hope we can draw upon to better understand why one can be both critical and hopeful. First, we can think of *hope-as-utopia* – an imagined state different from present conditions. Hope-as-utopia represents the imaginative capacity of human beings to envisage a better future. This kind of hope appears, for instance, in Thomas More's (1516/2005) *Utopia* – a text depicting a fictional society free of coercion, tyranny and cruelty. Although one may think of this notion of hope as idealistic, it lay the foundations for future actions. More's publication was intended as a critique of England's social conditions in the 15th century, and as observed by leisure scholar Zuzanek (2016), it expressed 'wishes and doubts about England's future and the importance of a socially just distribution of work and leisure' (p. 307). Zuzanek also explains that *Utopia* was 'an attempt to draw the Prince's [Henry VIII] attention to the social problems facing England and an invitation to seek a solution for them' (p. 311). In a broader sense, hope-as-utopia encompasses the visions we may hold for tourism when we inject it with optimism and the promise of thriving communities, increased social and economic benefits, and the lessening of cultural boundaries. However, as this is often not enough, we may require additional forms of hope.

Hope that is accompanied by speaking against dominant, despotic systems is *critical hope*. This form of hoping comes with the awareness that 'the idea that hope alone will transform the world, and action undertaken in that kind of naïveté, is an excellent route to hopelessness, pessimism, and fatalism' (Strazds, 2019, p. 10).

Drawing on the insights from Coté et al. (2007), Strazds (2019) points out that we can further discern between hoping that does not necessarily have a 'point of departure', and hoping that promotes collective action and pronounces a 'point of arrival'. Whereas the first resembles critical hope, the latter, she argues, is *transformative hope*. Transformative hope differs in that it has a goal towards which it mobilises people – what Strazds terms as 'goal directed social praxis' (p. 4). Between critical and transformative hope is yet another hope – *radical hope* or *critical-transformative hope* – accomplished through action. This radical variety of hope develops when academics, including many tourism scholars, call to arms and demand active engagement (e.g. Bianchi, 2009; Boluk et al., 2019; Higgins-Desbiolles et al., 2019).

In a similar light, Webb (2013) identifies five modes of hoping: *patient hope*, *critical hope*, *sound hope*, *resolute hope* and *transformative hope*. Whereas *patient hope* has no specific destination or direction, *critical hope* is the 'process of criticising present negatives in light of their promised negation' (p. 403). *Sound hope*, Webb argues, is more concrete and comes with direction and specific goals. *Resolute hope* emerges as an utter dedication, if not an embodied state, to maintaining a hopeful course – cognitively, emotionally and through action – despite any odds and probabilities. In this regard, Webb notes that, 'to hope resolutely is to be a dogged anti-determinist' (p. 407). *Transformative hope*, similarly to *resolute hope,* is oblivious to odds and evidence, but is depicted as a more widespread, collective and 'instrumental goal-directed social praxis' (p. 409). The articulations of hope by Strazds (2019) and Webb (2013) allow us to observe the subtle differences and similarities, facilitating the recognition that hope can be adopted to different degrees and effects.

In addition, and under the broad umbrella of *meliorism* (the view that humans can make the world better), we may also consider *pragmatic hope*. Herein, hope and pragmatism come together within pragmatism philosophy. Rorty's (1999) pragmatic hope is a plea to our imaginative capacity, urging us to worry less about whether or not our beliefs are well justified, and engaging instead in interesting alternatives (see Grippe, 2020). Whilst this philosophical tenet is likely to enrage those fighting for justice, it should not be dismissed outright. Pragmatic hope may serve as a temporary alternative adopted by practitioners who recognise that the challenges they are combatting can be enduring, and that small and steady increments are better than no progress at all. In this regard, Koopman (2006) describes pragmatism as 'a philosophical way of taking hope seriously' (p. 106). In his view, 'hope names the effort of prospective energy, self-creation looking forward, reliance on ourselves, trust that we shall manifest better values in the world' (p. 113). Koopman's point of view is helpful also in that it enables a deeper understanding as to why colleagues such as Pritchard et al. (2011) take hopeful tourism to be a serious endeavour.

What these examples amount to is an interwoven image of hope and criticality, and its rightful place in tourism scholarship. It goes without saying that this special issue is an expression of hope. We practice hope when we remain true to moral and ethical principles and continue building the foundations for change. We practice hope when we seek practical solutions and viable alternatives. We practice hope when we name the wrongs and strive to correct them. We practice hope when we remain resilient in combatting gender, economic, political, health or environmental injustices. And we practice hope, too, when we stand in solidarity through action. Hopeful research thus becomes the intentional effort to promote respect, dignity, justice, diversity and the active advancement of human rights. But here we must also add a caveat and rec- ognise that research in this realm can be arduous. Caton's (2012) sentiment about the 'fraught space that is tourism practice' (p. 1918) is a reminder that individual fulfilment and social consequences are notoriously difficult to synthesise, bringing to attention another element that is interconnected with hopefulness, criticality and tourism: aca- demic fragility.

Recognising academic fragility and humanness in scholarly work

Fragility is present in tourism generally as people navigate uncertainty – environ- ments, experiences and encounters that are unpredictable. Fragility can arrive dur- ing the most vulnerable moments, such as when we fall ill while overseas, or when experiencing direct prejudice because of our body shape, skin colour, sexuality, religion or nationality. Fragility can paralyse in flashes of hatred, racism and vio- lence. It can also become a companion for life. Those impacted by conflict, natural disasters, genocide or loss of homelands due to changing climate fall under large scale, blanket fragility that enwraps landscapes and populations – covering entire nations and generations (as recognised by the World Health Organisation, 2017). Critical tourism researchers work in these frail territories, yet we seldom acknow- ledge this academic variety of fragility that is part of having to balance hope and criticality.

Academic fragility can reach us in different stages of our academic careers, such as when we question the worth of our work – i.e. when we see that the communities and individuals we strive to help are left suffering, that the environment we hope to save is not improving, and that the policies we hope to change are likely to remain the same. Indeed, to witness poverty, conflict, diasporas and refugee crises is to invite fragility into one's life, as unmistakably captured in Alison Phipps and Tawona Sitholé's (2018) book of poems titled *The Warriors Who Do Not Fight*. One of these is shared below:

The academic border guard

And they will say of me
that despite it all, I was a border guard.
That I assigned my signature to the papers
which monitored and revealed the whereabouts
of students from other lands, whose learning
was in my care.

And they will have evidence,
when they look again, once again,
at the only question we can ever have
of history,
'How did this happen?
How can human beings
do this?'

They will say it of me and of my friends
and also of those who comply easily
and don't question, as I do, as I do daily.

They will say it also of those
who made the new rules gleefully
rejoicing in expulsions.

Maybe they will look at
my practices of resistance,
but I doubt it,
the weighing of evidence is rarely
that subtle in such matters
of life and death, as implicate me now.

Maybe they will read the minutes
of the Graduate Studies Committee
of 2007 where we said 'No.'
Maybe they will
examine my chaotic filing system,
my resistance to demands, the way
I spoke to those I am to sign off.
Maybe my accuracy will be found wanting.
But I doubt it. That is probably
not my way, even if I might wish it
to be so.

If justice comes quickly, hopefully
they will say it to my face.
It will help with the healings,
the clearing away of the detritus of the past.

If there is forgiveness in that future,
the one for which I work and pray,
then perhaps they
will say it kindly, and see that,
on balance I was 'only doing my job'.

These, of course, are the words which
haunt me most.

But if truth be told, my truth be told,
every time I sign my name, I know my
guilt, and shame and believe, that
when the day comes,
and the question is asked,
and the just verdict falls,
for every form filled out
and signed

you should spit in my face.

And if I am dead, then
desecrate my grave
with my guilt.

The inclusion of this poem serves the function of reinforcing the human nature of scholarly work, as alluded to at the start of this paper. It brings humanness to the centre stage of research, underscoring the limitations of Cartesian objectivism in the social sciences – sciences of which tourism is a part. It is not too often that we see poetry in 'serious' scholarly outlets; still, Phipps and Sitholé (2018) demonstrate – through poems – that academic work could not get any more serious. They show, also, that fragility, hope and criticality are connected in elementary ways, and that we are neither disconnected from the phenomena and human beings we study, nor untouched by the encounters we experience. Thus, objectivity is not the only measure of quality in research; hope, criticality and fragility facilitate valuable directions and insights necessary for understanding a phenomenon that is entirely made and remade by humans. This foresight was aptly communicated nearly a century ago by Bisbee (1937) who stated that:

> At every new turn a sign-post marks it as the Highway of Objectivity in order to keep up the confidence that it is Scientific. Subjectivity and Individual Purpose, nevertheless, determine each turn it takes, however objectively it can be followed once the turns have been established and made clear for those who may subsequently travel the road. (p. 382)

Conclusion

So what can we say about hope, tourism and criticality amid the COVID-19 pandemic? Ought hope to be part of tourism scholarship? The answer offered in this paper is a resolute 'yes'. In the same way that critical tourism studies scholars are fuelled by hope in their efforts to enact positive change in the world, we must have hope for tourism, which is not to be mistaken for naïve hope that things will go back to the way they once were. We ought to have *hope-as-utopia* and draw on the imaginative capacities of tourism scholars, students and professionals to envisage and articulate social realities vis-à-vis tourism that are more just, equitable and considerate towards fellow human beings and the natural world. We ought to have *critical hope* that disrupts the status quo – revealing, naming and articulating that which may be missing or lacking for some members of our societies, as well as other species. We ought to employ *resolute hope* in our determination to create opportunities without succumbing to dooming odds and statistics – a form of optimistic confidence that manifests through action and should be nurtured in every classroom. We ought to have *transformative hope*, which, as emphasised by Webb (2013), is 'not a desire plus a probability estimate grounded in a survey of the evidence, but rather a utopia plus a sense of possibility grounded in a confidence in the powers of human agency' (p. 409). We ought to have *pragmatic hope* and continue seeking alternatives despite the challenges and obstacles that may come along the way. And we, too, ought to have *patient*, *sound* and *resolute hope*, because it is the richness and plurality of hoping that makes hopeful tourism a powerful and worthwhile endeavour. Through a hopeful lens, our momentary loss of tourism may bring with it a renewed appreciation and care, which has been eroded by rampant commodification and comatose consumerism. The hope driving post COVID-19 visions of tourism lies in more thoughtful and responsible engagement with tourism, and in our ability to positively transform it. After all, tourism is a human construct; our responsibility is to advocate for the varieties that are beneficial to humanity and the planet. To this end, we are critical brokers of hope.

Disclosure statement

No potential conflict of interest was reported by the author.

ORCID

Tomas Pernecky http://orcid.org/0000-0001-6418-8020

References

Ateljevic, I., Morgan, N., & Pritchard, A. (2011). *The critical turn in tourism studies: Creating an academy of hope*. Routledge.
Ateljevic, I., Pritchard, A., & Morgan, N. (2007). *The critical turn in tourism studies: Innovative research methodologies*. Elsevier.
Bianchi, R. V. (2009). The 'critical turn' in tourism studies: A radical critique. *Tourism Geographies, 11*(4), 484–504. https://doi.org/10.1080/14616680903262653
Bisbee, E. (1937). Objectivity in the social sciences. *Philosophy of Science, 4*(3), 371–382. https://doi.org/10.1086/286468
Boluk, K. A., Cavaliere, C. T., & Higgins-Desbiolles, F. (2019). A critical framework for interrogating the United Nations Sustainable Development Goals 2030 Agenda in tourism. *Journal of Sustainable Tourism, 27*(7), 847–864. https://doi.org/10.1080/09669582.2019.1619748
Caton, K. (2012). Taking the moral turn in tourism studies. *Annals of Tourism Research, 39*(4), 1906–1928. https://doi.org/10.1016/j.annals.2012.05.021
Caton, K. (2016). A humanist paradigm for tourism studies?: Envisioning a collective alternative to epistemic literalism. In A. M. Munar & T. Jamal (Eds.), *Tourism research paradigms: Critical and emergent knowledges* (Vol. 22, pp. 35–51). Emerald Group Publishing.
Coté, M., Day, R., & de Peuter, G. (2007). *Utopian pedagogy: Radical experiments against neoliberal globalization*. University of Toronto Press.
Freire, P. (1994). *Pedagogy of hope: Reliving pedagogy of the opressed*. Bloomsbury.
Gergen, K. J. (2009). *Relational being: Beyond self and community*. Oxford University Press.
Grippe, E. (2020). Richard Rorty (1931–2007). Internet Encyclopedia of Philosophy. https://www.iep.utm.edu/rorty/
Higgins-Desbiolles, F., Carnicelli, S., Krolikowski, C., Wijesinghe, G., & Boluk, K. (2019). Degrowing tourism: Rethinking tourism. *Journal of Sustainable Tourism, 27*(12), 1926–1944. https://doi.org/10.1080/09669582.2019.1601732

Higgins-Desbiolles, F., & Whyte, K. P. (2013). No high hopes for hopeful tourism: A critical comment. *Annals of Tourism Research, 40*(1), 428–433. https://doi.org/10.1016/j.annals.2012.07.005

Koopman, C. (2006). Pragmatism as a philosophy of hope: Emerson, James, Dewey, Rorty. *The Journal of Speculative Philosophy, 20*(2), 106–116. https://doi.org/10.1353/jsp.2006.0020

Lew, A. A. (2020). A very special issue – Call for papers. *Tourism Geographies.* https://www.tgjournal.com/transformation.html

More, T. (2005). *Utopia.* (H. Morley, Ed.). Sage. https://www.gutenberg.org/files/2130/2130-h/2130-h.htm (Original work published 1516).

Morgan, N., Pritchard, A., Causevic, S., & Minnaert, L. (2018). Ten years of critical tourism studies: Reflections on the road less traveled. *Tourism Analysis, 23*(2), 183–187. https://doi.org/10.3727/108354218X15210313504535

Phipps, A., & Sitholé, T. (2018). *The warriors who do not fight.* Wild Goose Publications.

Pritchard, A., Morgan, N., & Ateljevic, I. (2011). Hopeful tourism: A new transformative perspective. *Annals of Tourism Research, 38*(3), 941–963. https://doi.org/10.1016/j.annals.2011.01.004

Ren, C., Pritchard, A., & Morgan, N. (2010). Constructing tourism research: A critical inquiry. *Annals of Tourism Research, 37*(4), 885–904. https://doi.org/10.1016/j.annals.2009.11.006

Rorty, R. (1999). *Philosophy and social hope.* Penguin Books.

Strazds, L. M. (2019). Radical hope: Transforming sustainability. *Journal of Sustainability Education, 12*, 21. http://www.susted.com/wordpress/content/radical-hope-transforming-sustainability_2019_12

Webb, D. (2013). Pedagogies of hope. *Studies in Philosophy and Education, 32*(4), 397–414. https://doi.org/10.1007/s11217-012-9336-1

World Health Organisation. (2017). *Climate and health country profile – 2017: Kiribati.* Retrieved February 20, 2020, from https://apps.who.int/iris/bitstream/handle/10665/260411/WHO-FWC-PHE-EPE-15.51-eng.pdf%3Bjsessionid%3DD410499E458E5E2A4A2B12AC8C405B84%3Fsequence%3D1

Zuzanek, J. (2016). Work and leisure in Thomas More's. *Utopia. Leisure Studies, 36*(3), 1–314. https://doi.org/10.1080/02614367.2016.1182200

Lessons from COVID-19 can prepare global tourism for the economic transformation needed to combat climate change

Bruce Prideaux (iD), Michelle Thompson (iD) and Anja Pabel (iD)

ABSTRACT

The COVID-19 pandemic led to the cessation of almost all international travel in the first half of 2020. A return to pre-pandemic growth patterns will take time and depend on the depth and extent of the recession sparked by COVID-19. The recovery phase will overlap with global efforts to deal with the evolving climate crisis. For the tourism industry to thrive in a future world it must look beyond the temptation of adopting strategies based on a return to the pre-COVID-19 normal of the past and instead seek to understand how it should respond to the emerging transformation of the global economy to carbon neutrality. Many of the lessons that emerged from the pandemic can be applied to strategies to deal with climate change. Of most interest is the success of strategies such as "flattening the curve". Application of similar strategies plus adoption of the circular economy model to wind back Green House Gas emissions will help avert the global environmental disaster that will occur if global temperatures continue to increase. These strategies point to what a future carbon-neutral economic production system might look like, the path to which could offer the tourism industry numerous opportunities to transform from the current model that favours a high resource consumption model to one that is environmentally friendly and resource neutral.

摘要

新冠状病毒肺炎（COVID-19）导致2020年上半年几乎所有国际旅行的中止。若想恢复到病毒爆发前的旅游增长模式需要一些时间，而且取决于新冠状病毒引发的衰退的程度和范围。未来从病毒复苏的阶段，全球同时还需努力应对不断演变的气候危机。为了在未来世界中蓬勃发展，旅游业必须抵制想要回归到新冠病毒爆发前常规发展模式的诱惑，转而寻求理解自身该如何应对全球经济向碳中和方向的新转型。从这次新冠爆发中汲取的许多经验教训都可以用于应对气候变化的战略中。其中最令人感兴趣的是例如"压平曲线"这样策略的成功。应用类似的策略，外加采用循环经济模式来减少温室气体的排放，将有助于避免全球气温持续升高所带来的全球环境灾难。这些策略指明了未来碳中和经济生产系统的样貌，这为旅游业提供了许多机会，使其从目前高资源消耗的模式转变为环境友好和资源中立的模式。

Introduction

Transformation is a process of change from one state to another. From an organisational perspective, transformation is necessary to ensure an organisation's long-term survival and involves processes that often require radical changes in the products, customer segments and markets it operates in (Davis et al., 2010). On a global scale, political transformations and economic revolutions (the Agricultural Revolution, the Industrial Revolution and more recently Digital Revolution have radically reshaped the global political system, global economic systems, national economies, societal norms, lifestyles and the way people spend non-work time.

The tourism industry has been a major beneficiary of the wealth created by these revolutions and by 2018 generated 10.4% of global GDP (WTTC, 2019), with year-on-year growth only briefly interrupted by crisis events such as SARS, the 9/11 terrorist attack on the USA and the Global Financial Crisis of 2007/08. Recovery occurred within a neoliberal global economic production system where continued economic growth was viewed as more important than the long-term impacts on the global environment. However, recovery from COVID-19 (caused by severe acute respiratory syndrome 2 (SARS-CoV-2)), is unlikely to follow the pattern of earlier post-crisis recovery.

Post-COVID-19 recovery of the tourism industry will be tied in the short-term to the rate of global economic recovery. Long-term recovery will overlap with the transformation of the current linear economic production system into a carbon-neutral economic production system and set new parameters for the future direction of global tourism recovery. While numerous countries have acknowledged the need to transition to a carbon-neutral economy (Edmond, 2019), most have deferred decisive action. Hesitancy to transform the global economy yet willingness to respond quickly to COVID-19 points to the core problem facing the tourism industry, and the global community. An immediate danger or crisis is much easier to respond to quickly and decisively than long-term dangers or known future crises. The response to crisis events of the scale of COVID-19 provides insights into opportunities to challenge and change the current global economic status quo.

This paper postulates that for the tourism industry to thrive in a future world it must look beyond the temptation of adopting strategies based on a return to the normal of the past and instead seek to understand how it should respond to the future transformation of the global economy. Lessons that will emerge from the successes or failures of countries in their response to COVID-19 will provide useful guidelines for the tourism industry in its future transformation.

Existing state of knowledge

The literature offers very few insights into how the tourism industry may emerge and be restructured in the post-pandemic period. The academic literature does however offer a range of insights into how disruption may be managed (Faulkner & Vikulov, 2001; Prideaux et al., 2003), how the global economic system responds to a range of shocks (Lee et al., 2001), various forms that future tourism pathways may take (Brouder, 2020) and approaches to dealing with pandemics (Bootsma & Ferguson, 2007). From another perspective, anticipated (by some) but unexpected (by most) events such as COVID-19 can be described as a Black Swan event. These events (Taleb, 2007) are extraordinary but seemingly unlikely events that are able to be explained but only in retrospect.

Much of the discussion in this paper is based on media reports rather than the peer reviewed literature, which in the case of the tourism literature is often reflective and generally written with the advantage of hindsight. The rapid unfolding and uncertainty about the ultimate outcome of events occurring while this paper was being written provides a unique insight into current concerns, why specific policy initiatives have been made in the face of future uncertainty and the learning that has occurred so far. This approach provides a unique opportunity to understand concerns and responses to the pandemic without the later filtering of interpretation that occurs in in post-crisis analysis of past events.

A 100-day timeline (Safi, 2020) provides a useful base line for the current state of knowledge about COVID-19 and a reference point for decisions that are now being made about how to respond to the pandemic. By Day 100 (9 April 2020), 85,521 people had died, and 1,436,198 people had been infected (WHO, 2020a). This stands in contrast to Day 50 (19 February 2020) when the coronavirus was present in 25 countries, had claimed 2006 lives in China and the US had 15 confirmed cases (WHO, 2020b). At that stage, the coronavirus was viewed as a problem for China and few nations apart from Taiwan and Singapore had implemented non-pharmacological (public health) interventions (NPI) to deal with the virus. The state of uncertainty about the course of events after Day 100 (when this passage was written) is demonstrated by concerns about the economic fallout of the pandemic. Some commentators have raised concerns about a deep recession, others are concerned about a potential depression. Many governments have responded by announcing very large stimulus packages (IMF, 2020). The success or otherwise of these decisions will be apparent in the future, illustrating the difficulty that decision makers face in developing policies in circumstances of uncertainty and an unknown future.

The literature on disruption (Christensen, 2006; Buhalis et al., 2019) and resilience (Hall et al., 2018) offer some insights into the likely impact of COVID-19 on tourism. Typical responses to disruptive change at individual, organisational and government levels include flight, fight, freeze or accept (Wester, 2011; Webster et al., 2016) where flight refers to an unwillingness to accept change, fight results in active opposition to change, freeze leads to uncertainty and acceptance refers to accepting change and adapting to it.

The medical literature offers evidence-based insights into how pandemics emerge and can be managed. Morse et al. (2012, p. 1956) note that 'Most pandemics—e.g., HIV/AIDS …. —originate in animals, are caused by viruses, and are driven to emerge by ecological, behavioural, or socioeconomic changes'. They suggested a three-stage progression commencing with a pre-emergency stage where there is encroachment on wildlife habitats and/or change in land use, a second stage where local emergence occurs and a third stage of pandemic emergence.

The development of vaccines and antiviral agents are important tools in dealing with infectious diseases such as influenza. However, vaccines take time to develop and test. Despite 40 years of research, a HIV/AIDS vaccine has not been developed

(Eisinger & Fauci, 2018). As of April 1, 2020, there were at least 41 COVID-19 vaccine candidates in various stages of testing (Routley, 2020). Given the need for rigorous testing regimes it might be at least 12 to 18 months before a vaccine is available (Healthline Media, 2020), if at all.

Where a vaccine is not available, the most effective control measures in the local emergence and pandemic emergence stages are NPIs, which include frequent hand washing, avoidance of mass gatherings, isolation of symptomatic individuals, quarantine and social distancing (Narain et al., 2009). When applied, NPIs helped reduce the rate of infection during the Great Manchurian Plague of 1910 (Summers, 2012) and the Spanish Flu (H1N1) pandemic of 1918/19 (Narain et al., 2009; Bootsma & Ferguson, 2007). However, these measures may be ineffective where there are individuals who are either presymptomic or asymptomatic and not aware that they are spreading the disease (Chastel, 2012).

A study of the Spanish Flu pandemic in US cities using the susceptible-exposed-infected-recovered (SEIR) epidemic model (Bootsma & Ferguson, 2007) found that NPIs reduced the level of mortality. Their findings demonstrated the positive impacts of NPIs and the potential for a second wave of infections if NPIs are lifted too early.

Echoing comments made by many researchers, Pike et al. (2010, p. 1639) stated that the next pandemic will occur from 'cross-species transmission from animals to humans'. Avoidance of future pandemics requires a system for detecting transmission early in the emergence process. As events in Wuhan indicate, failure of existing detection systems to respond to the initial phase of cross-species transmission can lead to a pandemic.

Transformation

Transformation requires change (Davis et al., 2010) and usually causes disruption. Saarinen (2004, p. 172) described transformation as a process where the destination 'is produced and reproduced by the discursive practices, and even competing discourses, through which the destination receives its identities and meanings, not only one after another, but also concurrently'. From this perspective, transformation is an ongoing almost linear process where multiple and at times competing ideas of destinations emerge. As Saarinen (2004) warns, actors involved in the process of transformation should consider conflicting discourses of development, the ethical dimensions of development and use of tourists' vs locals' space. From this perspective, transformation may lead to future conflict between local communities, the tourists who make use of the local community for their touristic activities and the business and government elites who control the shape and form of development. The transformation narrative adopted by destinations will become particularly important in how they respond to climate change and a carbon-neutral economy.

On a global scale, COVID-19 will accelerate transformations that have already commenced on a small scale with increased use of renewables and initial acceptance of models such as the circular economy (Ellen MacArthur Foundation, 2013). As change accelerates, groups of winners and losers will emerge (O'Brien & Leichenko, 2003). In the long-term, industries that depend on the fossil fuel industry will lose as nations transition to renewable energy and new production systems. In the short-term these firms will fight rather than accept change and continue to cause significant environmental damage.

Consideration must also be given to global geopolitics. The tourism literature rarely looks beyond the bubble of tourism activity to consider how geopolitics shapes and reshapes tourism activity. In 1989 US political scientist Francis Fukuyama (2006, p. 1) argued that liberal democracy may be the 'final form of human government'. Fast forward to 2020 and we find a world where globalism and multilateralism are under immense pressure from Brexit's rejection of centralised European power, the US swing to isolation under the slogan 'Make America Great Again', the rise of a strong nationalistic China, the election of popularist nationalist governments and the retreat of neoliberalism. Grant (2020) talks about a post-American world where US authority has been severely eroded and may be replaced by Chinese nationalism. In this new world order, the cries for leadership on climate change may not be heard over ideological clashes between the west and China, leading to catastrophic environmental damage.

COVID-19 has already transformed the global tourism industry from one that was concerned about how to manage rapid growth to one that is undergoing massive disruption and possible failure of key firms in the airline, hotel and attraction sectors. The outcomes of these changes and how tourism will be transformed will not be clear for some time.

Climate change

There is abundant evidence (IPCC, 2019) that climate change is rapidly changing the global environment. Solutions have been suggested but take-up has been slow. The circular economy model is one solution that is gaining increasing support as a strategy to deal with the economic factors that have caused climate change. The current global economy is based on the linear economic production system described as a 'take, make, dispose' model where limited effort is made to recycle on a large scale (Ellen MacArthur Foundation, 2013). The circular economy model changes this narrative to 'recycle, reuse, repair'. The circular economy model is based on old strategies such as reducing, reusing and recycling and new strategies such as an increased focus on renting rather than owning, moving from inbuilt obsolescence to repair and reuse, and localising production. Unlike alternative models such as degrowth, the circular economy model does not require a cessation of growth as an economic objective, rather one of its aims is to bend humanities' use of resources to achieve harmony with nature (Kunzig, 2020).

Building a circular economy will require an enormous cultural shift on the scale of the Industrial Revolution (Kunzig, 2020). Transforming the global economy will also require divergent thinking that will produce multiple answers through processes such as shifting our perspectives on existing information (seeing it in a new way) or transforming it through unexpected combinations of elements usually not regarded as belonging together (Cropley, 2015).

The role of experts

Expert knowledge is essential for long-term organisation survival particularly in operating environments that are subject to rapid change (Spruijt et al., 2014). Failure to employ expert knowledge increases the risk of financial loss (Aledort et al., 2007). When expert knowledge on pandemic management is ignored, and economic considerations given a higher priority than health considerations, less than optimal outcomes have occurred.

Leadership

Leadership is a key element in responding to crisis events. Boin et al. (2010, p. 707) observed that 'effective crisis leadership entails recognizing emerging threats, initiating efforts to mitigate them and deal with their consequences, and, once an acute crisis period has passed, re-establishing a sense of normalcy'. Unfortunately, it is not uncommon for leaders at all levels to seek to transfer responsibility for their poor decisions to others. Following Hurricane Katrina in 2005, US President George W. Bush's attempts to deflect blame based on 'unforeseenability' made matters worse (Boin et al., 2010). Similar comments in relation to blame for COVID-19 have been made about US President Donald Trump (Lopez, 2020), UK Prime Minister Boris Johnson and Indonesian President Joko Widodo (Lindsey & Mann, 2020). In other countries (Papua New Guinea and New Zealand for example), leaders were quick to respond to WHO advice and able to avert large-scale infections.

Key issues national leaders need to consider in crisis situations such as COVID-19 include decisions on the priority given to health, the economy, the cost of implementing (or not implementing) recovery strategies and the role given to experts. In parallel with these decisions, consideration of the long-term implications of responses is required. One of the lessons from the current response to COVID-19 is that there is considerable expert knowledge of what works and what doesn't (Bootsma & Ferguson, 2007) but unless governments are willing to listen, serious mistakes will continue to be made.

Current situation

The following discussion summarises the situation at the time the paper was written. The global situation on 13 April 2020 was 1,773,084 infections and 111,652 deaths. Future deliberations on the validity of observations made during COVID-19 will have the benefit of hindsight and knowledge of the outcomes. This knowledge was not available at the time of writing.

COVID-19 emerged in China in December 2019 and spread globally via the same air, land and sea travel networks used by the tourism industry. The initial response of the Chinese Government was flight, but this rapidly changed to fight, and many parts of China were placed in total lockdown. In a similar way, the US government initially adopted a policy of flight based on the view that the problem was not theirs and would go away. The US later changed course and adopted a policy of fight when it realised the problem would quickly escalate into a major health crisis.

By early April 2020 most countries had closed their international and in some instances internal borders, halting international travel for an indeterminate time and transforming the tourism industry in a manner never seen outside of wartime. The

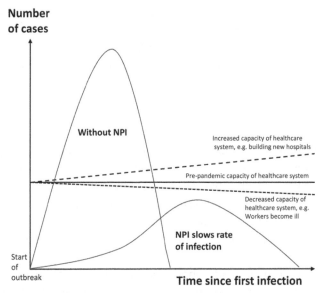

Figure 1. Flattening the curve.
Source: Authors

result has been a large-scale disruption of international and domestic tourism flows causing an unparalleled crisis for the global tourism industry. From a wider perspective, the disruption of tourism flows is only part of the larger disruption faced by the global economic system as it responds to the dramatic slowdown in economic activity. The way that the global economic system responds to the pandemic will ultimately determine the speed and volume of tourism activity in the post-pandemic period.

Response strategies

A report by the Imperial College (Ferguson et al., 2020) in mid-March 2020 illustrated the health and economic costs of two approaches to COVID-19. The first is based on suppression, described as policies designed to drive the 'reproduction number (the average number of secondary cases each case generates), R, to below 1 and … eliminate human-to-human transmission' (p. 3). The second is mitigation where NPIs are used to 'reduce the health impact of an epidemic, akin to the strategy adopted by some US cities in 1918, and by the world more generally in the 1957, 1968 and 2009 influenza pandemics (p. 3)'. The flattening the curve model illustrated in Figure 1 is a very simplified version of the suppression/mitigation approach outlined in Ferguson et al. (2020).

The key idea behind the widely accepted 'flattening the curve' approach is that measures taken to slow the rate of infection will allow a nation's healthcare system to cope with the number of hospital admissions and use of Intensive Care Unit (ICU) resources. The alternative curve illustrates a situation where measures to slow the rate of infection are either not implemented or are ineffective and the virus quickly overwhelms the healthcare system.

By early April 2020 variations of both approaches appear to have been successful. China's total lock down in Wuhan broke the cycle of transmission. In Australia, the Federal government's response (Gratton, 2020) struck a balance between health and keeping the economy running at a reduced pace and by 13 April the reproduction number (R), had fallen to below 1.

Discussion

COVID-19 has illustrated the fragility of life, but the same understanding has yet to be applied to addressing climate change which is about the fragility of resources required to sustain human life. The objective of this paper was to test the proposition that for the tourism industry to thrive in a future world it must look beyond the temptation of adopting strategies based on a return to the normal of the past and instead seek to understand how it should respond to the future climate change driven transformation of the global economy.

Four observations can be made about the factors that determine the outcome of strategies employed to deal with crisis events such as COVID-19. First, governments must identify the major objectives of the strategies adopted to deal with a crisis event. In the case of COVID-19, the primary objective for most countries was either health-care or the economy. Governments that identified healthcare as the key objective generally experienced fewer deaths and infections than governments that put the needs of business and politics first. Second, leadership is an important element in determining the success or failure of crisis response. Allied with leadership is the need for clear, honest, accurate and regular communications with the public and business. Third, the need to take advice from experts on developing strategies to respond to crisis events such as COVID-19 has emerged as a key lesson for governments at all levels. Fourth, the need to respond rapidly to the threat, rather than defer responses until the future, is now widely accepted. Each of these factors can be applied in dealing with the climate crisis that is becoming increasingly critical.

The pathway of the initial resumption of tourism activity post-COVID-19 is likely to be staged commencing with domestic tourism (stage 1), followed later by international travel (stage 2). In the long-term (stage 3), recovery will be influenced by the extent to which governments respond to the climate crisis and endorse the shift to a carbon-neutral economy. Domestic travel in stage 1 is also likely to be staged commencing with local travel.

Because there is potential for a second wave of infections generated by international arrivals, it is probable that international travel will resume only when a vaccine is developed and widely administered. The timing of stage 2 is unknown, and the level of restrictions placed on arrivals is likely to be very high and include documentary proof of vaccination. Within the tourism sector, it can be expected that there will be considerable disruption as major firms including hotels, transport companies and attractions collapse and are absorbed by new firms.

Long-term recovery (stage 3) will be influenced by the speed of the transformation of the current linear production system. This transformation will present significant challenges but also offer significant opportunities for the tourism industry. The response options to COVID-19 (Figure 1) have parallels with strategies for dealing with climate change. Currently, the world remains on the first trajectory and has failed to implement measures to mitigate climate change and risks catastrophic ecosystem collapse. The Australian bush fires and coral bleaching of the Great Barrier Reef in the summer of 2019/20 are graphic examples of damage that may lead to ecosystem collapse. The second approach is to rapidly respond to the problem and minimise the consequences. Drawing on the lessons of COVID-19, adoption of the second response (flattening the curve) is preferable to the first approach and much less costly in terms of human life and environment damage. The observations made earlier about the need to identify desired outcomes, leadership, use of experts and rapid response will need to be applied in stage 3 of post-COVID-19 recovery if the tourism industry is to flourish in a climate affected world. This approach also offers numerous opportunities for the tourism industry to transform from its current model that favours high resource consumption to a model that supports the circular economy model.

Conclusion

Prior to COVID-19 many governments acknowledged the possibility of a global pandemic but saw little value in funding research and stockpiling of medical resources to deal with a future event of this type. Similarly, many governments have acknowledged the threat of climate change, but most have hesitated to respond decisively and address the problem. The victory of decisiveness in the war to conquer COVID-19 provides a useful metaphor for the need to act decisively with climate change if that war is to be won.

Climate change poses a far greater threat to humanity, but because the danger is not immediate action continues to be deferred. The success of strategies to flatten the COVID-19 curve point to the potential for fighting climate change by adopting a 'flattening the curve' approach rather than flight.

The transformations required to restart global tourism flows post-COVID-19 will be just the first of a long series of overlapping economic and political transformations that the global tourism industry will need to respond to in coming decades. Beyond COVID-19, the global economy and political system will be forced to respond to climate change, a process that will necessitate further transformation of the global economy on a scale that has not been experienced since the Industrial Revolution. In parallel to economic transformation, global tourism will need to respond to the physical, social and economic changes that climate change will drive.

Disclosure statement

No potential conflict of interest was reported by the author(s).

ORCID

Bruce Prideaux (iD) http://orcid.org/0000-0002-3577-1951
Michelle Thompson (iD) https://orcid.org/0000-0002-7909-3523
Anja Pabel (iD) http://orcid.org/0000-0003-1409-5496

References

Aledort, J. E., Lurie, N., Wasserman, J., & Bozzette, S. A. (2017). Non-pharmaceutical public health interventions for pandemic influenza: An evaluation of the evidence base. *BMC Public Health, 7*(1), 208. https://doi.org/10.1186/1471-2458-7-208

Boin, A., Hart, P. 'T., McConnell, A., & Preston, T. (2010). Leadership style, crisis response and blame management: The case of Hurricane Katrina. *Public Administration, 88*(3), 706–723. https://doi.org/10.1111/j.1467-9299.2010.01836.x

Bootsma, M., & Ferguson, N. (2007). The effect of public health measures on the 1918 influenza pandemic in U.S. cities. *Proceedings of the National Academy of Sciences, 104*(18), 7588–7593. https://doi.org/10.1073/pnas.0611071104

Brouder, P. (2020). Reset Redux: Possible evolutionary pathways towards the transformation of tourism in a COVID-19 world, *Tourism Geographies*, https://doi.org/10.1080/14616688.2020. 1760928

Buhalis, D., Harwood, T., Bogicevic, V., Viglia, G., Beldona, S., & Hofacker, C. (2019). Technological disruptions in services: Lessons from tourism and hospitality. *Journal of Service Management, 30*(4), 484–506. https://doi.org/10.1108/JOSM-12-2018-0398

Chastel, C. (2012). Eventual role of asymptomatic cases of dengue for the introduction and spread of dengue viruses in non-endemic regions. *Frontiers of Psychology, 30*(3), 70. https://doi.org/10.3389/fphys.2012.00070

Christensen, C. (2006). The ongoing process of building a theory of disruption. *Journal of Product Innovation Management, 23*(1), 39–55. https://doi.org/10.1111/j.1540-5885.2005. 00180.x

Cropley, D. H. (2015). *Creativity in engineering: Novel solutions to complex problems*. Elsevier.

Davis, E., Kee, J., & Newcomer, K. (2010). Strategic transformation process: Toward purpose, people, process and power. *Organization Management Journal, 7*(1), 66–80. https://doi.org/10. 1057/omj.2010.6

Edmond, C. (2019). Zero by 2050: How the world's economy has planned to battle climate change. *We Forum*. https://www.weforum.org/agenda/2019/07/zero-emissions-target-climate-change-impact/

Eisinger, R., & Fauci, A. (2018). Ending the HIV/AIDS pandemic. *Emerging Infectious Diseases, 24*(3), 413–416. https://doi.org/10.3201/eid2403.171797

Ellen MacArthur Foundation. (2013). *Towards the circular economy* (Vol. 1). Ellen MacArthur Foundation.

Faulkner, B., & Vikulov, S. (2001). Katherine, washed out one day, back on track the next: A post-mortem of a tourism disaster. *Tourism Management, 22*(4), 331–344. https://doi.org/10.1016/S0261-5177(00)00069-8

Ferguson, N., Laydon, D., Nedjati Gilani, G., Imai, N., Ainslie, K., Baguelin, M., Bhatia, S., Boonyasiri, A., Cucunuba Perez, Z., Cuomo-Dannenburg, G., Dighe, A., Dorigatti, I., Fu, H.,

Gaythorpe, K., Green, W., Hamlet, A., Hinsley, W., Okell, L., van Elsland, S., … Ghani, A. (2020). Impact of non-pharmaceutical interventions (NPIs) to reduce COVID-19 mortality and health-care demands. *Imperial College, London*, 1–20. https://doi.org/10.25561/77482

Fukuyama, F. (2006). *The End of History and the Last Man*. Free Press.

Grant, S. (2020). *Coronavirus has sped up changes to global order and sovereignty is making a comeback*. Australian Broadcasting Corporation. https://www.abc.net.au/news/2020-04-13/coronavirus-changes-to-global-order-us-china/12139216

Hall, C. M., Prayag, G., & Amore, A. (2018). *Tourism resilience: Individual, organisational and destination perspectives*. Channel View.

Healthline Media (2020). *Why it'll still take more than a year to develop a COVID-19 vaccine*. Healthline. https://www.healthline.com/health-news/covid-19-vaccine-more-than-one-year-before-available#The-race-for-a-COVID-19-vaccine

International Monetary Fund. (2020). *Policy responses to COVID-19*. International Monetary Fund. https://www.imf.org/en/Topics/imf-and-covid19/Policy-Responses-to-COVID-19

IPCC. (2019). *The ocean and cryosphere in a changing climate*. IPCC.

Kunzig, R. (2020). The end of trash. *National Geographic*, *237*(3), 42–71

Lee, B. R., Lee, K., & Ratti, R. (2001). Monetary policy, oil price shocks, and the Japanese economy. *Japan and the World Economy*, *13*(3), 321–349. https://doi.org/10.1016/S0922-1425(01)00065-2

Lindsey, T., Mann, T. (2020). *Coronavirus is on the verge of exploding in Indonesia and 240,000 die*. Australian Broadcasting Corporation. https://www.abc.net.au/news/2020-04-08/coronavirus-could-cause-240,000-deaths-in-indonesia/12131778.

Lopez, G. (2020). *The Trump administration's botched coronavirus response, explained*. Vox. https://www.vox.com/policy-and-politics/2020/3/14/21177509/coronavirus-trump-covid-19-pandemic-response

Morse, S., Mazet, J., Woolhouse, M., Parrish, C., Carroll, D., Karesh, W., Zambrana-Torrelio, C., Lipkin, I., & Daszak, P. (2012). Prediction and prevention of the next pandemic zoonosis. *The Lancet*, *380*(9857), 1956–1965. https://doi.org/10.1016/S0140-6736(12)61684-5

Narain, J., Kumar, R., & Bhatia, R. (2009). Pandemic (H1N1) 2009: Epidemiological, clinical and prevention aspects. *The National Medical Journal of India*, *22*(5), e1–e6.

O'Brien, K. L., & Leichenko, R. M. (2003). Winners and losers in the context of global change. *Annals of the Association of American Geographers*, *93*(1), 89–103. https://doi.org/10.1111/1467-8306.93107

Pike, B. L., Saylors, K. E., Fair, J. N., Lebreton, M., Tamoufe, U., Djoko, C. F., Rimoin, A. W., & Wolfe, N. D. (2010). The origin and prevention of pandemics. *Clinical Infectious Diseases*, *50*(12), 1636–1640. https://doi.org/10.1086/652860

Prideaux, B., Laws, E., & Faulkner, B. (2003). Events in Indonesia: Exploring the limits to formal tourism trends forecasting methods in complex crisis situations. *Tourism Management*, *24*(4), 475–520. https://doi.org/10.1016/S0261-5177(02)00115-2

Routley, N. (2020). *Every vaccine and treatment in development for COVID-19, so far*. Visual Capitalist. https://www.visualcapitalist.com/every-vaccine-treatment-covid-19-so-far/

Saarinen, J. (2004). Destinations in change' The transformation process of tourist destinations. *Tourist Studies*, *4*(2), 161–179. https://doi.org/10.1177/1468797604054381

Safi, M. (2020). It started as a warning. It changed into a pandemic that that has transformed life as we know it. *The Guardian*. https://www.theguardian.com/world/ng-interactive/2020/apr/08/coronavirus-100-days-that-changed-the-world

Spruijt, P., Knol, A. B., Vasileiadou, E., Devilee, J., Lebret, E., & Petersen, A. C. (2014). Roles of Scientists as policy advisers on complex issues: A literature review. *Environmental Science & Policy*, *40*, 16–25. https://doi.org/10.1016/j.envsci.2014.03.002

Summers, W. (2012). *The great Manchurian plague of 1910-1911: The geopolitics of an epidemic disease*. Yale University Press.

Taleb, N. (2007). *The black swan – the impact of the improbable*. Random House.

Webster, V., Brough, P., & Daly, K. (2016). Fight, flight or freeze: common responses for follower coping with toxic leadership. *Stress and Health : journal of the International Society for the Investigation of Stress, 32*(4), 346–354. https://doi.org/10.1002/smi.2626

Wester, M. (2011). Fight, flight or freeze: assumed reactions of the public during a crisis. *Journal of Contingencies and Crisis Management, 19*(4), 207–214. https://doi.org/10.1111/j.1468-5973.2011.00646.x

WHO. (2020a). *Coronavirus Disease 2019 (COVID-19) Situation Report 80*. World Health Organisation. https://www.who.int/docs/default-source/coronaviruse/situation-reports/20200409-sitrep-80-covid-19.pdf?sfvrsn=1b685d64_6

WHO (2020b). *Coronavirus Disease 2019 (COVID-19) Situation Report 30*. World Health Organisation. https://www.who.int/docs/default-source/coronaviruse/situation-reports/20200219-sitrep-30-covid-19.pdf?sfvrsn=3346b04f_2

World Travel and Tourism Council. (2019). *Travel and Tourism Continues Strong Growth Above Global GDP*. World Travel and Tourism Council. https://www.wttc.org/about/media-centre/press-releases/press-releases/2019/travel-tourism-continues-strong-growth-above-global-gdp/

Reconsidering global mobility – distancing from mass cruise tourism in the aftermath of COVID-19

Luc Renaud (iD)

ABSTRACT

The mass cruise tourism industry (MCTI) is inscribed in a neoliberal production of tourism space that promotes the economic, sociocultural and environmental marginalization of cruise destinations. With cruise tourism halted as a result of the COVID-19, but likely to resume in 2021, I question the relevance of this form of tourism and propose future development alternatives aligned with deglobalisation and degrowth of the industry. Power relations with destinations communities can be critiqued using the concepts of global mobility and local mobility to show that the former, imperative for the deployment of mass cruise tourism, is a weakness for the industry in a post-pandemic perspective of reduced mobility. Destinations must use the industry's dependence on global mobility as leverage to transform the balance of power in their favor and promote local mobility. They must embrace radical solutions to take control of their territory to favor a transition from "Growth for development" to "Degrowth for liveability". Host territories, relying on national and regional governance, should gradually ban or restrict the arrival of mega-cruise ships, implement policies that promote the development of a niche cruise tourism industry (NCTI) with small ships and develop a fleet controlled by local actors.

摘要

大众邮轮旅游业促进了邮轮目的地经济、社会文化和环境的边缘化, 被认为是一种新自由主义的旅游空间生产。因新型冠状病毒肺炎疫情而暂停的邮轮旅游可能会在2021年得以恢复, 但作者质疑了当前邮轮旅游业发展的意义, 并提出了与去全球化和去增长相一致的邮轮旅游业未来发展替代方案。全球流动性是发展大众邮轮旅游业的必要条件, 但亦可能成为该行业的一个弱点, 新型冠状病毒肺炎疫情大流行后流动性降低就明证了这一点, 可以使用全球流动性和当地流动性的概念来批判大众邮轮旅游业与目的地社区的权力关系。目的地社区要善于利用大众邮轮旅游业对全球流动性的依赖这一特点, 努力将权力平衡向有利于自己的方向调节, 并促进本地流动性的杠杆作用。同时, 目的地社区也必须采取彻底的解决方案来控制自己的领土, 进而实现从"增长换发展"向"缩减换宜居"的过渡。最后, 东道国还应依托国家和地区的治理, 逐步禁止或限制巨型邮轮的抵达, 实施旨在促进小型邮轮旅游业发展的政策, 并发展由当地参与者控制的船队。

Introduction

In the midst of the COVID-19 crisis, sociologist and philosopher Bruno Latour asserted that we must reject the idea of restarting production as soon as the spread of the virus shows the first signs of weakening: "the last thing to do is to repeat everything we did before" (Latour, 2020). Latour proposes taking advantage of this forced "break" in globalization to reflect on the modes of production favored by the current global socio-economic structure so as to contest these modes of production, rather than to simply reflect on them from the perspective of wealth distribution. The challenge is to think up and then establish a new economic system that includes what is desirable, and excludes what is not.

Through its capacity to produce and reproduce consumption spaces on a global scale (Fletcher, 2011), the expansion of tourism is one of these modes of production. In a recent text, and in line with Latour, the editorial team at Degrow.info also proposed taking some time to carefully analyze the situation:

> "our hyper-mobile and interconnected global capitalist societies have exacerbated the spread of covid-19 through frequent long-distance travel, massive cruise ships, and short-distance flights (for example from Belgium to Italy for ski vacations). Covid-19 has grounded our hyper-mobility to a halt. We're forced to stay rooted, and maybe it's a moment to reflect on why we constantly feel compelled in contemporary society to be always on-the-go" (Degrowth.info, 2020).

The "COVID-19 break" implies stopping the expansion of a tourism standardized and homogenized by the forces of capitalism, what Hollinshead (2007) calls Worldmaking. Characterized by a hegemonic imposition - conscious or unconscious - of an ideological narrative framework supported by the actors of transnational tourism, Worldmaking marginalizes local stakeholders. Given its ability to expand geographically, and due to the ubiquity of tourism in the living spaces of receiving communities, Worldmaking is also involved in the production of new spaces that are incompatible with a sustainable development approach.

One of the current emblematic manifestations of transnational capitalist tourism is the mass cruise tourism industry (MCTI). Overall, this industry is able to take full advantage of all the mechanisms of the neoliberal economy that allow it to accumulate and geographically fix the capital necessary for its expansion. The MCTI promotes the creation of relational spaces around port areas in the periphery, but also throughout host territories' regional and national space (Gutberlet, 2019) where new power games appear (Renaud, 2019). It goes without saying that this creates collisions at the economic, environmental and socio-cultural level. Cruises are not a simple form of travel or an ordinary tourist product: they involve interrelations and spatio-temporal repercussions on multiple levels that require renewed critical questioning. Exacerbated socio-territorial exclusions, precarious regional livelihood, disturbed marine ecosystems and increased air pollution are just a few examples of the acute problems brought by the MTCI.

This contribution is part of Gibson's (2019) reflections on the excesses of tourism in the Anthropocene. Gibson grouped these excesses according to three analytical frameworks: fixed capital and territorial; excessive mobilities and accompanying material struggles; and biopolitical limits and excesses (Gibson, 2019, p. 2). The context of the present health crisis has transformed and reconfigured the nature of the excesses that characterize mass cruise tourism. The focus of the following discussion is on the concept of mobility as an excess of tourism as illustrated by the shutdown of the world economy. In addition, Ferreira et al. (2017) concept of mobility topology will be used to propose an alternative to the excessive mobility of MCTI. I argue that hopes for a return to pre-COVID-19 tourist mobility must be urgently questioned especially since calls for a reactivation of the pre-COVID-19 globalized economy are already being made even though the pandemic has yet to be stabilized on a global scale.

An uncertain future – time for reflection

The fundamental distinction between the mass cruise tourism industry and the exclusively land-based tourism industry is the former's extreme mobility (Timothy, 2006). Extreme mobility characterizes the MCTI, which exists to transport tourists through a circuit of destinations. The extreme mobility of the MCTI, however, ensures another fundamental function for the development of the industry: in the current neoliberal economic context, it gives the industry a particularly advantageous balance of economic and political power, allowing it to more easily negotiate the conditions in which cruise companies invest in destination territories when setting up their activities, very much to the detriment of receiving communities (Pinnock, 2012; Vogel, 2011).

In fact, the mobility from which the industry benefits thanks to its floating infrastructure allows it to easily break the geographic ties that link it to the destinations with which it comes in contact. If the conditions for the deployment of its activities do not meet its commercial expectations, the possibility exists to move to other places (Lester & Weeden, 2004). Obviously, unbalanced power relations become even more unbalanced in regions that offer few comparative advantages, such as the Caribbean. While we might expect the contrary, the balance of power may also be favorable to the MCTI in regions with distinctive ports of call (Renaud, 2017).

The COVID-19 pandemic put an abrupt end to the mobility on which the MCTI relies. First, destinations began to refuse to receive stopover vessels that were still at sea when the virus began to spread at an alarming rate. Then, most western countries closed their borders to nonessential transit. As a result, the industry ceased operations pending stabilization of the health situation. The question that arises is whether transnational cruise corporations will recover from this situation and to what extent this break in mobility will affect territorial relations in the destinations. In other words, is the MCTI resilient enough to deal with the crisis? No one has a crystal ball that allows us to answer this question with certainty. However, a recent analysis conducted by Sachs et al. (2020) on behalf of Carnival Cruise Line (CCL) sheds light on economic projections for the post-COVID-19 period. CCL, the world's largest cruise corporation, requested the analysis in the context of the company's plan to recapitalize part of their assets in the stock market to obtain liquidity, thereby allowing them to curb the pandemic's impact on its activities.

According to this document, the industry is counting on a reduced revival of its activities in 2021. This optimism is based on four expectations: a vaccine, the relaxation of travel restrictions, implementation of additional health measures for passengers to access the ships and, above all, the presence of a loyal clientele. In this regard, CCL continues to receive deposits for cruise bookings scheduled for 2020-2021, and 45% of customers who have had their trip canceled have accepted credits for a future cruise in lieu of a refund, a trend that seems to be widespread throughout the industry (Panetta, 2020). The industry's optimistic outlook is also based on the industry's financial resilience. Recall that at the beginning of 2020, the stocks of the three largest cruise corporations that together hold more than 80% of the world market - Royal Caribbean Cruise Lines, CCL and Norwegian Cruise Line - dropped an average of 84.2% in 62 days, between a high on January 17 and a low on March 18.

This sharp fall could threaten the very survival of these industry giants, especially since these corporations are, at the time of writing, being refused a bailout from the US government because they are incorporated outside the US[1] (O'Connell, 2020). Yet despite the decline in stock prices and the US government's stance, investors continue to be confident, as demonstrated by the recent influx of liquidity to CCL bank accounts. CCL has received billions of dollars in market capitalization from its assets and orders from investors-bondholders, despite the $4 billion debt backed by their fleet (Smith, 2020). This shows that even in times of acute crisis, investors are there to support the industry's recovery.

Certainly, Sachs et al. (2020) analysis was reserved, despite the optimism of the cruise lines and their industry partners. In fact, their predictions are written using "may", "should", "depends", "could", etc., demonstrating a certain degree of realism. There are, as well, significant uncertainties on the horizon, including the inability to travel to different regions because of health-related restrictions and passengers' financial capacity given the deterioration of the global economy. As well, despite the relative loyalty of "repeat cruisers", it is impossible to predict customers' reaction to the industry's battered reputation.

In a context where the industry must constantly attract new customers to ensure growth, and in a context where a majority of passengers are relatively elderly and often have fragile health, outbreaks on several ships (Diamond Princess, Oasis of the Sea, Costa Luminosa, Ruby Princess, Costa Magica and Grand Princess, etc.) risk having lasting consequences. The image of cruise ships as "Floating Petri dishes" (Nikiforuk, 2020) presents a marketing challenge. A final uncertainly relates to destinations' continued hospitality and willingness to receive ships. With confirmed or feared outbreaks on board, several ships have struggled to find somewhere to dock. As the cruise industry struggles to get back in business, it is possible that access to certain destinations could be refused.

Despite recovery challenges for the industry, the fact remains that, sooner or later, companies will be able to gradually redeploy their fleets. In the meantime, this gives the different places that dealt with the MCTI before the pandemic a unique opportunity to question their collaboration with an industry that "is not a charitable enterprise serving regional development" (Dehoorne et al., 2012, p.12) but that is, instead, inclined to promote its own interests. In this, destinations would be well advised to take advantage of the industry's weakness to promote a variety of development that counteracts the effects of Worldmaking, of which MCTI is an important vector.

Given that the idea of mobility is at the center of the tourist phenomenon, it must also be at the center of reflections that seek to encourage the emergence of new approaches to tourism. Thus, while mobility is generally structured along a center/periphery axis, and more generally operates on a neocolonial dynamic, it would be advisable to refocus its control within the spaces of tourist destinations, allowing these to determine their own territorial development. Following this approach, it becomes possible to envision a world where the quality of living spaces takes precedence over the production of tourism spaces, and all this in a context characterized by a push to go local, deglobalize trade and promote the sustainable development of tourist territories. This also has the potential to contribute to a paradigm shift that takes us from the "Growth for development" that characterizes the MCTI to "Degrowth for liveability," which is more focused on the concept of community quality of life throughdeseasonalization, decongestion, decentralization, diversification and deluxe tourism (Milano et al., 2019). However, to achieve this and build a better post-COVID-19 world, it is essential to restructure the balance of power between the mass tourism industry and destination stakeholders.

About mobilities

I rely on the idea of mobility to reflect on the question of power relations. I draw inspiration from Ferreira's et al. (2017) theoretical framework that mobilizes the two linked notions of "motility"– the capacity for movement as a form of social capital – and "immotility" – a reduction in the capacity for movement, also a form of social capital. Ferreira argues that reducing capacity for movement, and therefore of mobility, makes it possible to anchor an individual's relationships with her space within a local sphere, which tends to favor the sustainable development of living spaces. Conversely, increasing the capacity for movement favors a more globalized relationship that is socio-culturally disembodied from space and a greater consumption of environmental resources. The latter scenario seems incompatible with the concept of "Degrowth for liveability."

In other words, Ferreira's distinction between motility and immotility makes it possible to express the transition from a society where global mobility prevails and where the capacity for movement is economically and socially valued to one where local mobility dominates and where a societal alternative linked to a reduction in mobility is also valued. In the context of cruise tourism, an approach that values local mobility takes advantage of possible changes in power relations in a post-COVID-19 world. It becomes the new engine of social capital within a system that will be de-globalized and it promotes the transition to the degrowth mentioned above. In the following pages, I propose to explore these implications more fully to show how the MTCI is dependent on global (and excessive) mobility and how destinations can use this dependence to counter the industry's power to favor local mobility in future cruise tourism activity.

The tourist is a privileged individual who is able to travel; she is associated with a discretionary ability to move. Thanks to her global mobility, the tourist who travels by choice will seek socially constructed holistic experiences and consume produced landscapes that meet her needs. These experiences lead her to come into contact, on a global scale, with a multitude of social and geographic resources nested in a globalized transit network that requires the mobilization of various means of transport. It goes without saying that the tourist's travels require a significant amount of resources. This kind of travel can be characterized as reversible global mobility, reversible because this kind of mobility is not necessary in a search for otherness. The economic and social forces linked to tourism seek to create highly publicized markers that push individuals to embark on journeys to a commodified elsewhere (Lapointe et al., 2018).

Yet, each individual can choose other ways of enhancing her identity, including discovering her own environment and thereby reducing her personal mobility. It goes without saying that the local geographic, social and cultural environment also has the resources to meet an individual's various aspirations. What is more, there is a good chance that this individual will feel especially in tune with the familiar aspects of her space that she discovers (or rediscovers), all the while using a minimum of resources and contributing more directly to the concept of degrowth. In short, the individual has the ability to transit from one mobility to another, from global to local mobility, the latter of which is also reversible.

From the point of view of cruise tourism, the question of mobility arises differently. Neoliberal economic mechanisms have strengthened the oligopolistic position of the three large cruise corporations which, as mentioned above, control over 80% of the world market (Chin, 2008). In this context, global mobility is one of the fundamental conditions for the viability of the MCTI. For the cruise industry, mobility is irreversible: growth is rooted in the notion of space production and spatially fixing capital (Harvey, 2001), the latter of which is the basis of the production of the tourism space necessary to the cruise industry's survival. It goes without saying that the heart of the industry lies in its fleet of ships (mobile capital), and that the industry fixes its capital in these mobile structures according to this dynamic of continual reinvestment. This allows it to solve, among other things, the problem of obsolescence; that is to say, investing in ships solves a "technological fix".

Yet even if the industry's business model is strongly oriented towards the development of ever larger, more efficient, and more entertaining and technologically avant-garde vessels, ultimately the "cruise tourism" product is inseparable from the concept of destination. To ensure the sustainability of their investments in their ships, corporations therefore must also move their mobile capital around the world. Corporations find themselves in a double dynamic of irreversible global mobility because, in addition to having to transport their clients, they have to make sure they have access to territories to offer as stopovers, which is the purpose of the trip in the first place. This implies the creation of tourism spaces whose financial burdens, in the current state of power relations, are mainly borne by destinations. Therein lies the Gordian knot, in the ability of destinations to reverse this balance of power.

Transforming power relations

The power to act that characterizes the individual in relation to her mobility has no equivalent when it comes to MCTI mobility. As far as large corporations are concerned, they are stuck in a double dynamic of irreversible global mobility, which generates many types of weaknesses for them. Irreversible mobility will have repercussions in terms of power relations between the industry and host destinations, but only if the latter understand that the former are dependent on mobility and therefore on access to their potential hosts' territories. For example, even in its favorite Caribbean strong-hold, where the industry has historically established its economic power (Pinnock, 2012), there is now a bottleneck with several companies competing for access to new territorial resources. As a result, we can observe a significant paradigm shift: cruise lines are investing hundreds of millions of dollars to access new spaces while, not so long ago, destinations were rolling out the red carpet to attract the cruise companies to their ports, even adapting their own port infrastructure (at their own expense) to the needs of mega-ships (Renaud, 2019).

This competitiveness between cruise lines is a recent phenomenon because novel destinations are getting scarce in that part of the world. In this regard, irreversible glo-bal mobility weakens the industry in relation to potential destinations and helps to reverse the traditional dynamics of power relations in favor of the latter. Another example comes from regional spaces where destinations have distinctive characteris-tics, such as the St. Lawrence River in Canada. In this type of host territory, certain stopovers are unique and are not interchangeable, which prevents the MCTI from using its mobility as leverage in negotiations, as it has done throughout the Caribbean. In these regional contexts, there is significant potential to transform the dynamics of negotiating power, which could benefit destinations and counter the power of cruise lines (Renaud & Sarrasin, 2019). This potential must still be harnessed by host territories, something that represents a major challenge. In other words, desti-nations or groups of destinations on a regional or national scale must take advantage of their political and social capital to use the irreversible global mobility of the MCTI against it to promote "Degrowth for liveability".

Different options exist for a slow transition towards degrowth. For the purposes of this discussion, I will explore two that can work to transform the relationship between the MCTI and cruise destinations. These suggestions will surely provoke debates as to their feasibility, but I believe it is necessary to be radical in times of crisis and to bring approaches to the conversation that seek to change an unsustainable reality. As Fletcher et al. (2020) suggest, in a situation where the COVID-19 crisis offers a historic "moment" of questioning, this is a first step toward fairer and more sustainable tourism. Destinations should consider confronting the mass cruise tourism industry in the following ways:

- In a context where the economic benefits linked to cruise tourism are low and where the socio-environmental impacts are significant, destinations must forbid mega-ships from docking that exceed a certain number of passengers. The various levels of local government in some destinations can already limit the height of hotels using zoning or other restrictions; a regulation on the size of the ships could follow this line of reasoning.
- In a situation where a destination still chooses to accommodate mega-ships, their presence could be conditional on more aggressive operating modalities in terms of taxation. A progressive taxation system that increases as the size of the ship increases would make it possible to compensate for mega-ships' impact on infra-structure or the environment. This less radical suggestion would economically dis-criminate against larger ships without prohibiting them, but might also convince

them to avoid these newly less profitable destinations. This kind of taxation scheme would make cruise lines financially accountable for their impact on destinations and, above all, would bring significant economic benefits to communities.

The main goal of these suggestions is to eliminate the presence of the MTCI from a given space, or at least reduce the number of ships. Admittedly, for destinations heavily dependent on mass cruises, for example the Caribbean and a few other places in the world, these options would be highly damaging for local and even national economies in the short term. Unfortunately, several of these places have poorly diversified economies and structural solutions to these countries' economic woes go beyond the question of tourism development. However, in most places around the world, the MTCI is not vital to the economy. This type of tourism complements a larger tourism industry and is often marginal to their economy as a whole.

Readers will note that my suggestions are not intended to completely eliminate cruise tourism. This position is ideologically indefensible and undesirable because it is not a question of judging the value of cruise tourism per se. It is a question of favoring a transformation of cruise tourism toward increased sustainability. This can be accomplished with a cruise tourism paradigm shift involving either a decrease in the size of the ships and transition from mass cruises to niche cruises (NCTI), or a decrease in mobility and corresponding shift from global to proximity mobility.

The first approach to degrowth involves favoring a NCTI with small ships (for the sake of this discussion, let's say about 1000 passengers or less) that are able to enter into a more equitable relations with the receiving communities. The advantages linked to these smaller vessels are numerous: they offer proportionately greater economic benefits, require lighter infrastructure and are more environmentally friendly. For example, they are able to obtain local products during a stopover, they do not have to burn the same amount of fuel to sail from port to port and their energy needs are impossible to compare to those of mega-ships that must burn fuel to generate electricity for casinos, wave pools, ice rinks, etc.

The second degrowth approach would be to develop a fleet of local cruise ships within different regional spaces that could gradually integrate into the foreign cruise ship fleet. The goal would be to inscribe NCTI in local mobility where local actors take territorial control of their maritime and land spaces according to governance regimes established by different levels of local government. This would promote the increased resilience of transport structures, as well as that of the tourism industry as a whole, in addition to allowing better control over the direction territorial development, of which tourism is part, takes. In the event of a health crisis where local mobility remains effective, it would be possible to rely on a local fleet to continue domestic tourist activities. In the end, it is a question of emancipating destinations from the MTCI to move towards a NCTI made up of both local and foreign stakeholders.

Concluding remarks – envisioning distancing from mass cruise tourism

Will humanity start traveling again? Yes, and the mass cruise tourism industry will do everything in its power to regain its hegemonic position. The uncertainties we mentioned earlier - restrictions on international mobility, both the industry and travelers' financial precarity, travelers' fears of moving around in an uncertain world, the fears these travelers create for receiving communities, etc. - will one day be behind us. Are we going to travel as we did before? The short answer is no. Probably the only certainty for the tourism industry, and indeed for all human activities, is that nothing will be like it was in the pre-COVID-19 era. The solutions to some of the problems of cruise tourism proposed above seek to awaken a state of mind, a new way of dialoguing with mass tourism. Local stake-holders have an opportunity to decide what is best for their own communities, rather than having these decisions imposed on them from more powerful actors. Local stake-holders will have to fill the vacuum this pandemic leaves, circumscribing the ambitions of the mass tourism industry and so preventing a return to the old "normal".

Returning to the pre-COVID-19 status quo will only perpetuate an intolerable situ-ation in terms of sustainable tourism. In an era when Worldmaking can no longer be ignored (Lapointe et al., 2018) and when global mobility seems to have saturated receiv-ing communities by favoring overtourism (Milano et al., 2019), a major shift is needed, and quickly. As Fletcher et al. (2020) also noted, this window of opportunity to reflect on how tourism works - or should not work –is closing quickly, as evidenced by the actions of global stakeholders who are trying to implement the precepts of disaster cap-italism (Klein, 2010). For example, airlines, hotel and restaurant groups are quickly mov-ing to monopolize the bailout funds various national governments have proposed to rescue their economies as a whole. It is therefore a question of thinking about the future of tourism before the agents of neoliberal globalization once again impose a mode of production of space that is counter to the challenges tourism poses in the Anthropocene era (Gibson, 2019). I hope that this contribution and the highlighting of certain weaknesses of the MCTI that can be exploited in the post-COVID period offers elements of reflection in this collective effort to address the upcoming transformation of the cruise tourism industry (Cheer, 2020). I reiterate my humble call for change by join-ing my voice to other scholars and insisting that now is the time to distance ourselves from the mass cruise tourism industry, to fight against its hegemonic power and to put forward alternatives as part of what Higgins-Desbiolles (2020) defines as the socialization of tourism in order to promote a kind of tourism truly sustainable for communities.

Note

1. If this remains the case, it would be an ironic reversal: up to now, the big cruise corporations have taken full advantage of their extraterritorial status to evade US tax laws, making them floating duty-free zones.

Disclosures statement

No potential conflict of interest was reported by the author.

ORCID

Luc Renaud (iD) http://orcid.org/0000-0003-1195-5665

References

Cheers, J. (2020, April 21). Not drowning, waving: Where to for cruise tourism post-COVID-19? Monash Lens. https://lens.monash.edu/@politics-society/2020/04/21/1380110/not-drowning-waving-where-to-for-cruise-tourism-post-covid-19

Chin, C. B. N. (2008). *Cruising in the global economy: profits, pleasure and work at sea*. Ashgate.

Degrowth.info. (2020, March 19). A degrowth perspective on the coronavirus crisis. Degrowth. https://www.degrowth.info/en/2020/03/a-degrowth-perspective-on-the-coronavirus-crisis/#more-473015

Dehoorne, O., Petit-Charles, N., & Theng, S. (2012). Le tourisme de croisière dans le monde: Permanences et recompositions. *Études Caribéennes*, (18). https://doi.org/10.4000/etudescaribeennes.5629

Ferreira, A., Bertolini, L., & Naess, P. (2017). Immotility as resilience? A key consideration for transport policy and research. *Applied Mobilities*, 2(1), 16–31. https://doi.org/10.1080/23800127.2017.1283121

Fletcher, R. (2011). Sustaining tourism, sustaining capitalism? The tourism industry's role in global capitalist expansion. *Tourism Geographies*, 13(3), 443–461. https://doi.org/10.1080/14616688.2011.570372

Fletcher, R., Murray Mass, I., Blázquez-Salom, M., & Blanco-Romero, A. (2020, March 24). Tourism, Degrowth, and the COVID-19 Crisis. POLLEN. https://politicalecologynetwork.org/2020/03/24/tourism-degrowth-and-the-covid-19-crisis/amp/

Gibson, C. (2019). Critical tourism studies: new directions for volatile times. *Tourism Geographies*, 1–19. https://doi.org/10.1080/14616688.2019.1647453

Gutberlet, M. (2019). Geopolitical imaginaries and Cultural Ecosystem Services (CES) in the desert. *Tourism Geographies*, 19(4), 1–29. https://doi.org/10.1177/1468797619850117

Harvey, D. (2001). Globalization and the "Spatial Fix. *Geographische Revue*, 2, 23–30.

Higgins-Desbiolles, F. (2020). Socialising tourism for social and ecological justice after COVID-19, *Tourism Geographies*, 1–14. https://doi.org/10.1080/14616688.2020.1757748

Hollinshead, K. (2007). Worldmaking' and the transformation of place and culture. In I. Ateljevic, N. Morgan, & A. Pritchard (Eds.), *The critical turn in tourism studies: Innovative research methods* (pp. 165–193). Routledge.

Klein, N. (2010). *The shock doctrine: The rise of disaster capitalism*. Metropolitan Book.

Lapointe, D., Sarrasin, B., & Benjamin, C. (2018). Tourism in the sustained hegemonic neoliberal order. *Revista Latino-Americana de Turismologia*, 4(1), 16–33. https://doi.org/10.34019/2448-198X.2018.v4.13915

Latour, B. (2020, March 30). Imaginer les gestes-barrières contre le retour à la production avant-crise. AOC. https://aoc.media/opinion/2020/03/29/imaginer-les-gestes-barrieres-contre-le-retour-a-la-production-davant-crise/

Lester, J.-A., & Weeden, C. (2004). Stakeholders, the natural environment and the future of Caribbean cruise tourism. *International Journal of Tourism Research*, 6(1), 39–50. https://doi.org/10.1002/jtr.471

Milano, C., Novelli, M., & Cheer, J. M. (2019). Overtourism and degrowth: A social movements perspective. *Journal of Sustainable Tourism*, 27(12), 1857–1875. https://doi.org/10.1080/09669582.2019.1650054

Nikiforuk, A. (2020). COVID-19, brought to you by globalization. The Tyee. https://thetyee.ca/Analysis/2020/03/13/COVID-19-Brought-By-Globalization/

O'Connell, J. (2020, March 13). Cruise line companies cut out of the $500 billion federal bailout, industry group says. The Washington Post. https://www.washingtonpost.com/business/2020/03/26/cruise-line-bailout/

Panetta, G. (2020, April 12). Cruise ship bookings for 2021 are already on the rise despite multiple COVID-19 outbreaks. Business Insider. https://www.businessinsider.com/cruise-ship-bookings-are-increasing-for-2021-despite-coronavirus-2020-4

Pinnock, F. H. (2012). *Caribbean cruise tourism: Power relations among stakeholders*. LAP Lambert Academic Publishing.

Renaud, L. (2017). Résister au débarquement: Tourisme de croisière et dynamiques territoriales Québec/Caraïbe. *Revue Interdisciplinaire de Travaux Sur Les Amériques, 10*. http://www.revue-rita.com/thema/resister-au-debarquement-tourisme-de-croisiere-et-dynamiques-territoriales-quebec-caraibe.html

Renaud, L. (2019). *Résister au débarquement: tourisme de croisière et dynamiques d'appropriation territoriale dans la Caraïbe* [Unpublished Ph.D thesis]. Université de Montréal.

Renaud, L., & Sarrasin, B. (2019). Géographie politique du tourisme: Le cas des croisières en Gaspésie. In H. Bélanger & D. Lapointe (Eds.), *Les approches critiques: Quelles perspectives pour les études urbaines, régionales et territoriales*. PUQ. https://doi.org/10.2307/j.ctvq4bz4m.11

Sachs, G., Morgan, J. P., Securities, B. (2020). Common stock - Prospectus supplement Rule 424(b)(5). *Carnival Corporation*. https://www.sec.gov/Archives/edgar/data/815097/000119312520092049/d897344d424b5.htm

Smith, R. (2020, April 6). Why cruise ship-backed bonds drew $17bn of demand. Financial Time. https://www.ft.com/content/d85cf0bc-1c6b-4680-bee3-b32eb9c598f9

Timothy, D. J. (2006). Cruises, supranationalism and border complexities. In R. K. Dowling (Ed.), *Cruise ship tourism* (pp. 407–413). CABI. https://doi.org/10.1079/9781845930486.0407

Vogel, M. P. (2011). Critical cruise research: In the age of performativity. In P. Gibson, A. Papathanassis, & P. Milde (Eds.), *Cruise sector challenges: Making progress in an uncertain world* (pp. 227–244). Gabler.

The COVID-19 crisis: Opportunities for sustainable and proximity tourism

Francesc Romagosa (iD)

Introduction: the impact of COVID-19 on tourism

In light of the health crisis arising from the COVID-19 pandemic—and which has now become a global economic and social crisis—a large number of questions are being raised about its impact, in the near and long term, on the tourism sector. The crisis is so far-reaching and has developed so suddenly and unexpectedly that it has become very difficult to make predictions that are even slightly realistic. To paraphrase Pliny the Elder, the great Roman naturalist who lived 2,000 years ago, the only certainty right now is uncertainty. No-one knows what will happen, even in the short term, the almost immediate future. However, there is consensus that nothing will ever be the same again. Moreover, there are likely to be socioeconomic changes that will have a very significant impact on tourism as we have come to know it: changes in mobility, socialisation and consumption patterns, our leisure and work, and many other dimensions of our social lives. Based on the evidence we have and on recent trends in the tourism sector up until now, we reflect on the implications that this crisis may have for the sustainability of the sector and the challenges it faces.

Based on the latest preventative measures being taken by countries, recent developments in Asia and the pattern of previous crises (SARS in 2003, the economic and financial crisis in 2008–2009), the UN World Tourism Organisation (UNWTO) has estimated a decrease of between 20% to 30% in international tourist arrivals and corresponding economic earnings in 2020 compared with 2019. However, the UNWTO acknowledges that such estimates must be treated with considerable caution, given the magnitude, volatility and wholly different profile of this crisis with respect to previous ones (UNWTO, 2020). For now, the evidence we have is of the closure, albeit temporarily, of most of the world's tourism destinations and, consequently, of all the companies, large and small, that depend directly or indirectly on the sector (air transport, cruises, hospitality, travel agencies, leisure and cultural activities, etc.). The level of economic and social upheaval is unprecedented.

Furthermore, it is not yet known how long the crisis will last; nor do we know its implications, from the point of view of restrictions on our mobility or so-called social distancing that must be maintained to prevent the spread of contagion. In this sense, from a sociological and anthropological point of view there are also a number of questions concerning the social impact of this crisis—at least until the pandemic is over—especially in those places that until very recently welcomed tourists. Apart from a considerable sense of bewilderment, suffering and social unrest among the population, could tourists be seen as potential carriers of the virus and therefore a threat (Korstanje, 2020)? Could this be the start of tourismophobia or, in those destinations where it already exists, cause it to increase? The role that social media could play in disseminating pandemic-induced perceptions and discrimination that affect the image of companies and destinations has already been identified as being a major one (Yu et al., 2020).

A (new) opportunity for a more sustainable tourism

It has often been argued that the tourism sector has high resilience and the capacity to adapt to and recover from catastrophic or unexpected phenomena. This time, however, the sector will have a very severe stress test to pass. There are analysts who believe that once the worst moments have passed, we will gradually return—they do not venture to offer a timescale—to a certain level of normality, or at least to a situation relatively similar to that which existed pre-crisis (Navarro Jurado et al., 2020). If this is the case, the black swan theory would be confirmed. That theory posits that once an unexpected event of great socioeconomic impact, such as this crisis, has passed, it becomes rationalised, making it seem predictable or explicable and giving the impression that its occurrence was anticipated (Taleb, 2007). According to such a point of view, the current crisis would not imply substantial change to the tourism sector, at least in terms of its future management and planning. Rather, a 'business as usual' philosophy would prevail. This would be worrying, if we consider the repeated warnings that the sector has received both for its unsustainability (lack of long-term vision) and for the increasingly recurring risks it poses with respect to climate change and global health emergencies (Jamal & Budke, 2020). Ignoring these risks would be reckless.

In light of the current situation, there have been calls for taking advantage of this period of stoppage in order to make far-reaching structural changes to the tourism sector, starting with a reflection on its sustainability. This is particularly relevant if we are to take account of criticisms levelled in recent years, mainly by the academic field, around the concept of sustainable tourism.Those criticisms highlight the need to rethink that concept and bring it closer in line with resilience (Bosak, 2016; Cheer & Lew, 2017; Hall et al., 2018). With the current crisis, this need has become more evident than ever.

Higgins-Desbiolles (2020), for example, wonders whether the COVID-19 crisis is really an epic disaster. Given that human activities need to change if we are to avoid the worst effects of climate change, this crisis, she says, presents us with an unexpected opportunity. Rather than return to our previous operating model as soon as possible, COVID-19 challenges us to think about the unsustainability of the pre-crisis travel and tourism industry. This links into another debate that began a few years earlier, which highlighted the need to curb what appeared to be the unchecked (and, therefore, unsustainable) growth of international tourism travel and to opt instead for degrowth strategies, especially in oversaturated destinations suffering from 'overtourism' (Higgins-Desbiolles et al., 2019). However, suddenly and unexpectedly, those destinations that previously suffered from this problem are now faced with the completely opposite concern: 'undertourism' or, rather, the absence of tourism. It should be said that this crisis has nothing to do with degrowth, which entails voluntary and planned contraction. Nevertheless, as authors such as Fletcher et al. (2020) suggest,

> … even if the COVID-19 crisis ends relatively soon, we cannot afford to return to levels of travel experienced previously, particularly by the wealthiest segment of the world's population. This is not only because of the social unrest overtourism provoked, but also because the industry's environmental damages (including climate change as well as pollution and resource depletion) which were already beyond unsustainable.

According to the same authors, the current restrictions and controls on mobility of people imposed by the health crisis show how, where there is the will and political consensus to do so, it would be possible to regulate tourist flows according to certain sustainability standards—when it had often been argued that this was not possible (Fletcher et al., 2020).

Despite the uncertainty we referred to at the beginning of the article, one of the most likely consequences of this crisis is the bolstering of proximity tourism (Navarro Jurado et al., 2020), understood it as doing tourism and travelling near home (Diaz-Soria, 2017; Jeuring & Haartsen, 2017). This prediction is based on the fact that with greater social and environmental awareness (Lew, 2020), post-crisis tourists will probably choose to travel to destinations closer to their place of residence. In the context of growing insecurity and uncertainty, nearby destinations could be considered 'less risky' by many potential tourists who, having been noticeably affected by the economic crisis arising from the health crisis, have seen their purchasing power reduced. Added to this, there may in fact be restrictions on international (long-distance) travel, at least for a while; in helping to reduce overall emissions, this would certainly be in line with both the promotion of more sustainable tourism and the concept of degrowth.

Conclusions

Needless to say, there is considerable concern over the sustainability of destinations and tourism companies (in this case, sustainability in the sense of survival). Faced with an uncertain future, destinations that appear to be in a less disadvantaged, more resilient, position are those that have a more diversified offer, are less dependent on a particular market and have opted for qualitative rather than quantitative criteria (i.e. development instead of growth). As for the tourism companies, the larger ones may have more wriggle room compared with small ones, although nothing is guaranteed (consider the collapse of giant Thomas Cook, in September 2019). If we consider the above-mentioned predictions, companies that have believed in and been loyal to the principles of sustainable tourism, regardless of their size, are those that could be well positioned in the new context. At this point, we should make special reference to the myriad of micro and small enterprises that are deeply rooted in the destination: those companies that offer ecotourism products or products based on the local natural and cultural heritage and do not contribute to overcrowding, offering both high-quality experiences for tourists and high added value to the destination. In any case, as Lew (2020) has pointed out, companies that survive the pandemic will need to make their products more resilient to future pandemics—which health experts warn will continue to occur—and be able to adapt to the predicted change in consumer interests, which will include greater demand for sustainable products.

In developed countries and emerging economies, where most of the world's tourism demand is concentrated and where proximity tourism is expected to help save the sector, the situation is more promising than it is in developing countries. The latter are highly dependent on outbound markets that come mostly from developed countries. Therefore, the challenge to the global tourism sector is major. Sustainability tells us to look for balances (i.e. between the environment, society and the economy). Thus, the challenge for global sustainable tourism will be to strike a balance between maintaining activity in rich countries, while avoiding overcrowding, and bringing activity to poor countries, some of which are overly dependent on the sector and markets that will need a lot of incentives to recover. Tourism can be a good tool for local development, but it should not be the only one. Thus, it will also be necessary to find a social balance in terms of equity and justice, as well as an economic one, in every destination. This is where tourism planning and management policies come into play, in terms of implementing sustainability and resilience at all scales (local, national and international) and with appropriate forms of governance, integrating the public and private sectors in a co-ordinated manner.

In brief, all stakeholders, including us as researchers, have a task of great responsibility: to help redirect tourism—from the point of view of both supply and demand—towards a truly sustainable and resilient profile that is fit for a future that is constantly changing and full of new challenges.

Disclosure statement

No potential conflict of interest was reported by the author(s).

ORCID

Francesc Romagosa (ID) http://orcid.org/0000-0002-9963-4227

References

Bosak, K. (2016). Tourism, development, and sustainability. In S. F. McCool, & K. Bosak (Eds.), *Reframing sustainable tourism* (pp. 33–44). Springer.

Cheer, J. M., & Lew, A. A. (Eds.). (2017). *Tourism resilience and sustainability: Adapting to social, political and economic change*. Routledge.

Diaz-Soria, I. (2017). Being a tourist as a chosen experience in a proximity destination. *Tourism Geographies, 19*(1), 96–117. doi: 10.1080/14616688.2016.1214976

Fletcher, R., Murray Mas, I., Blázquez-Salom, M., & Blanco-Romero, A. (2020). Tourism, degrowth, and the COVID-19 Crisis. *Political Ecology Network*, 24 March 2020. https://politicalecologynet-work.org/2020/03/24/tourism-degrowth-and-the-covid-19-crisis/.

Hall, C. M., Prayag, G., & Amore, A. (2018). *Tourism and resilience: Individual, organisational and destination perspectives.* Channelview.

Higgins-Desbiolles, F. (2020). The end of global travel as we know it: an opportunity for sustainable tourism. *The Conversation,* 17 March 2020. https://theconversation.com/the-end-of-glo-bal-travel-as-we-know-it-an-opportunity-for-sustainable-tourism-133783.

Higgins-Desbiolles, F., Carnicelli, S., Krolikowski, C., Wijesinghe, G., & Boluk, K. (2019). Degrowing tourism: Rethinking tourism. *Journal of Sustainable Tourism, 27*(12), 1926–1944. doi: 10.1080/09669582.2019.1601732

Jamal, T., & Budke, C. (2020). Tourism in a world with pandemics: local-global responsibility and action. *Journal of Tourism Futures,* ahead-of-print(ahead-of-print) https://www.emerald.com/insight/content/doi/10.1108/JTF-02-2020-0014/full/pdf. doi: 10.1108/JTF-02-2020-0014

Jeuring, J. H. G., & Haartsen, T. (2017). The challenge of proximity: the (un)attractiveness of near-home tourism destinations. *Tourism Geographies, 19*(1), 118–141. doi: 10.1080/14616688.2016.1175024

Korstanje, M. (2020). *Tourism and the war against a virus?.* University of Leeds, 1 April 2020. https://northernnotes.leeds.ac.uk/tourism-and-the-war-against-a-virus-also-in-spanish/

Lew, A. (2020). How to create a better post-COVID-19 World. *Medium,* 16 March 2020. https://medium.com/@alanalew/creating-a-better-post-covid-19-world-36b2b3e8a7ae

Navarro Jurado, E., Ortega Palomo, G., & Torres Bernier, E. (2020). Propuestas de reflexión desde el turismo frente al COVID-19. *Incertidumbre, impacto y recuperación.* Universidad de Málaga. http://www.i3t.uma.es/wp-content/uploads/2020/03/Propuestas-Reflexiones-Turismo-ImpactoCOVID_i3tUMA.pdf

Taleb, N. N. (2007). *The black Swan: The impact of the highly improbable.* Random House.

UNWTO. (2020). *Impact assessment of the COVID 19 outbreak on international tourism. Updated 27 March 2020.* https://www.unwto.org/impact-assessment-of-the-covid-19-outbreak-on-inter-national-tourism.

Yu, M., Li, Z., Yu, Z., He, J., Zhou, J. (2020). Communication related health crisis on social media: a case of COVID-19 outbreak. *Current Issues in Tourism.* doi: 10.1080/13683500.2020.1752632.

The *transformational festival* as a subversive toolbox for a transformed tourism: lessons from Burning Man for a COVID-19 world

Ian Rowen

ABSTRACT

Examining transformational festivals can offer conceptual resources for a transformation of tourism into a more responsible and sustainable practice. By thinking together two usually distinct scholarly treatments of "transformation"—those of transformational tourism and those of transformational festivals—the COVID-19 pandemic can itself also be treated as a spatiotemporal threshold for the transformation of the travel industry. This approach can also help deconstruct the mechanisms that sustain deleterious aspects of tourism's guest-host divide. As borders reopen and mobility and recreation recommences, the capacity of transformational festivals—both within and beyond their highly porous time-spaces– to transform their participants offer lessons for the blurring, if not the outright obliteration of the demarcation between guests and hosts. The creative and pro-social responses of members of one such transformational festival culture—Burning Man– to this and past crises are presented as examples for how values such as participation and civic responsibility may help people overcome shared conditions of hardship, and support more sustainable tourism practices in the post-COVID-19 world. Such subversive inter-subjective inversions may bring the recognition, in-itself, and production, for-itself, of a shared humanity of co-creators and participants in not just ephemeral, but accretive transformational social and environmental projects.

摘要

研究非传统节日能够为旅游产业转变为更有社会责任、可持续发展提供概念性思路。通过同时考量两种截然不同的关于"非传统"的学术讨论（即非传统旅游与非传统节日），新冠状病毒自身可作为旅游产业转型的时空阈值。这种方法有助于解构旅游主客体间分歧带来的持续负面影响机制。随着边界的重新开放，以及新一轮的娱乐活动与旅游者流动的再次兴起，非传统节日的承载力（即从时空范围内外调控参与者的能力），能够为削弱而非彻底消除主客之间的界限提供经验教训。我们以具有创新性、亲社会行为特征的非传统节日文化的代表活动——火人节作为案例，分析在过去及当前危机中，公民参与和公民责任等价值观如何帮助人们克服共同的困境，以及旅游产业如何在全球性新冠状病毒危机中实现可持续发展。这种颠覆性主体间转

This article has been republished with minor changes. These changes do not impact the academic content of the article.

化将会引发共同创造者和参与者对于共享型人性认知的形成、生
产与发展，其影响不仅在暂时性的，而且在增值性的非传统社会与
环境项目中得以体现。

Transformational festivals and transformational tourism

Burning Man, the paradigmatic example of what has since been termed a
"transformational festival," may not seem like the most obvious event culture from
which to draw lessons towards a transformation of tourism for a post-COVID-19 world.
A resource-intensive and brazenly hedonistic ephemeral urban agglomeration, it has
for decades attracted tens of thousands of participants on a pilgrimage to construct
an annual temporary city in the harsh and remote Nevada desert and then clean it up,
more or less, without a trace. Despite an organizational commitment to move towards
carbon neutrality—one that is no more enforceable than the United Nation's
Sustainable Development Goals—it is by no means a thoroughly benign or even low
impact activity. Yet, the exemplary and creative response of some of its participants to
this and past waves of disaster and crisis can offer lessons for the formation and maintenance of community and connection that may support more sustainable social and
environmental economies. Moreover, thinking transformational tourism and transformational festivals together can also provide conceptual resources for treating the pandemic itself as a spatiotemporal threshold for the transformation not only of the travel
industry, but the transformation of the usual discursive and material mechanisms that
sustain the divide between guests and hosts.

Even before the great travel freeze of 2020, various approaches have been promoted by tourism scholars, including "responsible tourism" (Sin, 2014), "multi-stake-
holder approaches" (Timothy, 2007), and so on, to address tourism's capacity to
amplify socioeconomic inequality and inflict irreversible ecological damage. As conceptual starting points or ethical orientations for practice, these approaches are laudable
and useful, even as they approach the limits and contradictions of capitalist political
economy. I submit here that a further part of the problem are the usual modes of distinction between the spaces and communities of guests and hosts, which can impede
efforts at collective action. Many of these problems have been further masked by the
ephemerality and fragmentation of global industry practice, which effaces and displa-
ces such problems as climate change as economic externalities, to be solved by future
generations, or by someone else, somewhere else.

Complementing the normative approaches mentioned above, "transformational
tourism" is another turn that has been proposed to address the longstanding social
and environmental challenges of tourism. Through "the transformation of our way
of seeing, being, doing and relating in tourism worlds", so one story goes, we can
effect "the creation of a less unequal, more sustainable planet through action-oriented, participant-driven learnings." In the process, argue some of its proponents,
scholars can "translate essentially individual and often transitory experiences into
transformation at a societal and global level" (Pritchard & Morgan, 2013, pp. 3
and 4).

My modest contribution here is to suggest that the transformative features of some festivals—particularly those that subvert social hierarchies while spurring pro-social behavior (Crockett, 2014)—may offer yet further inspiration for rethinking and refashioning tourism more broadly. In particular, these include a commitment to an ethos of participation and responsibility, experience with a collective overcoming of hardship, and the flattening or inversion of social hierarchies.

Part of the confusion and challenge of using a notion like "transformation" to effect transformation in industry and in academia is the ambiguity of the term itself, as different scholarly streams draw its meanings from distinct genealogies. Much of the work on "transformative tourism" stems from Mezirow's development of "transformational learning theory" to explain how US women returning to the workforce could be better integrated via the personal transformation of values and behaviors (Lean, 2009; Reisinger, 2013), although transformation can also refer to the effects of travel on a place (Lean, 2012), often in deleterious ways (Bruner, 1991).

Distinct from the term's appearance within tourism studies, the nascent "transformational festival" literature has drawn inspiration from the classic work of Victor Turner on liminality and rites of passage. The denotation itself has origins in pop culture that precede its academic uptake—the term was promoted via a TEDx talk by a regular festival goer and documentarian, and later taken up by scholars to describe festivals with most of the following characteristics:

> "an ecstatic core ritual provided through electronic dance music; visionary art, performance, art installations, and live art; a workshop curriculum covering a spectrum of New Paradigm subjects; the creation and honoring of sacred space; ceremony and ritual; a social economy of artisans and vendors (or, alternative gift economy); a natural, outdoor setting to honor the Earth; and a multiple (typically 3–7) day duration" (Schmidt, 2015, p. 47).

Key to this is the "the co-creation of an immersive, participant-driven reality" that produces a sense of empowerment while effacing distinctions between performers and spectators. Following Turner, transformational festival scholars treat these rites as occasions during which participants enter threshold spaces where the usual rules of social order don't apply, but by emerging personally transformed, they produce an effect of communitas and a shared reference point for emergent social structures. As put by Graham St. John (2015, pp. 6 and 7),

> As festal citizens, participants are afforded passage into a transitional world possessing liminal conditions and carnivalesque logics (or illogics) to which inhabitants are compelled to surrender… [This affords conditions for] a rite of passage, a structured ritual which possesses the power to transform an individual's status, identity and life; only, the liminality of the modern festival holds heterogenous, elective and hyper-mediated characteristics … [for] entrants who become liminars (literally: threshold dwellers) while occupying the demarcated time-space framework of the event.

Transformational festival as social movement, and Burning Man's culture of crisis response

Although transformational festivals could themselves be analyzed as temporary tourist destinations, their propensity to spawn mediated manifestations of community, both in person and virtually, complicates efforts to bind them to a singular "natural, out-door" setting. Furthermore, considering these phenomena from the perspective of the so-called "mobilities paradigm," one might remember that there are "many other ways one travels (e.g. communicatively, virtually and imaginatively) during corporeal travel" (Lean, 2012, p. 154), and transformational festivals are no exception. Such a point can be made by observing how the progenitor of this typology, Burning Man, has evolved into a wider cultural field with regional events and regular meetups worldwide in both on and offline worlds. This has come not simply through the repetition of ritual in bounded-time-spaces, but through the invention of new forms of identification and subjectivity—basically, by transforming tourists to transformational festivals into partic-ipants in a broader movement.

What are some examples of how this might matter when contemplating the trans-forming role of mobility in producing more positive futures? Many Burning Man partic-ipants, or 'burners', had responded to past crises by upping their participation and sharing gifts developed through years of experimenting with temporary intentional community in adverse environmental circumstances. As the COVID-19 pandemic unfolded, regional 'Burn events' began cancelling worldwide. Plans for the main event, which had been held in the desert annually since 1990, and which through ticket sales covers most of the costs for a year-round office staff based in San Francisco, also fell into question. Yet, while still facing the potential impossibility of meeting face-to-face en masse, the organization and community that supports it returned to its roots, emphasizing participation, connection, and civic engagement in the face of isolation.

Of course, such community mobilization is not unique to Burning Man. Initial efforts are illustrative, if not entirely distinct from those of other event communities. Monthly 'burner pub' socials became weekly online chat sessions, drawing not just city dwellers but participants from remote rural areas. Dance camps moved their gatherings and fundraisers into cyberspace, beaming bass lines and good vibes across the planet. Artists from San Francisco to Berlin to Bucharest set up virtual sessions to share pieces from productions and performances that were canceled in the wake of the outbreak, offering exposure not only for a limited number of established names, but potentially limitless participation from less well-known creators.

But far more profound and useful to those outside the community were the attempts to apply technical and organizational skills developed through years of experimentation in the hardship conditions of the Black Rock Desert. The first notable such case was in 2004, when Hurricane Katrina devastated New Orleans and the US Gulf Coast during the same week that Burning Man took place. As thousands of the region's residents fled to take temporary shelter, hundreds of burners in Nevada real-ized they either did not have homes to return to, or had skills and tools they could bring from the desert to help people who had lost their basic material and social sup-port systems. This sparked the volunteer campaign later incorporated as Burners Without Borders, a non-profit relief organization that went on to rebuild a flooded Vietnamese Buddhist Temple in Mississippi (Chen, 2009, 2011). The establishment of Burners Without Borders also prefigured the later transformation of the privately held Burning Man company itself into a non-profit umbrella organization, the Burning Man Project, dedicated, per its mission statement, to "bring experiences to people in grand, awe-inspiring and joyful ways that lift the human spirit, address social problems, and inspire a sense of culture, community, and civic engagement" not only in the Burning Man event itself, but in "the wider world".

In the early days of the COVID-19 crisis in the US, it quickly became evident that face masks, which had long been fashion items of both practical necessity and creative expression for burners accustomed to desert conditions, were dangerously scarce. As frontline health care workers faced an acute shortage of personal protective equipment, Burners who had accumulated stockpiles of desert-ready dust masks and other supplies that would be useful for frontline health workers facing shortages, began coordinating collection and donation drives. Burners Without Borders sprung into action, collaborating with Harvard microbiologist Ethan Garner to acquire and distribute masks and other necessary gear through a coalition and website #GetUsPPE getusppe.org (Chason, 2020; Graham, 2020). Designers developed methods to mass-produce homemade masks, and makers prototyped 3 D printing technology to decentralize and spur the production of mechanical ventilators to help compensate for widespread hospital shortages.

COVID-19 as an agent of liminality, and the possibility of more pro-social mobilities

Turning from this festival realm back towards travel more broadly, I would like to submit that several of the principles designed to both describe and spur such pro-social behavior could be of use for a reimagined and reconfigured tourism. Like tourists, most burners visit their destinations temporarily. Unlike tourists, burners have embraced norms and principles of "participation" and "civic responsibility" that have served community formation and crisis relief functions in the Black Rock Desert, as well as in authorized regional events in the so-called "default world" beyond Burning Man. As an ethos, participation implies that everyone has agency and parts to play. Unlike a conventional concert or staged cultural performance, there are, at least in theory, no spectators. Civic responsibility suggests that successful collaboration relies on understanding of local conditions and respect for local practices, also values which support more sustainable forms of tourism.

The unrealized promises of the capacity of responsible tourism, and its various permutations including "voluntourism", to manifest positive personal and spatial transformations are in part constrained by the reproduction of the fundamental divide between guests and hosts. However, echoing the transformative festival's cultural injunction against spectators, the physical immobility impelled by the pandemic, for a time, effectively *rendered almost no one a tourist*. Considering COVID-19 as an agent of global liminality that has subverted the usual social roles and subjectivities of tourism, I suggest that values such as participation and civic responsibility can inform and transform not only festivals and festival goers, but guests and hosts as we renegotiate our places within, between, and out of place and fixed subject positions.

Although the COVID-19 pandemic, like climate change, has affected nearly everyone on the planet, it has not done so in any kind of fair or uniform way – New York governor Andrew Cuomo's facile mischaracterization of the pandemic as "the great equalizer" to the contrary. Tourism likewise will continue to unevenly affect guests and hosts. Still, as borders reopen and mobility and recreation recommences, transformational festivals and event communities, in their evident capacity to transform participants both within and beyond the time-space of their highly porous events, offer some hope for the blurring, if not the outright obliteration of the demarcation between guests and hosts. Such a subversive inter-subjective inversion may bring the recognition, in-itself, and production, for-itself, of a shared humanity of co-creators and participants in not just ephemeral, but accretive transformational social and environmental projects.

Facing the unfolding pandemic, the Burning Man Project announced in April 2020 that it would not construct a physical Black Rock City that year in Nevada. Instead the movement would manifest virtually and physically elsewhere in the world, if and when possible. It was therefore even more felicitous that the 2019 theme was "Metamorphoses", and the 2020 event theme had already been chosen as "The Multiverse", a topological notion drawn from quantum physics meant to explore,

> the quantum kaleidoscope of possibility, the infinite realities of the multiverse, and our own superpositioning as actors and observers in the cosmic Cacophony of resonant strings. It is an invitation to ponder the real, the surreal and the pataphysical, and a chance to encounter our alternate selves who may have followed, or are following, or will follow different decision-paths to divergent Black Rock City realities.

With their usual desert pilgrimage beyond the realm of possibility, burners found themselves approaching a liminal threshold, in which the annual distinction between the burner world and "default world" could no longer be made, and the definition of participation and scope of gift giving would have to be radically expanded. A Brooklyn-based Burners Without Borders organizer wrote on her social media account, "…we talk a lot about black rock city as a place for prototyping and exploration. It feels a little bit like the training wheels are off and now we are doing it live".

While housebound burners considered ways to move their projects out of the event time-space and towards the wider world, some segments of the travel and tourism industry, for their part, briefly adjusted towards more altruistic operations. Hotels and airlines offered otherwise unusable food to charities, delivered emergency supplies and personnel, and arranged to rescue or host stranded travelers (Morris, 2020).

It remains to be seen if and how these ephemeral convergences of gift and market economy may translate into communitas, for whom, and for how long. It is not hard to imagine that the tourism industry and the transformational festival scene may get back to (mostly) usual soon enough. Yet, it is heartening that at a time when a virus threatened the health and well-being of billions of individuals and the global biopolitical assemblage they constitute, many voices took the opportunity to push for collective action to address longer term (and often tourism-accelerated) threats such as socioeconomic inequality, mass extinction, and global warming (Robinson & Reddy, 2020). Indeed, even as COVID-19 compelled participants in the human event to surrender to liminal conditions of immobility, uncertainty, and extraordinary risk, many not only encountered their alternate selves, but conceived other, more sustainable worlds that may take yet more subversive experiments to realize.

Disclosure statement

The author has created art and facilitated Burning Man regional events on a volunteer basis.

ORCID

Ian Rowen ⓘ http://orcid.org/0000-0002-9674-5669

References

Bruner, E. M. (1991). Transformation of self in tourism. *Annals of Tourism Research*, *18*(2), 238–250. https://doi.org/10.1016/0160-7383(91)90007-X

Chason, R. (2020, March 23). Coronavirus leads hospitals, volunteers to crowdsource. *Washington Post*. https://www.washingtonpost.com/local/social-issues/donate-ppe-hospitals-gloves-masks-doctors-nurses/2020/03/23

Chen, K. K. (2009). *Enabling creative chaos: The organization behind the burning man event*. https://doi.org/10.1073/pnas.0703993104

Chen, K. K. (2011). Lessons for creative cities from Burning Man: How organizations can sustain and disseminate a creative context. *City, Culture and Society*, *2*(2), 93–100. https://doi.org/10.1016/j.ccs.2011.05.003

Crockett, M. (2014, September 26). Gifts in the desert: the psychology of Burning Man. *The Guardian*. https://www.theguardian.com/science/head-quarters/2014/sep/26/gifts-in-the-desert-psychology-burning-man-altruism

Graham, M. (2020, April 1). How the Burning Man community is helping to get masks and other supplies to hospitals. *CNBC*. https://www.cnbc.com/2020/04/01/burning-man-community-helping-to-get-masks-supplies-to-hospitals.html

Lean, G. L. (2009). Transformative travel: inspiring sustainability. In R. Bushell & P. J. Sheldon (Eds.), *Wellness and tourism: mind, body, spirit, place* (pp. 191–205). Cognizant. https://www.cognizantcommunication.com/books/wellness-and-tourism

Lean, G. L. (2012). Transformative travel: A mobilities perspective. *Tourist Studies*, *12*(2), 151–172. https://doi.org/10.1177/1468797612454624

Morris, S. (2020, March). Delta air lines offers free flights to medical workers traveling to coronavirus hotspots. *Newsweek*. https://www.newsweek.com/delta-air-lines-medical-volunteers-free-round-trip-flights-michigan-georgia-louisiana-1495021

Pritchard, A., & Morgan, N. (2013). Hopeful tourism: A transformational perspective. In Y. Reisinger (Ed.), *Transformational tourism: tourist perspectives*. CABI. https://doi.org/10.1079/9781780642093.0017

Reisinger, Y. (2013). Transformation and transformational learning theory. In *Transformational tourism: Tourist perspectives* (pp. 17–26). CABI.

Robinson, M., Reddy, D. (2020, April 1). Tackling climate change with COVID-19 urgency. *Project Syndicate*. https://www.project-syndicate.org/commentary/tackling-climate-change-with-covid19-urgency-by-mary-robinson-and-daya-reddy-2020-04

Schmidt, B. (2015). Boutiquing at the raindance campout: Relational aesthetics as festival technology. *Dancecult*, *7*(1), 35–54. https://doi.org/10.12801/1947-5403.2015.07.01.02

Sin, H. L. (2014). Realities of doing responsibilities: Performances and practices in tourism.
Geografiska Annaler: Series B, Human Geography, *96*(2), 141–157. https://doi.org/10.1111/geob.
12042

St John, G. (2015). Introduction to weekend societies: EDM festivals and event-cultures.
Dancecult, *7*(1), 1–14. https://doi.org/10.12801/1947-5403.2015.07.01.00

Timothy, D. J. (2007). Empowerment and stakeholder participation in tourism destination communities. In A. Church & T. Coles (Eds.), *Tourism, power and space* (pp. 199–216). Routledge.

A mindful shift: an opportunity for mindfulness-driven tourism in a post-pandemic world

Uglješa Stankov, Viachaslau Filimonau and Miroslav D. Vujičić

ABSTRACT

Many see the COVID-19 pandemic as a turning point for tourism, a chance to reflect on the pressing environmental and socio-economic concerns of the industry, and an opportunity to pinpoint a more desirable direction. However, for tourism to revive as a less impactful and more meaningful industry, more mindful consumers are needed to take factual benefits from the gravity of the current situation. Mindfulness as a practice of bringing a certain quality of attention to moment-by-moment experiences has become an important asset for individuals to cope with the problems of modern life. It is even seen as a significant driver of lifestyle change in Western societies, resulting in an increasing number of more conscious consumers and mindfulness-driven products and services. The COVID-19 pandemic is a wake-up call and opportunity for the tourism industry to embrace the mindfulness movement, trusting in its capacity to reflect on the current problems and to pave a new way forward towards more compassionate and meaningful tourism for both hosts and guests.

摘要

许多人将新型冠状病毒肺炎（COVID-19）疫情视为旅游业的转折点。这让人们有机会反思该行业紧迫的环境和社会经济问题，并指明未来行业发展更理想的方向。但是，为了让旅游业恢复成影响小、意义大的产业，这需要更多正念的消费者从当前严峻的形式中获取到实际收益。正念作为一种对即时即地体验给予一定关注的实践，已经成为个人应对现代生活问题的重要能力。它甚至被视为西方社会生活方式改变的重要驱动力，也导致正念的消费者数量的增加与正念驱动类的产品服务的增多。新型冠状病毒肺炎（COVID-19）疫情是旅游产业接受正念运动的警钟和机会，也让人们相信正念具有能力反映现在问题，开辟一条主人和宾客更富有同情心、意义更深远的旅游业道路。

Introduction

The COVID-19 pandemic is likely to cause the largest downturn that the tourism industry had ever experienced in its history (Becker, 2020). After the 9/11 terrorism attack the global tourism industry was also severely damaged, and as a result, a new normal was established, primarily with new safety percussions (Taylor & Toohey, 2005). However, the current downturn is unprecedented, hitting everyone across the globe, thus creating a common challenge for all tourism stakeholders (Gössling et al., 2020). Alternative calls have also emerged: these claim, for example, that in a time when a society is witnessing the collapse of, sometimes to be believed, stable and rigid structures of the capitalist world, a positive shift with more holistic perspectives to the world should/can potentially emerge (Ateljevic, 2020; Nepal, 2020; Rowen, 2020). We concur with the current stream of academic commentaries on COVID-19 by calling for a revisioning tourism in a post-pandemic world from a mindfulness perspective. We build our vision on the momentum of mindfulness movements in Western societies (Gotojones, 2013; Kabat-Zinn, 2006; Wilson & Pile, 2015), where mindfulness-driven tourism has the potential to set an important agenda for the long-term sustainability of the tourism and travel industry and spark the creation of more compassionate tourism. With this call, we will elaborate on our vision of mindfulness-driven tourism, its organization, and the main downturns of the current tourism industry that mindful tourists could help to resolve at a time of the 'new normal'.

Leaning into the mindfulness momentum

In simple terms, mindfulness can be defined as 'an approach for increasing awareness and responding skillfully to mental processes that contribute to emotional distress and maladaptive behavior' (Bishop et al., 2006, 230). As such, mindfulness is perceived in various ways, it is a therapy, a technology, or a lifestyle choice, and it is present everywhere, within schools, universities, military facilities, parliaments, and other realms (Kabat-Zinn, 2014). It became publicly recognized as a means to heal the manifold ills of modern societies (Kristensen, 2018). In the tourism domain, mindfulness has been recognized for its beneficial effects on tourist wellbeing and transformative influences on tourist experiences (Chen et al., 2017; Kirwin et al., 2019; Loureiro et al., 2019), as well as for its potential impact on the industry's sustainability agenda and its employees' performance (Jang et al., 2020; Lengyel, 2018). Gradually, the tourism industry is becoming aware of this potential of mindfulness, and commercial applications are increasingly emerging to leverage the benefits of meta-awareness within tourist experiences (McGoarty et al., 2020).

The practical knowledge of the profile of mindful tourists and how they behave in real-life tourism situations are rare (Chen et al., 2017). According to Loureiro et al. (2019, 4) mindful tourists are '... those who pay attention to the present moment (not the past or the future), attending to the actual somatic sensations lived at the destination in an open, non-reactive and non-judgement, rather than tourists who accept their present emotions and thoughts'. However, this definition can be seen just as a novel paradigm for further categorisation of tourist typologies, allowing for building appropriate consumer profiles. From a mindful tourist perspective, providing mindfulness services in the tourism domain can be seen as a genuine gesture of sincere care for consumer wellbeing which respects contemporary consumers' needs, compliments the etiquette of services in the tourism industry, and creates space for improving consumer loyalty (Stankov & Filimonau, 2019a). At the same time, mindful consumers could become more aware of the social contacts (Kang & Gretzel, 2012) which would prompt them to provide more genuine and sincere feedback on tourist services received (Stankov et al., 2020)

The effects of the adoption of mindfulness practice in the tourism domain would go beyond the intra- and interpersonal levels. Many calls are pointing out the transformational power of mindfulness and advocating that more present-awareness can be healing for the socio-economic and environmental problems of a global society (Gotojones, 2013; Wamsler et al., 2018; Wilson & Pile, 2015). However, the transformative potential of the mindfulness movement across the whole tourism industry is still understeered (Stankov et al., 2020).

The COVID-19 pandemic as a wake-up call for the tourism industry

Lessons from eco-evolutionary dynamics teach us that an environmental change can trigger a rapid evolution among living organisms (Pelletier et al., 2009). Nevertheless, the factual change that causes visible transformations, comes from within, from the genomic level. In terms of society, the initiator of today's prevailing understanding of contemplative mindfulness Jon Kabat-Zin (2006) believes that mindfulness is the next evolutionary step of democratic societies, driven by the individuals that are more compassionate and with the experience of ultimate freedom. Indeed, mindfulness as a movement has entered the cultural mainstream of Europe and North America, with all beneficial effects of this contemplative practice to individuals and potential dangers to be wrongly exploited by the propagators of capitalist societies (Gotojones, 2013). Having that said, people's needs and desires are that 'genomic levels' that shape the current outness, appearance, and dynamics of the tourism industry, and we believe that any long-lasting change can only be induced by the transformation of the demand side of the tourism market (Lew, 2018). Thus, the global pandemic creates, ironically, that external change in the tourism ecosystem and provides a space and time (in literal) for many consumers to reflect on their past and future travel behaviors.

The lessons so far and a mindful way ahead

What we have seen so far with the pandemic is probably not enough for making a strong statement from a tourism-specific, socio-economic, perspective, but we believe that the biblical proposition of its influence over the tourism industry allows us this kind of speculation. What we have witnessed during the pandemic gives us more arguments for advocating the adoption of mindfulness by the tourism industry's mindset. The following will summarize our main points on what we have learned so far, and how a mindful shift could help a post-pandemic tourism industry.

Wherever you go, there you are – tourism marketing should cater to more conscious tourists

The title of an iconic book 'Wherever you go, there you are' whiten by Jon Kabat-Zinn (1994) resonates well with the paradoxical condition of modern tourism. While most providers insist on promoting and designing enhanced tourist experiences, constantly pleading for more engagement, more enhancement, sometimes going to the extremes, much fewer providers focus is put on the authentic wellbeing of a tourist as a human (Stankov & Filimonau, 2019b). Tourism marketing tries to let tourists believe that participating in tourism experiences will make them happier (Nawijn, 2011). Although tourists are promised with happiness, they are not told that it cannot be granted, since it is not entirely in the hand of the providers. Tourists will be amused, but just for a brief moment in time, as that kind of excitement will quickly fade away. The anticipation of holidays or even the reflection on how they went may, in fact, be a more enjoyable and, therefore, happier experience, than the holidays themselves (Gilbert & Abdullah, 2002).

The self-isolation and the limitations imposed on freedom of movement in light of COVID-19, like in any other recession, have led the consumers to return to more primary, essential and non-negotiable needs (Starr, 2011). However, the sudden discontinuity from usual everyday routines and the freedom from social and business obligations and support have prompted people to also face anxiety and stress (Usher et al., 2020). Apart from reported negative behaviors, a portion of people has increasingly started searching for self-help, including meditation, pilates, and healthy lifestyles (Johnson, 2020). These were not just standalone attempts of the consumers left to cope with the problems on their own devices, as the media and organizations involved in the research of mindfulness, as well as the commercial providers of mindfulness-related services, generously offered assistance with advice, free seminars and access to a premium version of their services (The Mindfulness Initiatives, 2020).

A post-pandemic tourism industry could benefit from more conscious consumers that are more aware of their unconscious behaviors, purchasing patterns, and increased ability to resist the promise of false happiness. Thus, we assume that more mindful tourists will be more preoccupied with the question of happiness and it is likely that they will be more self-aware of delusive tourism marketing (Ivakhiv, 2003). In that sense, traditional approaches to tourism marketing (e.g. promotion of the 3S – sea, sex, and sun) might seem somewhat trivial to them and could be perceived as patronizing advertising (Szmigin & Carrigan, 2000). Therefore, a mindfulness-driven tourism industry could limit the shorthand of tiring stereotypes in favor of a more sincere approach such as promoting vacations as a means of expression of life diversity, active participation, socially and environmentally responsible traveling and not as a final product that can fulfill people's 'dreams and desires' (Stankov et al., 2018).

Quality over quantity of experiences

Despite the constant efforts to change the face of the current tourism industry, attracting mass tourists is still its major feature. Longer, but rare, holidays become gradually replaced with shorter, but more frequent, holiday journeys. Finally, the constant growth of international and domestic trips and air travel clearly shows the point that modern tourism expands dramatically (Schubert et al., 2020).

COVID-19 has forced mass tourism to face the wall and stop expanding almost instantly. Indeed, media reports on COVID-19 on cruise ships exposed the problems of the travel industry in almost caricatural fashion (Higgins-Desbiolles, 2020). Inevitably, in the following recovery phase, the tourism industry will attempt to attract as much as it can from the declined mass demand. However, the pandemic, seen as a global event, could be perceived as a chance for adding more quality to future tourist experiences, by making them more memorable (Pizam, 2010). In other words, travel will be less frequent, but this opens up the space to make it less trivial and more valuable. Indeed, market reports show that post-pandemic tourists will ask for more basic experiences insisting on domestic travel (stay-cation) and valuing more spending quality time with friends and relatives (Wootton, 2020). Some destination marketing organizations (e.g. Peru and Cyprus) started campaigns to remind tourists about some basic physical experiences of visits to their countries, like the common sounds of water and nature, food preparation and serving, and other similar tactile experiences that were unavailable to most of the self-isolated consumers during the lockdowns. Indeed, according to some popular advice given for mindful travel, it could awaken sensory perceptions, taking sensory delights of focused attention to the new external and inner spaces (Currie & Jim, 2000).

Technology is not a holy grail, an enemy nor a simple servant

Contemporary tourism is a technology-driven industry, that highly values technology-enhanced experiences and insists on using state-of-the-art technologies to amplify competitiveness in a digital society (Cimbaljević et al., 2019). However, the everyday use of technology and its spill overs during travel cause various problematic scenarios of technology usage (Dickinson et al., 2016; Pearce & Gretzel, 2012). Indeed, Kabat-Zinn (2019) emphasizes that the habit of filling every moment with mental content continues even during travel, which ultimately leaves travelers unsatisfied.

We have witnessed that, in a time of a crisis created by COVID-19, people turned towards technology asking for help. For example, there has been an increase in demand for mental health applications during the pandemic (Gordon & Doraiswamy, 2020). There have been various examples of robots replacing people, mobile applications tracking people's contacts, or Big Data analytics predicting the spread of the virus among the population. Most importantly, technology has been used to connect people and replace physical interactions. The reports show an increased public trust in technology, willingness to engage, and to change the attitudes towards it, while some are even willing to temporarily forget about privacy issues for a greater good (Geist, 2020).

Tourism marketing has switched to some already existing and new virtual solutions to satisfy people's desire for travel. However, for most tourists, despite the advances in visual and immersive technologies (Wagler & Hanus, 2018), virtual tourism could serve just as a temporary fix, not a viable substitute to travel. The tourism industry and academics were aware of that fact even before the pandemic, admitting that the overdependency of tourism experiences on digital technology had to be managed carefully, by limiting its use or by creating more meaningful instances of use (Dickinson et al., 2016). The pandemic exposed, even more, the complexity of human-technology interactions reaffirming some of the recent calls that more mindful tourists will be more capable of self-reflection when interacting with technology in tourist experiences (Stankov, Filimonau, & Slivar et al., 2019).

A path to compassionate tourism

For a long time, modern tourism has been described with some catchy slogans, such as, a 'passport to peace', or 'the peace industry' which is to promote peaceful cohabitation across national and cultural borders (Bechmann Pedersen, 2020). The current COVID-19 reality of that and other idealistic visions of modern tourism reminds all tourism stockholders that such goals are hardly achievable/manageable and that tourism, as an industry, could hardly keep up with the highest projected expectations. As we mentioned earlier, the idea of tourism being a responsible and sustainable industry is still a far-to-reach goal, as some of the game-changing and promising attempts quickly face the harsh reality of a highly competitive market. For instance, instead of leaving more space for profitability for smaller hotels, new online travel intermediaries impose high commissions and interfere with restrictive price policies and the sharing economy sites very quickly turn into the likes of their commercial, excessive profit-making, counterparts (Slivar et al., 2019).

Here, consumers largely contribute to the story. A significant portion of consumers is still showing high inconsistency in their proclaimed and actual behavior. The most notable example is a discrepancy between declarative support of the pro-environmental and sustainability agendas and acting oppositely, for example, many tourists are not willing to pay extras for environmental initiatives without having additional personal benefits (Pulido-Fernández & López-Sánchez, 2016). Similarly, the current trend of increasing demand for air travel is in opposition to climate-related sustainability goals (Kantenbacher et al., 2019).

During crisis events, the values of solidarity, altruism, and compassion emerge as extremely important, not just in the realms of professions directly involved in the crisis, but as higher-level, collective values, such as when wearing a face mask in the community to protect others (Cheng et al., 2020). Indeed, compassion has been neglected for a long period, as a powerful and universal motivator for enabling aspiration for sustainable tourism or enlightening mass tourism (Weaver & Jin, 2016). A vision of more compassionate tourists leans on the evidence of the emergence of new consumer segments in tourism that are already attracted to mindfulness-themed products and services. With the increased awareness of their behavior as consumers, tourists might be more interested in the global and local impacts, as their purchasing behavior may influence the local economy and the environment (Bechwati et al., 2016; Geiger et al., 2017). By being supported with honest support from tourists, the sustainability agendas in the tourism industry would become less difficult to reach. If tourists are more immersed within the present moment, there are better chances to notice what is wrong with the current state of tourism. Tourists may, therefore, become susceptible to notice fake smiles of overworked reception staff or housekeepers taking double shifts that often come from low-income countries. Tourists may further become better aware of the devasting, from the environmental but also socio-economic viewpoint, the context of isolated resorts often placed in those countries

(Taranath & Bolisay, 2019). Tourists may not be able to act upon these immediately, nor it is needed at this moment, but these experiences could become transformational in a long-run making from, what is now pejorative called, a mass tourist, to a driver of a mass mindful change and, ultimately, to more compassionate tourism.

Concluding remarks

The COVID-19 pandemic has mobilized the global society pleading to the responsible behavior of every individual. This has forced a shift in global awareness towards the revived views that collective values start from within the mindful individuals (Steidle, 2017), and this capacity, we think, could serve as an ignition to a more mindful solution for the future. We believe that the current pandemic could give rise to more mindful tourists whilst these, in turn, can give rise to more mindful and, ultimately sustainable tourist experiences. These, in turn, should prompt tourism providers to respond to a new demand by adjusting their, currently unsustainable, product offers. According to that vision, more mindful tourists could act as an underlying web that connects, supports, and nurtures the whole tourism ecosystem for the benefit of all.

Disclosure statement

No potential conflict of interest was reported by the author(s).

References

Ateljevic, I. (2020). Transforming the (tourism) world for good and (re)generating the potential 'new normal. *Tourism Geographies*, 1–9. doi: 10.1080/14616688.2020.1759134

Bechmann Pedersen, S. (2020). A passport to peace? Modern tourism and internationalist idealism. *European Review*, 1–14. doi: 10.1017/S1062798719000516

Bechwati, N. N., Baalbaki, A. M., Nasr, N., & Baalbaki, I. (2016). Mindful consumer behavior: A cross-cultural compariosn. *Journal of International & Interdisciplinary Business Research*, 3(1), 100–113.

Becker, E. (2020). How hard will the coronavirus hit the travel industry? Retrieved May 6, 2020, from https://www.nationalgeographic.com/travel/2020/04/how-coronavirus-is-impacting-the-travel-industry/

Bishop, S. R., Lau, M., Shapiro, S., Carlson, L., Anderson, N. D., Carmody, J., Segal, Z. V., Abbey, S., Speca, M., Velting, D., & Devins, G. (2006). Mindfulness: A proposed operational definition. *Clinical Psychology: Science and Practice*, 11(3), 230–241. doi: 10.1093/clipsy.bph077

Chen, I.-L., Scott, N., & Benckendorff, P. (2017). Mindful tourist experiences: A Buddhist perspective. *Annals of Tourism Research*, 64, 1–12. doi: 10.1016/j.annals.2017.01.013

Cheng, K. K., Lam, T. H., & Leung, C. C. (2020). Wearing face masks in the community during the COVID-19 pandemic: altruism and solidarity. *The Lancet*, 1–2. doi: 10.1016/S0140-6736(20)30918-1

Cimbaljević, M., Stankov, U., & Pavluković, V. (2019). Going beyond the traditional destination competitiveness – reflections on a smart destination in the current research. *Current Issues in Tourism*, 22(20), 2472–2477. doi: 10.1080/13683500.2018.1529149

Currie, J. D., & Jim, D. (2000). *The mindful traveler: a guide to journaling and transformative travel*. Open Court.

Dickinson, J. E., Hibbert, J. F., & Filimonau, V. (2016). Mobile technology and the tourist experience: (Dis)connection at the campsite. *Tourism Management*, 57, 193–201. doi: 10.1016/j.tourman.2016.06.005

Geiger, S. M., Otto, S., & Schrader, U. (2017). Mindfully green and healthy: An indirect path from mindfulness to ecological behavior. *Frontiers in Psychology, 8*, 2306. doi: 10.3389/fpsyg.2017.02306

Geist, M. (2020). Opinion: After the tech-lash: new digital policy priorities in the post-pandemic world. Retrieved May 6, 2020, from https://www.theglobeandmail.com/business/commentary/article-after-the-tech-lash-new-digital-policy-priorities-in-the-post/

Gilbert, D., & Abdullah, J. (2002). A study of the impact of the expectation of a holiday on an individual's sense of well-being. *Journal of Vacation Marketing, 8*(4), 352–361. doi: 10.1177/135676670200800406

Gordon, J., Doraiswamy, M. (2020). High anxiety calls for innovation in digital mental health. Retrieved April 27, 2020, from https://www.weforum.org/agenda/2020/04/high-anxiety-calls-for-innovation-in-digital-mental-health-6b7b4e7044/

Gössling, S., Scott, D., & Hall, C. M. (2020). Pandemics, tourism and global change: a rapid assessment of COVID-19. *Journal of Sustainable Tourism*, 1–20. doi: 10.1080/09669582.2020.1758708

Gotojones, C. (2013, September 1). Zombie Apocalypse as Mindfulness Manifesto (after Žižek). *Postmodern Culture*. Johns Hopkins University Press. doi: 10.1353/pmc.2013.0062

Higgins-Desbiolles, F. (2020). Socialising tourism for social and ecological justice after COVID-19. *Tourism Geographies*, 1–14. doi: 10.1080/14616688.2020.1757748

Ivakhiv, A. (2003). Nature and self in new age pilgrimage. *Culture and Religion, 4*(1), 93–118. doi: 10.1080/01438300302812

Jang, J., Jo, W., & Kim, J. S. (2020). Can employee workplace mindfulness counteract the indirect effects of customer incivility on proactive service performance through work engagement? A moderated mediation model. *Journal of Hospitality Marketing & Management*, 1–18. doi: 10.1080/19368623.2020.1725954

Johnson, C. (2020). The coronavirus pandemic offers an opportunity to go back to the basics with health. Retrieved May 6, 2020, from https://www.abc.net.au/news/health/2020-04-21/back-to-basics-health-during-a-pandemic/12164400

Kabat-Zinn, J. (1994). *Wherever you go, there you are mindfulness meditation in everyday life*. Hachette Books.

Kabat-Zinn, J. (2006). *Coming to our senses: healing ourselves and the world through mindfulness*. Hachette Books.

Kabat-Zinn, J. (2014). Meditation is everywhere. *Mindfulness, 5*(4), 462–463. doi: 10.1007/s12671-014-0323-1

Kabat-Zinn, J. (2019). Filling up all our moments. *Mindfulness, 10*(4), 772–773. doi: 10.1007/s12671-018-1086-x

Kang, M., & Gretzel, U. (2012). Effects of podcast tours on tourist experiences in a national park. *Tourism Management, 33*(2), 440–455. doi: 10.1016/j.tourman.2011.05.005

Kantenbacher, J., Hanna, P., Miller, G., Scarles, C., & Yang, J. (2019). Consumer priorities: what would people sacrifice in order to fly on holidays? *Journal of Sustainable Tourism, 27*(2), 207–222. doi: 10.1080/09669582.2017.1409230

Kirwin, M., Harper, N. J., Young, T., & Itzvan, I. (2019). Mindful adventures: a pilot study of the outward bound mindfulness program. *Journal of Outdoor and Environmental Education, 22*(1), 75–90. doi: 10.1007/s42322-019-00031-9

Kristensen, M. L. (2018). Mindfulness and resonance in an era of acceleration: a critical inquiry. *Journal of Management, Spirituality and Religion, 15*(2), 178–195. doi: 10.1080/14766086.2017.1418413

Lengyel, A. (2018). *Spatial aspects of sustainablity mindfulness and tourism*. Szent István University.

Lew, A. A. (2018). Why Travel? – Travel, tourism and global consciousness. *Tourism Geographies, 20*(4), 742–749. doi: 10.1080/14616688.2018.1490343

Loureiro, S. M. C., Stylos, N., & Miranda, F. J. (2019). Exploring how mindfulness may enhance perceived value of travel experience. *The Service Industries Journal*, 1–25. doi: 10.1080/02642069.2019.1600672

McGoarty, B., Ellis, S., Chapman, J., Eadon-Clarke Peter, Panek, R., Raphael, R. (2020). *Global Wellnes Trends Report - The Future of Wellness 2020*. Miami. Retrieved from https://www.global-wellnesssummit.com/wp-content/uploads/2020/04/GlobalWellnessTrends2020.pdf

Nawijn, J. (2011). Happiness through vacationing: Just a temporary boost or long-term benefits? *Journal of Happiness Studies, 12*(4), 651–665. doi: 10.1007/s10902-010-9221-y

Nepal, S. K. (2020). Travel and tourism after COVID-19 – business as usual or opportunity to reset? https://Doi.Org/10.1080/14616688.2020.1760926. doi: 10.1080/14616688.2020.1760926

Pearce, P., & Gretzel, U. (2012). Tourism in technology dead zones: documenting experiential dimensions. *International Journal of Tourism Sciences, 12*(2), 1–20. doi: 10.1080/15980634.2012.11434656

Pelletier, F., Garant, D., & Hendry, A. P. (2009). Eco-evolutionary dynamics. *Philosophical Transactions of the Royal Society B: Biological Sciences, 364*(1523), 1483–1489. doi: 10.1098/rstb.2009.0027

Pizam, A. (2010). Creating memorable experiences. *International Journal of Hospitality Management, 29*(3), 343. doi: 10.1016/j.ijhm.2010.04.003

Pulido-Fernández, J., & López-Sánchez, Y. (2016). Are tourists really willing to pay more for sustainable destinations? *Sustainability, 8*(12), 1240. doi: 10.3390/su8121240

Rowen, I. (2020). The transformational festival as a subversive toolbox for a transformed tourism: lessons from Burning Man for a COVID-19 world. *Tourism Geographies*, 1–8. doi: 10.1080/14616688.2020.1759132

Schubert, I., Sohre, A., Ströbel, M. (2020). The role of lifestyle, quality of life preferences and geographical context in personal air travel. doi: 10.1080/09669582.2020.1745214. https://doi.org/10.1080/09669582.2020.1745214

Slivar, I., Stankov, U., & Pavluković, V. (2019). Case study: Delegated distribution: Hotels should be warned! An example from Croatia. *Transnational Marketing Journal, 7*(2), 245–256. doi: 10.33182/tmj.v7i2.838

Stankov, U., & Filimonau, V. (2019a). Co-creating "Mindful" Holiday Resort Experience for Guests' Digital Well-Being. In J. Pesonen & J. Neidhardt (Eds.), *Information and communication technologies in tourism 2019* (pp. 200–211). Springer International Publishing. doi: 10.1007/978-3-030-05940-8_16

Stankov, U., & Filimonau, V. (2019b). Reviving calm technology in the e-tourism context. *The Service Industries Journal, 39*(5–6), 343–360. doi: 10.1080/02642069.2018.1544619

Stankov, U., Filimonau, V., Gretzel, U., & Vujičić, M. D. (2020). E-mindfulness – the growing importance of facilitating tourists' connections to the present moment. *Journal of Tourism Futures*, ahead-of-print(ahead-of-print). doi: 10.1108/JTF-11-2019-0135

Stankov, U., Filimonau, V., & Slivar, I. (2019). Calm ICT design in hotels: A critical review of applications and implications. *International Journal of Hospitality Management, 82*, 298–307. doi: 10.1016/j.ijhm.2018.10.012

Stankov, U., Čikić, J., & Armenski, T. (2018). *Should tourism sector be responsive to New Age lifestyles? [Paper presentation]*. 5th International Conference on Contemporary Marketing Issues (ICCMI) 2017, Thessaloniki (p. 636). Thessaloniki: Alexander Technological Educational Institute (ATEI) of Thessaloniki; Manchester Metropolitan University. June 21–23, 2017.

Starr, M. A. (2011). Recession and the social economy. In *Consequences of economic downturn* (pp. 189–214). Palgrave Macmillan. doi: 10.1057/9780230118355_10

Steidle, G. K. (2017). *Leading from within: Conscious social change and mindfulness for social innovation*. MIT PRess.

Szmigin, I., & Carrigan, M. (2000). Does advertising in the UK need older models? *Journal of Product & Brand Management, 9*(2), 128–143. doi: 10.1108/10610420010322170

Taranath, A., & Bolisay, R. (2019). *Beyond guilt trips: mindful travel in an unequal world*. Between the Lines.

Taylor, T., & Toohey, K. (2005). Impacts of terrorism-related safety and security measures at a major sport event. *Event Management, 9*(4), 199–209. doi: 10.3727/152599506776771544

The Mindfulness Initiatives. (2020). COVID-19 Mindfulness Resources for Health Care Staff. Retrieved May 6, 2020, from https://www.themindfulnessinitiative.org/Handlers/Download. ashx?IDMF=d83f9973-dae4-4267-a67f-f11a83502f8d

Usher, K., Bhullar, N., & Jackson, D. (2020). Life in the pandemic: Social isolation and mental health. *Journal of Clinical Nursing*, 1–2. doi: 10.1111/jocn.15290

Wagler, A., & Hanus, M. D. (2018). Comparing virtual reality tourism to real-life experience: Effects of presence and engagement on attitude and enjoyment. *Communication Research Reports*, *35*(5), 456–464. doi: 10.1080/08824096.2018.1525350

Wamsler, C., Brossmann, J., Hendersson, H., Kristjansdottir, R., McDonald, C., & Scarampi, P. (2018). Mindfulness in sustainability science, practice, and teaching. *Sustainability Science*, *13*(1), 143–162. doi: 10.1007/s11625-017-0428-2

Weaver, D. B., & Jin, X. (2016). Compassion as a neglected motivator for sustainable tourism. *Journal of Sustainable Tourism*, *24*(5), 657–672. doi: 10.1080/09669582.2015.1101130

Wilson, J., & Pile, T. (2015). *Mindful America the mutual transformation of Buddhist meditation and American culture*. Oxford University Press.

Wootton, H. (2020). Consumers go "back to basics" post pandemic. Retrieved May 6, 2020, from https://www.afr.com/companies/tourism/consumers-go-back-to-basics-post-pandemic-20200417-p54kpu

The novel spaces and power-geometries in tourism and hospitality after 2020 will belong to the 'local'

Lucia Tomassini and Elena Cavagnaro

ABSTRACT

The global crisis we have experienced due to the COVID-19 pandemic emergency challenges our perception of the global and local context in which we live, travel, and work. This crisis has spread novel uncertainties and fears about the future of our world, but at the same time, it has also set the ground to rethink the future scenario of tourism and hospitality to bring about a potentially positive transformation after 2020. Such a scenario can be understood in light of the work of Doreen Massey and the pivotal theorisations on 'space' and 'power-geometry' she presented in her book *For Space* (2005). Massey conceives space as the product of multiple relations, networks, connections, as the dimension of multiplicity, the result of an ongoing making process, and in a mutually constitutive relationship with power. Interweaving Massey's theorisations with a critical examination of the neoliberal capitalism approach to the conceptualization of space, the COVID-19 global crisis prompts us to rethink the space inside and outside of tourism and hospitality by re-focusing on the local dimension of our space as the only guarantee of our own wellbeing, safety, and security. While the global dimension seems more broken than ever, the urgency of belonging to the local is more and more evident. Hence, we propose a critical reflection on the implications of such a scenario in the space of tourism and hospitality, foreseeing a potentially positive transformation in terms of activation of local relations, networks, connections, and multiplicities able to open up such space to multiple novel functions designed not just for tourists and travelers but also for citizens.

摘要

我们所经历的新型冠状病毒全球流行性疾病突发事件所造成的全球危机，挑战了我们对我们所生活、旅行和工作的全球和地方环境的认知。这场危机散播了对我们未来世界的新的不确定性和恐惧，但与此同时，它也为重新思考旅游接待业未来的前景奠定了基础，以便在2020年后实现潜在的积极转变。这种前景可以从多琳·马西(Doreen Massey)的工作和她在2005年出版的《空间》(For space)一书中提出的"空间"和"权力几何学"的关键理论中来理解。马西认为空间是多种关系、网络、联系的产物，是多样性的维度，是不断创造过程的结果，具有与权力相互构成的关系。结合马西的理论对新资本主义空间概括的方法进行批判性的考察，新型冠状病毒全球危机促使我们重新聚焦空间在地层面为自身健康与安全的唯一保证, 进而重新思考旅游接待业的内外空间。尽管全球层面似乎比以往任何时候都更加支离破碎, 但归属于地方的紧迫性却越来越明显。因此,我们提出需要批判性地反思这种前景在旅游接待业空间中的启示, 以预见通过激活当地的关系、网络、连接以及各种多元性以促进发生一个潜在的正向的转型, 不仅为旅游者也为当地居民开辟具有多元创新功能的空间。

Introduction

The COVID-19 global crisis is redesigning our perception of geographical distances and our feeling of belonging to a community, to a country, and to a global or local dimension. The intense worldwide mobility we have been experiencing in recent decades was suddenly stopped, leaving many unanswered questions and a diffuse sense of uncertainty. In this commentary, we aim to explore this novel scenario through two lenses: the conceptualization of 'space' and 'power-geometry' that Doreen Massey presents in her '*For Space*' (2005) and the neoliberal capitalism approach to space, and its commodification. In doing so, we aim to lay the groundwork for a critical reflection of how novel spaces and power-geometries could emerge inside and outside tourism and hospitality after the 'reset' caused by the COVID-19 global crisis.

For Massey (2005; 2009), space is the dimension of multiplicity and the result of relations, connections, networks, and exchanges. Space is the dimension of the social, imbued with relations of power, since power is itself relational. The brutal lock down we have been experiencing as citizens and travelers prompts a critical reflection on the future of 'space' inside and outside tourism and hospitality. Such space - as we knew it before - has now been silenced. The social dimension of this space has dissolved: on the one side the touristic dimension has disappeared; on the other side the daily multiplicity of relations, networks, and connections has been shocked and altered. Our reflection on this scenario is conceptually driven by Massey's (2005) ruminations on how our spatial imagination is largely embedded in neoliberal globalization. We have been used to imagining space as a surface, continuous and given, and as a land stretching out around us. Space has been largely understood as a surface in which people, capital, and products transit. "So, easily this way of imagining space can lead us to conceive of other places, peoples, cultures simply as phenomena on 'this' surface" (Massey, 2005, p. 4). The challenge is letting go of this spatial imagination by embracing an alternative approach to space that – as Massey explains (2005, p. 9) – is rooted in three pivotal propositions:

> "*First*, that we recognise space as the product of interrelations, as constituted through interactions, from the immensity of the global to the intimately tiny [...]. *Second*, that we understand space as the sphere of the possibility of the existence of multiplicity in the sense of contemporaneous plurality; as the sphere in which distinct trajectories coexist; as the sphere therefore of coexisting heterogeneity. Without space, no multiplicity; without multiplicity, no space. If space is indeed the product of interrelations, then it must be predicated upon the existence of plurality. Multiplicity and space are co-constitutive. *Third*, that we recognise space as always under construction [...] it is always in the process of being made. It is never finished; never closed. Perhaps we could imagine space as a simultaneity of stories-so-far."

Therefore, in this contingent global crisis, we would like to prompt a critical reflection on the future of the 'space' of tourism and hospitality and the transformation of its power-geometry (i.e. space is imbued with and a product of relations of power, which have their own geography), likely soon shifting from the understanding of space as a flat surface where tourists move as products in transit, to a space where novel multiplicities, relations, connections and networks occur. We have seen hotels offering their rooms as extra Intensive Care temporary units and restaurants offering to cook meals for hospital staff intensively working on the emergency cases. At the same time, we witnessed 'tourists' ignoring restrictions, trying to sneak out, or simply departing for a leisure journey despite the global crisis and emergency. Hence, while the 'global' dimension appears scattered, broken, and disconnected; conversely, the 'local' dimension of citizens, professionals, inhabitants, neighbors seems actively and positively connected to the crisis. Whereas our global interconnection now appears riskier, the micro dimension of local citizenship seems more and more crucial to guarantee us safety and wellbeing.

Space and power-geometry of tourism and hospitality in the neoliberal globalized world

Tourism and hospitality have been largely investigated as an industry highly representative of our neoliberal globalized world (UNWTO, 2020). For this reason, it has been increasingly understood as an industry reflecting the unbalanced power-relations, injustices, and inequalities that are rooted in our neoliberal, market-driven, pro-growth economic model (Bianchi, 2009; Burrai et al., 2019; Boluk et al., 2019; Higgins-Desbiolles et al., 2019; Jamal, 2019). The tension between a neoliberal economic model driven by unlimited growth and the limited resources available on earth has caused worsening conditions for a growing number of people due to climate, social, and political crises (Higgins-Desbiolles et al., 2019). In conjunction with the increasing global mobility and its impact on destinations – i.e. in terms of 'overtourism' (Milano et al., 2019) - tourism space appears an assertion of the privilege and power imbalance. Hence, our reflection is drawn upon the relationship between the unbalanced power-relations and power-geometries emerging in the space of the tourism and hospitality, and the conceptualization of the urban space and the power-geometries that have emerged, first, in the industrial revolution period and, afterwards through the neoliberal capitalism. In other words, we claim that the contemporary 'space' of tourism and hospitality is intimately interwoven with the way space has been constructed and made sense of within the neoliberal city, which function is primarily to create economic value (Gainsforth, 2019, p. 102).

Marco D'Eramo (2017) - in his critical reflection on the age of tourism and the pivotal role such industry has in the 21st century - makes a comparison between the seriality, anonymity, and automatization of the touristic procedure and touristic space with the seriality, anonymity, and automatization of activities inside a traditional industrial plant. In his analysis both serialities are informed by the 20th century concept of *urbanity* and the notion of *zoning* in urban planning (D'Eramo, 2017, p. 128). Since the beginning of the 20th century, urban planning has revolved around *zoning*, a principle assigning to each urban space a specific mono-functional destination like housing, industrial activities, trade, and leisure activities (Moskowitz, 1998). That meant that the space to live, to work, and to have leisure had to be physically and temporally separated (D'Eramo, 2017). Therefore, cities were designed with urban spaces to be used during working time as industry plants and offices, other spaces to be inhabited during the evening as houses, and yet other spaces to be visited during the weekends for leisure and recreation. This meant not only fragmentation of the space and its functions, but also a flattening of the multiplicity and richness of the relations taking place in such spaces according to Massey's (2005; 2009) propositions on space. Jane Jacobs (2011) in 'The Death and Life of Great American Cities' criticizes an abstract functional urban planning and urges the coexistence of multiple functions within the same space to have people on the streets at all hours of the day and preserve a rich and various social capital (Hospers, 2006; Jacobs, 2011; Sassen, 2016).

Such contemporary rationalization, fragmentation, and flattening of space in terms of a physical and temporal separation of the different moments of our daily life is reflected in the space of tourism and hospitality. Tourism has set a clear divide between residents and tourists. Dwellers and tourists – despite occupying the same space – are actually disconnected, moving in parallel dimensions due to the impossibility of being a tourist and a resident at the same time or in the same space. This is arguably why an excess of tourism threatens to kill the urban space: because it cancels its urbanity by creating an invisible wall between residents and visitors and consequently disactivating the capacity of the urban space for multiplying contacts, relations and networks (D'Eramo, 2017, p. 142). Our contemporary society seems actually to be suffering from a 'tourism syndrome' since we largely experience the condition of rootless individuals disconnected from places and, living experiences limited in space and time (Bauman, 2000; Franklin, 2003). Moreover, the presence of tourism prompts the commodification of space (Gainsforth, 2019). Sarah Gainsforth (2019, p. 9) in her critical analysis of the impacts of Airbnb on our urban spaces claims that: "[…] a change of perspective is needed: it is not 'sustainable' tourism that makes cities 'livable', but the possibility for everyone to *inhabit* the cities […]".

In contrast to Airbnb's ambiguous mantra 'Belong to anywhere' (https://www.airbnb. co.uk/belong-anywhere) enhancing the myth of being a root-less global citizen able to belong to anywhere and feel at home anywhere, the global crisis prompted by the COVID-19 is urging us to rethink and re-focus on our sense of belonging and our connection to the space we experience and inhabit, by reactivating its multiplicity. Only in a space understood as a continuous surface to transit, can travelers 'belong to everywhere', while – on the contrary – within a spatial imagination rooted in multiple interconnections and networks travelers are called to be proactively engaged co-producing such multiplicity. This historical moment is showing us how much our wellbeing and survival is primarily rooted in our belonging to the 'local' and the multiple relations, connections, and networks we can activate within the local space we inhabit and experience. The new-felt urgency of belonging to the local and staying connected to the multiplicity of 'space' can be understood using the space propositions of Massey (2005).

Space is – by nature – 'relational'. Therefore, space is 'produced' through the establishment - or denial - of relations. Space emerges as a product of our on-going world and, therefore, it is also open to the future (Massey, 2009). If space is constantly produced by multiple relations and connections, then space is a social and political dimension. The political dimension of space – as Massey stresses – reminds us of the importance of making sense of space not as a fixed static entity, potentially 'dead' or wrongly perceived as in opposition to the dynamicity of time. Space is not an a-temporal dimension because it is constantly produced (Massey, 2005; 2009). 'Space', as understood by Massey, prompts us to reflect on how we live together, challenging us to reflect on the social and political dimension of living together, acknowledging the existence of 'others' by entering into relationship with them (Massey, 2009, p. 18). Moreover, space is imbued with and a product of relations of power; power itself has a geography that Massey identifies as 'power-geometry'. The existence of a 'power geometry' in spaces is evident in the centralization of power-relationships in certain spaces like the financial district in the city of London or the geography of the relations of production and distribution within a nation (Massey, 2005, 2009). With regards to power-geometries in action, Massey claims that: "in itself the term power-geometry does not imply any specific form (any specific geometry). It is a concept through which to analyse the world, in order perhaps to highlight inequalities, or deficiencies in democracy. It is in this mode an instrument through which to imagine, and maybe to begin to build, more equal and democratic societies […]" (Massey, 2009, p. 19). The new-felt urgency of belonging to the local and staying connected to the multiplicity of 'space' is here understood using the space propositions of Massey (2005).

Novel spaces and power-geometries in tourism and hospitality after 2020

What does Massey's theorization of space and power geometry (2005; 2009) mean with regards to the future of space in tourism and hospitality after 2020? Which are the implications of disentangling us from the space of 'belong to anywhere' to re-focus on our belonging to local space? Which is the novel power-geometry we can foresee? Acknowledging that it is too early to give any definitive answers to these questions, we believe that we can already glimpse some features, that are still *'in fieri'* but, nevertheless, indicate potentialities for a positive transformation of the space of tourism and hospitality with regards to the local dimension. The resilience, adaptation, and functional multiplicity we are seeing in some hospitality facilities that have opened to the needs of the local community in this COVID-19 crisis, can be embraced and developed further. This would mean re-thinking these spaces in terms of multiple relations, more networks than the strict tourism-related ones, a multiplicity of functions going beyond commercial hospitality, and a different power-geometry opening up these spaces to the local community and making them also a resource for local residents. Spaces that can be used all year long, not only during the tourist seasons, rooms that can be rented to students during the academic year, meeting rooms available for local associations and local groups, spaces to be used by children. Public urban spaces, services and infrastructure conceived and designed to favor human encounters, connections, and spontaneous interactions, together with the coexistence of a diversity of inhabitants and visitors.

A critical re-rethinking of the neoliberal approach to space, of the touristification and commodification of our spaces should urge a radical discussion for a novel conceptualization of space - both inside and outside - tourism and hospitality. This would mean – for instance – setting the ground for a novel spatial imagination for destination dynamics welcoming the unintended, unexpected, indeterminate multiplicity of 'untidy guests' (Veijola et al., 2014) as Hazel Tucker stressed in her key note at ATLAS Conference 2018 (www.atlas.org).This historical moment is prompting us to enact a deeper connection with our space and local dimension to release novel connections, relations, and multiplicities rooted in more democratic, just, and balanced power-relations.

Disclosure statement

No potential conflict of interest was reported by the author(s).

References

Bauman, Z. (2000). *Liquid Modernity*. Polity Press.

Bianchi, R. V. (2009). The 'critical turn' in tourism studies: A radical critique. *Tourism Geographies*, *11*(4), 484–504. doi:10.1080/14616680903262653

Boluk, K. A., Cavaliere, C. T., & Higgins-Desbiolles, F. (2019). A critical framework for interrogating the united nations sustainable development goals 2030 agenda in tourism. *Journal of Sustainable Tourism*, *27*(7), 847–864. doi:10.1080/09669582.2019.1619748

Burrai, E., Buda, D.-M., & Stanford, D. (2019). Rethinking the ideology of responsible tourism. *Journal of Sustainable Tourism*, *27*(7), 992–1007. doi:10.1080/09669582.2019.1578365

D'Eramo, M. (2017). *Il selfie del mondo. Indagine sull'età del turismo*. Feltrinelli.

Franklin, A. (2003). The Tourist Syndrome: an interview with Zygmunt Bauman. *Tourist Studies*, *3*(2), 205–217. doi:10.1177/1468797603041632

Gainsforth, S. (2019). *Airbnb città merce. Storie di resistenza alla gentrificazione digitale*. DeriveApprodi.

Higgins-Desbiolles, F., Carnicelli, S., Krolikowski, C., Wijesinghe, G., & Boluk, K. (2019). Degrowing tourism: rethinking tourism. *Journal of Sustainable Tourism, 27*(12), 1926–1944. doi:10.1080/09669582.2019.1601732

Hospers, G.-J. (2006). Jane Jacobs: her life and work. *European Planning Studies, 14*(6), 723–732. doi:10.1080/09654310600779444

Jacobs, J. (2011). *The death and life of great American cities*. Penguin Random House.

Jamal, T. (2019). *Justice and ethics in tourism*. Routledge.

Massey, D. (2009). Concepts of space and power in theory and in political practice. *Documents D'anàlisi Geogràfica, 55*, 15–26.

Massey, D. (2005). *For Space*. Sage Publications Ltd.

Milano, C., Cheer, J. M., & Novelli, M. (2019). *Overtourism: Excesses, discontents and measures in travel and tourism*. CABI.

Moskowitz, M. (1998). Zoning the industrial city: Planners, commissioners, and boosters in the 1920s. *Business and Economic History, 27*(2), 307–317.

Sassen, S. (2016, May 4). How Jane Jacobs changed the way we look at cities. *The Guardian*. https://www.theguardian.com/cities/2016/may/04/jane-jacobs-100th-birthday-saskia-sassen

Veijola, S., Molz, J., Germann, P., Hockert, O., Grit, E., Molz, A., Germann, J., & Höckert, E. (2014). *Disruptive tourism and its untidy guests: Alternative ontologies for future hospitalities*. Palgrave Macmillan.

UNWTO. (2020, January 20). *International tourism growth continues to outplace the global economy*. UNWTO. https://unwto.org/international-tourism-growth-continues-to-outpace-the-economy

COVID-19 leads to a new context for the "right to tourism": a reset of tourists' perspectives on space appropriation is needed

Sabrina Tremblay-Huet

We already know that the COVID-19 pandemic has changed the way actors see transnational mobility, as well as the appropriation of spaces for leisure purposes, for the foreseeable future. But will this be to the advantage of host communities? I argue, and hope, that it will.

In September 2017, the UNTWO's *Framework Convention on Tourism Ethics* was adopted by the organization's Assembly (it has yet to enter into force, as ten ratifications are needed for this to be the case. The Convention is thus not legally binding as of yet, from a formal international law perspective). Article 10 provides for a "right to tourism." Therefore, "The prospect of direct and personal access to the discovery and enjoyment of the planet's resources constitutes a right equally open to all the world's inhabitants; the increasingly extensive participation in domestic and international tourism should be regarded as one of the best possible expressions of the sustained growth of free time, and obstacles should not be placed in its way."

A "right to tourism" has been part of the UNWTO's discourse on tourism long before the adoption of the Convention, including in its 1999 *Global Code of Ethics for Tourism*. However, this consecration in an instrument destined to be legally binding on states, and eventually enforceable, underlines the normative status the right to be a (leisure) tourist has attained.

Parallel to this consecration, and to continuously exponential numbers of tourist arrivals per year, activists and researchers raised alarms about the environmental cost of these increases in travel. The UNWTO simply emphasized its "sustainable development"/"sustainable tourism" component of the "right to tourism" discourse, never questioning the sector's growth. In the words of then-Secretary General, Taleb Rifai, "Growth is not the enemy; it's how we manage it that counts." (UNWTO, 2017).

At the same time, Font and Hindley wrote about reactance, environmental degradation of tourism spaces, and an increase in tourists' interest for theses spaces (Font and Hindley, 2017). Reactance theory, developed by Jack Williams Brehm, posits that an individual will react to a perceived threat to freedom of choice in a potentially contradictory manner. Thus, increased attention directed towards a destination in order to showcase its environmental fragility could result in a similarly increased interest from tourists for this destination. We have also observed this in the context of greater consciousness about the environmental impact of air travel itself, as tourist arrivals essentially followed the same upwards curve as greenhouse gas emissions awareness campaigns.

In March 2020, COVID-19 was officially declared a pandemic by the World Health Organization. Travel was highly restricted, either by government advisories and orders, or by common sense. A Quebec couple decided to drive up to the North of Canada, and then fly, to Old Crow, Yukon (Blatchford, 2020). Home of the Vuntut Gwitchin First Nation, its population is estimated at 221 (Statistics Canada, 2016). The couple, seeking refuge from the pandemic, was swiftly placed in isolation, and sent back packing. Dana Tizya-Tramm, the Nation's chief, is quoted as saying: "Our community, albeit remote, is not a life raft for the rest of the world." It is not suggested that the couple harbored intentions to put the community at risk. But with scarce medical resources and difficult access, that could have been the result, had they not been removed.

Late 2019 and early 2020 saw an important tourism promotion campaign from the Government of Yukon's Department of Tourism & Culture (Travel Yukon). On March 22nd, however, Dr. Brendan Hanley, Yukon's Chief Medical Officer of Health, published an update on COVID-19 in which he "strongly advises the suspension of all non-essential travel into and out of Yukon."

Whereas the adoption of the "right to tourism" in an internationally legally binding instrument followed the momentum of its logic of unlimited occupation of space for leisure purposes, will the near-term and medium-term future see the rise of a reset of tourists' perspectives on space appropriation?

This pandemic has awakened realizations of how interconnected our world truly is, and about the effects of shared spaces. Concerted collective efforts should be made to lead to more deliberate decisions as to if, how and when we appropriate other spaces than our "own," including through leisure travel. There is hope for this to be so, because we will have seen the deleterious effects nonchalant and irresponsible appropriation of space can have, when people around us do not respect stay-at-home advisories and orders for non-essential motivations.

While being confined at home, we also mourn unrestricted movement, within our community but also to others. Through thoughtful leadership by the UNWTO and all other tourism actors involved in the inevitable reboot of the sector, our collective self-isolation experience could result in increased awareness of the situation of people whose freedom of circulation is impaired. Some people's mobility is characterized not by choice, but by disastrous life events and situations: the UN Refugee Agency estimates that there are around 26 million refugees worldwide, in addition to around 41 million internally displaced people and 3.5 million asylum seekers (numbers available online as of April 2020: UNHCR). Some people's transnational mobility is prohibited by their nationalities (Mau et al., 2015) or lack thereof. And of course, mobility for leisure purposes is not accessible to a number of the world's population for a host of other social and economic reasons. A "right to tourism" without a strict association with, namely, social tourism, renders it ethically senseless.

This reboot should also constitute an opportunity for communities to increasingly seize their power to decide who may visit them. This could be so, as it is now impossible to refuse to acknowledge that wealth accumulation cannot be accomplished without prioritizing the physical, mental and social health of host communities (e.g. on social sustainability: Jover & Díaz-Parra, 2020). Hopefully, this also dissipates the mirage of "sustainable development," in which "development" trumps the "sustainable" component, or in which "sustainable" is defined according to the neo-liberal elite's interests (e.g. on sustainable development and neoliberalism: Lapointe et al., 2018; Higgins-Desbiolles, 2020).

And, importantly, this halt in the lightness of decisions to pursue tourism for leisure purposes should lead the leisure class (MacCannell, 2013) to truly take notice of its privileges. In turn, when we travel again, may we act more gracefully, and with more gratefulness towards the people who have agreed to host us. May we have a deeper understanding of the challenges facing remote communities and act consequently. May we demonstrate greater empathy for those who lack the possibility of trans-national mobility.

Disclosure statement

No potential conflict of interest was reported by the author(s).

References

Blatchford, A. (2020, March 30). *Couple flees to north of the Arctic Circle in bid to escape Covid-19*. Politico. https://www.politico.com/news/2020/03/30/couple-flees-north-arctic-circle-corona-virus-155878.

Font, X., & Hindley, A. (2017). Understanding tourists' reactance to the threat of a loss of freedom to travel due to climate change: a new alternative approach to encouraging nuanced behavioural change. *Journal of Sustainable Tourism*, *25*(1), 26–42. https://doi.org/10.1080/09669582.2016.1165235

Framework Convention on Tourism Ethics, Off doc GA UNWTO, 22nd sess, A/RES/707(XXII) (2017).

Government of Yukon. *Updates on COVID-19 from the Office of the Chief Medical Officer of Health*. https://yukon.ca/en/coronavirus-updates.

Higgins-Desbiolles, F. (2020). Socialising tourism for social and ecological justice after COVID-19. *Tourism Geographies*, 1–15. https://doi.org/10.1080/14616688.2020.1757748.

Jover, J., & Díaz-Parra, I. (2020). Who is the city for? Overtourism, lifestyle migration and social sustainability. *Tourism Geographies*, 1–24. https://doi.org/10.1080/14616688.2020.1713878.

Lapointe, D., Sarrasin, B., & Benjamin, C. (2018). Tourism in the Sustained Hegemonic Neoliberal Order. *Revista Latino-Americana de Turismologia*, *4*(1), 16–33. https://doi.org/10.34019/2448-198X.2018.v4.13915

MacCannell, D. (2013). *The tourist: A new theory of the leisure class*. University of California Press.

Mau, S., Gülzau, F., Laube, L., & Zaun, N. (2015). The global mobility divide: How visa policies have evolved over time. *Journal of Ethnic and Migration Studies*, *41*(8), 1192–1213. https://doi.org/10.1080/1369183X.2015.1005007

Old Crow – Yukon – Home of the Vuntut Gwitchin First Nation. https://www.oldcrow.ca/.

Statistics Canada. (2016). *Census Profile, 2016 Census – Old Crow, Settlement [Census subdivision], Yukon and Yukon [Territory]*. https://www12.statcan.gc.ca/census-recensement/2016/dp-pd/prof/details/page.cfm?Lang=E&Geo1=CSD&Code1=6001043&Geo2=PR&Code2=60&SearchText=Old%20Crow&SearchType=Begins&SearchPR=01&B1=All&GeoLevel=PR&GeoCode=6001043&TABID=1&type=0.

Travel Yukon. https://www.travelyukon.com/en.

UNHCR. (2020). *Figures at a glance – statistical yearbooks*. https://www.unhcr.org/figures-at-a-glance.html.

UNWTO. (2017, August 15). *Tourism: Growth is not the enemy; It's how we manage it that counts*. https://www.unwto.org/archive/global/press-release/2017-08-15/tourism-growth-not-enemy-its-how-we-manage-it-counts.

From high-touch to high-tech: COVID-19 drives robotics adoption

Zhanjing Zeng, Po-Ju Chen (iD) and Alan A. Lew (iD)

ABSTRACT

Global economic and social life has been severely challenged since the World Health Organization (WHO) declared the COVID-19 disease a pandemic. Travel, tourism and hospitality, in particular, has been massively impacted by the lockdowns used to maintain social distance to manage the disease. Robotics, artificial intelligence, and human-robot interactions have gained an increased presence to help manage the spread of COVID-19 in hospitals, airports, transportation systems, recreation and scenic areas, hotels, restaurants, and communities in general. Humanoid robots, autonomous vehicles, drones, and other intelligent robots are used in many different ways to reduce human contact and the potential spread of the SARS-CoV-2 virus, including delivering materials, disinfecting and sterilizing public spaces, detecting or measuring body temperature, providing safety or security, and comforting and entertaining patients. While controversial in the past due to concerns over job losses and data privacy, the adoption of robotics and artificial intelligence in travel and tourism will likely continue after the COVID-19 pandemic becomes less serious. Tourism scholars should seize this opportunity to develop robotic applications that enhance tourist experiences, the protection of natural and cultural resources, citizen participation in tourism development decision making, and the emergence of new 'high-touch' employment opportunities for travel, tourism and hospitality workers.

摘要

在世界卫生组织宣布新型冠状病毒肺炎（COVID-19）成为大流行病之后, 全球经济和社会生活受到了严峻挑战。为保持社交距离和控制疫情发展而实施的限制出行政策也对交通、旅游和接待业造成了巨大的影响。在这种情况下, 机器人技术、人工智能和人机交互得到了越来越多的关注。它们在帮助医院、机场、交通系统、景区、酒店、餐饮和社区抵抗新冠疫情的传播普遍发挥重要作用。管理者使用人形机器人、自动驾驶汽车、无人机和其他智能机器人, 通过多种途径来避免人与人的直接接触和降低潜在传染风险。这些措施包括运送物资、清洁消毒公共空间、测量或检测体温、提供安全保障、安抚并娱乐病患等。尽管曾由于担心会带来失业或者数据隐私问题而饱受争议, 但在新冠疫情减轻后, 机器人和人工智能仍将在交通和旅游业中继续发挥作用。旅游学者应该抓住这次新冠疫情带来的科技变革机会，发掘机器人技术的潜力以增强旅游体验，保护自然和文化资源，并致力于为交通、旅游和接待从业人员提供"非接触式"就业机会。

1. Introduction

As of mid-April 2020, more than two million cases of COVID-19 infections had been reported worldwide, and over 160,000 people have reportedly died from the disease (WHO, 2020). First reported in 2019, the World Health Organization (WHO) declared this strain of coronavirus (SARS-CoV-2) a global pandemic on March 11, 2020 (X. Yang et al., 2020). In only a few months, the coronavirus disease of 2019 (COVID-19) has impacted social and economic aspects of everyday life across the globe. Tourism, as a "high-touch" industry, has come to a grinding halt under social distancing guidelines and travel bans (Jamal & Budke, 2020). While it is too early to know exactly what travel and tourism will look like when it emerges from the COVID-19 lockdowns, it is very likely that various forms of technology being used to manage this disease will continue to play a significant role. If developed properly, such technological innovations may also help to achieve some of the goals of a more sustainable form of travel and tourism. Evidence from China and elsewhere shows how robotics, in particular, has advanced in its applications during the COVID-19 pandemic.

Due to the highly contagious nature of the SARS-CoV-2 virus, ensuring a safe social distance between people has proven to be an effective way to reduce viral infections in communities (Fong et al., 2020). Initially implemented with the onset of COVID-19 (believed to have originated in Wuhan, China), social distancing measures include the closing public areas (such as parks and plazas) and the maintenance of physical distances between people in areas that cannot be closed (such as markets and health care facilities). These social distancing practices have had a major impact on industries that rely on high levels of human interaction, such as hospitality and tourism, which are suffering greatly during this period (Hoque et al., 2020).

COVID-19 is not the first virus to impact travel and tourism. In recent decades, virus epidemics such as SARS (also known as SARS-CoV-1), MERS, the swine flu, Ebola, Zika, and yellow fever have also threatened public health around the world (Buheji & Ahmed, 2020). According to the WHO, globally, more than 5,000 disease early-warning signals have been received on average per month in recent years, with hundreds of those warnings prompting in-depth investigations. None of these past disease outbreaks, however, were on the global scale and impact as has been experienced with COVID-19.

History has shown that a crisis can bring about technological innovation and development (Colombo et al., 2016). Due to advances in artificial intelligence (AI), miniaturization, and other technologies, robotics have grown increasingly more viable in hospitality and tourism industry settings to provide concierge, housekeeping, food, and other service tasks (Cain Lisa et al., 2019; Ivanov et al., 2019; Yu, 2020). Although some researchers previously believed that the adoption of social robots is not optimistic, mostly due to the tourism industry's desire to maintain high-touch amenities

Table 1. The classification of robots interact with humans.

Classification Name	Definition	Function	Types of Robots
Telerobot	Robots that can sense the environment and make limited automatic reactions through computer programs to complete routine tasks	Routine tasks	Picking and placing robots, welding robots, cleaning robots, delivery robots, self-guard gate, ultraviolet-light-disinfection robots
Teleoperator	Robots that deal with nonroutine tasks in hazardous or inaccessible environments with continuous remote control from humans.	Nonroutine tasks	Drones, unmanned spacecraft, undersea robotic vehicles, unscrewed aerial vehicles
Social robot	Robots that have autonomous agents with social intelligence to interact with humans in an acceptable manner.	Entertainment, teaching, comfort, and assistance	Guiding robots, teaching robots, communication robots, assistive healthcare robots, autonomous vehicles

(Bhimasta & Kuo, 2019; Osawa et al., 2017), the COVID-19 public health crisis has brought forth new application and prospects for robots.

Robots, which includes drones, delivery robots, and service robots, are now being used to manage COVID-19 (Marr, 2020; G.-Z. Yang et al., 2020). These developments raise new questions such as "What roles can robots fulfill in hospitality and tourism?", "How will people's attitudes be affected after seeing the roles robots played during the COVID-19 pandemic?" and "What is the future of robots in hospitality and tourism?"

2. Robot types and applications

While robots have played an essential role in industrial environments and high-risk jobs for many years, little attention has been given to the roles robots could play in "high-touch" or "high interpersonal" interactive environments, such as the hospitality sector. Researchers use the word "robotics" to describe the research area related to information engineering, computer science and other technical fields (McKerrow & McKerrow, 1991) in which a robot is defined as an "actuated mechanism programmable in two or more axes with a degree of autonomy, moving within its environment, to perform intended tasks" (Ivanov et al., 2019).

With the development of artificial intelligence (AI), robots are becoming equipped with "social intelligence" – the capability to be socially aware and able to interpret emotional signals and react as would a real human being (Breazeal, 2003; Lazzeri et al., 2013). Different from industrial robots that are widely used in agriculture, manufacturing, and medicine (Engelberger, 2012), a socially intelligent robot emphasizes interaction with humans through its use of artificial intelligence (Dautenhahn & Billard, 1999). In hospitality and tourism, these robots are used to help customers or tourists with tasks such as providing directions, checking in and out of hotel rooms, delivering food or amenities, cleaning, and providing safety and security services (Ivanov et al., 2017).

Researchers have gradually come to classify human-robot interaction (HRI) into three categories: robot-centered approaches, human-centered approaches, and robot cognition-center approaches (Dautenhahn, 2007). Based on the nature of the application, (Sheridan, 2016) further classified robots interacting with humans into "telerobot," "teleoperator," and "social robot" (Table 1).

Robots have often been used in response to disasters and crises, such as the Fukushima nuclear plant meltdown in 2011 (Nagatani et al., 2013). However, unlike many other disasters or crises where there is an easily identified cause that endangers human life (Schmude et al., 2018; Woosnam & Kim, 2014), the highly infectious disease crisis of COVID-19 is caused by close contact between random people. In one similar example, robots were discussed for use in the 2015 Ebola outbreak in Africa. The US White House Office of Science and Technology Policy identified three broad areas where robotics assistance could help that epidemic: clinical care, logistics, and reconnaissance (G.-Z. Yang et al., 2020).

In the COVID-19 pandemic, robots were initially found to be particularly effective in China for routine or nonroutine tasks using ultraviolet (UV) for surface disinfection. Robot technology, however, rapidly matured with different types of robots appearing to manage COVID-19 in various settings, including hospitals, airports, transportation, recreation and scenic areas, hotels, and in communities in general.

2.1. Robots in hospitals

Due to the sudden and rapid outbreak of COVID-19 in China, the influx of patients into hospitals caused a severe workload for medical staff. To place more patients, Wuhan Hongshan Stadium was transformed into a robot-led smart field hospital (Katz, 2020; O'Meara, 2020). Fourteen robots were deployed in this field hospital by the robotics company CloudMinds. They were used to clean and disinfect, measure patient temperatures, deliver medicine and food, and entertain and comfort patients by communicating and dancing with them. In Italy, another place with high levels of COVID-19 disease incidents, robots (named 'Tommy') have been used to help medical teams look after their patients and reduce direct contact between patients and medical staff (Romero, 2020). Tommy has a monitor and a tablet for patients to communicate both visually and acoustically with nurses and doctors in a remote location. Robots like Tommy can measure two crucial patient parameters; blood pressure and oxygen saturation. Hospitals around the world are turning to tireless robots to get rid of viruses and bacteria on rooms, halls, and on door handles (Blake, 2020; Mean, 2020). They are increasingly able to make initial tests, complete routine tasks, and assist doctors with remote diagnoses, thereby reducing the fear of spreading diseases.

2.2. Robots in communities

Robots used in the communities have two primary tasks, one is to protect the health of residents by disinfecting and monitoring spaces, and the other is to ensure the adequate supply of foods and materials in the community. Disinfection or sterilization robots have been adopted in the COVID-19 pandemic around the world. Danish company UVD Robots shipped robots to Chinese hospitals first, and later spread their usage throughout China. Robots with sprayers or a dispenser for hand sanitizers also travel around neighborhoods in Shanghai (Sharma, 2020). Delivery robots and self-delivery autonomous cars also occupy an essential position for the food supply in China, where people use JD.com or Meituan, a delivery app, allowing them to stay at home and reduce human-to-human contact during the COVID-19 pandemic. "Contactless delivery" by robots has also been used by Alibaba (China's largest online retailer), which has been very popular.

Robots have a long history in communities where most of the permanent population is elderly or disabled (Dubowsky et al., 2000; Pollack et al., 2002). Because these populations are at high-risk for COVID-19 infections, robots have become especially important to deliver telemedicine for physical health and telecommunication for psychological health.

2.3. Robots in airports

Most large airports manage a tremendous flow of people, many of whom have needs for information, navigation, and pick-up transportation services. Before the COVID-19 pandemic, some airports had started piloting the use of robots to assist managers in ensuring airport safety, provide information and directional services, help with passenger check-ins, deliver luggage, and some other routine services.

As the COVID-19 pandemic placed a greater value on public health, opportunities and trust of airport robots increased. Disinfection and sterilization robots have now gained a secure place in many airports around the world. Robots with the ability to track or detect high-touch or high-risk areas that may not seem obvious to the human eye are also gaining in importance in busy public areas like airports and shopping complexes (Gent, 2020). In addition, it is suggested that a kind of ambulance robot, operated remotely and supplied with medical tools such as a thermometer, automatic external defibrillator (AED), coronavirus test kit, and other instruments, could be used to instruct the public on appropriate actions to take in public spaces in an emergency (Samani & Zhu, 2016).

2.4. Robots in transportations

Because of the COVID-19 lockdown in China, transportation during the Chinese New Year period in late January dropped 50% from levels in 2019. The public's panic over health has increased trust in autonomous vehicles (self-driving cars). In Wuhan, people have gradually accepted self-driving vehicles to deliver supplies to hospitals and communities, and to transport COVID-19 tests to the clinics and labs. Self-driving cars can also transport tourists, residents, and business people to specific locations safely in many situations that involve small passenger loads.

Public transportation in China that involves longer distances, such as subways, light rail, and high-speed rails, use robots or intelligent gates to measure body temperatures to detect possibly infected travelers. The combination of infrared (heat detection) cameras and facial recognition systems has proven successful in detecting a person with high temperatures, even if he or she is wearing a mask in the public transportation station (Chun, 2020). These robotic uses in large public spaces can scan many passengers simultaneously, thereby reducing the workload for public transportation system staff.

2.5. Robots in recreation, attraction and scenic areas

The management committee of the Huangshan (Yellow Mountain) Scenic Area, in Anhui Province, China, had to close the park in April when an early morning crowd of 20,000 people showed up after it reopened following the lockdown with a special free admission day. In addition to many of the robotic applications cited above, scenic areas throughout China are planning to rely heavily on smart monitoring and management systems to detect and control the number of visitors they receive so as not to overwhelm their ecosystems and create potential disease outbreaks.

The COVID-19 pandemic has also brought the use of drones (flying robots) to the attention of scenic area managers (Marr, 2020). Drones that were originally used to spray pesticides on agriculture fields have been repurposed to spray disinfectants in areas heavily visited by tourists in scenic areas. Unlike flat city roads, the complex terrain of many scenic areas makes it difficult for larger car-like robots to manage the disinfection. Drones are also used to provide an overhead view to better monitor the density and movement of tourists in a scenic area. In Hawaii, drones have further been used to convey voice instructions to remind people to maintain social distance in public areas, including on beaches (The Honolulu Fire Department, 2020). More broadly, drones have been shown to be helpful in efforts to prevent wildlife poaching in nature reserves in Africa.

2.6. Robots in hotels and restaurants

In 2015, the Henn Na Hotel in Nagasaki, Japan, opened as the first to be almost completely operated by robots (Alexis, 2017). Robots in this hotel are responsible for 70% of the hotel's work, allowing only seven people to operate the entire hotel. The robots could carry luggage and guide guests through front desk services. Miscellaneous tasks such as cleaning rooms and pouring coffee were also done by robots. However, soon after opening, Hen Na Hotel stopped half of the robotic services because of the poor performance that they were providing (Bhimasta & Kuo, 2019). By comparison, "Connie Robot" in Hilton Hotels is more fortunate. Connie, developed by IBM, is a concierge who helps guests to figure out places to visit and dine, and to find things on the hotel's property (Trejos, 2016). With some ability to think or judge, intelligent robots are gaining opportunities in hospitality and with the pandemic. Such service robots, equipped with AI, can potentially provide information, do housekeeping work, provide food services, and help to comfort and entertain the customer in a safe way.

Restaurants have also adopted robots to transfer goods from warehouses to trucks and customers amid the COVID-19 pandemic to limited potential virus contamination (Demaitre, 2020). Concerns for food preparation safety is also placing more trust in robots during the pandemic (Meisenzahl, 2020). At the Hema restaurant in China, developed by Alibaba, robots not only cook fried rice for customers but also deliver the dishes autonomously (Bhardwaj, 2018).

3. Robots for a better tourism and hospitality industry?

Researchers generally agree that the adoption of robots in tourism and hospitality can increase the efficiency of work, the quality of services, and reduce the financial costs (Ivanov & Webster, 2019a). During the COVID-19 pandemic, the advantage of robots in helping to maintain social distance has also been shown to the public. Robots can accomplish tasks related to logistics, disinfection, and provide COVID-19 information to people and reduce the threat of infection.

However, many also see major challenges in the adoption of robotics. For example, wide application and use of robots in the service industries could cause a large number of people to lose their jobs (Boyd & Holton, 2018; Huang & Rust, 2018). Concerns are also acute over the vulnerability of robot security systems to being compromised, the confidentiality of private data, and the lack of human contact in a traditionally high-touch service industry (Tussyadiah, 2020; Tussyadiah et al., 2018). In addition, some people have negative feelings about robots and experience anxiety when they encounter these cold machines (Nomura et al., 2006; 2008). These are certainly serious issues that can be exploited and abused by governments and others without proper oversight. On the other hand, robotics are part of the digital democracy movement, which envisions the application of technology to enhance citizen freedoms and participation in governance. Taiwan's use of technology to stave off the spread of COVID-19 from China through rapid monitoring and information sharing is often cited as an example of what can be accomplished through a digital democracy policy. Robots could potentially assist local communities in monitoring the impacts of tourism on natural and cultural resources and preventing overtourism impacts, for example.

If recent robotic development continues, and proper oversight policies are implemented, some industry experts predict that between 400 million and 800 million of today's jobs around the world, and one-quarter of the hospitality jobs in the USA, will be automated by the 2030s (Bowen & Morosan, 2018). A mostly robot economy is predicted by the 22nd century, driven by innovative and labor-saving technologies (Webster & Ivanov, 2019). While some human jobs will be lost to robots, others argue that robots will fill gaps in the negative demographic growth and limited labor that many countries will increasingly experience (Webster, 2019). Robots can also help people transfer from low-skilled jobs to high-skilled jobs.

In the future, robots serving in tourism and hospitality may change the tourist experience in terms of expectations, service quality, and image (Ivanov & Webster, 2019b). Research has shown how technologies can mediate and, to some extent, enhance tourism experiences (Tussyadiah & Fesenmaier, 2009; Zhang, 2018), which is equally applicable to robotics. Judging from attitudes towards robots in China during the pandemic crisis, people's acceptance of high-tech services may be greater than some scholars have speculated. For example, robots dancing with patients in the Wuhan Fangcang field hospital has been widely viewed as a benefit. Tourists, on the other hand, are more likely to accept the technology if it is trustworthy, free of risk, competent, and easy to use (Kaushik et al., 2015). The relationship of "tourists – guides – destinations" will increasingly include "tourists – robots – destinations" in a post-COVID-19 world.

COVID-19 will be a driver to technology innovation in tourism (Ivanov et al., 2020). The arrival of COVID-19 has given robotics a boost in its existing practical applications. Travel and tourism scholars should seize this opportunity and consider new areas in which robotics can further enhance the quality and sustainability of the travel and tourism experience. Some of these are hinted at above, and might include:

- better monitoring and protection of fragile natural and cultural resources;
- navigational systems that automatically re-route tourists to prevent overcrowding and overtourism;
- concierge information systems that match tourist interests to a greater variety of local high-touch providers, and thereby spread the economic benefits of tourism more equitably; and
- public informational systems that detect inappropriate behavior and educate tourists on culturally acceptable behavior when necessary.

Creative innovations such as these, and potentially many more, can create whole new high-touch and high-quality tourism services. In this way, a new paradigm can emerge in which robotics and artificial intelligence can facilitate a better tourism than we knew prior to the COVID-19 pandemic.

Disclosure statement

No potential conflict of interest was reported by the author(s).

Funding

National Natural Science Foundation of China (41971173).

ORCID

Po-Ju Chen ⒾⒹ https://orcid.org/0000-0002-1741-0589
Alan A. Lew ⒾⒹ http://orcid.org/0000-0001-8177-5972

References

Alexis, P. (2017). R-Tourism: Introducing the potential impact of robotics and service automation in tourism. *Ovidius University Annals, Series Economic Sciences, 17*(1), 211–216.

Bhardwaj, P. (2018, July 02). *Robots are replacing waiters and delivering fresh seafood right to people's tables at Alibaba's high-tech restaurant in Shanghai.* https://www.businessinsider.com/alibaba-shanghai-restaurant-robothe-robots-waiters-photos-2018-7

Bhimasta, R. A., & Kuo, P. Y. (2019, September). *What causes the adoption failure of service robots? A case of Henn-na Hotel in Japan [Paper presentation].* Adjunct Proceedings of the 2019 ACM International Joint Conference on Pervasive and Ubiquitous Computing and Proceedings of the 2019 ACM International Symposium on Wearable Computers, London, UK. https://doi.org/10.1145/3341162.3350843

Blake, R. (2020, April 17). *In Coronavirus fight, robots report for disinfection duty.* https://www.forbes.com/sites/richblake1/2020/04/17/in-covid-19-fight-robots-report-for-disinfection-duty/#7a8dc2c72ada

Bowen, J., & Morosan, C. (2018). Beware hospitality industry: The robots are coming. *Worldwide Hospitality and Tourism Themes, 10*(6), 726–733. https://doi.org/10.1108/WHATT-07-2018-0045

Boyd, R., & Holton, R. J. (2018). Technology, innovation, employment and power: Does robotics and artificial intelligence really mean social transformation? *Journal of Sociology, 54*(3), 331–345. https://doi.org/10.1177/1440783317726591

Breazeal, C. (2003). Toward sociable robots. *Robotics and Autonomous Systems, 42*(3-4), 167–175. https://doi.org/10.1016/S0921-8890(02)00373-1

Buheji, M., & Ahmed, D. (2020). Foresight of Coronavirus (COVID-19) opportunities for a better world. *American Journal of Economics, 10*(2), 97–108. https://doi.org/10.5923/j.economics.20201002.05

Cain Lisa, N., Thomas John, H., & Alonso, M. Jr, (2019). From sci-fi to sci-fact: The state of robotics and AI in the hospitality industry. *Journal of Hospitality and Tourism Technology, 10*(4), 624–650. https://doi.org/10.1108/JHTT-07-2018-0066

Chun, A. (2020, March 18). *In a time of coronavirus, China's investment in AI is paying off in a big way.* https://today.line.me/hk/pc/article/In+a+time+of+coronavirus+China%E2%80%99s+investment+in+AI+is+paying+off+in+a+big+way-2596oj

Colombo, M. G., Piva, E., Quas, A., & Rossi-Lamastra, C. (2016). How high-tech entrepreneurial ventures cope with the global crisis: Changes in product innovation and internationalization strategies. *Industry and Innovation, 23*(7), 647–671. https://doi.org/10.1080/13662716.2016.1196438

Dautenhahn, K. (2007). Socially intelligent robots: Dimensions of human–robot interaction. *Philosophical Transactions of the Royal Society B: Biological Sciences, 362*(1480), 679–704. https://doi.org/10.1098/rstb.2006.2004

Dautenhahn, K., Billard, A. (1999, April). Bringing up robots or—the psychology of socially intelligent robots: From theory to implementation. In *Proceedings of the Third Annual Conference on Autonomous Agents* (pp. 366–367).

Demaitre, E. (2020, March 18). *COVID-19 pandemic prompts more robot usage worldwide.* https://www.therobotreport.com/covid-19-pandemic-prompts-more-robot-usage-worldwide/

Dubowsky, S., Genot, F., Godding, S., Kozono, H., Skwersky, A., Haoyong, Y., Long Shen, Y. (2000, April). PAMM - a robotic aid to the elderly for mobility assistance and monitoring: A "helping-hand" for the elderly. *Proceedings 2000 ICRA. Millennium Conference.* IEEE International Conference on Robotics and Automation. San Francisco, CA, USA

Engelberger, J. F. (2012). *Robotics in practice: Management and applications of industrial robots.* Springer Science & Business Media.

Fong, M. W., Gao, H., Wong, J. Y., Xiao, J., Shiu, E., Ryu, S., … Cowling, B. J. (2020). Nonpharmaceutical measures for pandemic influenza in nonhealthcare settings—Social distancing measures. *Emerging Infectious Diseases, 26*(5), 976–984. https://doi.org/10.3201/eid2605.190995

Gent, E. (2020, April 01). *Robots to the rescue: How they can help during Coronavirus (and future pandemics).* https://singularityhub.com/2020/04/01/robots-to-the-rescue-how-they-can-help-during-coronavirus-and-future-pandemics/

Hoque, A., Shikha, F. A., Hasanat, M. W., Arif, I., & Hamid, A. B. A. (2020). The effect of Coronavirus (COVID-19) in the tourism industry in China. *Asian Journal of Multidisciplinary Studies, 3*(1), 52–58. https://asianjournal.org/online/index.php/ajms/article/view/213

Huang, M. H., & Rust, R. T. (2018). Artificial intelligence in service. *Journal of Service Research, 21*(2), 155–172. https://doi.org/10.1177/1094670517752459

Ivanov, S., Gretzel, U., Berezina, K., Sigala, M., & Webster, C. (2019). Progress on robotics in hospitality and tourism: A review of the literature. *Journal of Hospitality and Tourism Technology, 10*(4), 489–521. https://doi.org/10.1108/JHTT-08-2018-0087

Ivanov, S., & Webster, C. (2019a). Conceptual Framework of the Use of Robots, Artificial Intelligence and Service Automation in Travel, Tourism, and Hospitality Companies. In I. Stanislav & W. Craig (Eds.), *Robots, Artificial Intelligence, and Service Automation in Travel, Tourism and Hospitality* (pp. 7–37). Emerald Publishing Limited. https://doi.org/10.1108/978-1-78756-687-320191001

Ivanov, S., & Webster, C. (2019b). *Robots, artificialiIntelligence, and service automation in travel, tourism and hospitality*. Emerald Publishing Limited.

Ivanov, S. H., Webster, C., & Berezina, K. (2017). Adoption of robots and service automation by tourism and hospitality companies. *Revista Turismo & Desenvolvimento, 27*(28), 1501–1517. https://ssrn.com/abstract=2964308

Ivanov, S., Webster, C., Stoilova, E., & Slobodskoy, D. (2020). Biosecurity, automation technologies and economic resilience of travel, tourism and hospitality companies. https://doi.org/10.31235/osf.io/2hx6f

Jamal, T., & Budke, C. (2020). Tourism in a world with pandemics: local-global responsibility and action. *Journal of Tourism Futures*. https://doi.org/10.1108/JTF-02-2020-0014

Katz, L. (2020, March 14). *Coronavirus care at one hospital got totally taken over by robots*. https://www.cnet.com/news/coronavirus-care-at-one-hospital-got-taken-over-by-robots/

Kaushik, A. K., Agrawal, A. K., & Rahman, Z. (2015). Tourist behaviour towards self-service hotel technology adoption: Trust and subjective norm as key antecedents. *Tourism Management Perspectives, 16*, 278–289. https://doi.org/10.1016/j.tmp.2015.09.002

Lazzeri, N., Mazzei, D., Zaraki, A., & De Rossi, D. (2013, July). *Towards a believable social robot* [Paper presentation]. Conference on Biomimetic and Biohybrid Systems, London, UK.

Marr, B. (2020, March 18). *Robots and drones are now used to fight COVID-19*. https://www.forbes.com/sites/bernardmarr/2020/03/18/how-robots-and-drones-are-helping-to-fight-coronavirus/#f29aee32a12e

McKerrow, P. J., & McKerrow, P. (1991). *Introduction to robotics*. Addison-Wesley Sydney.

Mean, N. (2020, March 05). *Robot to deliver meals, medication to Covid-19 patients at Alexandra Hospital to reduce exposure of healthcare workers*. https://www.todayonline.com/singapore/robot-deliver-meals-medication-covid-19-patients-alexandra-hospital-reduce-exposure

Meisenzahl, M. (2020, April 02). *How China, the US, and Europe are using robots to replace and help humans fight coronavirus by delivering groceries, sanitizing hospitals, and monitoring patients*. https://www.businessinsider.com/robots-fighting-coronavirus-in-china-us-and-europe-2020-3

Nagatani, K., Kiribayashi, S., Okada, Y., Otake, K., Yoshida, K., Tadokoro, S., Nishimura, T., Yoshida, T., Koyanagi, E., Fukushima, M., & Kawatsuma, S. (2013). Emergency response to the nuclear accident at the Fukushima Daiichi Nuclear Power Plants using mobile rescue robots. *Journal of Field Robotics, 30*(1), 44–63. https://doi.org/10.1002/rob.21439

Nomura, T., Kanda, T., Suzuki, T., & Kato, K. (2008). Prediction of human behavior in human–robot interaction using psychological scales for anxiety and negative attitudes toward robots. *IEEE Transactions on Robotics, 24*(2), 442–451. https://doi.org/10.1109/TRO.2007.914004

Nomura, T., Suzuki, T., Kanda, T., & Kato, K. (2006). Measurement of negative attitudes toward robots. *Interaction Studies, 7*(3), 437–454. https://doi.org/10.1075/is.7.3.14nom

O'Meara, S. (2020, March 09). *Coronavirus: Hospital ward staffed entirely by robots opens in China*. https://www.newscientist.com/article/2236777-coronavirus-hospital-ward-staffed-entirely-by-robots-opens-in-china/

Osawa, H., Ema, A., Hattori, H., Akiya, N., Kanzaki, N., Kubo, A., … Ichise, R. (2017). *What is real risk and benefit on work with robots? From the analysis of a robot hotel* [Paper presentation]. Proceedings of the Companion of the 2017 ACM/IEEE International Conference on Human-Robot Interaction, Vienna, Austria. (pp. 241–242). https://doi.org/10.1145/3029798.3038312

Pollack, M. E., Brown, L., Colbry, D., Orosz, C., Peintner, B., Ramakrishnan, S., Engberg, S., Matthews, J. T., Dunbar-Jacob, J., & McCarthy, C. E. (2002). Pearl: A mobile robotic assistant for the elderly. AAAI workshop on automation as eldercare.

Romero, M. E. (2020, April 08). *Tommy the robot nurse helps Italian doctors care for COVID-19 patients.* https://www.pri.org/stories/2020-04-08/tommy-robot-nurse-helps-italian-doctors-care-covid-19-patients

Samani, H., & Zhu, R. (2016). Robotic automated external defibrillator ambulance for emergency medical service in smart cities. *IEEE Access, 4,* 268–283. https://doi.org/10.1109/ACCESS.2016.2514263

Schmude, J., Zavareh, S., Schwaiger, K. M., & Karl, M. (2018). Micro-level assessment of regional and local disaster impacts in tourist destinations. *Tourism Geographies, 20*(2), 290–308. https://doi.org/10.1080/14616688.2018.1438506

Sharma, P. (2020, March 17). *How robots and AI can help fight Coronavirus.* https://www.rediff.com/business/special/how-robots-and-ai-can-help-fight-coronavirus/20200317.htm

Sheridan, T. B. (2016). Human-Robot interaction: Status and challenges. *Human Factors: The Journal of the Human Factors and Ergonomics Society, 58*(4), 525–532. https://doi.org/10.1177/0018720816644364

The Honolulu Fire Department. (2020, April 10). *Drones to assist in enforcement of stay at home order on Oahu.* https://www.khon2.com/coronavirus/drones-to-assist-in-enforcement-of-stay-at-home-order-on-oahu/

Trejos, N. (2016, March 09). *Introducing Connie, Hilton's new robot concierge.* https://www.usatoday.com/story/travel/roadwarriorvoices/2016/03/09/introducing-connie-hiltons-new-robot-concierge/81525924/

Tussyadiah, I. P. (2020). A review of research into automation in tourism: Launching the Annals of Tourism Research Curated Collection on Artificial Intelligence and Robotics in Tourism. *Annals of Tourism Research, 81,* 102883. https://doi.org/10.1016/j.annals.2020.102883

Tussyadiah, I. P., & Fesenmaier, D. R. (2009). Mediating tourist experiences: Access to places via shared videos. *Annals of Tourism Research, 36*(1), 24–40. https://doi.org/10.1016/j.annals.2008.10.001

Tussyadiah, I. P., Wang, D., Jung, T. H., & Tom Dieck, M. C. (2018). Virtual reality, presence, and attitude change: Empirical evidence from tourism. *Tourism Management, 66,* 140–154. https://doi.org/10.1016/j.tourman.2017.12.003

Webster, C. (2019). Halfway there: the transition from 1968 to 2068 in tourism and hospitality. *Zeitschrift Für Tourismuswissenschaft, 11*(1), 5–23. https://doi.org/10.1515/tw-2019-0002

Webster, C., & Ivanov, S. (2019). Future tourism in a robot-based economy: A perspective article. *Tourism Review, 75*(1), 329–332. https://doi.org/10.1108/TR-05-2019-0172

WHO. (2020, April 12). Coronavirus disease 2019 (COVID-19) Situation Report. https://www.who.int/docs/default-source/coronaviruse/situation-reports/20200412-sitrep-83-covid-19.pdf?sfvrsn=697ce98d_4

Woosnam, K. M., & Kim, H. (2014). Hurricane impacts on southeastern United States coastal national park visitation. *Tourism Geographies, 16*(3), 364–381. https://doi.org/10.1080/14616688.2013.823235

Yang, G. Z., J. Nelson, B., Murphy, R. R., Choset, H., Christensen, H., H. Collins, S., Dario, P., Goldberg, K., Ikuta, K., Jacobstein, N., Kragic, D., Taylor, R. H., & McNutt, M. (2020). Combating COVID-19 - The role of robotics in managing public health and infectious diseases. *Science Robotics, 5*(40), eabb5589. https://doi.org/10.1126/scirobotics.abb5589

Yang, X., Yu, Y., Xu, J., Shu, H., Xia, J., Liu, H., Wu, Y., Zhang, L., Yu, Z., Fang, M., Yu, T., Wang, Y., Pan, S., Zou, X., Yuan, S., & Shang, Y. (2020). Clinical course and outcomes of critically ill patients with SARS-CoV-2 pneumonia in Wuhan, China: A single-centered, retrospective, observational study. *The Lancet Respiratory Medicine.* https://doi.org/10.1016/S2213-2600(20)30079-5

Yu, C. E. (2020). Humanlike robots as employees in the hotel industry: Thematic content analysis of online reviews. *Journal of Hospitality Marketing & Management, 29*(1), 22–38. https://doi.org/10.1080/19368623.2019.1592733

Zhang, J. (2018). Big data and tourism geographies - An emerging paradigm for future study?. *Tourism Geographies, 20*(5), 899–904. https://doi.org/10.1080/14616688.2018.1519719

Reflections and discussions: tourism matters in the new normal post COVID-19

Patrick Brouder, Simon Teoh, Noel B. Salazar (iD), Mary Mostafanezhad, Jessica Mei Pung, Dominic Lapointe (iD), Freya Higgins Desbiolles, K. Michael Haywood, C. Michael Hall (iD) and Helene Balslev Clausen

The large number of commentaries in this special issue reflect the need that so many people have to express themselves as a way of releasing the anxieties and integrating the hopes that the COVID-19 pandemic has engendered in individuals and groups around the world. The guest editors of this special issue provide the following comments in reflecting on the major themes that are envisioned for travel and tourism in a COVID-19 world. Comments from the guest editors are individually identified in this conclusion editorial.

Importance of the local

Jessica Mei Pung: In relation to **Benjamin, Dillette and Alderman's** paper, overtourism may correspond to more than just people visiting renowned destinations that are already crowded and far from where they reside. I interviewed restaurateurs who worked in a small tourism destination with only 7000 residents. They faced competition from 60 other restaurants, and almost exclusively relied on revenue from tourists, even if the majority only visited the destination on a day trip. When considering locals as potential customers, restaurateurs complained that their restaurant was not appealing because of its perceived high prices. Regarding regional travel, hopefully the pandemic will make people more aware of their nearby lesser known destinations and increase their support for local businesses when safety measures are in place.

Dominic Lapointe: Tourism in the context of COVID-19 reveals how the local is a locus of change. As tourism grinds to a halt and social distancing measures are enforced, the micro mobilities at the local level become highly impaired. It is at this scale that the post COVID-19 world may be redefined through tension between a desire to "go back to normal" and a rejection of what could be called the new normal (**Benjamin, Dillette & Alderman**). Local communities in the spring of 2020 are severely impacted in large part by the loss of livelihoods. Yet, from within this loss, the opportunity exists to rebuild tourism with a triple bottom line which will secure a more resilient and sustainable local economy (**Cooper & Alderman; Romagosa**). This rebuilding has the potential to regenerate short circuit economies (**Ateljevic**), reinvigorate environmental hope and remediation (**Crossley**) and promote institutional innovation (**Brouder**). The tourism industry could take this path with local communities, but this path would need leadership and creativity from academics as well as researchers and educators (Benjamin, Dillette & Alderman; **Edelheim; Pernecky**).

This possible transformation at the local level is also an occasion to contest capitalism as the main narrative and replace neocolonial and neoliberal subjectivities (**Everhingham; Tremblay-Huet; Renaud**). On the other hand, it is important to keep in mind that degrowth and slow tourism might benefit developed countries while impacting developing countries more negatively (**Tomassini & Cavagnaro**). This shows the asymmetrical power relations in tourism development, especially when negotiated through the lens of North-South relationships (Tremblay-Huet).

Tomassini and Cavagnaro similarly expose the relational nature of tourism space where an industrial structuring of tourism activities creates a symbolic "wall" between local resident and tourism functions of the cities, which is also described by **Lapointe** as a paradoxical twofold alterity. Both commentaries suggest that a refocus of tourism business towards local needs might become more permanent than a quick on the surface adaptation to the crisis. While this local scale perspective present throughout the special issue is important for thinking about the future of tourism, **Hall, Scott and Gössling** warn of selfish nationalism as an infringement of global sustainability which stresses the importance of scale in our analyses.

Helene Balslev Clausen: Following the thinking of several papers, questions for resetting tourism circulate around whether such proposals can be sustainable forms that will translate into equitable development. One of the vast challenges seems to be that tourism often places a focus on the individual and innovations rather than on collectives and communal-owned transactions. Even though tourism redirects and seeks to integrate "communities" in decision-making processes, what often fails is the unpacking of complexities of the historical- and sociopolitical context of societies, regions, or localities. The consequences typically strengthen existing power asymmetries in the decision-making process instead of embedding an inclusive approach. These asymmetries often determine the tensions or conflicts arising during the collaborative process we seek to enhance.

Cave and Dredge's paper offers fascinating frameworks for the reshaping of tourism business models. The complexities of tourism require more profound insights into multiple world perspectives to break down the dichotomies we work with and within. How can we incorporate knowledge produced in other languages and cultures without using Western concepts to identify sustainable development? Cave and Dredge's lens of alternative economies brings critical understanding to how to create resilience in communities using tourism as a tool. The COVID-19 context provides a space to rethink how we might redefine, represent, and enact the tourism economy. During the COVID-19 pandemic lockdowns, experiences of solidarity have emerged with, for example, residents supporting social enterprises to sustain these businesses in their communities. These exchanges strengthen resilience and are values-based. These types of transactions create a value not accounted for in traditional economic models. Nevertheless, they are essential to build on to support community resilience in tourism.

These transactions underpin communities and make it possible to cope with future vulnerabilities. A notable example is the Zapatista Movement in Chiapas (Mexico) that believes in a world where many worlds fit. Through exploiting the tourism toolbox, the Zapatista Movement and linked communities have generated benefits to the residents in the communities. These varied dimensions of transactions of modes and practices have consequences for our understanding of sustainable-oriented, sociocultural, and political development. They challenge us to think about sustainability considering new contexts, new questions, and maybe new modes of research.

Inequalities

Jessica Mei Pung: Regarding **Benjamin, Dillette and Alderman's** commentary, tourists should reconsider their travel patterns and be aware of how beneficial their vacation would be to the destination they intend to visit, especially when engaging in air travel. Local and regional tourism is a great practice that should be encouraged to benefit all stakeholders. However, the stigmatization of air (and long-haul) travel is an argument that seems to be persistent among people with a certain degree of privilege because they have already travelled around the world, built their travel experience, and can now rely on their memories of famous landmarks and picturesque or exotic places.

What about young people or people from developing countries that either were not born yet or could not afford to travel across the globe when this was glamourized and appreciated by the West? What about families and loved ones who want to visit each other but are separated by oceans because of work? For the latter, travel is a necessity, but travel is also a leisure activity that should not be unequal.

While we as travelers are called to adjust our priorities (**Hall, Scott & Gössling**), travel operations should also adapt to the necessities of travelers as people. To survive, air travel should be made safer by changing the logic of profit maximization which favors overcrowded airport queues and planes and prioritizing the safety and hygiene of air travel procedures.

To still benefit destinations, long-haul travel should consist of trips that last longer. In my studies, I found that long stays are especially transformative for tourists, in terms of opportunities for reflection in the destination and for positive encounters with fellow travelers and local residents, which in turn translate to long-term positive changes in behavior. It is also true that tourist transformation is especially facilitated by challenges and cultural differences which are probably not faced when visiting a familiar destination.

On a different note but still linked to travel and inequality, while air travel is condemned, during the pandemic more and more people are travelling by car, which is considered the "safest" means of transport, when compared to crowded trains and buses. If this is still the case after lockdowns around the world are eased, not only would it make the reduction of air travel vain in terms of carbon footprint, but disincentivizing public transport would also create inequalities for those who do not own or cannot afford a car. Therefore, we should not give up on public transport, but we should still encourage it and make sure that measures are put in place for people to safely use trains and buses.

Also, I agree that hospitality workers are too vulnerable to these uncertain times, even when working in established workplaces and long-standing businesses. With many restaurants closed during the lockdown, what can we practically do about it? In the case of restaurants, should we as consumers encourage food deliveries, but still support the riders' right to work in safety? What should restaurant owners do about their employees? What should governments do about the current sector vulnerability? What kind of revolution should take place to make sure that hospitality workers are not so vulnerable to crises? **Higgins-Desbiolles** proposes some relevant actions in her agenda.

Noel Salazar: **Galvani, Lew and Sotelo Perez** reflect on how tourism may help to solve some of the challenges our planet is currently facing. One of the underlying ideas is that tourism (and, by extension, travel in general) can be transformational, particularly at the level of the individual tourist. However, while tourism certainly has transformational potential, not every tourist is interested in change and not everybody looking for transformation (through tourism or other means) will find it.

This raises multiple questions. At what cost should we maintain a system (or install a new one) that only "transforms" some? Do the authors imply that even more people should travel (so that the number of potential transformers can multiply)? How should we treat the people necessary to enable the travels and, thus, transformations of others (the so-called service providers)? It would, of course, be much easier if we would all be equal at the start of rethinking the organization of our planetary life. The problem is that we are not (and most likely never will be).

If there is one thing a crisis like the one at hand teaches us, it is that we cannot solve complex challenges alone and that we need to collaborate. As this contribution convincingly argues, such collaboration can and should lead to an expanded global consciousness. Whether tourism will play a leading role in this effort will depend on the sustained efforts by many stakeholders, some who are already transformed and some who are in "happy expectancy".

Michael Hall: While scholars have called for a 'Transformative Turn' in post COVID-19 tourism, this "turn" may indeed become an addition to the fashion stakes of the contemporary social sciences. Like all the other critical, resilient, and sustainable tourisms [and which are often not] the desire for transformative tourism highlights this ongoing, sometimes desperate, search for something other, an alternative tourism that does not melt into air and which provides meaning to those who seek it. Yet the promise of such meaning has usually been transitory if not illusory as tourism studies moves on to another turn, always travelling never arriving. Is the potential catalyst of COVID-19 going to change tourism at a global scale or will it be 'Business as Usual'? Despairingly, there is reason to believe that it will be the latter. This is not to say that greater justice is not possible in all its forms, nor that enlightened individuals cannot create their own transformative spaces for those around them, nor that an ecologically rich future cannot be. We desperately do want all these things - but the signs are not good.

Mary Mostafanezhad: **Crossley's** article is a fascinating description of a collective feeling of ecogrief that has been triggered by the pandemic. This is an important psychological framing of what might drive post COVID-19 tourism behavior. Of course, as noted above in the context of flight shaming, not everyone will feel ecofatigue equally and in rural areas, we may find that people that transitioned from ecologically destructive livelihoods will return to those livelihoods because tourism is no longer viable. **Niewiadomski**, for instance, offers a sort of cautious hope when he describes how "the path of re-development and transformation which the global tourism production system will follow once the COVID-19 crisis has been resolved is yet to be determined." Moreover, it will be important to frame this kind of reaction in class terms. Thus, whether framing the local or global dynamics, neither is a homogeneous whole. This framing points to how a political ecology framework adds a bit of nuance to what we might call the "politics of hope" in post COVID-19 tourism, especially around ideas of what it means to "collectively" hope. Who, for instance, is the collective?

This framing is echoed in several papers in this issue. For example, **Hall, Scott and Gössling** describe how the response to "planetary limits and sustainable tourism requires a global approach. Despite clear evidence of this necessity, the possibility for a comprehensive transformation of the tourism system remains extremely limited without a fundamental transformation of the entire planet". In a similar vein, **Mostafanezhad** describes how the consequences of so-called "natural" disasters are unevenly distributed. Drawing on Doreen Massey, **Tomassini and Cavagnaro** describe disentangling the local and global. They write: "While the global dimension seems more broken than ever, the urgency of belonging to the local is more and more evident".

Complex globalizations

Jessica Mei Pung: **Mostafanezhad** sheds a light on how tourists are great when they generate profit, and are immediately thrown under the bus when it comes to geopolitical issues. We should not forget how this pandemic unfolded from a geopolitical perspective. When COVID-19 first spread in Wuhan, several national governments stopped travel connections to and from China. Other countries, while previously promoting themselves as welcoming and warm tourism destinations, also closed their borders as a primary measure against COVID-19, ordering travelers to quarantine, and threatening them with deportation in case of disobedience.

At the same time, citizens were invited to travel back home, almost as if foreign travelers were the only probable carriers of COVID-19. In Italy, for example, stopping travel connections with China was the primary measure taken by the government on January 31st to prevent COVID-19 from reaching its population. However, this decision backfired because no additional limitations or checks were made, and people travelling from China still managed to reach Italy through indirect routes.

While Italian media outlets focused on two Chinese tourists who became infected in Rome, an outbreak of COVID-19 was taking place in Lombardy in northern Italy, initiated by Italian citizens who had come back from overseas. When developing a strategy to prevent COVID-19, closing borders or stopping connections with selected countries were considered by governments as a panacea, which mostly ended up perpetuating geopolitical anxieties and sometimes the illusion of "the foreigner" as sole plague spreader. Instead, governments should have directed their energies to funding and equipping their health system to proactively fight COVID-19.

Noel Salazar: Geologists have suggested that we currently live in the Anthropocene, an era during which human activity is the dominant influence on climate and the environment. As a result, disasters are increasingly anthropogenic.

Although some have described the coronavirus crisis as an equalizer, this may not be accurate. While international travel, for instance, has been reduced, it certainly has not stopped. A simple analysis of flight tracking websites and apps confirms this. Much of this is deemed "essential transport" (e.g. of food and medical supplies), but some people still manage to travel for leisure. This situation, as **Niewiadomski** points out, is quite dramatic with COVID-19 causing a reduction in global connectedness. European Union dynamics show nicely how the national and the supranational each play their role and how a crisis may (temporarily) alter the assigned roles. It is not always clear what role those involved in tourism—at various levels— can play. What is clear is that we are paying a high price to deal with the containment of the coronavirus, but the crucial question is who the "we" are in this whole story.

Freya Higgins-Desbiolles: On the issue of global-local views, COVID-19 is a critical moment on the pathway to implementing some form of globalization. Tourism has certainly benefited from a globalized world (as per Pete Burns's classic analysis). While there is a branch of tourism management scholarship that seeks to depoliticize tourism, there are important reasons to repoliticize tourism within the current context. Significantly, tourism scholars did not extensively address anti-Islam rhetoric and actions after "9/11", racism against certain groups including Asians in the West or human rights in tourism realms. One possible outcome after COVID-19 is travel becomes localized or regionalized (this is applauded in **Higgins-Desbiolles** and in **Tomassini and Cavagnaro**) because of nationalistic thinking, distrust, fear, and hatred; do we hold a view on that? Are we cosmopolitan in our stance by nature or not?

A new normal?

Simon Teoh: COVID-19 presents an opportunity for the tourism industry to pause and consider what we want out of a post COVID-19 tourism landscape. It presents an opportunity to not only focus on the economic, but also the socio-cultural and environmental aspects of the industry. It is, for example, important for industry to act as stewards towards Mother Earth. In this context we may ask how in a post-lockdown world, tourism will be reestablished in a crippled global economy? Two issues come to mind: first, the economic imbalance and hence power between tourism in the Global North (richer, developed countries) vs. Global South (poorer, developing countries); and second, each jurisdiction's own tourism agenda. Whilst tourists from the richer countries will most likely continue to want to take their holidays in the Global South, tourism stakeholders in the poorer countries would likely also want them to, because of their economic needs and their government's need for the tourism dollar.

However, this might transform post COVID-19, at least in the next two to four years. Those richer countries will need to recover themselves first and will most likely look to domestic or 'proximity tourism' (**Romagosa**). The call for a post COVID-19 evolutionary reset with new tourism pathways (**Brouder**) would most likely dominate in Global South tourism, given the realization that their ability to rely on the tourism dollar has now vanished. This will require looking for fresh sources of alternative revenue to the tourism dollar. Sufficiency economy or regenerative economy (**Alteljevic**) will most likely play an important role here.

Jessica Mei Pung: In the context of animals and tourism, **Crossley's** paper made me think about the pandas who mated for the first time in the Hong Kong zoo while visitors were absent due to the lockdown (Watts, 2020). Apart from making for "cute" headlines on media outlets, will this make certain zoo operators more aware of the fact that they are prioritizing profit over the preservation of species, or will they go back to "business as usual"?

Patrick Brouder: The temporary break in tourist activity shows some possibility of institutional innovation towards 'socializing' tourism but the challenge will be in embedding the new normal for the long-term and for the greater good (Brouder, 2019). As **Ateljevic** points to in her opening quote, there never was a 'normal' but rather a 'normalized' way of doing things. **Crossley** and **Higgins-Desbiolles** both suggest that for true transformation to occur, entrenched ways of doing things need to be broken. The call for a move towards 'regenerative tourism' addresses the important question of how we can embed change in the aftermath of the present crisis.

Romagosa notes the potential 'regionalization of tourism' as tourists start to 'think local and act local'. This would favor destination regions which already have advantages of infrastructure, population, and income. It would also undermine two of the traditional rationales for tourism development: (1) tourism as a path to regional economic development (rural, peripheral, and remote destinations may well be left behind even though many are dependent on tourism, and (2) tourism as a source of foreign currency and contributor to GDP (a regional approach would see an increasing share of gains made within the same currency regime or within the same nation state).

In a similar vein, **Hall, Scott and Gössling** demonstrate that a regional reset is as likely to bolster selfish regionalism based on pre-existing power dynamics and growth-focused development as it is to lead to regional reorientation towards sustainable practices. They further describe how the potential of the present transformative moment will likely be swept aside in many regions as governments urgently pursue job growth to mitigate the increased unemployment. Hall, Scott and Gössling conclude with a classic geographical phrasing: "Changes to tourism as a result of COVID-19 will be uneven in space and time" so while we may see a new regionalism, it will likely be a patchwork of old and new approaches to tourism.

Dominic Lapointe: With large cities being identified as hotspots of the COVID-19 contagion and social distancing measures creating challenges in densely populated areas, we could see a movement to the countryside by the higher economic class, just as when, at the beginning of the 19th century aristocrats would escape dirty and polluted cities for the seaside for health and hygiene to *prendre les eaux* (take to the waters) or the sanatorium to "cure" tuberculosis which is still an important health issue of our time.

Freya Higgins-Desbiolles: **Crossley's** paper makes an important contribution to understanding our ecological imaginations. She asks us to consider what it means when we collectively hope nature is rapidly repairing itself in our absence under lockdown. In this context, are we willing to transform our choices and actions so that ecology can survive and thrive? Can we as academics foster tourism in these many ways (whether we are aware we are doing it or not) and yet hope for a world with less tourism? Are we able to reconcile the needs of the environment with the demands of the industry? In other words, what potential do these sentimental scenes have for transformative sustained action? This connects back to what I tried to get at in my paper on the false promise.

Simon Teoh: **Lapointe's** notion of the '6 foot tourism world' sanity safety scenario, can be very real in the immediate post COVID-19 tourism. Domestic tourists' movements may be restricted to those who are immune and those who are not. Would post COVID-19 jurisdictions impose a health passport, like the olden days of the yellow colored health passport that travelers needed to carry?

Ateljevic's notion of 'conscious citizens', much likened to **Cheers's** notion of 'human flourishing', is the basis for transforming tourism, one that deserves more attention post COVID-19, as does **Higgins-Desbiolles'** call for tourism benefits to recenter on the public good. For instance, Higgins-Desbiolles's example of the cruise industry echoes **Renaud's** call for smaller size cruise ship operations to combat the impacts of seasonality in the aftermath of COVID-19.

There is also much 'ecological grief' (**Crossley**), which the tourism Industry must face and deal with. There will be much soul searching within the tourism Industry. However, to transform tourism post COVID-19, a 'philosophical reset' (**Benjamin, Dillette & Alderman**) is necessary. The important question of the value of tourism will most likely dominate the tourism industry discourse in the future, as the consensus as to what tourism post COVID-19 will look like will still be up for discussion for some time to come.

Helene Balslev Clausen: One of the underlying issues in most of the papers is the importance of the state. Tourism scholarship would benefit from political geographers' analyses of the state. Perhaps it is time to bring the state back, as Evans et al. (1985) reminded us several decades ago. Indeed, the tourism industry is dependent on states and the way they regulate. However, COVID-19 also reveals the state's vulnerability and tight bonds to the industry. The state should support and secure the "clean industries"; the living world, and "bail out the living world not its destroyers" although European governments have been quick to provide loans to airlines (Monbiot, 2020).

One of the extraordinary responses to COVID-19 has been how communities mobilized the commons. In Copenhagen, people supported older people by delivering food to their doorsteps; in Mexico, self-organized groups provided aid packages to people without savings, and in Johannesburg, young people have on a massive scale handed out hand sanitizer, bottled water, and food in informal settlements. Might this be a potential eye-opener for context-based co-creation with the communities (that are not homogenous either) for tourism enterprises? These transactions are all sensible but the transformations they represent will be far from easy to scale up. The underlying causes of poverty and the unsustainable tourism system need to be addressed.

Mary Mostafanezhad: Rowen describes the annual Burning Man festival in Nevada, USA, as a model of an "alter- or anti-tourism, tourism". Originally developed as an anti-capitalist festival, it continues to serve as an alternative space for non- or not-fully capitalist forms of exchange. There are numerous critiques against its ongoing corporatization both in popular and academic literature. Yet, the concept of thinking differently about economic exchange is an important way forward in a post COVID-19 tourism landscape.

Higgins-Desbiolles' paper addresses related themes in her call for socialized tourism that is "recentred on the public good". While the tourism industry is dependent on monetary exchanges, there is potential to incorporate other forms of non or not fully capitalist exchange. In this way, Rowen's framing of Burning Man as a metaphor for the potentiality of tourism is apt: both tourism and Burning Man have the potential to both depend on capitalist exchange but also offer opportunities for non or not fully capitalist exchange. These forms of exchange also depend on mutual trust and solidarity.

In a post COVID-19 tourism recovery, these sentiments are going to be necessary. Trust that people have washed their hands, do not travel when they feel sick, and will be cared for if they become ill. Trust also depends on mutual respect between hosts and guests who see each other not as consumers and producers but rather as equal partners in the exchange. In this sense, the entire notion of hospitality will require a new kind of trust between hosts and guests.

Michael Hall: While there are pockets of action and resistance, the bailouts for airlines and carbon emitters are already happening. The race to the bottom of special offers and discounts has begun. Government funded holidays in Sicily at half price? Sure.

While tourism is founded on the promise of mobility and freedom, COVID-19 has only reinforced the systems of surveillance and control in many countries, including in some cases on research and publication on COVID-19 itself. The selfish nationalism and leadership of many countries only serves to reflect the selfish individualism that characterizes much tourism and, perhaps in the drive for research assessment and impact, the tourism academy as well.

Utopias are, just like the newspeak of critical, resilient, sustainable, and transformative tourisms, illusory, and, in the wrong hands, with an inherently contradictory, rather than emancipatory, nature. It is almost as if the more you repeat something the less power, explanatory or otherwise, it has – the entropy of meaning.

Transformations lie somewhere in the eddies in the multiple scales between structure and agency. But structure is not fashionable in the tourism world where the consumptive agent is king. We remain in search of common ground even as the commons are eroded away while we muddle through and talk too much, or perhaps not talk enough at all.

My mutable self can no longer tell as it becomes commodified on a commercial transformational journey – Eat, Love, Prey. If the best path to utopia to hope for is local or individual transformative tourisms – whatever they might be – without living within the limits of the ecosystems of which we are a part, then what future is there for our pale blue dot that we travel round let alone for our children? Ontological shifts as well as more practical turns are needed. I despair.

Mary Mostafanezhad: The papers in this issue highlight the tension among tourism industry practitioners to, on the one hand, "return to normal" and by tourism academics to recreate a "new normal". **Nepal's** paper brings this to the fore when he describes how "The tourism industry in Nepal has always worked under the assumption that things will be normal, and that tourists would continue to flock to Nepal, as long as there is growth in international travel." While he may hope that the present crisis affords the "global adventure tourism industry an opportunity to reset," recently unemployed Sherpas may be hoping for things to quickly get "back to normal" so they can feed their families.

There are many examples of local governments now realizing that putting all their eggs in the tourism basket was a vulnerability and mistake that they do not want to repeat. For instance, headlines in Hawaii state newspapers describe the urgent need to diversify the economy and move away from the state's heavy reliance on tourism. **Nepal** makes this point in his conclusion when he writes: "There is a fundamental disconnect between what the UNWTO preaches (sustainability), and what it practices (growth expansion). This disconnect must be fixed first before we can consider the future of tourism."

Other authors make similar points. For example, **Ioannides and Gyimóthy** describe how, "although policymakers seek to strengthen the resilience of post-pandemic tourism, their subsidies and other initiatives serve to maintain a fundamentally flawed market logic". In a fascinating description of the potential role of robotics in post COVID-19 tourism, **Zeng, Chen and Lew** call for a radical normalization of "robotic applications that enhance tourist experiences, the protection of natural and cultural resources, and the emergence of new 'high-touch' employment opportunities for travel, tourism and hospitality workers".

Ateljevic similarly grapples with what a new normal may engender, writing: "New ways of being, knowing and doing in the world are emerging as conscious citizens, consumers, producers, travelers, entrepreneurs, and community leaders are calling and acting upon the necessary transformation towards the regenerative paradigm and regenerative economic systems." This is all to say the current set of papers offers multiple pathways forward for dealing with the trouble with "normal".

What really matters

Michael Haywood: The aftermath of the COVID-19 pandemic as it plays out in the travel and tourism industry will reveal the importance of tourism (community-by-community) through its absence. It's revival is not in doubt, but if it is to serve "purpose" (the why of tourism determined by individual communities-as-destinations) then consideration definitely has to be given to what Arjun Appadurai refers to as the "ethics of probability" to which I would add, the "ethics of possibility", which has to be revealed through thought, behavior and action associated with those in leadership positions.

Freya Higgins-Desbiolles: I think it says something that so many people, including tourism academics, were looking for something that could catalyze change. We have all responded rapidly as we draw on the values, training, and knowledge that we have been accumulating to try to make sense of the possibilities this moment may hold. I note there are a few blind spots that I see, and I think they are telling:

- This is a moment of life and death for many so what is the value of a journal article and particularly on tourism?
- Our own discipline risks being on the scrap heap as does the university sector, but we said nothing of that.
- There is immense ugliness sitting in this moment including anti-Asian sentiment and violence and we have failed to relate this to the rapid rise in dependency on Chinese tourists in many regions. That is underpinned by racism that has been there all along.
- Geo-politics is totally changing in this crisis and the world on the other side will be totally different. Tourism will be shaped by those realities and we as academics have no influence on that.

Yet the crisis has shown that tourism matters in our societies and that, in the impacts of quarantine measures, this fact has been brought into sharp relief. Given that tourism scholars have never agreed on what tourism is, we have been especially challenged to agree on why it matters. It is perhaps in this moment that we may come together to think otherwise as the industry rebuilds itself from the ground up.

Michael Haywood: As I read through these comments I cannot help but wonder what the average person involved within tourism-related enterprises might be thinking or how they may be reacting to what is being said (how it is being said … use of language) about post COVID-19 change or transformation; it's all rather obtuse to all but the contributors! Yet, the day-to-day struggle that is going on right now within all types of enterprises is immense. Not only is adaptation on the minds of everyone, but so is survival (survival in the short-term in which cash is, and will remain, king). Strategy and policy changes will have to wait until operational adjustments are made (all tactical decisions) and a degree of stability returns. Everything that is happening now is experimental; moreover, the actual learning that is taking place is occurring only through the actual acts of doing, seeing what works and what does not, what resonates and what does not.

It is perhaps telling that so few of the papers and comments in this conclusion acknowledge where the groundswell of actual change (demand- and supply-related) is occurring and will continue to occur.

Patrick Brouder: As the natural environment exhibits hope through the short-term change of behavior of animals there may be a change in the perceptions of would-be tourists. Increased environmental sensitivity is a precursor to behavior change. As **Crossley** and **Pernecky** each note, the question remains how to transform the hope of this moment into changed behavior as we begin to adapt the tourism sector to the new reality. The fact that the return of tourism activities will be gradual means there is a chance that positive change can be slowly embedded in a temporarily protected tourism system and that, given time, as temporary tourism restrictions are lifted a more enlightened tourism may have had time to flourish.

Michael Hall: Fundamentally, the COVID-19 pandemic reinforces how it is not tourism that matters. Rather, tourism is a means to an end. What really matters is planet, people, and our families. *He mea nui. Ko te papaorangarewa, ko te taangata, he whanau.*

Disclosure statement

No potential conflict of interest was reported by the author(s).

ORCID

Noel B. Salazar ⓘ http://orcid.org/0000-0002-8346-2977
Dominic Lapointe ⓘ http://orcid.org/0000-0002-5696-1471
C. Michael Hall ⓘ http://orcid.org/0000-0002-7734-4587

References

Brouder, P. (2019). Towards a geographical political economy of tourism. In D. K. Müller (Ed.), *A research agenda for tourism geographies* (pp. 71–78). Elgar.
Evans, P. B., Rueschemeyer, D., & Skocpol, T. (1985). *Bringing the state back in*. Cambridge University Press.
Monbiot, G. (2020, April 29). Airlines and oil giants are on the brink. No government should offer them a lifeline (opinion). *The Guardian*. https://www.theguardian.com/commentisfree/2020/apr/29/airlines-oil-giants-government-economy
Watts, J. (2020, April 7). Hong Kong's pandas mate for first time in decade in privacy of coronavirus lockdown. *The Guardian*. https://www.theguardian.com/world/2020/apr/07/in-the-mood-for-love-hong-kongs-middle-aged-pandas-rediscover-their-mojo

Index

Note: **Bold** page numbers refer to tables; *italic* page numbers refer to figures.

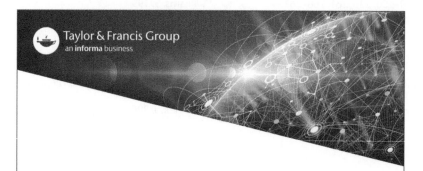

For Product Safety Concerns and Information please contact our
EU representative GPSR@taylorandfrancis.com Taylor & Francis
Verlag GmbH, Kaufingerstraße 24, 80331 München, Germany